# Women in Jazz

**Recent Titles in**
**Discographies**

*Series Editor: Michael Gray*

V-Discs: A History and Discography
*Richard S. Sears*

Melodiya: A Soviet Russian L.P. Discography
*Compiled by John R. Bennett*

The Chess Labels: A Discography
*Compiled by Michel Ruppli*

The Al Jolson Discography
*Compiled by Larry F. Kiner*

The Metropolitan Opera on Record:
A Discography of the Commercial Recordings
*Compiled by Frederick P. Fellers*

International Discography of Women Composers
*Compiled by Aaron I. Cohen*

Walter Legge: A Discography
*Compiled by Alan Sanders*

The Rudy Vallee Discography
*Compiled by Larry F. Kiner*

Rockin' the Classics and Classicizin' the Rock:
A Selectively Annotated Discography
*Janell R. Duxbury*

The American 45 and 78 RPM Record Dating Guide, 1940-1959
*William R. Daniels*

The Johnny Cash Discography
*Compiled by John L. Smith*

A Discography of Hindustani and Karnatic Music
*Compiled by Michael S. Kinnear*

# Women in Jazz
## A Discography of Instrumentalists, 1913-1968

*Compiled by* **JAN LEDER**

Discographies, Number 19

**Greenwood Press**
Westport, Connecticut • London, England

**Library of Congress Cataloging-in-Publication Data**

Leder, Jan.
  Women in jazz.

  (Discographies, 0192-334X ; no. 19)
  Includes index.
  1. Women jazz musicians—Discographies. 2. Jazz
music—Discographies. I. Title. II. Series.
ML156.4.J3L44   1985   016.7899'12542'088042   85-17657
ISBN 0-313-24790-0 (lib. bdg. : alk. paper)

Library of Congress Catalog Card Number: 85-17657
ISBN: 0-313-24790-0
ISSN: 0192-334X

First published in 1985

Greenwood Press
A division of Congressional Information Service, Inc.
88 Post Road West
Westport, Connecticut 06881

Printed in the United States of America

The paper used in this book complies with the
Permanent Paper Standard issued by the National
Information Standards Organization (Z39.48-1984).

10  9  8  7  6  5  4  3  2  1

This book is dedicated to three special people who inspired and encouraged my work:

To my mother, Claire Leder Billings, who continues to show me how creative a woman can be;

To the late Lennie Tristano, who believed in me and so many other women and men players, and helped us to believe in ourselves;

And to Connie Crothers, for her sensitivity and integrity, and her never-ending musical devotion and inspiration.

# Contents

Introduction    ix

Instrument Abbreviations    xiii

Record Label Abbreviations    xv

1.   **Discography of Women in Jazz**    **3**

2.   **Collective Section**    **291**

Index    307

# Introduction

In the last eight years there has been an explosion of interest and activity in the field of women in jazz, as evidenced by the annual Kansas City Women's Jazz Festival, the publication of the first two books on the subject, as well as a proliferation of local festivals and concerts. And, while women vocalists have enjoyed well-deserved recognition for their skill and innovation throughout the history of recorded jazz it is the women players who have not gotten their due. This discography attempts to present a complete picture of women instrumentalists' recording activity from 1913 to 1968. Indeed, since 1968 the number of recording sessions with women players has probably doubled. However, it has been my intention to show the large extent to which women players participated in jazz, and the fact that they have been on the scene, playing, since jazz began.

The task of compiling a hopefully complete discography of women jazz instrumentalists has been quite difficult. While discography in general struggles with the management of vast amounts of data, the subject of women players presents additional problems. My biggest problem has been in the identification of gender by first name, as there are quite a few names that are not gender-specific. Unless a woman with a potentially male name was specifically known to me (i.e., Terry Pollard) these ambiguous names had to be assumed to be men. This same problem extended to almost all European sessions, as these names seem even more ambiguous to Americans.

This discography is based on four pioneer sources: Delauney's New Hot Discography; Rust's Jazz Records 1897-1942; Jepsen's Jazz Records 1942-1968; and Bruyninckxy's 60 Years of Recorded Jazz, 1917-1977. The only exceptions are Stash's ST109 - Jazzwomen, A Feminist Retrospective and one session mentioned to me by Phil Schaap on the Everybody label. Some corrections and additions have been made from discussions with other scholars. The question of what "jazz" is has been discussed by these four discographers and I have decided to include most sessions found in their discographies. Hence the inclusion of recordings that may go into the gospel, blues and r&b areas. The only sessions I did not include which were in their discographies are unissued recordings and airchecks, since I felt it important to stay within the guideline of recording sessions that either were or are commercially available.

The discography is split into two sections: the first section is alphabetical by last name of the player and chronological within each player's section; the second is a chronologically listed collective section containing recordings with two or more women players. Following the collective section is an index with all women players and the pages on which their recordings may be found.

The layout of each session is as follows:

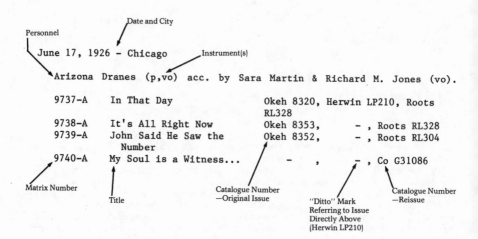

Occasionally a title will be followed by a set of initials, preceded by a small "v," in brackets (i.e., (vAZ)). This identifies the vocalist on a particular title. If a vocalist is listed in the personnel section and this notation does not appear after any of the titles in the session, it indicates that the vocalist sings on all the titles of that date. "Acc." stands for "accompanied." City designations such as "New York City" or "Los Angeles" include the Greater New York and Greater Los Angeles areas, and may include sessions done on Long Island or in Hollywood. Letters in parentheses in the Catalogue Number area usually refer to foreign releases, such as (G) for Germany, etc. Reissue numbers standing alone refer to the previous Company Code (i.e., Co 1862, 1863). Quite often the personnel area reads "so-and-so added" or "so-and-so replaced by ..." Whenever a full listing of personnel is not presented, these notes refer to the personnel of the previous session. "c" in the date area means "circa." "(Prob)" means the personnel are not certain but are believed to be the players (this, again, according to my four main source discographies).

For great reading on this subject I recommend Sally Placksin's American Women in Jazz (Wideview Books, 1982). Also, included in the Stash ST109 package was a fine survey written by Frank Driggs in 1977, which I believe was the first piece written on the subject.

An interesting note: There are 250 women players in the discography, including over 120 pianists; 21 harp players; 21 guitarists; 20 reed players; 16 trumpeters; 13 bassists; 10 drummers; 9 organists; and 9 trombonists. (Note the tendency toward string instruments!) Many of the pianists and guitarists also sang on their records.

Additions and corrections are welcome. Please address any correspondence to me at 24 Caryl Avenue, Apt. 4A, Yonkers, New York, 10705.

      I wish to thank the following people for their valuable time and
help:  Dr. James Sabin of Greenwood Press; Dan Morganstern, Marie Griffin
and Ed Berger of the Institute of Jazz Studies at Rutgers University;
Phil Schaap; Marian McPartland; Sally Placksin; Karl Van Ausdale, Michael
Hammond, Bob Stein and Marcia Cavell of S.U.N.Y. Purchase;     Bernard
Brightman of Stash Records; Richard Piro; and my best friend and husband,
Julio Cesar Leder-Luis.

# Instrument Abbreviations

| | | |
|---|---|---|
| acc | = | accordian |
| alto-fl | = | alto flute |
| arr | = | arranger |
| as | = | alto saxophone |
| b | = | bass |
| b-cl | = | bass clarinet |
| b-g | = | bass guitar |
| b-tb | = | bass trombone |
| b-vn | = | bass violin |
| bars | = | baritone saxophone |
| bass-sax | = | bass saxophone |
| bgs | = | bongos |
| bj | = | banjo |
| c | = | cornet |
| cga | = | conga |
| cl | = | clarinet |
| c-mel sax | = | c-melody saxophone |
| cond | = | conductor |
| d | = | drums |
| dir | = | director |
| el-b | = | electric bass |
| el-p | = | electric piano |
| EngH | = | English Horn |
| fl | = | flute |
| flhn | = | flugelhorn |
| FrH | = | French Horn |
| g | = | guitar |
| h | = | harp |
| hca | = | harmonica |
| ldr | = | leader |
| mand | = | mandolin |
| org | = | organ |
| p | = | piano |
| pic | = | piccolo |
| perc | = | percussion |
| sax | = | saxophone |
| sop | = | soprano saxophone |
| tamb | = | tamborine |
| tb | = | trombone |
| tp | = | trumpet |
| ts | = | tenor saxophone |
| uk | = | ukelele |
| vo | = | vocal |
| v-tb | = | valve trombone |
| wbd | = | washboard |

# Record Label Abbreviations

| | | |
|---|---|---|
| A.F.C.D.J. | = | Association Francaise des Collectioneurs de Disques du Jazz |
| AmMusic | = | American Music |
| ARS | = | American Record Society |
| Atl | = | Atlantic |
| B.D. | = | Boogie Disease |
| Bilt | = | Biltmore |
| Br | = | Brunswick |
| BRS | = | British Record Society |
| Clx | = | Claxtonola |
| Co | = | Columbia |
| Contemp | = | Contemporary |
| Cq | = | Conqueror |
| CRC | = | Coltrane Recording Company |
| De | = | Decca |
| El | = | Electrola |
| Esq | = | Esquire |
| Fnt | = | Fontana |
| Gz | = | Gazelle |
| Ha | = | Harmony |
| Har | = | Harmograph |
| HMV | = | His Master's Voice |
| Imp | = | Imperial |
| JA | = | Jazz Archives |
| JC | = | Jazz Collector |
| JCOA | = | Jazz Club of America |
| JD | = | Jazz Document |
| JI | = | Jazz Info |
| JS | = | Jazz Selection |
| Jzt | = | Jazztone |
| Merc | = | Mercury |
| Met | = | Metronome |
| MW | = | Montgomery Ward |
| NOM | = | New Orleans Memories |
| Od | = | Odeon |
| Par | = | Parlophone |
| Pby | = | Playboy |
| Pm | = | Paramount |
| Prest | = | Prestige |
| Pur | = | Puritan |
| Re | = | Rendition |
| Rmg | = | Remington |
| RZ | = | Regal Zonophone |
| Sig | = | Signature |
| Slvt | = | Silvertone |
| SpEd | = | Special Editions |
| Stv | = | Storyville |
| UHCA | = | United Hot Clubs of America |
| Vg | = | Vogue |
| VJR | = | Vinylite Jazz Reissues |
| Vo | = | Vocalion |
| WRC | = | World Record Club |

# Women in Jazz

# 1
# Discography of Women in Jazz

### ADAMI, MADAME (piano)

March 6, 1913 - London

Olly Oakley (bj) acc. by Madame Adami (p).

Ab-16373e  The College Rag                Zonophone 1060


### AGOSTINI, GLORIA (harp)

May 27, 1949 - New York City

ARTIE BAKER'S SALON SWINGTET:    Artie Baker (cl); Gloria Agostini (h);
Mike Colicchio (p); Allen Hanlon (g); Bert Nazer (b).

|  | Microphonics | Royal 180, Par(E)R3082 |
|  | Mellow Moments | - | - |
|  | Platter Chatter Jump | Royal 181 | - |
|  | Reading Upside Down | - | - |


September 10, 1959 - New York City

Don Hammond (as,fl); Harry Lookofsky, Leo Kahn, Dana Nadien, Paul Gersh-
man, Julius Held, Max Cahn, Alex Cores, Harry Katzman, Leonard Posner,
George Ockner (vln); Al Brown, Dave Mankowitz, Bert Fisch, Harold
Coletta (viola); George Ricci, Charlie McCracken, Harvey Shapiro
(cello); Gloria Agostini (h); Jimmy Jones (p); Milt Jackson (vib); Barry
Galbraith (g); Bill Crow (b); Connie Kay (d); Quincy Jones (arr, cond).

| 3770 | Alone Together | Atl LP1342 |
| 3771 | The Cylinder | -    , SD2-319 |
| 3772 | Makin' Whoopie | - |


September 9, 1961 - New York City

PAUL DESMOND AND HIS FRIENDS:    Paul Desmond (as); u (strings); Phil
Bodner, Romeo Penque (woodwinds); Gloria Agostini (h); Jim Hall (g);

Milt Hinton (b); Robert C. Thomas (perc); Bob Prince (cond).

| M2PB4816 | Late Lament | Victor LPM(S)2438,RCA(SF)7501 |
|----------|-------------|---------------------------------|
| M2PB4817 | Like Someone in Love | – – |
| M2PB4818 | I Should Care | – – |

October 2, 1961 - New York City

Paul Desmond (as); Albert Richman (FrH); Romeo Penque, Stan Webb (woodwinds); Gloria Agostini (h); Jim Hall (g); Milt Hinton (b); Robert C. Thomas (perc); Bob Prince (cond).

| M2PB2841 | I've Got You Under My Skin | Victor LPM(s)2438,RCA(SF)7501 |
|----------|---------------------------|-------------------------------|
| | Ill Wind | – – |
| | Then I'll Be Tired of You | |
| | Desmond Blue | – – |
| | Body and Soul | – – |

January 22, 1962 - New York

Jackie Paris (vo) acc. by Bill Hammond (fl); Phil Bodner (b-cl); George Dessinger (oboe); Gene Orloff, Harry Lookofsky, Arnold Eidus, Paul Geishman (vln); David Schwartz (viola); Charles McCracken (cello); Gloria Agostini (h); Barry Galbraith (g); Jack Lesberg (b); Ted Somer (d).

| | Jenny | Impulse A(S)17 |
|--|-------|----------------|
| | If Love Is Good To Me | – |

January 26, 1962 - New York

Jackie Paris (vo) acc. by Dick Berg, Don Corrado, Art Cery, Ray Alonge (FrH); Bill Hammond (fl); Phil Bodner (as,fl); Romeo Penque (ts,fl); George Dessinger (bassoon); Gloria Agostini (h); Barry Galbraith (g); George Duvivier (b); Sol Gubin (d).

| | Duke's Place | Impulse A(S)17 |
|--|--------------|----------------|
| | My Very Good Friend in the Looking Glass | – |
| | 'Tis Autumn | – |

April 5, 1966 - New York

Herbie Mann (fl); Richard Davis (b); Gloria Agostini (h); David Nadien, Anahid Ajemian, Alfred Brown, Bernhard Eichen, Leo Kahn, Leo Kruczek, Charles Libove, Dave Mankowitz, Charles McCracken, Marvin Morganstern, George Ockner, Raoul Poliakin, Max Pollikoff, George Ricci, Aaron Rosand, Tosha Tamaroff, Karen Tuttle, Al & Sylvan Schulman, Emanuel Vardi, Jack Zayde (vn, viola, cello); Arif Mardin (arr, cond).

| 10090 | Sports Car | Atl SD1490 |
|-------|------------|------------|
| 10091 | Eli Eli | Atl SD1475 |
| 10092 | Gloomy Sunday | Atl SD1490 |

```
10093       I Get Along Without You
            Very Well                         -
```

April 6, 1966 - New York

same personnel.

```
10105       Hold Back                   Atl SD1490
10107       Flight of the Bluebird            -
```

Jimmy Owens (flhn) added.

```
10113       Please Send Me Someone      Atl SD1490
            to Love
10114       It Was A Very Good Year            -
```

Owens out.

```
10115       Yesterday's Kisses                 -
```

April 27 & 28, 1966 - New York

Ernie Royal (tp); Jerome Richardson (ts,fl); Lalo Schiffrin (p); Gene
Bertocini (g); Richard Davis (b); Grady Tate (d); Gloria Agostini (h);
Rose Marie Jun (vo); u (strings).

```
100174      Renaissance                 Verve 8654
100175      Beneath A Weeping Willow
            Shade                             -
100176      Arie                              -
```

c. 1966

```
            Sumadija                    Cambridge CRS1820
            ..Their Silence                   -
            Night Music                       -
            Densities 1                       -
            Elegy for Dolphy                  -
```

See Collective Section for Additional Recordings


AKIYOSHI, TOSHIKO (piano)

1954 - Tokyo

Toshiko Akiyoshi (p); Herb Ellis (g); Ray Brown (b); J.C. Heard (d).

```
            Toshiko's Blues             Norgran EPN-47, MGN-22
            What Is This Thing Called
            Love                              -            -
```

| | | |
|---|---|---|
| I Want To Be Happy | - | - |
| Gone With the Wind | - | - |
| Squatty Roo | Norgran EPN-48 | - |
| Solidado | - | - |
| Shadrock | - | - |
| Laura | - | - |

## 1954 - Boston

Toshiko Akiyoshi (p); Paul Chambers (b); Ed Thigpen (d).

| | |
|---|---|
| Between Me and Myself | Storyville SLP-912, SLP-916 |
| It Could Happen to You | - |
| Kyo-Shu | -            - |
| Homework | - |
| Manhattan Address | - |
| Softly As in a Morning Sunrise | - |
| Soshu No Yora | - |
| Sunday Afternoon | - |
| Blues for Toshiko | - |

## 1954-1955 - Boston

Toshiko Akiyoshi (p); Oscar Pettiford (b); Roy Haynes (d).

| | |
|---|---|
| No Moon At All | Storyville SLP-918 |
| I'll Remember April | - |
| Thou Swell | - |

## 1954-1955 - Boston

Boots Mussuli (as); Toshiko Akiyoshi (p); Wyatt Ruther (b); Ed Thigpen (d).

| | |
|---|---|
| Kelo | Storyville SLP-918 |
| Salute to Shorty | - |
| Pee Bee and Lee | - |
| Takin' A Chance on Love | - |
| All the Things You Are | - |

## July 5, 1957 - Newport

Toshiko Akiyoshi (p); Gene Cherico (b); Jake Hanna (b).

| | | |
|---|---|---|
| Between Myself and I | Verve MGV-8236,Co(E)33CX10110 | |
| Blues for Toshiko | - | - |
| I'll Remember April | - | - |
| Lover | - | - |

## September 28, 1957 - New York City

same personnel.

| | |
|---|---|
| After You've Gone | Verve MGV-8273,Co(E)LB10098, SEB10107 |
| Studio J. | -    -    - |
| Bags Groove | -    '    - |
| The Man I Love | - |
| Minor Moods | - |
| We'll Be Together Again | - |
| Tosh's Fantasy | - |
| Imagination | - |

June 13, 1958 - New York City

TOSHIKO AND HER INTERNATIONAL JAZZ SEXTET:   Doc Severinson (tp); Rolf
Kuhn (cl,as); Bobby Jaspar (fl,ts); Toshiko Akiyoshi (p); Rene Thomas
(g); John Drew (b); Bert Dale (Nils Dahlander) (d).

| | |
|---|---|
| Broadway | Metrojazz (S) E1001 |
| Sukiyaki | - |
| Singin' Till the Girls Come Home | - |
| Civilized Folk | - |

Nat Adderly (c) replaces Severinson.

| | |
|---|---|
| United Notions | - |
| Strike Up the Band | - |
| Jane | - |

December 5, 1960 - New York City

TOSHIKO MARIANO QUARTET:   Charlie Mariano (as); Toshiko Akiyoshi Mariano
(p); Gene Cherico (b); Eddie Marshall (d).

| | |
|---|---|
| When You Meet Her | Candid CM8012, CS9012 |
| Little T | -       - |
| Toshiko's Elegy | -       - |
| Deep River | -       - |
| Long Yellow Road | -       - |

1963 - New York City

TOSHIKO AKIYOSHI - STEVE KUHN:   Toshiko Akiyoshi, Steve Kuhn (p); Barry
Galbraith (g); Dave Izenson, John Neves (b); Pete LaRocca (d).

| | |
|---|---|
| Trouble in Mind | Dauntless DM-4308, DS-6308 |
| Hang Your Head in Shame | -       - |
| May the Lord Bless and Keep You | -       - |
| Someday You'll Want Me to Want You | -       - |
| Down in the Valley | -       - |
| Beautiful Brown Eyes | -       - |
| It is No Secret | -       - |
| Nobody's Darling But Mine | -       - |

Along the Navajo Trail      -          -
Foggy Foggy Dew           -          -

**March 30, 1963 - Tokyo**

MARIANO - TOSHIKO QUARTET: Charlie Mariano (as); Toshiko Mariano (Akiyoshi) (p); Gene Cherico (b); Albert Heath (d).

| | |
|---|---|
| Tonight | Takt Jazz 12 |
| Something Coming | - |
| America | - |
| Maria | - |
| Cool | - |
| Plaisir D'Amour | - |
| Malaguena | - |
| Oleo | - |

**c. 1964**

Hisao Maro, Shigeru Takemura, Tetsuo Fushimi, Terumasa Hino (tp); Hiroshi Suzuki, Mitsuhiko Matsumoto, Teruhiko Kataora, Takeshi Aoki (tb); Hirishi Okazaki, Shigeo Suzuki, Akira Miyazawa, Hidehiko Matsumoro, Tadayuki Harada (saxes); Toshiko Mariano (Akiyoshi) (p); Paul Chambers (b); Jimmy Cobb (d).

| | |
|---|---|
| Kisarazu Jink | Vee-Jay LP2505 |
| Lament | - |
| The Shout | - |
| Israel | - |
| Land of Peace | - |
| Walkin' | - |
| Santa Barbara | - |

**January 18, 1965 - Tokyo**

BUDDY RICH & LOUIE BELLSON ACC. BY THE GEORGE KAWAGUCHI ORCHESTRA: Blue Mithcell (tp); Y. Tomoto (tb); Junior Cook (ts); Toshiko Mariano (Akiyoshi) (p); Gene Taylor (b); Buddy Rich, Louie Bellson (d); u (brass, reeds); Benny Carter (arr).

| | |
|---|---|
| Slides & Rides | Roost (S)LP2263 |

## ALEXANDER, ZACKY (reeds)

See Collective Section.

## AMADIO, JUDY (flute)

**January 27, 1953 - Town Hall, Melbourne, Australia**

William Flynn (dir); Fred Thomas, Bob Trenberth, Frank Arnold (tp); Jack
Glenn (tb); Gordon Grieve (horn); Ern Pettifer, Bob Storey, Splinyer
Reeves (cl); Bert Brigalia (bassoon); Tamata Coates (oboe); Judy Amadio
(fl); u (strings); Isadore Goodman (p); Jack O'Brien (b); Bruce Clarke
(g); Bill Fleming (d).

Rhapsody in Blue                Spotlight Varieties SV12


## AMBROSE, AMANDA (piano)

September 22-29, 1959 - Chicago

Amanda Ambrose (p,vo); acc. by John Frigs (b); Frank Rullo (d).

| | | |
|---|---|---|
| Time After Time | Stephany MF4007,Starlite(E)STLP7 | |
| You're Nobody Till | | |
|   Somebody Loves You | - | - |
| You've Got Me Crying Again | - | - |
| My Melancholy Baby | - | - |
| There Will Never Be | | |
|   Another You | - | - |
| Everywhere | - | - |
| This Can't Be Love | - | - |
| Someday Sweetheart | - | - |
| A Good Man is Hard to Find | - | - |
| Honeysuckle Rose | - | - |
| Taking a Chance on Love | - | - |
| Close Your Eyes | - | - |

1963 - "Village Gate" - New York City

Amanda Ambrose (p,vo); acc. by Sam Brown, Bill Salter (b); Osie Johnson
(d); Auchee Lee (perc).

| | | |
|---|---|---|
| This Can't Be Love | Victor LPM(S)2696,RCA(E)RD(SF)7572 | |
| Besame Mucho | - | - |
| Someone to Love | - | - |
| Come Rain or Come Shine | - | - |
| Sweet Georgia Brown | - | - |
| Too Ra Loo Ra Loo Ra | - | - |
| A Foggy Day | - | - |
| Tennessee Waltz | - | - |
| Lullaby for Toys | - | - |
| Lavender Blue | - | - |
| When Irish Eyes are Smiling | - | - |
| This Little Light of Mine | - | - |

August 5, 1963 - New York City

Joe Wilder (tp); Amanda Ambrose (p,vo); George Duvivier (b); Osie
Johnson (d).

| | | | |
|---|---|---|---|
| PPB15476 | Just in Time | Victor LPM(S)2742,RCA(E)RD(SF)7605 | |
| PPB15477 | C. C. Rider | - | - |
| PPB15478 | House of the Rising Sun | - | - |
| PPB15479 | What are the Parts of a Flower | - | - |

August 7, 1963 - New York City

Amanda Ambrose (p,vo); acc. by big band including Nick Travis (tp); Phil Bodner (as,fl); Bobby Scott (arr,dir).

| | | | |
|---|---|---|---|
| PPB15480 | God Bless the Child | Victor LPM(S)2742,RCA(E)RD(SF)7605 | |
| PPB15481 | Out of This World | - | - |
| PPB15482 | Goose Never Be a Peacock | - | - |
| PPB15483 | Hong Kong Blues | - | - |

similar personnel.

| | | | |
|---|---|---|---|
| PPB15484 | More Than You Know | Victor LPM(S)2742,RCA(D)RD(SF)7605 | |
| PPB15485 | Crawdad | - | - |
| PPB15486 | Indian Love Call | - | - |
| PPB15487 | While I Am Still Young | - | - |

## ANDREWS, ROSETTA (piano)

1946 - Los Angeles

Mary de Pina (vo) acc. by MONTE EASTER AND HIS ORCHESTRA: Monte Easter (tp); Maxwell Davis (ts); Rosetta Andrews (p); Ralph Hamilton (b); Charlie Blackwell (d).

| | |
|---|---|
| Boogie Woogie Man | Aladdin 147 |
| I Love My Man | - |
| Ooh Lawdy Lawdy | Aladdin 148 |
| It's Heaven | - |

1946 - Los Angeles

Jessie Mae Robinson (vo) acc. by MONTE EASTER'S ORCHESTRA: Monte Easter (tp); Maxwell Davis (ts); Rosetta Andrews (p); Ralph Hamilton (b); Charles Blackwell (d).

| | |
|---|---|
| That's My Secret | Discovery 1203 |
| Jessie Mae's Blues | - |

## ANSIDALE, ROSE (reeds)

See Collective Section.

## ARMSTRONG, LIL HARDIN (piano)

**March, 1923 - Chicago**

KING OLIVER'S JAZZ BAND: Joe "King" Oliver, Louis Armstrong (c); Honore
Dutray (tb); Johnny Dodds (cl); Lil Hardin Armstrong (p); u (bj,bass
sax); Baby Dodds (d).

| 1622-1-2 | Mabel's Dream | Paramount 20292, Clx40292, Steiner-Davis 100, Har890, Sig905 |
|---|---|---|
| 1623-1-2 | Southern Stomp | Paramount 12088, Century 3011 |
| 1624-2 | Riverside Blues | Paramount 20292, Clx40292, Steiner-Davis 100, Har890, Sig905 |

**April, 1923 - Richmond, Indiana**

KING OLIVER'S CREOLE JAZZ BAND: Joe Oliver, Louis Armstrong (c); Honore
Dutray (tb); Johnny Dodds (cl); Lil Hardin Armstrong (p); Bill Johnson
(bj); Baby Dodds (d).

| 11383 | Just Gone | Gennett 5133, Br(E)02202 |
|---|---|---|
| 11384 | Canal Street Blues | - Br(E)02200,JI-1,UHCA67-68 |
| 11385 | Mandy Lee Blues | Gennett 5134, Br(E)02201, JI-2, UHCA 69-70 |
| 11386 | I'm Going to Wear You Off My Mind | - Br(E)02201 |
| 11387 | Chimes Blues | Gennett 5135 |
| 11388 | Weather Bird Blues | Gennett 5132, Br(E)02202, JI-5, UHCA 75-76 |
| 11389 | Dipper Mouth Blues | - ,3076, Br(E)02202, JI-10, UHCA 77-78 |
| 11390 | Froggie Moore | Gennett 5135 |
| 11391 | Snake Rag | Gennett 5184 |

**June 22-23, 1923 - Chicago**

KING OLIVER'S JAZZ BAND: Joe Oliver, Louis Armstrong (c); Honore Dutray
(tb); Johnny Dodds (cl); Lil Hardin Armstrong (p); Bill Johnson (bj);
Baby Dodds (d).

| 8391 | Snake Rag | Okeh 4933 |
|---|---|---|
| 8392 | Sweet Loving Man | Okeh 4906 |
| 8393 | High Society Rag | Okeh 4933, HRS 12 |
| 8394 | Sobbin' Blues | Okeh 4906 |
| 8401 | Where Did You Stay Last Night | Okeh 4918, Br8223, HRS4 |
| 8402 | Dippermouth Blues | - |
| 8403 | Jazzin' Babies Blues | Okeh 4975 |

**July, 1923 - Chicago**

same personnel.

| 8475 | Buddy's Habits | Okeh 4000, HRS 12 |
| 8476 | Tears | - |
| 8477 | I Ain't Gonna Tell Nobody | Okeh 8148,Od(G)3198,(G)312872 |
| 8478 | Room Rent Blues | - - - |

## August, 1923 - Chicago

same personnel.

| 8484 | Riverside Blues | Okeh 40034,Od(G)3197,(G)312808 |
| 8485 | Working Man Blues | - - - |
| 8486 | Sweet Baby Doll | Okeh 8235 |
| 8487 | Mabel's Dream | - |

## October 15, 1923

KING OLIVER'S JAZZ BAND: Joe Oliver, Louis Armstrong (c); Ed Atkins or John Lindsay (tb); Jimmy Noone (cl); Lil Hardin Armstrong (p); Charlie Johnson (bass-sax); Baby Dodds (d).

| 81300 | Chattanooga Stomp | Columbia 13003D,(F)DF3079,(F)LF225 |
| 81302 | London (Cafe) Blues | Columbia 14003D |
| 81303 | Camp Meeting Blues | - |
| 81304 | New Orleans Stomp | Columbia 13003D,(F)DF3079,(F)LF225 |

## November, 1923 - Richmond, Indiana

King Oliver, Louis Armstrong (c); Honore Dutray (tb); Johnny Dodds (cl); Stomp Evans (as); Lil Hardin Armstrong (p); Bill Johnson (bj); Baby Dodds (d).

|       | That Sweet Something | Gennett 5276 |
|       | If You Want My Heart | - |
| 11633 | Alligator Hop | Gennett 5274, Century 3008 |
| 11635 | Working Man Blues | Gennett 5275 |
| 11636 | Zulu's Ball | - |
| 11638 | Krooked Blues | Gennett 5274, - |

## November 8, 1924 - New York City

Josephine Beatty (Alberta Hunter) (vo) acc. by RED ONION JAZZ BABIES: Louis Armstrong (c); Aaron Thompson (tb); Buster Bailey (cl,sop); Lil Hardin Armstrong (p); Buddy Christian (bj).

| 9167 | Everybody Loves My Baby | Gennett 5594,3044,3049, Buddy 8025, JC L-94, Slvt 4033 |
| 9176-A | Texas Moaner Blues | Gennett 5594,3044, JC L-94, Slvt 4033 |
| 9177 | Of All the Wrongs You've Done to Me | Gennett 5627, HRS32, JC L-36, Tempo R-21, Slvt 4029, Storyville KB-104 |

November 26, 1924 - New York City

    same personnel.

| | | |
|---|---|---|
| 9206 | Terrible Blues | Gennett 5607, Br80062, Gz1040, JC L-62, Slvt 4023, Storyville KB-100, HRS32 |
| 9207 | Santa Claus Blues | Gennett 5607, Br80062, Gz1040, JC L-62, Slvt 4023, Storyville KB-100 |

December 22, 1924 - New York City

    same personnel.

| | | |
|---|---|---|
| 9246 | Nobody Knows the Way I Feel This Mornin'(*) | Gennett 5626, Slvt 4030 |
| 9247-A | Early Every Morn (*) | -      - ,Buddy 8024 |
| 9248-A | Cake Walking Babies * | Gennett 5627, Gz1038, JC L-36, JI-10, Slvt 4029, Tempo R-21, UHCA 77-78 |

   * Clarence Todd (vo)
  (*) Charlie Irvis (tb); replaces Thompson, Sidney Bechet (sop)
      replaces Bailey

November 12, 1925 - Chicago

LOUIS ARMSTRONG AND HIS HOT FIVE: Louis Armstrong (c, vo); Kid Ory (tb,vo); Johnny Dodds (cl,as); Lil Hardin Armstrong (p); John St. Cyr (bj).

| | | |
|---|---|---|
| 9484 | My Heart | Okeh 8320, Co36154,DO-3424, (S)DZ-540, Od(G)E60259 |
| 9485 | Yes, I'm in the Barrel | Okeh 8261, Co36152, (F)BF-474, (I)CQ-2301, (UK)DB02978, DO-3396, (G)DW-5143, DYC-127, (S)DZ-542 |
| 9486 | Gut Bucket Blues (vKO) | Okeh 8261, Co36152,(F)BF-474, (K)CQ-2301, (UK)DB02978, DO-3396, (G)DW-5143, DYC-127, (S)Dz542 |

February 22, 1926 - Chicago

    same personnel.

| | | |
|---|---|---|
| 9503 | Come Back, Sweet Papa | Okeh 8318, HJCA-HC-21, Od279790, SpEd 5018 |

February 26, 1926 - Chicago

    same personnel.

| | | |
|---|---|---|
| 9533 | Georgia Grind (vLHA) | Okeh 8318,HJCA-HC-21, Od279790, SpEd 5018 |
| 9534 | Heebie Jeebes (vLA) | Okeh 8300, Co35660,36153, Od031939, 279826 |
| 9535 | Cornet Chop Suey | Okeh 8320,Co36154,(F)BF-309, (I)CQ-2125,(UK)DB-2624, (G)DW-5069,(S)DZ-540, HRS 2, OdA-60259, (G)E60259 |
| 9536 | Oriental Strut | Okeh 8299, Co36155, DO-3424, DZ-544, HRS-10, Od C291480 |
| 9537 | You're Next (vLA) | Okeh 8299, Co36155, DZ-544, HRS-10, OdC291480 |
| 9538 | Muskrat Ramble | Okeh 8300, Co(J)M-665,DZ-543, Od031939, 279826 |

**May 28, 1926**

LIL'S HOT SHOTS: Louis Armstrong (c); Kid Ory (tb); Johnny Dodds (cl); Lil Hardin Armstrong (p); Johnny St. Cyr (bj).

| | | |
|---|---|---|
| C340; E3156W | Georgia Bo Bo | Vocalion 1037, Br80060, (E)02065, (F)500319, Od D284029, Oriole(E)1009 |
| C341-42; E3157-58W | Drop That Sack | Vocalion 1037, Br80060, (E)02502, Oriole(E)1009 |

**June 16, 1926 - Chicago**

LOUIS ARMSTRONG AND HIS HOT FIVE: Louis Armstrong (c,vo); Kid Ory (tb); Johnny Dodds (cl,as); Lil Hardin Armstrong (p); Johnny St. Cyr (bj).

| | | |
|---|---|---|
| 9729-A | Don't Forget to Mess Around | Okeh 9343, JHCA-HC-10, JS(F)AA-519, VJR 13 |
| 9730-A | I'm Gonna Gitcha | - - - - |
| 9731-A | Dropping Shucks | Okeh 8357, BRS14,HJCA-HC-30, JS(F)AA-518, VJR 14 |
| 9732-A | Who's It (vLA)* | - - - - - |

* Louis plays slide whistle

Butterbeans and Susie (vo) added.

| | | |
|---|---|---|
| 9750-A | He Likes it Slow* | Okeh 8355 |

**June 23, 1926**

same personnel.

| | | |
|---|---|---|
| 9776-A | The King of the Zulus | Okeh 8396, BRS1, CoCQ02640, DB-3340,DCH-280,DF-3484, DO-3635,DZ-988,HJCA-HC-22, Odeon 279827, Okeh 41581 |

| | | |
|---|---|---|
| 9777-A | Big Fat Ma and Skinny Pa | Okeh 8379, HJCA-HC-9, Odeon 279789 |
| 9778-A | Lonesome Blues | Okeh 8396,BRS1,CoCQ-2640, DB03340,DCH0280,DF-3484, DO-3635,DZ-988,HJCA-HC-22, Od 279827, NOM(F)M-10, Okeh 41581 |
| 9779-A | Sweet Little Papa | Okeh 8379,HJCA-HC-9, Odeon 279789 |

July 13, 1926 - Chicago

NEW ORLEANS WANDERERS: George Mitchell (c); Kid Ory (tb); Johnny Dodds (cl); Stomp Evans (as); Lil Hardin Armstrong (p); Johnny St. Cyr (bj); Baby Dodds (d).

| | | |
|---|---|---|
| 142426 | Perdido Street Blues | Columbia 698D,BF-417,CQ-2239, DB-2860,DZ-789,GN-5086,GNS5092, M-199 |
| 142427 | Gatemouth | Columbia 698D,BF-417,CQ-2239, DB-2860,DZ-789,GN-5086, GNS5092,M-199,SpEd 6008-S, UHCA 15-16 |
| 142428 | Too Tight Blues | Columbia 735D,CQ-2240,DB-2920, DW-5080,DZ-813,GNS-5093,VJR 20 |
| 142429 | Papa Dip | Columbia 735D,CQ-2240,DB-2920, DW-5080,DZ-813,GNS-5093,VJR 20 |

July 14, 1926 - Chicago

NEW ORLEANS BOOTBLACKS: George Mitchell (c); Kid Ory (tb); Johnny Dodds (cl); Stomp Evans (as); Lil Hardin Armstrong (p); Johnny St. Cyr (bj); Baby Dodds (d).

| | | |
|---|---|---|
| 142436-1 | Mixed Salad | Columbia 14465-D,Bilt 1085, HJCA-HC-31, VJR-2 |
| 142437-3 | I Can't Stay | Columbia 14465-D,Bilt 1085, HJCA-HC-31, VJR-2 |
| 142438-1 | Flat Foot | Columbia 14337-D, CQ-2780, DB-3422, DCH-250, DZ-883, BF-618, HJCA-HC-26, VJR-1 |
| 142439-1 | Mad Dog | Columbia 14337-D, CQ-2780, DB-3422, DCH-112, DZ-883, BF-618, HJCA-HC-26, VJR-1 |

November 16, 1926 - Chicago

LOUIS ARMSTRONG AND HIS HOT FIVE: Louis Armstrong, (c); Kid Ory (tb); Johnny Dodds (cl,as); Lil Hardin Armstrong (p); Johnny Dodds (bj).

| | | |
|---|---|---|
| 9890-A | Jazz Lips | Okeh 8436,Co36153,DZ-543, Od279828,          HJCA-5 |
| 9891-A | Skid-Dat-De-Dat | —    —    —    — |

May Alix, Louis Armstrong (vo) added.

| 9892-A | Big Butter and Egg Man | |
| | From the West | Okeh 8423,HJCA-HC-16, |
| | | Od279788,     A-2384 |
| 9893-A | Sunset Cafe Stomp (vMA) | −     −     −     − |

November 27, 1926 − Chicago

LOUIS ARMSTRONG AND HIS HOT FIVE:  Louis Armstrong (c,vo); John Thomas
or Henry Clark (tb); Johnny Dodds (cl); Lil Hardin Armstrong (p); Johnny
St. Cyr (bj).

| 9980 | You Made Me Love You | Okeh 8447, Odeon 279787 |
| 9981-A | Irish Black Bottom | −          − |

April 27, 1927

Johnny Dodds (cl); Lil Hardin Armstrong (p); Bud Scott (g).

| C-775; | San | Brunswick 3574,7016,HJCA-615, |
| E-22704 | | JS AA-596,Temple 548,Vo-V1025 |
| C-776/7; | Oh Lizzie | Brunswick 3585,7015,HJCA-615, |
| E-22706/7 | | Vo-V1025 |
| C-779; | Clarinet Wobble | Brunswick 3574,7016,   − |
| E-22710 | | Temple 548, Vo-V1025 |
| C-781; | New St. Louis Blues | Brunswick 3585,7015,   − |
| E-22709 | | Vo-V1025 |

May 7, 1927 − Chicago

LOUIS ARMSTRONG AND HIS HOT SEVEN:  Louis Armstrong (c); Kid Ory (tb);
Johnny Dodds (cl); Lil Hardin Armstrong (p); Johnny St. Cyr (bj); Pete
Briggs (tuba); Baby Dodds (d).

| 80847-C | Willie the Weeper | Okeh 8482,Co20676,Od(F)277006, |
| | | Par A7595,B-71120,PZ-11120, |
| | | R2392, Vo 3381 |
| 80848-C | Wild Man Blues | Okeh 8474, CoDZ-353, |
| | | Od(I)A-2373, Par 6391, |
| | | Par(F)85190,DO-3,R113,R2162, |
| | | R3492, Vo 3193, SpEd 5003-S |

May 10, 1927 − Chicago

same personnel.

| 80854-B | Alligator Crawl | Okeh 8482, Par A6450, R2185 |
| 80855-C | Potato Head Blues | Okeh 8503,Co DZ-344,Par A6450 |

May 11, 1927

  same personnel.

| 80862-A | Melancholy Blues | Okeh 8496, Co 20028, 20177,<br>Od279829, Par6391, B71199,<br>B71247, Do-3, PZ-11238, R2162,<br>Vo 3137 |
|---|---|---|
| 80863-A | Weary Blues | Okeh 8519, Co 20056, Od 028427,<br>277006, A-2413, Par A-7595,<br>PZ-11120, R2392, Vo 3210,3216 |
| 80864-A | Twelfth Street Rag | Columbia 35663,20280,291358,<br>(F)Bf-505, CQ-2860, DB-3477,<br>DCH-112, DO-2215, DZ-884,<br>Od C291358 |

May 13, 1927 - Chicago

  same personnel.

| 80877-D | Gully Low Blues | Okeh 8474, Co(S)DZ-353,<br>Par R113, SpEd5003-S, Vo 3193 |
|---|---|---|
| 80876-B | Keyhole Blues | Okeh 8496, BRS 6, Co 20028,<br>HJCA-67, Od 279829 |

May 13, 1927 - Chicago

LOUIS ARMSTRONG AND HIS HOT SEVEN: Louis Armstrong (c,vo); Johnny Dodds
(cl); Kid Ory (tb); Lil Hardin Armstrong (p); Johnny St. Cyr (bj); Pete
Briggs (tuba); Baby Dodds (d).

| 81126-B | S.O.L. Blues | Columbia 35661, Par A-7513,<br>B-71121, PZ-1128, (E)R2774 |
|---|---|---|

May 14, 1927 - Chicago

LOUIS ARMSTRONG AND HIS HOT SEVEN: Louis Armstrong (c); Kid Ory (tb);
Johnny Dodds (cl); Lil Hardin Armstrong (p); Johnny St. Cyr (bj); Pete
Briggs (tuba); Baby Dodds (d).

| 80884-B | That's When I'll Come<br>Back to You | Okeh 8519, Co 20056, D-5039-S,<br>Od 031806, Od 272266, A2348,<br>A2339, OR-2704, A-7581, A-7595,<br>Par R113, R2704 |
|---|---|---|

September 2 & 6, 1927 - Chicago

LOUIS ARMSTRONG AND HIS HOT FIVE: Louis Armstrong (c); Kid Ory (tb);
Johnny Dodds (cl); Lil Hardin Armstrong (p); Johnny St. Cyr (bj).

| 81302-B | Put 'Em Down Blues | Okeh 8503, Co 37537, CQ-2934,<br>DB-3524,DZ-344, UHCA 59-60 |
|---|---|---|

| 81310-D | Ory's Creole Trombone | Columbia 35838,1400,37534, DS-1410,DZ-339,Od 277005, Par A-7392,B71121,DO-15,DPE-8,- DPY-1057,PZ-11356,R2792 |
| 81317-A | The Last Time | Columbia 35838,1400,37534, DS-1410,DZ-339, Par A-7392, DO-15,DPE-8,DPY-1507,PZ-11356, R2792 |

December 9, 1927 - Chicago

same personnel.

| 82037-B | Struttin' With Some Barbecue | Okeh 8566,Co37535,DS-1428, Par A7625,DO-16,PZ-11228, PZ-11233, R2829 |
| 82038-B | Got No Blues | Okeh 8551, Co 37536, DZ-343, Okeh 3204,Par DO-14,PZ-11160, R2449, Vo 3204,3237 |

December 10, 1927 - Chicago

| 82039-B | Once in a While | Okeh 8566, Co 37535, Par PZ-11228, R2242 |
| 82040-B | I'm Not Rough | Okeh 8551, Co 37536,DB-3524, DZ-343, Vo 3237 |
| 82055-B | Hotter Than That (vLA) | Okeh 8535, CoD-5039-S,-2766, Od272266,A-2339,A-2348,A-2339, OR-2704,ParA-7581,B71122,R2704, Vo 3237 |
| 82056-A | Savoy Blues | Okeh 8535, Co37537,J-2766, ParB71198,DO-9,PZ-11149,R2127, Vo 3217 |

July 5, 1928

JOHNNY DODDS TRIO:   Johnny Dodds (cl); Lil Hardin Armstrong (p); Bill Johnson (b).

| 46055 | Blue Clarinet Stomp | Victor 21554, HMV-JK2179 |
| 40656 | Blue Piano Stomp | -          Bluebird B10238 |

July 6, 1928

JOHNNY DODDS' WASHBORAD BAND: Natty Dominique (c); Honore Dutray (tb); Johnny Dodds (cl); Lil Hardin Armstrong (p); Bill Johnson (b); Baby Dodds (wb).

| 46063-2 | Bucktown Stomp | Victor V38004, Bluebird B8549 |
| 46064-2 | Weary City | -, Bluebird B10238,HMV-JK-2154 |
| 46065 | Blue Washboard Stomp | Victor 21552 |
| 46066 | Bull Fiddle Blues | - , Bluebird B8549,B10239, - |

January 16, 1929 - Chicago

  same personnel.

                Pencil Papa                    Cameo CAL-339,CDN-139,HMV7EG-8233


January 30, 1929 - Chicago

  same personnel.

  48798-3   Heah Me Talkin        Victor LPV-558,RD-7983,Swaggie 33755
  48841-1   Sweet Lorraine            -             -             -
  48842     My Little Isabelle    Victor V38541, Bilt 1092, Bb B10241,
                                   BRS-22, HMV-JK-2137
  48869     Indigo Stomp*         Victor 23396, El EG-7844

  * (cl,p,b) only


July 16, 1930 - Hollywood

  Jimmie Rodgers (vo) acc. by Louis Armstrong (c); Lil Hardin Armstrong
  (p).

  54867-2   Blue Yodel No. 9      Victor 23580,Co MZ-315,HMV-MH-194
            (Standin' on the Corner) MW M-4209, M-8124, RZ MR-3208,
                                   Twin FT-9832


January 21, 1938

  JOHNNY DODDS AND HIS CHICAGO BOYS:  Charlie Shavers (tp); Johnny Dodds
  (cl); Lil Hardin Armstrong (p); Teddy Bunn (g); John Kirby (b); O'Neill
  Spencer (d,vo).

  63189     Wild Man Blues        Decca 2111,3519,BrA-505199,VoS231
  63190     Melancholy            Decca 1676,3864,M30400,MU60514,
                                   BrA-505200, Vo S207
  63191     29th and Dearborn     Decca 2111,M30402,MU60514,Vo S215
  63192     Blues Galore          Decca 7413, M30402, Br03205,
                                   A-505200, Vo S215
  63193     Stack O'Lee Blues     Decca 1676, M30400, Vo S207
  63194     Shake Your Can        Decca 7413, Br 88044


May 19, 1938 - New York City

  Frankie "Half Pint" Jaxon (vo) acc. by Barney Bigard (cl); Lil Hardin
  Armstrong (p); Wellman Braud (b); Sid Catlett (d).

  65607     Don't Pan Me          Decca 7638
  65610     Fan It Boogie Woogie      -

July 20, 1938 - New York City

| 64325-A | I Got a Feeling For You | Decca 7593 |
|---------|-------------------------|------------|
| 64236-A | Someday, Someday | Decca 7496 |
| 64237-C | Oh That Nasty Man | - |
| 64328-A | Mailman Blues | Decca 7593 |
| 64329-A | Mayberry Blues | Decca 7520 |
| 64330-B | Evil Hearted Woman | - |

September 9, 1938

LIL HARDIN AND HER ORCHESTRA: Renald Jones (tp); J.C. Higginbotham (tb); Buster Bailey (cl); Lil Hardin Armstrong (p,vo); Wellman Braud (b); O'Neill Spencer (d).

| 64604 | Safely Locked Up in My Heart | Decca 2234,Br02732,82039,80046 |
|-------|------------------------------|--------------------------------|
| 64605 | Everything's Wrong Ain't Nothin' Right | Decca 2542, Br 02824 |
| 64606 | Harlem on Saturday Night | Decca 2234,Br02732,82039,88046 |
| 64607 | Knock Kneed Sal | Decca 2542, Br 02824 |

May 19, 1939 - New York City

Frankie "Half Pint" Jaxon (vo) acc. by Barney Bigard (cl); Lil Hardin Armstrong (p); Wellman Braud (b); Sid Catlett (d).

| 65608 | Callin' Corrine | Decca 7619 |
|-------|-----------------|------------|
| 65609 | You Can't Put That Monkey On My Back | - |

June 8, 1939 - New York City

Rosetta Howard (vo) acc. by HARLEM BLUES SERENADERS: (prob) Charlie Shavers (tp); Buster Bailey (cl); Lil Hardin Armstrong (p); Ulysses Livingston (g); Wellman Braud (b); O'Neil Spencer (d).

| 65756-A | Come Easy Go Easy | Decca 7627 |
|---------|-------------------|------------|
| 65757-A | My Blues is Like Whiskey | Decca 7640 |
| 65758-A | The Jive is Here | Decca 7618 |
| 65759-A | My Downfall | Decca 7687 |
| 65760-A | Hog Wild Blues | Decca 7658 |

June 14, 1939 - New York City

Henry Allen (tp) replaces Shavers; Sid Catlett (d) replaces Spencer.

| 65811-A | Plain Lenox Avenue | Decca 7627 |
|---------|--------------------|------------|
| 65812-A | Men Are Like Street Cars | Decca 7618 |
| 65813-A | He's Mine, All Mine | Decca 7658 |

August 15, 1939 - New York City

Alberta Hunter (vo) acc. by Charlie Shavers (tp); Buster Bailey (cl);
Lil Hardin Armstrong (p); Wellman Braud (b).

| 66104-A | Chirpin' the Blues | Decca 7644, 48066 |
|---------|-------------------|-------------------|
| 66105-A | Down-Hearted Blues | Decca 7727 |
| 66106-A | I'll See You Go | Decca 7644 |
| 66107-A | Fine and Mellow | Decca 7633, 48066 |
| 66108-A | Yelpin' the Blues | - |
| 66109-A | Someday Sweetheart | Decca 7727 |

August 30, 1939 - New York City

Blue Lu Barker (vo) acc. by Charlie Shavers (tp); Buster Bailey (cl);
Lil Hardin Armstrong (p); Ulysses Livingston (g); Wellman Braud (b);
O'Neill Spencer (d).

| 66245-A | You Ain't Had No Blues | Decca 7648 |
|---------|------------------------|------------|
| 66246-A | Marked Woman | - |
| 66247-A | Midnight Blues | Decca 7683 |
| 66248-A | Down in the Dumps | Decca 7713 |

October 13, 1939 - New York City

Helen Proctor (vo) acc. by (prob) Henry Allen (tp); Buster Bailey (cl);
Lil Hardin Armstrong (p); Ulysses Livingston (g); Wellman Braud (b);
Sidney Catlett or O'Neill Spencer (d).

| 66764-A | Cheatin' On Me | Decca 7666 |
|---------|----------------|------------|
| 66765-A | Let's Call It a Day | Decca 7703 |
| 66766-A | Take Me Along With You | - |
| 66767-A | Blues at Midnight | Decca 7666 |

March 6, 1940 - New York City

Frankie "Half Pint" Jaxon (vo) acc. by Henry Allen (tp); Rupert Cole
(cl); Lil Hardin Armstrong (p); Walter Martin (wb).

| 67271-A | When They Play Them Blues | Decca 7742 |
|---------|---------------------------|------------|
| 67272-A | Something's Goin' On Wrong | - |
| 67273-A | Wasn't It Nice | Decca 7733 |
| 67274-A | You Know Jam Don't Shake | - |

March 17-18, 1940 - New York City

LIL ARMSTRONG'S DIXIELANDERS: Jonah Jones (tp); Don Stovall (as);
Russell Jones (ts); Lil Armstrong (p); Wellman Braud (b); Manzie Johnson
(d); Midge Williams (vo).

| 67331 | Sixth Street (vMW) | Decca 7739, Br(G)82679 |
|-------|--------------------|------------------------|
| 67332 | Riffin' the Blues | Decca 7803 |

| 67333 | Why Is a Good Man So Hard to Find | - , 18121 |
| 67334 | My Secret Flame | Decca 7739 |

April 4, 1940 - New York City

Peetie Wheatstraw (vo) acc. by Jonah Jones (tp); Lil Hardin Armstrong (p); Sid Catlett (d).

| 67481-A | Big Apple Blues | Decca 7753 |
| 67482-A | Big Money Blues | Decca 7738 |
| 67483-A | Chicago Mill Blues | Decca 7788 |
| 67484-A | Five Minute Blues | Decca 7738 |
| 67485-A | Two Time Mama | Decca 7753 |
| 67486-A | Jaybird Blues | Decca 7798 |
| 67487-A | Suicide Blues | Decca 7788 |
| 67488-A | Pocket Knife Blues | Decca 7778 |

April 17, 1940 - New York City

Frankie "Half Pint" Jaxon (vo) acc. by Henry Allen (tp); Rupert Cole (cl); Lil Hardin Armstrong (p); Walter Martin (wb).

| 67565-A | Let Me Ride Your Train | Decca 7786 |
| 67566-A | Be Your Natural Self | - |
| 67567-A | Turn Over | Decca 7806 |
| 67568-A | Take Off Them Hips | Decca 7795 |
| 67569-A | Gimme a Pig's Foot | - |
| 67570-A | You Can't Tell | Decca 7806 |

April 18, 1940 - New York City

Georgia White (vo) acc. by Jonah Jones (tp); Fess Williams (cl); Lil Hardin Armstrong (p); Walter Martin (d).

| 67573-A | Jazzin' Babies Blues | Decca 7741 |
| 67574-A | Papa Pleaser | Decca 7783 |
| 67575-A | Sensation Blues | Decca 7754 |
| 67576-A | Late Hour Blues | Decca 7741 |
| 67577-B | Panama Limited Blues | Decca 7783 |
| 67578-A | You Ought to Be Ashamed of Yourself | Decca 7754 |

May 28, 1940 - New York City

RED ALLEN AND HIS ORCHESTRA or ZUTTY SINGLETON AND HIS ORCHESTRA: Henry "Red" Allen (tp); Benny Morton (tb); Ed Hall (cl); Lil Hardin Armstrong (p); Bernard Addison (g); Pops Foster (b); Zutty Singleton (d).

| 67839 | Down in Jungle Town | Decca 18092,Br(E)03166,De25101, MU-03166 |
| 67840 | Canal Street | - - - - |

| 67841 | King Porter Stomp | Decca 18093,M30320,Br(E)03167 |
| 67842 | Shim-Me-Sha-Wabble | - - - |

## August 28, 1940 - New York City

Peetie Wheatstraw (vo) acc. by Jonah Jones (tp); Lil Hardin Armstrong (p); Sid Catlett (d).

| 68022-A | Gangster's Blues | Decca 7815 |
| 68023-A | Cuttin' 'Em Slow | Decca 7798 |
| 68024-A | Look Out for Yourself | Decca 7815 |
| 68025-A | No 'Count Woman | Decca 7823 |
| 68026-A | What's That | - |

## September 23, 1940 - New York City

Jonny Temple (vo) acc. by Henry Allen (tp); Buster Bailey (cl); Lil Hardin Armstrong (p).

| 68136-A | Baby Don't You Love Me No More | Decca 7825 |
| 68137-A | My Pony | Decca 7817 |
| 68138-A | Jive Me, Baby | Decca 7800 |
| 68139-A | Corrine Corrina | Decca 7825 |
| 68140-A | Bow Leg Woman | Decca 7817 |
| 68141-A-B | Fix It Up and Go | Decca 7800 |

## February 7, 1941

Lonnie Johnson (g,vo) acc. by Lil Hardin Armstrong (p); Andrew Harris (b).

| 059205 | Crowin' Rooster Blues | Bluebird B8804 |
| 059206 | That's Love Blues | - |
| 059208 | Lazy Woman Blues | Bluebird B8748 |
| 059210 | Chicago Blues | Bluebird B8779 |
| 059211 | I Did All I Could | - |
| 059212 | In Love Again | Bluebird B8748 |

## November 11, 1941 - Chicago

Peetie Wheatstraw (vo) acc. by Lil Hardin Armstrong or Jack Dupree (p); u (b).

| 93843-A | Don't Put Yourself on the Spot | Decca 7894 |
| 93844-A | Old Organ Blues | Decca 7901 |
| 93845-A | Hearse Man Blues | Decca 7886 |
| 93846-A | Bring the Flowers While I'm Living | - |
| 93847-A | Pawn Broker Blues | Decca 7894 |
| 93848-A | Southern Girl Blues | Decca 7904 |

| 93849-A | Mister Livingood | Decca 7879 |
| 93851-A | Separation Day Blues | Decca 7901 |

**January 9, 1945 - New York City**

| C5 | Let's Get Some | Black & White 104 |
| C6 | Boogie Boo Blues | Black & White 105 |
| C7 | I'm Hip to These Women | - |
| C8 | I Got the Blues | Black & White 104 |

**January 9, 1945 - Chicago**

LIL ARMSTRONG AND HER ALL STAR BAND:  Jonah Jones (tp); J.C. Higgin-botham (tb); Al Gibson (cl,bars); Lil Hardin Armstrong (p,vo); Sylvester Hickman (b); Baby Dodds (d).

| BW82 | Little Daddy Blues | Black & White 1211, Jazztone J1039 |
| BW83 | Lady Be Good | - | - |
| BW84 | Confessin' | Black & White 1210 | - |
| BW85 | East Town Boogie | - |

**1947 - Chicago**

Lil Armstrong (p, vo).

| 101 | East Town Boogie | Eastwood 1181 |
| 102 | Walkin' On Air | Eastwood 1180 |
| 103 | Little Daddy Blues | Eastwood 1182 |
| 104 | Rock It | Eastwood 1183 |

**1947 - Chicago**

personnel unknown.

| Joogie Boogie | Gotham 241 |
| Baby Daddy | - |
| Rock It | Gotham 256 |
| Brown Gal | - |

**July 13, 1949 - New York City**

BOB CAMP AND HIS BUDDIES:  Lil Hardin Armstrong (p); Bob Camp, Brownie McGhee (g,vo); Billy Taylor (b); Herbie Cowans (d).

| 75061 | Reading Blues | Decca 48112 |
| 75062 | When You Surrender To Me | Decca 48118 |
| 75063 | Between You and Me | - |
| 75064 | My Little Rose | Decca 48112 |

October 7, 1952 - Paris

SIDNEY BECHET TRIO: Sidney Bechet (sop); Lil Hardin Armstrong (p);
Zutty Singleton (d).

| V4326 | Limehouse Blues | Vogue(F)V5138,(F)LD096,LDE069,Jzt1213 |
|-------|-----------------|------------------------------------------|
| V4327 | Milenberg Joys | − − − − |
| | Rockin' Chair | − − − |
| | Big Butter and Egg Man | − − − |
| | My Melancholy Baby | − − − |
| | Black Bottom | − − − |
| | I've Got a Right to Sing the Blues | − − − |
| V4604 | Stars Fell on Alabama | Vogue(F)V5156, Embassy 181 |
| V4605 | Lazy River/Baby's Prayer | − − |

May 20, 1953 - Paris

Lil Hardin Armstrong (p); Marcel Blanche (d).

| 53V4556 | Maple Leaf Rag | Vogue (F)V5169 |
|---------|----------------|-----------------|
| 53V4557 | The Pearls | Vogue (F)V5157,Embassy (D)182 |
| 53V4558 | Lil's Boogie | − −,Vogue(E)V2234 |
| 53V4559 | Joogie Boogie | Vogue (F)V5169 |

c. 1953 - 1954

Lil Armstrong (p) solo.

| Lil's Boogie | Swing M33307 |
|--------------|--------------|

1954 - Chicago

NATTY DOMINIQUE AND HIS NEW ORLEANS HOT SIX: Natty Dominique (tp);
Floyd O'Brien (tb); Frank Chace (cl); Lil Hardin Armstrong (p); Israel
Crosby (b); Baby Dodds (d).

| Touching Blues | Windin' Ball WB104 |
|----------------|--------------------|
| Big Butter and Egg Man | − |
| Someday Sweetheart | − |
| You Rascal You | − |

1959 - Chicago

The Hardenaires (vocal group) acc. by Lil Hardin Armstrong (p).

| | A Memphis Man | Trend 30-017 |
|-------|----------------|--------------|
| K3608 | Let's Have a Ball | Ebony 1015 |

September 1, 1961 - Chicago

LOVIE AUSTIN'S BLUES SERENADERS: Jimmy Archey (tb); Darnell Howard (cl); Lil Hardin Armstrong replaces Lovie Austin (p); Pops Foster (b); Jasper Taylor (d).

| | | |
|---|---|---|
| After All These Years | Riverside RLP(S9) 390 | |

September 7, 1961 - Chicago

personnel unknown.

| 365 | Red Arrow Blues | Riverside RLP(S9) 401 | |
|---|---|---|---|
| 366 | Bugle Blues | -, | Riverside (S9) 389, |
| 367 | Basin Street Blues | - | |
| 368 | Muskrat Ramble | -, | Riverside (S9) 390 |
| 369 | Royal Garden Blues | - | |
| 370 | Easttown Boogie | - | |
| 371 | Clip Joint | - | |
| 374 | Boogie Me | -, | - |

October 31, 1961 - New York City

Lil Hardin Armstrong (p) solo.

| | |
|---|---|
| Original Boogie | Verve MGV8441 |
| Original Rag | - |

c. 1963

Little Ben Montgomery (vo,p) acc. by u (tp); Lil Hardin (p); The Hardinaires & The Folk Jazz Hootenanies (vocal groups)

| | |
|---|---|
| Gonna Raise Ruckus Tonite | Ebony 1030 |


## ASHBY, DOROTHY (harp)

1957 - New York City

Dorothy Ashby (h); Frank Wess (fl); Eddie Jones (b); Ed Thigpen (d).

| | |
|---|---|
| Thou Swell | Regent MG 6039 |
| Stella By Starlight | - |
| Aeolian Groove | - |
| Quietude | - |

Wendell Marshall (b) replaces Jones.

| | |
|---|---|
| Spicy | - |
| Dancing on the Ceiling | - |
| Lamentation | - |

March 21, 1958 - New York City

Dorothy Ashby (h); Frank Wess (fl); Gene Wright (b); Art Taylor (d).

| 1481 | Small Hotel | Prestige LP 7140 |
|------|-------------|------------------|
| 1482 | Charmaine | - |
| 1483 | Jollity | - |
| 1484 | Moonlight in Vermont | - |
| 1485 | Dancing in the Dark | - |
| 1486 | Back Talk | - |
| 1487 | Pawky | - |

September 19, 1958 - New York City

Dorothy Ashby (h); Frank Wess (fl); Gene Wright (b); Roy Haynes (d).

| Bohemia After Dark | New Jazz LP 8209 |
|--------------------|------------------|
| Yesterdays | - |
| Rascality | - |
| Autumn in Rome | - |
| It's a Minor Thing | - |
| Taboo | - |
| Alone Together | - |
| You'd Be So Nice to Come Home To | - |

August 16, 1961 - New York City

Dorothy Ashby (h); Gene Wright (b); John Toole (d).

| Lonely Melody | Argo 5406, LP(S) 690 | |
|---------------|----------------------|---|
| Secret Love | - | - |
| John R. | | - |
| Django | | - |
| Gloomy Sunday | | - |
| Satin Doll | | - |
| Li'l Darlin' | | - |
| Booze | | - |
| You Stepped Out of a Dream | | - |
| Stranger in Paradise | | - |

c. 1961

personnel unknown.

| Soft Winds | Jazzland JLP (S9) 61 |
|------------|----------------------|
| Wild is the Wind | - |
| The Man I Love | - |
| My Ship | - |
| Love is Here to Stay | - |
| I've Never Been in Love Before | - |
| With Strings Attached | - |
| Guns of Navarone | - |
| Misty | - |

| | |
|---|---|
| Gypsy | - |
| Laura | - |

**May 3, 1965 - New York**

Jimmy Cleveland, Quentin Jackson, Sonny Russo, Tony Studd (tb); Dorothy
Ashby (h); Richard Davis (b); Grady Tate (d); Willie Bobo (perc).

| | |
|---|---|
| What Did You Leave Me | Atlantic ATL 5047 |
| What Am I Here For | - |
| House of the Rising Sun | - |
| Nabu Carfa | - |
| Dodi Li | - |

**May 4, 1965 - New York**

same personnel.

| | |
|---|---|
| Flighty | Atlantic ATL 5047 |
| Essence of Sapphire | - |
| I Will Follow You | - |
| Invitation | - |
| Feeling Good | - |

**c. 1968**

Soul Vibrations: personnel unknown

| | |
|---|---|
| Soul Vibrations | Cadet 809 |
| Games | - |
| Action Live | - |
| Lonely Girl | - |
| Life Has Its Trials | - |
| Little Sunflower | - |
| Valley of the Dolls | - |
| Come Live With Me | - |
| Look of Love | - |

## AUSTIN, LOVIE (piano)

**c. 1923**

Ma Rainey (vo) ac. by LOVIE AUSTIN'S SERENADERS: Tommy Ladnier (c);
Jimmy O'Bryant (cl); Lovie Austin (p); The Pruitt Twins (g).

| | | |
|---|---|---|
| 1698 | Lost Wandering Blues | Paramount 12098 |
| 1699 | Dream Blues | - |

**June 1923 - Chicago**

Ida Cox (vo) acc. by Lovie Austin (p).

```
1437-1-2-   Any Woman's Blues            Paramount 12503, Har847*,
   3-4                                   Slvt 3559**
1438-1-2    'Bama Bound Blues            Paramount 12045, Har829
1439-1-2    Lovin' is the Thing I'm
            Wild About                        -          -
```

```
 *  listed as Julia Powers acc. by Goldie Hall
**  listed as Jane Smith (vo).
```

June, 1923 - Chicago

LOVIE AUSTIN'S SERENADERS:  Tommy Ladnier (c); Jimmy O'Bryant (cl);
Lovie Austin (p); Ida Cox (vo).

```
1442-1-2    Graveyard Dream Blues        Paramount 12044,Sig907,Har827,
                                         JC L-22
1443-1-2    Weary Way Blues                 -        -        -        -
```

September, 1923 - Chicago

Ida Cox (vo) acc. by Lovie Austin (p).

```
1486-1-2    Blue Monday Blues            Paramount 12053,Har 847*,
                                         Slvt 3559**, Stash ST 109
1487-1-2-4  I Love My Man Better Than
            I Love Myself                Paramount 12056, Har 858
1488-1-3-4  Ida Cox's Lawdy Lawdy Blues  Paramount 12064, Har 883*
1493-3,4    Moanin' Groanin' Blues          -      , Riverside 12-147
1496-1-2-
   3-4      Chattanooga Blues            Paramount 12063, Har 872
1503-1-2-
   3-4-5-6  Chicago Bound Blues          Paramount 12056, Har 858
1504-1-2    Come Right In                Paramount 12022
1509-1-2-   I've Got the Blues for       Paramount 12063, Har 872,
   3-4          Rampart Street           AmMusic 7
```

```
 *  listed as Julia Powers acc. by Goldie Hall and her Blues
       Serenaders
**  listed as Jane Smith (vo).
```

October, 1923 - Chicago

Alberta Hunter (vo) acc. by her PARAMOUNT BOYS:  Tommy Ladnier (c);
Jimmy O'Bryant (cl); Lovie Austin or Glover Compton (p).

```
1528-1      Experience Blues             Paramount 12065, Har873*,
                                         Slvt 3570
1529-1-     Sad 'N Lonely Blues             -        -        -
```

```
 *  listed as May Alix (vo) and her Harmograph Jazz Boys
**  listed as Helen Roberts (vo).
```

October, 1923 - Chicago

    Alberta Hunter (vo) acc. by John Obrigant (cl); Lovie Austin (p); u (d).

| 1530-1-2 | Miss Anna Brown | Paramount 12066 |
|---|---|---|
| 1531-1-2 | Maybe Someday | - |

October, 1923 - Chicago

    Ida Cox (vo) acc. by Lovie Austin (p).

| 1545-1-2 | Graveyard Dream Blues | Paramount 12022 |
|---|---|---|

December, 1923 - Chicago

LOVIE AUSTIN AND HER BLUES SERENADERS:  Ida Cox (vo); Tommy Ladnier (c);
Jimmy O'Bryant (cl); Lovie Austin (p).

| 1594-1- | Mama Doo Shee Blues | Paramount 12085, Har 897, JC L-76 |
|---|---|---|
| 1595-1-2 | Worried Mama Blues | -  -  - |

Ma Rainey (vo) replaces Cox.

| 1596-2 | Bad Luck Blues | Paramount 12081 |
|---|---|---|
| 1597-1-2 | Boweavil Blues | Paramount 12080, Poydras 78 |
| 1598-2 | Barrell House Blues | Paramount 12082, JC L-48, A.F.C.D.J. A-047 |
| 1599-1-2 | Those All Night Long Blues | Paramount 12081 |

Edmonia Henderson (vo) replaces Rainey.

| 1601-1 | Black Man Blues | Paramount 12084, Slvt 3562, 3521 |
|---|---|---|
| 1603-1-2 | Worried 'Bout Him Blues | -  -  - |

Ida Cox (vo) replaces Henderson.

| 1604-1-2 | So Soon This Morning Blues | Paramount 12086 |
|---|---|---|
| 1605-1 | Mailman Blues | Paramount 12087 |
| 1607-2 | Confidential Blues | Paramount 12086 |

Ma Rainey (vo) replaces Cox.

| 1608-1-2 | Moonshine Blues | Paramount 12083, Har 896, JC L-66 |
|---|---|---|
| 1609-2 | Last Minute Blues | Paramount 12080, Poydras 78 |
| 1612-2 | Southern Blues | Paramount 12083, Har 896, JC L-66 |
| 1613-2 | Walking Blues | Paramount 12082, JC L-48, A.F.C.D.J. A-047 |

c. 1924

Ethel Waters (vo) acc. by LOVIE AUSTIN'S SERENADERS:  Featuring Joe
Smith (tp); Lovie Austin (p).

```
1737        Tell 'Em 'Bout Me          Paramount 12214
1740        You'll Need Me When I'm
            Long Gone                     -  , Slvt 3537
```

February, 1924 - Chicago

Edmonia Henderson (vo) acc. by LOVIE AUSTIN AND HER BLUES SERENADERS:
Tommy Ladnier (c); Jimmy O'Bryant (cl); Charles Harris (as); Lovie
Austin (p).

```
1689-1-2    Brownskin Man             Paramount 12095
1690-2      Traveling Blues               -  , Slvt 3521
1691-2      Mama Don't Want Sweet     Paramount 12203, Tempo R-43
            Man Anymore
1692-2      Hateful Blues                 -          -
1693-2      If You Sheik On Your Mama Paramount 12097
            Mama's Gonna Sheba On You
```

February, 1924 - Chicago

LOVIE AUSTIN'S SERENADERS:   Ida Cox (vo); Tommy Ladnier (c); Jimmy
O'Bryant (cl); Charles Harris (as); Lovie Austin (p).

```
1708        Mean Papa, Turn Your Key  Paramount 12097
```

March, 1924 - Chicago

Ma Rainey (vo) acc. by HER GEORGIA BAND:   Tommy Ladnier (c); Jimmy
O'Braynt (cl); Charles Harris (as,ts); Lovie Austin (p).

```
1701-2      Honey Where You Been So
            Long                      Paramount 12200, JC L-82
1702-2-3    Ya-Da-Do                  Paramount 12257
1703-1      These Dogs of Mine        Paramount 12215, AmMusic 6,
                                      JC L-78
1704-2      Lucky Rock Blues              -          -          -
```

March, 1924 - Chicago

Edna Hicks (vo) acc. by LOVIE AUSTIN AND HER BLUES SERENADERS:   Tommy
Ladnier (c); Jimmy O'Bryant (cl); Lovie Austin (p).

```
1710-2      Down on the Levee Blues   Paramount 12204
1711-2      Lonesome Woman Blues          -,         Slvt 3520
```

Ethel Waters (vo) replaces Hicks.

```
1742-1-2    Craving Blues             Paramount 12313, Slvt 3536
```

March, 1924 - Chicago

Ethel Waters (vo) acc. by LOVIE AUSTIN'S SERENADERS:   Joe Smith (tp);
Buster Bailey (cl); Lovie Austin (p); prob. Kaiser Marshall (d).

| 1747-2 | Black Spatch Blues | Paramount 12230, Slvt 3535 |
| 1749-2 | I Want Somebody All My Own | – | – |

## April, 1924 – Chicago

Ma Rainey (vo) acc. by HER GEORGIA BAND:  Tommy Ladnier (c); Jimmy
O'Bryant (cl); Charles Harris (as,ts); Lovie Austin (p).

| 1741-1 | South Bound Blues | Paramount 12227, JC L-107, |
| | | A.F.C.D.J.A-101 |

## May, 1924 – Chicago

same personnel.

| 1758-1-2 | Lawd Send Me a Man Blues | – | – | – |
| 1759-2 | Ma Rainey's Mystery Record | Paramount 12200, JC L-82 |

## July, 1924 – Chicago

LOVIE AUSTIN'S SERENADERS:  Ida Cox (vo); Tommy Ladnier (c); Jimmy
O'Bryant (cl); Arville Harris (ts); Lovie Austin (p).

| 1843 | Worried In Mind Blues | Paramount 12237 |
| 1855 | My Mean Ma Blues | – |

## August, 1924 – Chicago

same personnel.

| 1705 | Last Time Blues | Paramount 12212 |
| 1706 | Worried Anyhow Blues | Paramount 12202 |
| 1707 | Chicago Monkey Man Blues | – |
| 1714 | Blues Ain't Nothing Else | |
| | But | Paramount 12212 |
| 1840 | Kentucky Man Blues | Paramount 12220 |
| 1841 | Cherry Pickin' Me | Paramount 12228 |
| 1842 | Wild Women Don't Have | |
| | the Blues | – |
| 1854 | Death Letter Blues | Paramount 12220 |

## August, 1924 – Chicago

same personnel.  (Arville Harris listed as Charles Harris).

| 1824-3 | Shave 'Em Dry | Paramount 12222 |
| 1825-2 | Farewell Daddy Blues | – |

## October, 1924 – Chicago

Ford & Ford (male & female vocal duets) acc. by Tommy Ladnier (c);
Johnny Dodds (cl); Lovie Austin (p).

```
1899-2     Skeeg-A-Lee Blues          Paramount 12244
1914-1     I'm Three Times Seven         -
```

October, 1924 - Chicago

Edmonia Henderson (vo) acc. by LOVIE AUSTIN AND HER BLUES SERENADERS:
Tommy Ladnier (c); Johnny Dodds (cl); Lovie Austin (p).

```
1897-1-2   Jelly Roll Blues           Paramount 12239,14402,JC L-21,
                                       Slvt 3523
```

Edmonia Henderson (vo) acc. by u (c,tb,cl,ts); Lovie Austin (p); u (b).

```
1905-1     Lazy Daddy Blues           Paramount  12239,14002,JC  L-21,
                                       Slvt 3523
```

October 15, 1924 - New York City

Ma Rainey (vo) acc. by her GEORGIA JAM BAND:  Howart Scott (tp); Charlie
Green (tb); Buster Bailey (cl); Lovie Austin (p); Kaiser Marshall (d).

```
1922-2     Booze and Blues            Paramount 12242
1923-2     Toad Frog Blues               -
1924-1-2   Jealous Hearted Blues      Paramount  12252,JI 9,UHCA 85-86
```

October 16, 1924 - New York City

Louis Armstrong (tp) replaces Scott.

```
1925-1-2   See See Rider Blues        Paramount  12252,JI 9,UHCA 85-86
1926       Jelly Bean Blues           Paramount  12238,JI 8,UHCA 83-84
1927       Countin' the Blues            -        -        -
```

November, 1924 - Chicago

Ma Rainey (vo) acc. by her GEORGIA JAM BAND:  Tommy Ladnier (c); Jimmy
O'Bryant (cl); Charles Harris (as); Lovie Austin (p).

```
10001-2    Cell Bound Blues           Paramount 12257
```

November, 1924 - Chicago

Julia Davis (vo) acc. by LOVIE AUSTIN AND HER BLUES SERENADERS:   Tommy
Ladnier (c); Jimmy Bryant (cl); Lovie Austin (p).

```
1002-4     Ska-Da-De                  Paramount 12248
1003-4     Black Hand Blues              -
1004-2     Steppin' On the Blues      Paramount 12255, Century 3017,
                                       JC L-41, A.F.C.D.J. A-06
1005-2     Travelin' Blues            Paramount 12255, Century 3102,
                                       JC L-41
```

April, 1925 - Chicago

LOVIE AUSTIN AND HER BLUES SERENADERS: Tommy Ladnier (c); Jimmy
O'Bryant (cl); Lovie Austin (p); W.E. Burton (d); Priscilla Stewart
(vo).

| 2094-1-2 | Charleston Mad | Paramount 12278, Century 3012, JC L-118 |
| 2095-2 | Charleston, South Carolina | - |
| 2096-1 | Heebie Jeebies | Paramount 12283, Slvt 3551, JC L-64 |
| 2097-2 | Peepin' Blues | Paramount 12277, Slvt 3572, JC L-118, VJR 16, A.F.C.D.J. A-04 |
| 2098-2 | Mojo Blues | Paramount 12283, Slvt 3552, JC L-64 |

April, 1925 - Chicago

Ida Cox (vo) acc. by LOVIE AUSTIN AND HER BLUES SERENADERS: u (c);
Jimmy O'Bryant (cl); Lovie Austin (p).

| 2103-2 | Black Crepe Blues | Paramount 12291 |
| 2104-2 | Fare Thee Well Poor Gal | - |
| 2105-2 | Cold Black Ground Blues | Paramount 12282 |
| 2106-2 | Someday Blues | - |

May, 1925 - Chicago

Ma Rainey (vo) acc. by her GEORGIA JAZZ BAND: Howard Scott (tp);
Charlie Green (tb); Buster Bailey (cl); Lovie Austin (p); Kaiser
Marshall (d).

| 2138-1 | Louisiana Hoodoo Blues | Paramount 12290 |
| 2139-1 | Goodbye Daddy Blues | - |

August, 1925 - Chicago

LOVIE AUSTIN AND HER SERENADERS: Bob Shaffner (c); Jimmy O'Bryant (cl);
Lovie Austin (p); W.E. Burton (d); Ethel Waters (vo).

| 2219-1 | Don't Shake It No More | Paramount 12300, Slvt 3552 |
| 2220-1 | Rampart Street Blues | - | Slvt 3551 |
| 2222-2 | Too Sweet for Words (vEW) | Paramount 12313 |

August, 1925 - Chicago

Ida Cox (vo) acc. by LOVIE AUSTIN AND HER SERENADERS: Bob Shaffner (c);
Jimmy O'Bryant (cl); Lovie Austin (p).

| 2242-1 | Mistreatin' Daddy Blues | Paramount 12298 |
| 2243-1- | Long Distance Blues | Paramount 12307 |

| 2244-2 | Southern Woman's Blues | Paramount 12298 |
| 2246-1 | Lonesome Blues | Paramount 12307 |

**September, 1925 - Chicago**

W.E. Burton (d) added.

| 2291-2 | How Can I Miss You When I've God Dead Aim | Paramount 12234 |
| 2292-2 | I Ain't Got Nobody | - |
| 2293-1 | Coffin Blues* | Paramount 12318 |
| 2294-2 | Ramblin' Blues | - |
| 2299-1 | One Time Woman Blues | Paramount 12325 |

* Joe Smith (c) replaces Shaffner; no (cl,d).

**September, 1925 - Chicago**

Viola Bartlette (vo) acc. by LOVIE AUSTIN'S BLUES SERENADERS: Jimmy O'Bryant (cl); Lovie Austin (p); W.E. Burton (d).

| 2300-2 | Go Back Where You Stayed Last Night | Paramount 12322 |
| 2301-1-2 | Tennessee Blues | - |

**November, 1925 - Chicago**

Ozie McPherson (vo) acc. by LOVIE AUSTIN'S SERENADERS: Bob Shaffner (c); Jimmy O'Bryant (cl); Lovie Austin (p); W.E. Burton (d).

| 11005-2 | You Gotta Know How | Paramount 12327, Slvt 3522 |
| 11006-2 | Outside of That He's All Right With Me | - | - |

**January, 1926 - Chicago**

Ozie McPherson (vo) acc. by LOVIE AUSTIN'S BLUES SERENADERS: u (c); Buster Bailey (cl); Charlie Green (tb); Lovie Austin (p); Kaiser Marshall (d).

| 2422 | Down To the Bottom Where I Stayed | Paramount 12362 |

Jimmy O'Bryant (cl) replaces Baily; Kid Ory (tb) replaces Green.

| 2423-1 | Standing on the Corner Blues | Paramount 12350, Slvt 3557 |
| 2425-2 | He's My Man | - | - |

January, 1926 - Chicago

Viola Bartlette (vo) acc. by LOVIE AUSTIN'S BLUES SERENADERS:    Jimmy
O'Bryant (cl); Lovie Austin (p); W.E. Burton (d).

2426-1    You Never Can Tell What       Paramount 12351
          Your Perfectly Good Man
          Will Do


February, 1926 - Chicago

Ida Cox (vo) acc. by Jimmy O'Bryant (c); Charlie Green (tb); Lovie
Austin (p); u (d).

2441-2    Trouble Trouble Blues         Paramount 12344
2443-1    Do Lawd Do                    Paramount 12353
2444-1    I'm Leaving Here Blues        Paramount 12344
2445-2    Night and Day Blues           Paramount 12353


April, 1926 - Chicago

LOVIE AUSTIN AND HER SERENADERS: Natty Dominique (c); Kid Ory (tb);
Johnny Dodds (cl); Lovie Austin (p); W.E. Burton (d).

11096-2   Jackass Blues                 Paramount 12361, Broadway 1018,
                                        Century  3007,  Puritan  11460,
                                        JC L-19
          Frog Tongue Stomp             Paramount 12361, Broadway 1018,
                                        Century  3007,  Puritan  11460,
                                        JC L-19, Stash ST109


April 20, 1926 - Chicago

Edmonia Henderson (vo) acc. by Johnny Dodds (cl); Lovie Austin (p).

          Who's Gonna Do Your Lovin'  Vocalion 1015, Br A-169
          (When Your Good Man's
          Gone Away)
          Nobody Else Will Do              -        Oriole 1005


May, 1926 - Chicago

Viola Bartlette (vo) acc. by LOVIE AUSTIN'S BLUES SERENADERS:  Kid Ory
(tb); Johnny Dodds (cl); Lovie Austin (p).

2545-2    Sunday Morning Blues          Paramount 12369
2546-1-2  You Don't Mean Me No Good     Paramount 12363
2552-1-2  Out Bound Train Blues              -


May, 1926 - Chicago

Viola Bartlette (vo) acc. by COBB'S PARAMOUNT SYNCOPATORS:  Jimmy Cobb
(c); u (tb); Johnny Dodds (cl); Lovie Austin (p).

| 2554-2 | Walk Easy 'Cause My Papa's Here | Paramount 12369 |
|--------|--------------------------------|-----------------|

**August, 1926 - Chicago**

LOVIE AUSTIN AND HER SERENADERS: Natty Dominique (c); Kid Ory (tb); Johnny Dodds (cl); Lovie Austin (p); Eustern Woodford (bj); W.E. Burton (d); Henry Williams (vo).

| 2621-1 | Chicago Mess Around (vHW) | Paramount 12380,14030,JC L-100, JD 018 |
|--------|----------------------------|-----------------|
| 2622-1 | Galion Stomp | —     —     —     — |
| 2623-2 | In the Alley Blues | Paramount 12391, AmMusic 4, JC L-30, A.F.C.D.J. A-04 |
| 2624-2 | Merry Makers Twin (vHW) | Paramount 12391, AmMusic 4, JC L-30 |

**September, 1926 - Chicago**

Ida Cox (vo) acc. by LOVIE AUSTIN'S SERENADERS: u (c,cl); Lovie Austin (p); W.E. Burton (d).

| 2633-2 | Don't Blame Me | Paramount 12381 |
|--------|----------------|-----------------|
| 2634-2 | Scottle-De-Do | — |

**November 17, 1926 - Chicago**

Hattie McDaniels (vo) acc. by LOVIE AUSTIN'S SERENADERS: u (c); Preston Jackson (tb); Darnell Howard (as); Lovie Austin (p); Johnny St. Cyr (bj).

| 9899-A | I Wish I Had Somebody | Okeh 8434 |
|--------|------------------------|-----------|
| 9900-A | Boo Hoo Blues | — |

**March, 1929 - Chicago**

Hattie McDaniels and "Dentist" Jackson (vocal duets) acc. by Papa Charlie Jackson (g); Lovie Austin (p).

| 21203-2 | Dentist Chair Blues, Pt. 1 | Paramount 12751 |
|---------|-----------------------------|-----------------|
| 21204-2 | Dentist Chair Blues, Pt. 2 | — |

**February 5, 1946 - Chicago**

Bertha "Chippie" Hill (vo) acc. by LOVIE AUSTIN'S BLUES SERENADERS: Lee Collins (tp); Lovie Austin (p); John Lindsay (b); Baby Dodds (d).

| C1 | Trouble in Mind | Circle J1003, Riverside RLP1059 |
|----|-----------------|---------------------------------|
| C2 | Careless Love | Circle J1004,     — |
| C3 | Around the Clock Blues | Circle J1013,    —,RLP12-113, RLP12-121 |

September 1, 1961 - Chicago

Alberta Hunter (vo) ac. by LOVIE AUSTIN'S BLUES SERENADERS: Jimmy
Archey (tb); Darnell Howard (cl); Lovie Austin (p); George "Pops" Foster
(b); Jasper Taylor (d).

| | | |
|------|-------------------------------|-------------------------------------|
| 312 | Downhearted Blues | Riverside RLP(S9)389,RLP(S9)418 |
| 313 | Moanin' Low | - |
| 314 | You Better Change | - |
| 315 | Now I'm Satisfied | - |
| 316 | I Will Always Be in Love With You | - |
| 317 | Streets Paved with Gold | - |
| 318 | St. Louis Blues | - |

Alberta Hunter out.

| | | |
|------|-------------------|-------------------------------------|
| 320 | Gallion Blues | Riverside RLP(S9)390,RSL(S9)418 |
| 321 | C Jam Blues | - |
| 322 | Sweet Georgia Brown | - |

date unknown

LOVIE AUSTIN'S BLUES SERENADERS: Tommy Ladnier (c); Johnny Dodds (cl);
Arville Harris (ts); Lovie Austin (p); u (d); Priscilla Steward (vo).

| | | |
|-------|-------------------------------|-----------|
| 2755 | O Katharina | Vox 1883 |
| 2756 | Shanghai Shuffle | - |
| 2757 | Alabamy Bound | Vox 1891 |
| 2758 | By the Waters of Minnetonka Melody | - |

See Collective Section for Additional Recordings

### BAILEY, JESSIE (reeds)

See Collective Section.

### BAKER, HELEN (guitar)

See Collective Section.

### BARRETT, "SWEET" EMMA (piano)

August 20, 1952 - New Orleans

Creole George Guesnon (bj,vo) acc. by Jimmy "Kid" Clayton (tp,vo); Joe
Avery (tb); Albert Burbank (cl); Emma Barrett (p); Sylvester Handy (b);
Alec Bigard (d).

```
              Gettysburg                    Fokways FA 2463, Topic(E) 12T55
              Jimmy's Blues                 -
              Corrine, Corrina              -              -
              In the Groove                 -              -
```

January 25, 1961 - New Orleans

SWEET EMMA BARRETT AND HER DIXIELAND BOYS: Percy Humphrey (tp); Jim
Robinson (tb); Willie Humphrey (cl); Emma "The Bell Gal" Barrett (p,
vo); Emanuel Sayles (bj,g); McNeal Breaux (b); Josiah Frazier (d).

```
180-1    Just a Little While           Riverside RLP(9S)364
181      St. Louis Blues               Riverside RLP(9S)356
182      Bill Bailey                   Riverside RLP(9S)364
183      Down in Honky Tonk Town       -
184      The Bell Gal's Careless Blues -
185      Tishomingo Blues              -
186      High Society                  Riverside RLP(9S)357
187      The Saints                    Riverside RLP(9S)364
188      Sweet Emma's Blues            Riverside RLP(9S)357
189      I Ain't Gonna Give...         Riverside RLP(9S)364
190      Chinatown My Chinatown        -
```

1963 - New Orleans

SWEET EMMA BARRETT AND HER NEW ORLEANS MUSIC: Alvin Alcorn (tp); Jim
Robinson (tb); Louis Cottrell (cl); Sweet Emma Barrett (p,vo); Emanuel
Sayles (bj); Placider Adams (b); Paul Barbarin (d).

```
              Jelly Roll Blues             Southland SLP 241
              A Good Man is Hard to Find   -
              Big Butter and Egg Man       -
              That's a Plenty              -
```

Raymond Burke (cl) added.  Don Alpert (tp) replaces Alcorn; Waldren
Joseph (tb); replaces Robinson.

```
              Breeze                       Southland SLP 241
              Bogakusa Strut               -
              Pagan Love Song              -
              Take Me Out to the Ballgame  -
```

1964 - New Orleans

Alvin Alcorn (tp); Andrew Morgan (cl); Capt. John Handy (as); Sweet Emma
Barrett (p,vo); "Creole" George Guesnon (bj); Joseph Butler (b); Josiah
"Cie" Frazier (d).

```
              Oh, Didn't He Ramble         New Orleans Rarities 2
              Pallet on the Floor          -
              In the Shade of the Old Apple Tree   -
              Big Lunch Blues              -
              Just a Closer Walk with Thee -
              Bill Bailey (vSEB)           -
```

September, 1964 - New Orleans

AT DISNEYLAND: Perry Humphrey (tp); Jim Robinson (tb); Willie Humphrey
(cl); Sweet Emma Barrett (p,vo); Emanuel Sayles (bj); Placide Adams (b);
Joseph "Cie" Frazier (d).

| | |
|---|---|
| Just a Closer Walk with | GHB 142 |
| Thee | |
| When I Grow Too Old to Dream | - |
| Just a Little While to | - |
| Stay Here | |
| Eyes of Texas | - |
| Down in Honky Town | - |
| I Ain't Gonna Give Nobody | - |
| None of My Jelly Roll | |
| Yes Sir, That's My Baby | - |
| Black & Blue | - |
| St. Louis Blues | - |

Thomas Jefferson (tp,vo) replaces Humphrey.

| | |
|---|---|
| All The Wrongs You've Done | GHB 142 |
| To Me | |
| Bill Bailey Please Come Home | - |
| Bye and Bye (vTJ) | - |
| It's a Long Way to Tipperary | - |

October 18, 1964 - "Tyrone Guthrie Theatre" - Minneapolis

Percy Humphrey (tp,vo); Jim Robinson (tb); Willie Humphrey (cl,vo);
Sweet Emma Barrett (p,vo); Emanuel Sayles (bj); Alcide "Slow Drag"
Pavageau (b); Josiah "Cie" Frazier (d).

| | |
|---|---|
| Basin Street Blues | Preservation Hall 2 |
| Clarinet Marmalade | - |
| Chimes Blues | - |
| Just a Closer Walk with | - |
| Thee (vSEB) | |
| Little Liza Jane (vWH) | - |
| I'm Alone Because I | - |
| Love You (vSEB) | |
| Ice Cream (vPH) | - |
| When the Saints...(vPH) | - |

November, 1965 - "Dixieland Hall"

Alvin Alcorn (tp); Jim Robinson (tb,vo); Willie Humphrey (cl); Sweet
Emman Barrett (p,vo,ldr), Marvin Kimball (bj); Josiah "Cie" Fazier (d).

| | |
|---|---|
| Somebody Stole My Gal | Nobility LP711 |
| (vSEB) | |
| Chinatown | - |
| Bye and Bye (vJR,vSEB) | - |

Whenever You're Lonesome,                    -
    Telephone Me (vSEB)
Bill Bailey (vSEB)                            -


### BARTON, LYNN (trombone)

1944 - Dallas

Don Potter (c); Lynn Barton (tb); Rupert Murphy (ts); Jim Cullum (bars);
Shub Fuertes (cl); Vincent Parrino (p); John Gilliland (tuba); Bob
McClendon (d).

             At the Jazz Band Ball      Dallas Jazz Club (no #)
             Royal Garden Blues         -


### BARTON, WILLENE (tenor sax)

August 8, 1956 - New York

Joe Medlin (vo) acc. by Willene Barton (ts); Don Abney (p); Mickey Baker
(g); Arvell Shaw (b); Granville T. Hogan (d).

K8804      Lord Knows I Tried         King 4970
K8806      After All I've Been To You  -


February 5, 1957 - New York

Willen Barton (ts); Dayton Selby (org); Skeeter Best (g); Milt Hinton
(b); Eddie Locke (d); Paul Livert (bgs).

H2PB1404   Teenagers Honky Tonk       Victor LPM1540
H2PB1405   Baryon's Blues             -
H2PB1406   Dayton's Dance             -
H2PB1407   Little Brown Bug           -


### BEAOUT MARILYN (cello)

See Collective Section


### BEATTY, WINI (piano)

See Collective Section.

BEAUCAMP, MARTHA (saxophone)

August 9-10, 1959 - Albuquerque, New Mexico

Buddy de Franco with the UNIVERSITY OF NEW MEXICO STAGE BAND: Dick Beaucamp, Duke Peer, Gordon Purslow, Ed Tucker (tp); Larry Case, John Cheaten, John Husler, Jim Richards (tb); Wayne Sharp (FrH); Buddy de Franco (cl); Art Chavez, Harvey Dove, Martha Beaucamp, Bruce Erdale, Larry Shetts (saxes); Dick van Dongen (fl); Bob O'Boyle (oboe); Pat Lewis (bassoon); Jim Bonnel (p); Pete Schoenfeld (b); Gerry Hauer (d).

| | |
|---|---|
| One Morning in May | Advance Guard LP 1001 |
| Danny Boy | - |
| If You Cared | - |
| My Man's Gone Now | - |
| I've Got the World on a String | - |
| Fancy Meeting Karen | - |
| Burnt Water | - |
| Intermezzo | - |
| Touch Me Softly | - |
| El Yorke | - |
| The Folks Who Live on the Hill | - |
| All Through the Night | - |

BERMAN, RUTH (harp)

January 13, 1956 - New York

Cora Woods (vo) acc. by Clifford Scott, Budd Johnson, Big John Greer (ts); Bill Doggett (org); Billy Butler (g); Al Lucas (b); Shep Shepard (d); Ruth Berman (h).

| | | |
|---|---|---|
| K8691 | Father Forgive Him | Federal 12256 |
| K8694 | Don't Fall in Love With Me | - |

January 13, 1956 - New York

Joe Medlin (vo) acc. by Clifford Scott, Budd Johnson, Big John Greer (ts); Bill Doggett (p,org); Billy Butler (g); Al Lucas (b); Shep Shepard (d); Ruth Berman (h).

| | | |
|---|---|---|
| K8692-1 | Suffering With the Blues | King 4886 |
| K8693-1 | Someone Made You For Me | - |

BIRDSONG, BLANCHE (harp)

March, 1960 - Baden-Baden

Stan Getz with RUSSELL GARCIA'S ORCHESTRA: Stan Getz (ts); Blanche Birdsong (h); Dave Hildinger (vib); Jan Johansson (p); Freddy Dutton (b); Sperie Karas (d); u (strings).

| | |
|---|---|
| Nature Boy | Verve 89193, Verve MGV(S6)8379, MGV8719, HMV7EG8689 |
| 'Round Midnight | Verve 89193,   -      - |
| A New Town is a Blue Town | -      - |
| Whisper Not | -      - |
| The Thrill is Gone | - |
| It Never Entered My Mind | Verve VSP-38,      - |
| Early Autumn | - |
| When I Go, I Go All the Way | - |
| Born To Be Blue | - |

## BLEY, CARLA (piano)

January 11 or 12, 1966 - Baarn, Holland

Mike Mantler (tp); Steve Lacy (sop); Carla Bley (p); Kent Carter (b); Aedo Romano (d).

| | |
|---|---|
| Doctor | Fort (Du) 88110124 |
| Oni Puladi | - |
| J.S. | - |
| Walking Batteriewoman | - |
| Closer | - |
| Communications No. 7 | - |

January 24, 1968 - New York City

THE JAZZ COMPOSERS ORCHESTRA: Don Cherry (tp); Lloyd Michaels, Randy Brecker (flhn); Bob Northern, Julius Watkins (FrH); Jimmy Knepper, Jack Jeffers (tb); Howard Johnson (tuba); Al Gibbons, Steve Lacy (sop); Bobby Donoson, Gene Hull (as); Gato Barbieri, Lew Tabackin George Barrow (ts); Charlie Davis (bars); Carla Bley (p); Kent Carter, Ron Carter, Richard Davis, Charlie Hoden, Reggie Workman (b); Andrew Cyrille (d); Mike Mantler (ldr).

Communications No. 8        Jazz Club of America LP 1001

May 8, 1968 - RCA Studios, New York

THE JAZZ COMPOSERS ORCHESTRA: Michael Mantler (comp,cond); Lloyd Michaels, Stephen Furtado (flhn); Jimmy Knepper, Roswell Rudd (tb); Jack Jeffers (b-tb); Bob Northern, Julius Watkins (FrH); Howard Johnson (tuba); Steve Marcus, Al Gibbons (sop); Frank Wess, Bob Donovan (as); Lew Tabackin, George Barrow, Pharoah Sanders (ts); Charlie Davis (bars); Carla Bley (p); Larry Coryell (g); Ron Carter, Eddie Gomez, Charlie Haden, Steve Swallow, Reggie Workman (b); Beaver Harris (perc).

| | |
|---|---|
| Communications No. 9* | Jazz Club of America LP1001 |
| Communications No. 10** | - |
| Preview*** | - |

  *   Larry Coryell (g) solo
 **   Roswell Rudd (tb) and Steve Swallow (b) solos
***   Pharoah Sanders (ts) solo

Note: The majority of Ms. Bley's extensive recording career lies outside the temporal scope of this discography.


## BLUNT, HILARY (guitar)

1959-1960 - Baton Rouge, Louisiana

Hilary Blunt (g,vo).

|  | | |
|---|---|---|
| A Thousand Miles from Nowhere | Storyville SLP129 |


Early 1960 - Baton Rouge, Louisiana

Sally Dotson (vo) acc. by Smoky Babe (Robert Brown) (g,vo); Hilary Blunt (g).

| Your Dice Won't Pass | Folk-Lyric FL-111 |
|---|---|


## BOOKER, BERYL (piano)

Early 1946 - New York City

DON BYAS QUARTET: Don Byas (ts); Beryl Booker (p); John Simmonds (b); Fred Radcliffe (d).

| S1-182 | You Go To My Head | Gotham 132, Blue Star (F) 83 |
|---|---|---|
| S1-183 | Don't You Know I Care | - - |
| S1-184 | Gloomy Sunday | Gotham 131 |

1948

| SI2020 | One for the Road | Sittin' In With 527 |
|---|---|---|
| SI2021 | Easy to Love | - |
| SI2023 | You've Changed | Sittin' In With 529 |
| SI2024 | I Can Dream | - |
| SI2025 | Someone to Watch Over Me | Sittin' In With 539 |
| SI2026 | That Old Black Magic | - |

January, 1952 - New York City

Don Elliott (mellophone,vib); Budd Johnson (ts,bars); Beryl Booker (p,vo); Slam Stewart (b); Charlie Smith (d).

| You'd Better Go Now | Mercury 8279,EmArcy EPI-6014, MG-26007 |
|---|---|
| A Handful of Stars | -   -   - |

1953 - New York City

Beryl Booker (p,vo); John Collins (g); Oscar Pettiford (b).

| | | |
|---|---|---|
| Love is the Thing | Mercury 8297,EmArcy EPI-6014, MG-26007 | |
| Stay As Sweet As You Are | - | - |
| Remember Me | - | ,EmArcy EPI-6013 |
| But Beautiful | - | - |
| Darn That Dream | - | - |
| Let's Fall in Love | - | - |
| When a Woman Loves a Man | - | ,Mercury 70041 - |
| Why Do I Love You | - | - |

See Collective Section for Additional Recordings

### BOOKER, CONNIE MAE (piano)

c. 1953

Connie Mae Booker (p,vo) with unknown small band.

| | | |
|---|---|---|
| 1194 | Loretta | Freedom 1520 |
| 1195 | My Baby Left Me | - |

### BORCHARD, HENRIETTA (violin)

See Collective Section.

### BOSWELL, HELVETIA "VET" (cello)

See Collective Section.

### BOSWELL, MARTHA
### (piano, cello, celeste)

March 22, 1925 - New Orleans

Connie Boswell (vo) acc. by Martha Boswell (p).

| | | |
|---|---|---|
| 32114-1 | I'm Gonna Cry (Crying Blues) | Victor 19639 |

October 3, 1930 - Los Angeles

THE THREE BOSWELL SISTERS: Connie Boswell, Helvetia "Vet" Boswell (vo) acc. by Martha Boswell (p).

404407-C  My Future Just Passed      Okeh 41444,Od A-221310,025223,
                                     Par R-787,R-1575,A-3112,
                                     B-49947, Od 193863, A-189369
404408-B  Heebie Jeebies            Okeh 41444,Od A-221310,
                                     Par R-821,R-1574,B-97065,
                                     Od 193830,A-2323,Od A-28026,
                                     025223, Har 1428-H, Clarion
                                     5476-C, Velvet Tone 2536-V
404410-B  Gee, But I'd Like To      Okeh 41470,Par R-854,R-1575,
          Make You Happy            A-3112,Par B-97065, Od 193863,
                                     A-221321


October 31, 1930 - Los Angeles

same personnel.

404414-B  Don't Tell Him What's     Okeh 41470, Par R-850, R-1574
          Happened to Me            Od 193830


July 27, 1931 - New York City

Connie Boswell (vo) acc. by Manny Klein (tp); Tommy Dorsey (tb); Jimmy
Dorsey (cl); Harry Hoffman (vn); Martha Boswell (p); Dick McDonough (g);
Joe Tarto (b); Chauncey Morehouse (d,vbs).

E-36987   I'm All Dressed Up With   Brunswick 6162, 01198
          A Broken Heart
E-36988   What is It


October 27, 1931 - New York City

Connie Boswell (vo) acc. by Manny Klein (tp); Will Bradley (tb); Jimmy
Dorsey (cl); Martha Boswell (p); Eddie Lang (g); Joe Tarto (b); Chauncey
Morehouse (d,vib).

E-37333-A Time on My Hands          Brunswick 6210, 01443
E-37334-A Concentratin' (On You)        -      , 01252


February 19, 1932 - New York City

THE BOSWELL SISTERS:  Connie Boswell, Helvetia "Vet" Boswell (vo); Bunny
Berigan, Manny Klein (tp); Tommy Dorsey (tb); Jimmy Dorsey (cl,as);
Harry Hoffman (vn); Martha Boswell (p); Dick McDonough (g); Joe Tarto
(b); Stan King (d).

B-11320-A Was That the Human Thing  Brunswick 6257,01284,A-9226,
          to Do                     Lucky 60128
B-11321-A (We've Got To) Put That       -      -    -    -
          Sun Back in the Sky

March 21, 1932 - New York City

Klein, Hoffman out. Eddie Lang (g) replaces McDonough.

| | | |
|---|---|---|
| B-11543-A | There'll Be Some Changes<br>Made | Brunswick 6291,01306,A-9244,<br>Co 36521 |
| B-11544-A | Between the Devil and the<br>Deep Blue Sea | -   -   - |

February 23, 1932 - New York City

Connie Boswell (vo) acc. by Manny Klein (tp); Tommy Dorsey (tb); Jimmy Dorsey (cl,as); u (ts); Harry Hoffman (vn); Martha Boswell (p); u (g,b); Chauncey Morehouse or Larry Gomar (d,vib).

| | | |
|---|---|---|
| B-11332 | I Cried For You | Brunswick 6267, 01298 |
| B-11333 | I Can't Believe That It's You | -   - |

February 24, 1932 - New York City

THE BOSWELL SISTERS: Connie Boswell, Helvetia "Vet" Boswell (vo) acc. by Bunny Berigan (tp); Tommy Dorsey (tb); Jimmy Dorsey (cl,as); Harry Hoffman (vn); Martha Boswell (p); Dick McDonough (g); Joe Tarto (b); Stan King (d).

| | | |
|---|---|---|
| B-11353-B | Stop the Sun, Stop the<br>Moon (My Man's Gone) | Brunswick 6271,01295,A-9232 |
| B-11354-A | Everybody Loves My Baby<br>(But My Baby Don't Love<br>Nobody But Me) | -   -   -, 6783,<br>4898, Columbia 36520,<br>Lucky 60021 |

April 9, 1932 - New York City

Connie Boswell (vo) acc. by Bunny Berigan (tp); Tommy Dorsey (tb); Jimmy Dorsey (cl); Harry Hoffman (vn); Martha Boswell (p); Eddie Lang (g); Artie Bernstein (b); Stan King (d).

| | | |
|---|---|---|
| B-11682-A | Lullably of the Leaves | Brunswick 6297, 01315 |
| B-11683-A | My Lips Want Kisses<br>(My Heart Wants Love) | -   - |

April 9, 1932 - New York City

THE BOSWELL SISTERS: Connie Boswell, Helvetia "Vet" Boswell (vo) acc. by Tommy Dorsey (tb); Jimmy Dorsey (cl); Martha Boswell (p,cello) Eddie Lang (g); Stan King (d).

| | | |
|---|---|---|
| B-11684-A | If It Ain't Love | Brunswick 6302,01330,A-9262 |
| B-11685-A | Got the South in My South | -   -   - |

June 17, 1932 - New York City

THE BOSWELL SISTERS: Connie Boswell, Helvetia "Vet" Boswell (vo) acc.
by Bunny Berigan, Manny Klein (tp); Tommy Dorsey (tb); Jimmy Dorsey
(cl,as); Larry Binyon (ts); Harry Hoffman (vn); Martha Boswell (p); Carl
Kress (g); Artie Bernstein (b); Stan King (d).

| | | |
|---|---|---|
| B-12639-A | It Don't Mean a Thing<br>(If It Ain't Got That<br>Swing) | Brunswick 6442,01436,A-9350,<br>4819,Vo4546,Rex 8873,Co DB-1994 |
| B-12640-A | Louisiana Hayride | Brunswick 6470,01625,A-9378,<br>A-9507, 4803 |
| B-12641-A | Minnie the Moocher's<br>Wedding Day | Brunswick 6442,01436,A-9350,<br>4879, Vo 4536 |

January 9, 1933 - New York City

Klein, Binyon, Hoffman out.  Eddie Lang (g) replaces Kress.

| | | |
|---|---|---|
| B-12858-A | It's All My Fault | Brunswick 6483,01443,Co 38298 |
| B-12859-A | Underneath the Arches | -                -   |
| B-12860-A | Mood Indigo | Brunswick 6470,A-9378,01543,<br>A-500230,Co 36521,DB-1960,<br>Rex 8910 |

April 11, 1933 - New York City

Dick McDonough (g) replaces Lang.

| | | |
|---|---|---|
| B-13222-A | Forty-Second Street | Brunswick 6545,01516,A-9416,<br>4825 |
| B-13223-A | Shuffle Off to Buffalo | -          -     -,4862 |

June 13, 1933 - New York City

Manny Klein (tp) replaces Berigan.  Add Larry Binyon (ts).

| | | |
|---|---|---|
| B-13450-A | The Gold Diggers' Song<br>(We're In the Money) | Brunswick 6596,01556,A-9443,<br>4830,A-500271 |
| B-13451-A | It's Sunday Down in<br>Caroline | Brunswick 6596,   -     -,4380,<br>A-500271 |

June 15, 1933 - New York City

same personnel.

| | | |
|---|---|---|
| B-13466-A | Puttin' It On | Brunswick 6625,01576,A-9440,<br>4849, Co DO-1228 |
| B-13467-A | Swanee Mammy | Brunswick 6625,   -     -,4849,<br>Co DO-1228 |

September 11, 1933 - New York City

THE BOSWELL SISTERS: Connie Boswell, Helvetia "Vet" Boswell (vo) acc.
by Manny Weinstock (tp); Charlie Butterfield (tb); Benny Goodman
(cl,as); Chester Hazlett (as); Harry Hoffman (vn); Martha Boswell (p);
Perry Botkin (bj); Dick Cherwin (b); Stan King (d).

| | | |
|---|---|---|
| B-13990-A | Sophisticated Lady | Brunswick 6650,01592,A-9484, A-500336, Co DO-1110 |
| B-13991-A | That's How Ryhthm Was Born | Brunswick 6650,01592,A-9484, A-500336, Co DO-1110,DB-1960, Br 4849, 4862 |

November 14, 1933 - New York City

THE BOSWELL SISTERS: Connie Boswell, Helvetia "Vet" Boswell (vo) acc.
by Manny Klein (tp); Tommy Dorsey (tb); Jimmy Dorsey (cl); Larry Binyon
(ts,fl); Fulton McGrath or Martha Boswell (p,celeste); Dick McDonough
(g); Artie Bernstein (b); Stan King (d).

| | | |
|---|---|---|
| B-14319-A | Song of Surrender | Brunswick 6733,01711,A-9512, 4888, Co DO-1526 |
| B-14320-B | Coffee in the Morning (Kisses in the Night) | Brunswick 6733,   -   -, 4888, Co DO-1526 |

March 23, 1934 - New York City

Add Bunny Berigan (tp); Chuck Campbell (tb).

| | | |
|---|---|---|
| B-14993-A | You Oughta Be in Pictures (My Star of Stars) | Brunswick 6798,01751,A-9575, 4915, Co DO-1221 |
| B-14994-A | I Hate Myself (For Being So Mean to You) | Brunswick 6798,   -   -,4915, Co DO-1221 |

May 23, 1934 - New York City

same personnel.

| | | |
|---|---|---|
| B-15254-A | Alexander's Ragtime Band | Brunswick 7412,01893,A-9688, A-500528, Vo 4239, Par R-2562, Co DO-1255 |
| B-15525-A | The Darktown Strutter's Ball | - |

June 21, 1934 - New York City

Campbell out.

| | | |
|---|---|---|
| B-15357-A | Don't Let Your Love Go Wrong | Brunswick 6929,01832,A-9616, 4928,Co DO-1269,DS-1462, Par R-2631, Od A-272287 |

B-15358-A  Why Don't You Practice      Brunswick 6929,01832,A-9616,
           What You Preach           4928, Co DO-1269

August 21, 1934 - New York City

Connie Boswell (vo) acc. by Bunny Berigan (tp); Tommy Dorsey (tb); Jimmy
Dorsey (cl); Harry Hoffman (vn); Martha Boswell (p); Dick McDonough (g);
Artie Bernstein (b); Chauncey Morehouse (d,vib).

B-15714-A  A New Moon is Over My      Brunswick 6962,01865
           Shoulder

July 19, 1935 - London

THE BOSWELL SISTERS:  Connie Boswell, Helvetia "Vet" Boswell (vo) acc.
by Martha Boswell (p); Joe Brannelly (g); Dick Ball (b); Max Bacon (d).

GB-7316-A  Fare Thee Well, Annabelle    Brunswick 02043,A-9823,
                                 Decca M-30070, Y-5012

Brannelly and Ball out.

GB-7317-3  Lullaby of Broadway       Brunswick 02043,A-9823,
                                 Decca M-30070, Y-5012

October 8, 1935 - New York City

THE BOSWELL SISTERS:  Connie Boswell, Helvetia "Vet" Boswell (vo) acc.
by Russ Case, Ed Wade (tp); Will Bradley (tb); Artie Shaw (cl,as);
Martha Boswell (p); Dick McDonough (g); Artie Bernstein (b); Stan King
(d).

60029-A    Top Hat, White Tie and     Decca 574, Y-5031, Br02067,
         Tails                    A-9854, Polydor A-61002
60030-A    Cheek to Cheek           Decca 574, Y-5031, Br 02067,
                                 A-9854, Polydor A-61002

January 6, 1936 - New York City

Wade out.  Russ Jenner (tb) replaces Bradley.

60302-A    I'm Gonna Sit Right Down   Decca 671, Y-5049, Br02142,
         And Write Myself a Letter A-9923,603003, Polydor A-61003
60303-A    The Music Goes 'Round      Decca 671, Y-5049, Br02142,
         And Around            A-9923,503003, Polydor A-61003

February 12, 1936 - New York City

Will Bradley (tb) replaces Jenner.  Dick Cherwin (b) replaces Bernstein.

| 60463-B | Let Yourself Go | Decca 709, F-42066, Y-5083, |
|---|---|---|
| | | Br02165,A-9959,Polydor A-61001 |
| 60464-B | I'm Putting All My Eggs | Decca 709, F-42066, Y-5083, |
| | In One Basket | Br02165,A-9959,Polydor A-61001 |

See Collective Section for Additional Recordings

BOWN, PATTI (piano, organ)

September 27, 1959

Patti Bown (p); Joe Benjamin (b); Ed Shaughnessy (d).

| CO-63564 | Sunshine Cake | Columbia CL 1379 |
|---|---|---|
| CO-63565 | G'Won Train | - |

October 8, 1959

same personnel.

| CO-63568 | Nothin' But the Truth | Columbia CL-1379 |
|---|---|---|
| CO-63607 | Give Me the Simple Life | - |
| CO-63608 | True to You | - |

October 27, 1959

same personnel.

| CO-63560 | It Might as Well Be Spring | Columbia CL 1379 |
|---|---|---|
| CO-63561 | Head Shakin' | - |
| CO-63562 | Waltz De Funk | - |
| CO-63563 | I Didn't Know | - |
| CO-63566 | I'm Gonna Wash That Man | - |
| | Right Outa My Hair | |

c. 1961 - Englewood Cliffs, New Jersey

AFRO-AMERICAN SKETCHES: Ernie Royal, Joe Newman, Jerry Kail, Joe Wilder (tp); Urbie Green, Britt Woodmer, Paul Faulise (tb); Eric Dixon (ts,fl); Arthur Clark (cl,bars); Oliver Nelson (as,ts,arr); Jerry Dodgion (as,fl); Bob Ashton (ts,fl,cl); Dan Butterfield (tuba); Charles McCracken, Pete Makis (cello); Patti Bown (p); Art Davis (b); Ed Shaughnessy (d); Ray Baretto (bgs,cga).

| 3230 | Disillusioned | Prestige PRLP7225 |
|---|---|---|
| 3231 | Freedom Dance | - |
| 3232 | Emancipation | - |

1961 - New York City

Oscar Brown, Jr. (vo); acc. by large band including Joe Newman (tp);
Patti Bown (p).

| | |
|---|---|
| Elegy | Columbia 42284,CL1774,CS8574, Philips(C)B47171L,CBS(S)BPG62016 |
| When Malindy Sings | Columbia 42284,CL1774,CS8574, Philips(C)B47171L,CBS(S)BPG62016 |
| Mr. Kicks | Columbia CL1774,CS8574,Philips (C)B47171L,CBS(S)BPG62016 |
| Hazel's Hips | Columbia CL1774,CS8574,Philips (C)B47171L,CBS(S)BPG62016 |
| Excuse Me for Living | Columbia CL1774,CS8574,Philips (C)B47171L,CBS(S)BPG62016 |
| Lucky Guy | Columbia CL1774,CS8574,Philips (C)B47171L,CBS(S)BPG52016 |
| Forbidden Fruit | Columbia CL1774,CS8574,Philips (C)B47171L,CBS(S)BPG62016 |
| Sam's Life | Columbia CL1774,CS8574,Philips (C)B47171L,CBS(S)BPG62016 |
| Opportunity Please Knock | Columbia CL1774,CS8574,Philips (C)B47171L,CBS(S)BPG62016 |
| Hymn to Friday | Columbia CL1774,CS8574,Philips (C)B47171L,CBS(S)BPG62016 |
| Love is Like a Newborn Child | Columbia CL1774,CS8574,Philips (C)B47171L,CBS(S)BPG62016 |
| World Full of Grey | Columbia CL1774,CS8574,Philips (C)B47171L,CBS(S)BPG62016 |

January 13, 1961 - New York City

Cal Massey (tp); Julius Watkins (FrH); Hugh Brodie (ts); Patti Bown (p);
Jimmy Garrison (b); G.T. Hogan (d).

| | |
|---|---|
| Father and Son | Candid DM 8019, CS 9019 |

March, 1961 - Zurich

Freddie Hubbard, Benny Bailey (tp); Curtis Fuller, Ake Persson (tb);
Phil Woods (as); Eric Dixon (ts); Sahib Shihab (bars,fl); Patti Bown
(p); Buddy Catlett (b); Stu Martin (d).

| | |
|---|---|
| Blue 'N Boogie | Smash MG S27034, SRS 67304 |
| Billie's Bounce | —            — |
| Stolen Moments | —            — |
| Scrapple from the Apple | —            — |

October 18, 1961 - Hackensack, New Jersey

Gene Ammons (ts); Patti Bown (p); George Duvivier (b); Art Taylor (d);
Ray Barretto (cga).

```
Five O'Clock Whistle          Prest PRLP 7208
I Sold My Heart to the Junkman    -
Song of the Islands           Prest PRLP 7445
Uptight                       Prest PRLP 7208
Travellin'                    Prest PRLP 7445
Soft Summer Breeze            Prest PRLP 7208
Don't Go to Strangers             -
```

April 6, 1962 - Hackensack, New Jersey

Etta Jones (vo) acc. by Patti Bown (p); Wally Richardson (g); George
Duvivier (b); Ed Shaughnessy (d).

```
3467    Good for Nothing Joe          Prestige PRLP 7241
3468    You Don't Know My Mind            -
3469    I'll Be There                     -
3470    I Miss You So                     -
3471    In the Dark                       -
3472    I Wonder                          -
3473    I'm Pulling Through               -
```

April 13, 1962 - Hackensack, New Jersey

Etta Jones (vo) acc. by Gene Ammons (ts); Patti Bown (p); George
Duvivier (b); Walter Perkins (d).

```
3482    But Not For Me                Prest PRLP 7275
3483    If You Are But a Dream (vEJ)      -
3485    Cool Cool Daddy (vEJ)             -
        The Party's Over              Prest PRLP 7287
        Lascivious                        -
        Soft Winds                        -
        Scam                          Prest PRLP 7400
```

April 14, 1962 - New York City

GENE AMMONS GROUP:  Gene Ammons (ts); Patti Bown (p); George Duvivier
(b); Ed Shaughnessy (d).

```
3489    Two Different Worlds          Moodsville MVLP-28
3490    But Beautiful                     -
3491    Skylark                           -
3492    On the Street of Dreams           -
3493    You'd Be So Nice to Come Home to  -
3494    Under a Blanket of Blue           -
3495    I'm Glad There's You              -
3496    Three Little Words                -
```

May 4, 1962 - Hackensack, New Jersey

LONELY AND BLUE: Etta Jones (vo) acc. by Budd Johnson (ts); Patti Bown
(p); Art Davis (b); Ed Shaughnessy (d).

| 3515 | Out in the Cold Again | Prestige PRLP 7241 |
|------|------------------------|--------------------|
| 3516 | My Gentleman Friend    | -                  |
| 3517 | Gee, Baby, Ain't I Good to You | -          |
| 3518 | Travelin' Light        | -                  |

October 3, 1962 - New York City

Don Goldie (tp); Leo Wright (as,fl); Patti Bown (p); Barry Galbraith
(g); Ben Tucker (b); Ed Shaghnessy (d); Ray Barretto (cga); Willie
Rodriguez (perc); Manny Album (arr,cond).

| Nightingale | Argo LP(S)708 |
|-------------|---------------|
| Fast Thought | - |
| I Hear a Rhapsody | - |
| Shiny Stockings | - |
| Goldie's Thing | - |
| There Will Never Be Another You | - |

January 22-23, 1963 - New York

Jimmy Rushing (vo) acc. by Bernie Glow, Snookie Young, Marky Markowitz,
Joe Newman (tp); Jimmy Cleveland, Urbie Green, Billy Byers, Willie
Dennis (tb); Gene Ovill, Phil Woods (as); Zoot Sims, Budd Johnson (ts);
Sol Schlinger (bars) Patti Bown (p); Freddie Green (g); Milt Hinton (b);
Gus Johnson (d); Al Cohn (arr)

| I'm Walking' Through | Colpix CP446,Pye(E)GGL0384 | |
|----------------------|------------|---|
| Heaven With You | | |
| Trouble in Mind | - | - |
| Heartaches | - | - |
| Did You Ever | - | - |
| Just Because | - | - |
| You Always Hurt the One You Love | - | - |
| Ooh! Looka There, Ain't She Pretty | - | - |
| T'Ain't Nobody's Business If I Do | - | - |
| My Bucket's Got a Hole in It | - | - |
| Please Come Back | - | - |

c. 1964

WARM WAVE: Seldon Powell, Jerome Richardson (ts); Cal Tjader (vib);
Patti Bown, Hank Jones, Bernie Leighton (p); Kenny Burrell, Jimmy Raney
(g); George Duvivier (b); Ed Shaughnessy (d); Willie Rodriguez (perc);
Les Double Six (vo); u (strings); Claus Agerman (arr,cond).

| Where or When | Verve V(S) 8585 |
|---------------|------------------|
| Violets for Your Furs | - |
| People | - |
| This Time the Dream's on Me | - |
| Ev'ry Time We Say Goodbye | - |
| The Way You Look Tonight | - |
| Passe | - |

strings out.

|                      |   |
|----------------------|---|
| Poor Butterfly       | - |
| I'm Old Fashioned    | - |
| Just Friends         | - |
| Sunset Boulevard     | - |

**June, 1964 - Chicago**

Art Hoyle, Snooky Young (tp); Roy Wiezand (tb); Tony Studd (b-tb); Phil
Woods (cl,as); Kenny Soderblom (ts,fl); Oliver Nelson (ts); Jerome
Richardson (bars,fl,alto-fl); Patti Bown (p); Ben Tudier (b); Grady Tate
(d).

|                    |            |
|--------------------|------------|
| Hobo Flats         | Argo LP737 |
| Post No Bills      | -          |
| A Bientot          | -          |
| Take Me With You   | -          |
| Daylie's Double    | -          |
| Teenie's Blues     | -          |
| Laz-ie Kate        | -          |
| Three and One      | -          |

**August 1 & 4, 1964 - New York**

Thad Jones (tp); James Moody (ts,as,fl); Patti Bown (p); Reggie Workman
(b); Albert Heath (d); Marie Volpee (vo).

|                          |                   |
|--------------------------|-------------------|
| Buster's Last Stand      | Scepter LP(S)526  |
| Paint the Town Red       | -                 |
| Em Prean Shore           | -                 |
| Capers                   | -                 |
| If You Grin (You're In)  | -                 |
| Wayward Plaint           | -                 |
| Figurine                 | -                 |
| Giant Steps              | -                 |

**June 15-16, September 3 and October 7, 1964**

Jimmy Cleveland (tb); Seldon Powell, Spencer Sinatra (fl); Patti Bown
(p); Gary McFarland (vib); Antonio Carlos Jobim, Kenny Burrell (g);
Richard Davis (b); Sol Gubin (d); Willie Bobo, Arnie Luise (perc).

|          |                          |                     |
|----------|--------------------------|---------------------|
|          | Ringo                    | Verve (E) VLP9095   |
|          | From Russia With Love    | -                   |
|          | She Loves You            | -                   |
| 64VK501  | A Hard Day's Night       | -                   |
|          | The Good Life            | -                   |
|          | More                     | -                   |
|          | And I Love Her           | -                   |
|          | I Love Goddess           | -                   |
|          | I Want to Hold Your Hand | -                   |
|          | Emily                    | -                   |

California Here I Come            -
La Vie En Rose                  -

**April 29, 1965 - New York**

SPECTRUM: Russell Jacquet (tp); Illinois Jacquet (ts); Patti Bown (p); George Duvivier (b); Gary Tate (d); Candido Camero (perc).

| 13907 | Blues for Bunny | Cadet/Argo LP754 |
|---|---|---|
| | Black Foot | - |
| | Big Music | - |

Russell Jacquet out.

Blue Horizon                  -

**c. 1967**

ROLL 'EM: Joe Turner (vo) acc. by Buddy Lucas (ts, hca); Patti Bown (p); Wally Richardson, Thornell Schwartz (g); Bob Bushnell (el-b); Herbie Lovelle (d).

| Well, Oh Well | Bluesway BLS6006, 6060 | |
|---|---|---|
| Joe's Blues | - | - |
| Since I Was Your Man | - | - |
| Roll 'Em Pete | - | - |

Panama Frances (d) replaces Lovelle.

| Bluer than Blue | - | - |
|---|---|---|
| Big Wheel | - | - |
| Poor House | - | - |
| Piney Brown Blues | - | - |
| Mrs. Geraldine | - | - |
| Cherry Red | - | - |

**February 15, 1967 - New York**

Marvin Stamm, Jimmy Nottingham, Thad Jones, John Frosh (tp); Tom Mitchell, Tom McIntosh, Paul Faulise (tb); Pee Wee Russell (cl); Phil Woods (as); Jerry Dodgion (as,fl); Bob Ashton (ts); Seldon Powell (ts,fl); Gene Allen (bars); Patti Bown (p); Howard Collins (g); George Duvivier (b); Grady Tate (d); Oliver Nelson (arr).

| Love is Just Around the Corner | Impulse A(S) 9147 |
|---|---|
| A Good Man is Hard to Find | - |
| Bopol | - |
| I'm Coming Virginia | - |
| 6 and 4 | - |

March, 1967 - New York

Eddie "Cleanhead" Vinson (as,vo); Buddy Lucas (ts,hca); Patti Bown (p,org); Mike Bloomfield (g); u (g,b,d).

| | |
|---|---|
| Cherry Red | Bluesway BL6007 |
| Cadillac Blues | - |
| Juice Head Baby | - |
| Alimony Blues | - |
| Somebody's Got to Go | - |
| Flat Broke Blues | - |
| Old Maid Got Married | - |
| Workin' Blues | - |
| Wee Baby Blues | - |
| Goodnight Baby Blues | - |

Late 1967 - New York

HIP VIBRATIONS: Ernie Royal, Marvin Stamm (tp,flhn); J.J. Johnson (tb); Alan Raph (b-tb); Jerome Richardson (fl,ts,bar); Patti Bown (p); Cal Tjader (vib); Richard Davis (b); Mel Lewis (d); Bobby Rosengarden (perc); Ray Barretto (cga); Bobby Bryant, Benny Golson (arr).

| | |
|---|---|
| Windy (BGarr) | Verve V(6)8730, (E)VLP 9215 |
| Hip Vibrations (BBarr) | -      - |

October, 1967 - New York

JAZZ INTERACTIONS ORCHESTRA:   Joe Newman (tp,cond); Ernie Royal, Ray Copeland, Bert Collins, Marv Stamm (tp); Benny Powell, Paul Faulise, Wayne Andre, Jimmy Cleveland (tb); Jimmy Buffington, Ray Alonge (FrH); Don Butterfield (tuba); Phil Woods, George Marsh (as,fl); Zoot Sims, Jerry Dodgion (ts); Danny Bank (bars,b-cl,fl); Patti Bown (p); Ron Carter, George Duvivier (b); Ed Shaughnessy (d); Bobby Rosengarden (perc); Oliver Nelson (arr,cond).

| | |
|---|---|
| A Typical Day in New York | Verve V(6)-8731,VOP(S)9202 |
| The East Side/The West Side | -      - |
| 125th and 7th Avenue | -      - |
| A Penthouse Dawn | -      - |
| One for Duke | -      - |
| Complex City | -      - |

See Collective Section for Additional Recordings

BRACKEEN, JOANNE (piano, organ)

June 22, 1966 - New York

Freddi McCoy (vib); Joanne Brackeen (p); Augustus Turner (b); George Scott (d).

58

| | |
|---|---|
| And I Love Her | Prestige PRLP 7470 |
| High Heel Sneakers | - |
| Moye | - |
| Theodora | - |
| Tough Talk | - |

April 10, 1967 - New York

Edward Williams, Dud Bascomb (tp); Freddie McCoy (vib); Joanne Brackeen (p,org); Wally Richardson (g); Eustis Guillemet (el-b); Ray Lucas (d); Dave Blum (arr,cond).

| | |
|---|---|
| Summer in the City | Prestige PRLP 7487 |
| Lightening Strikes | - |
| Call Me | - |
| One Cylinder | - |
| Huh! | - |

May 4, 1967 - New York

Freddie McCoy (vib); Joanne Brackeen (p); Eddie Gomez (b); Kahl Madhi (d); Dave Blum (arr).

| | |
|---|---|
| Peas 'n' Rice | Prestige PRST 7487 |
| My Funny Valentine | - |
| 1-2-3 | - |

October 2, 1967 - New York

Richard Williams, Dud Bascomb (tp); Freddie McCoy (vib); Joanne Brackeen (p); Dave Blum (org); Wally Richardson (g); Joseph Macho (el-b); Ray Lucas (d).

| | |
|---|---|
| A Whiter Shade of Pale | Prestige PRST 7542 |
| I Was Made to Love Her | - |
| You Keep Me Hanging On | - |
| Tony's Pony | - |
| Take My Love (and Shove It Up Your Heart) | |

October 4, 1967 - New York

Williams, Bascomb & Richardson out.    Don Payne (el-b) replaces Macho.

| | |
|---|---|
| Beans 'n' Greens | Prestige PRST 7542 |
| Makin' Whoopie | - |
| Doxie | - |
| 6th Avenue Stroll | - |

January 24, 1968 - New York

Freddie McCoy (vib); Joanne Brackeen (p,org); Wally Richardson (g);

Lawrence Evans (el-b); Ray Appleton (d); Steve Wolfe (sitar); Dave Blum (arr).

| | |
|---|---|
| Ride On | Prestige PRST 7561 |
| Pet Sounds | - |
| I Am a Walrus | - |
| Salem Soul Song | - |
| Sorry 'Bout That | - |

February 5, 1968 - New York

Freddie McCoy (vib); Manny Green, Peter Dimitriades, Joseph Malignaggi (vn); Joanne Brackeen (p); Lawrence Evans (b); Ray Appleton (d).

| | |
|---|---|
| Soul Yogi | Prestige PRST 7561 |
| What Now My Love | - |
| Mysterioso | - |
| Autumn Leaves | - |

June 10, 1968 - New York

Freddie McCoy (vib); Joanne Brackeen (el-p); Roy McKinney (b); Al Dreares (d).

| | |
|---|---|
| Listen Here | Prestige PRLP 7582 |
| Love for Sale | - |
| Short Circuit | - |
| Stone Wall | - |

See Collective Section for Additional Recordings

BRADLEY, RUTH
(clarinet, alto sax)

See Collective Section.

BRIM, GRACE (harmonica)

1950 - Detroit

JOHN BRIM COMBO: Grace Brim (hca,vo); Big Maceo Merriweather (p); John Brim (g); James Watkins (b).

| | |
|---|---|
| Strange Man | Fortune 801 |
| Mean Man Blues | - |

BROWN, CLEO (piano)

March 12, 1935 - New York City

Cleo Brown (p,vo) acc. by Perry Botkin (g); Artie Bernstein (b); Gene
Krupa (d).

| | | |
|---|---|---|
| 39393-A | Lookie, Lookie, Lookie<br>(Here Comes Cookie) | Decca 409, Br 02013, A-9780 |
| 39396-A | You're a Heavenly Thing | Decca 410, Br 02021 |
| 39397-A | I'll Take the South (You<br>Take the Eest, Take the<br>West, Take the North) | Decca 409, Br 02013,      - |
| 39398-A | The Stuff is Here and<br>It's Mellow | Decca 410,3683, Br 02021 |
| 39399-A | Boogie Woogie | Decca 477,3386,25265,Y-5073,<br>Br 02037 |

May 20, 1935 - New York City

solo piano.

| | | |
|---|---|---|
| 39531-A | Pelican Stomp | Decca 477, Y-5073, Br 02037 |

June 8, 1935 - New York City

Cleo Brown (p,vo) acc. by Mike McKendrick (g); Leonard Bibbs (b); Tubby
Hall (d).

| | | |
|---|---|---|
| 395 | Never Too Tired to Love | Decca 512, B402049 |
| 39579-A | Give a Broken Heart a<br>Break | Decca 486,      - |
| 39579-B | Give a Broken Heart a Break | - |
| 39580-A | Mama Don't Want No Peas<br>An' Rice An' Coconut Oil | Decca 512, Br 02047, A-9877 |
| 39581-A | Me and My Wonderful One | Decca 486,      -      - |

November 20, 1935 - Los Angeles

Cleo Brown (p,vo); acc. by Bobby Sherwood (g); Manny Stein (b); Vic
Berton (d).

| | | |
|---|---|---|
| DLA-270-A | When Hollywood Goes Black<br>and Tan | Decca 632, Br 02123 |
| DLA-271-B | When | -      - |
| DLA-272-A | You're My Fever | Decca 718, Br 02147,A-99656 |
| DLA-272-A | Breakin' In a Pair of Shoes | -      - |

1936 - Hollywood

HOLLYWOOD HOT SHOTS: Cleo Brown (p,vo), others unknown.

| | |
|---|---|
| The Girl from Kanhakee | Hot Shot 303 |
| Man, Be On Your Way | - |
| Men At Work | Hot Shot 350 |
| Tramp | - |

April 4, 1936 – Los Angeles

Cleo Brown (p,vo) acc. by Bobby Sherwood (g); Manny Stein (b); Vic Berton (d).

| DLA-337-A | Latch On | Decca 795, Br 02186 | |
|---|---|---|---|
| DLA-338-A | Slow Poke | – | – |
| DLA-339-A | Love in the First Degree | Decca 846, Br 02271 | |
| DLA-340-A | My Gal Mezzanine | – | – |

September 30, 1949 – Los Angeles

Cleo Brown (p,vo); Nappy Lamare (g); Leonard Bibb (b); Zutty Singleton (d).

| 4936 | Cleo's Boogie | Capitol 57-70057 |
|---|---|---|
| 4937 | I'd Climb the Highest Mountain | Capitol 57-887 |
| 4938 | Cook That Stuff | Capitol 57750057 |
| 4939 | Don't Overdo It | Capitol 57-887 |

## BROWN, LOUISE (piano)

1961 – Chicago

Louise Brown (p,vo) acc. by u (ts,g,b,d).

| S1331 | Son-In-Law | Witch 101 |
|---|---|---|
| S1332 | You Gave Me Misery | – |

## BRYANT, CLORA (trumpet)

July, 1957 – Los Angeles

Clora Bryant (tp,vo) acc. by Norman Faye (tp); Walter Benton (ts); Roger Fleming (p); Ben Tucker (b); Bruz Freeman (d).

| Gypsy in My Soul | Mode LP106 |
|---|---|
| Man With a Horn | – |
| Sweet Georgia Brown | – |
| Tea for Two | – |

Faye and Benton out.

| Making Whoopee | Mode LP106 |
|---|---|
| This Can't Be Love | – |
| Little Girl Blues | – |
| S'Posin' | – |

## CANTINE, SARAH (piano)

Early 1966 - New York

Sarah Cantine (p); Richard Davis (b); Chester Thompson (d).

| | |
|---|---|
| On Green Dolphin Street | Samar SE100 |
| Solitude | - |

unknown (b) replaces Davis.

| | |
|---|---|
| Chit'lins A La Carte | Samar SE 105 |
| Feeling Good | - |

## CAPERS, VALERIE (piano)

1965-1966

Valerie Capers (p); John Daley (b); Charlie Hawkins (d).

| | |
|---|---|
| Little David Swing | Atlantic SD3003 |
| Sabrosa | - |
| The Heather on the Till | - |

Vincent McEwen (tp); Robin Kenyatta (as); Frank Perowsky (ts); Richard Landrum (cga) added.

| | |
|---|---|
| Hey Stuff | Atlantic SD3003 |
| Kenne's Soul | - |
| Odyssey | - |

details unknown.

| | |
|---|---|
| Baby, Let's Make Some Love | Blue 119 |
| Blues Boogie | - |

## CARLISLE, UNA MAE (piano)

May 20, 1938 - London

UNA MAE CARLISLE AND HER JAM BAND: David Wilkins (tp); Bertie King (cl,ts); Una Mae Carlisle (p,vo); Alan Ferguson (g); Len Harrison (b); Hymie Schneider (d).

| | | |
|---|---|---|
| DR-3654-1 | Don't Try Your Jive on Me | Vocalion (E) S162 |
| DR-3655-1 | I Would Do Anything For You | Vocalion (E) S199 |
| DR-3656-1 | Hangover Blues | Vocalion (E) S198 |
| DR-3657-1 | Love Walked In | Vocalion (E) S162 |
| DR-3658-1 | Mean to Me | Vocalion (E) S198 |
| DR-3659-1 | I'm Crazy 'Bout My Baby | Vocalion (E) S199 |

January 30, 1939 - Paris

DANNY POLO AND HIS SWING STARS: Philippe Brun (tp); Danny Polo (cl);
Alix Combelle (ts); Una Mae Carlisle (p); Oscar Aleman (g); Louis Vola
(b); Jerry Mongo (d).

| 4862hpp | Montparnasse Jump | Decca F-6989, Br A-82071 |
| 4863hpp | China Boy | Decca F-7126, 59001 |

August 2, 1940 - New York City

Una Mae Carlisle (p,vo); John Hamilton (tp); Al Casey (g); Cedric
Wallace (b); Slick Jones (d).

| 054675-1 | Now I Lay Me Down to Dream | Bluebird B10853 |
| 054676-1 | Papa's In Bed With His | - |
| | Britches On | |
| 054677-2 | If I Had You | Bluebird B10898 |
| 054678-1 | You Made Me Love You | - |

November 13, 1940 - New York City

Una Mae Carlisle (p,vo); Benny Carter (tp,sax); Everett Bardsdale (g);
Slam Stewart (b); Zutty Singleton (d).

| 57641-1 | Walkin' By the River | Bluebird B11033 |
| 57642-1 | I Met You Then, I Know | - |
| | You Now | |

May 23, 1944 - New York City

Ray Nance (tp); Bud Johnson (ts); Una Mae Carlisle (p,vo); Snags Allen
(g); Bass Robinson (b); Shadow Wilson (d).

| 'Tain't Yours | Beacon 7170, Joe Davies 4-34 |
| Without Your Baby | - |
| You Gotta Take Your Time | Beacon 7171, Joe Davies 4-78 |
| I Like It 'Cause I Love You | - |
| I'm a Good Woman | Beacon 7172 |
| Ain't Nothin' Much | - |

August 30, 1944 - New York City

Billy Butterfield (tp); Vernon Brown (tb); Bill Stegmeyer (cl); Una Mae
Carlisle (p,vo); Bob Haggart (b); George Wettling (d).

| Teasing Me | Beacon 7174, Joe Davies 4-34 |
| You and Your Heart of Stone | - |
| You're Gonna Change Your | Beacon 7175, Joe Davies 4-12 |
| Mind | |
| I've Got a Crying Need | Beacon 7176 |
| For You | |

October 20, 1944 - New York City

    same personnel.

| | |
|---|---|
| The Best of My Life | Beacon 7175 |
| I Speak So Much About You | Beacon 7173 |
| He's the Best Little Yank | - |

July 3, 1946 - New York City

Johnny Letman (tp); Gene Sedric (ts); Una Mae Carlisle (p,vo); Jimmy Shirley (g); Cedric Wallace (b); Slick Jones (d).

| | | |
|---|---|---|
| S3313 | That's My Man | Savoy 616 |
| S3314 | If It Ain't Mine | Savoy 517 |
| S3315 | I'm Crazy About My Baby | - |
| S3316 | Throw It Out of My Mind | Savoy 616 |

December, 1947 - New York City

    same or similar personnel.

| | |
|---|---|
| Where the River Meets the Sea | National 9044 |
| Stop Going Through the Motions | - |

CARPENTER, MARIE (alto saxophone)

See Collective Section.

CARR, LADY WILL (piano)

1945 - Los Angeles

Al Hibbler (vo) acc. by Harry Carney's All Stars: Taft Jordon, Harold Baker (tp); Russell Procope (as); Jack McVea (ts); Harry Carney (bars); Lady Will Carr (p); Ralph Hamilton (g); Red Callender (b); Harold West (d).

| | | |
|---|---|---|
| 2700 | Don't Take Your Love | Aladdin 155,3328, Score LP4013, ImpA9185 |
| 2701 | I Got It Bad | Aladdin 154, -    -,ImpA9185 |
| | How Long | Aladdin 155,    -    - |
| | S'Posin' | Aladdin 154,    -    - |

April, 1946 - Los Angeles

Karl George (tp); Henry Coker (tb); Marshall Royal (as,cl); Willie Smith (as); Lucky Thompson (ts); Lady Will Carr (p); Irving Ashby (g); Charlie Mingus (b); Lee Young (d).

```
            Ashby De la Zooch          Four Star 1105
            Love on a Greyhound Bus    -
```

April 26, 1946 - Los Angeles

Lady Will Carr (p); Irving Ashby (g); Charlie Mingus (b).

```
388AS-2     After Hours                Four Star 1106c
```

Claude Trenier (vo) added.

```
393AS       Make Believe               Four Star 1107
394AS-1     Honey Take a Chance        Four Star 1108
              With Me (vCT)
395AS       Bedspread                  Four Star 1107
396AS-2     This Subdues My Passion    Four Star 1108
397AS-2     Pipe Dream                 Four Star 1106
```

April 26, 1946 - Los Angeles

Bob Parrish (vo) acc. by LUCKY THOMPSON TRIO: Lucky Thompson (ts); Lady
Will Carr (p); Irving Ashby (g); Red Callender (b).

```
385AS       Full Moon and Empty Arms   Four Star 1119
386AS       How Deep is the Ocean      -
```

## CARR, WYNONA (piano, guitar)

1961-1962 - Los Angeles

Wynona Carr (p,vo); others unknown.

```
448         Don't Come Cryin' to Me    Reprise R(S)6023
449         Willow Weep for Me         -
450         Strange                    -
451         Bring Back the Blues       -
545         I Wanna Be Around          -
546         The Lucky Old Sun          -
547         So Long                    -, Reprise 20043
548         My Faith                   -, Reprise 20033
549         I Gotta Stand Tall         -            -
631         Down By the Riverside      -, Reprise 20043
632         Love Love Love             -
633         Oh How I Love You          -
2079        We're Gonna Throw a        Reprise 20201
              Little Party
2080        Carrying a Torch           -
```

date unknown

SISTER WYNONA CARR: Wynona Carr (vo,g)

| | |
|---|---|
| Each Day | Specialty 324 |
| Lord Jesus | - |
| I Want to Go to Heaven and Rest | - |
| I Know That He Knows | - |
| Don't Miss That Train | - |
| I Heard Mother Pray One Day | - |
| I Know Someday God's Gonna<br>  Call Me | - |
| What You Gonna Do When<br>  You Get to Heaven | - |
| The Good Old Way | - |
| See His Blessed Face | - |

date unknown.

Sister Wynona Carr (vo,g)

| | |
|---|---|
| Did He Die in Vain | Specialty 826 |
| Conversation with Jesus | - |
| A Letter to Heaven | - |
| In a Little While | - |
| The Ball Game | - |
| I Know By Faith | - |

## CARROLL, BARBARA (piano)

1949

BARBARA CARROLL TRIO:    Barbara Carroll (p,vo); Danny Martucci (b);
Herbie Wasserman (d).

| | | |
|---|---|---|
| 256 | Dancing on the Ceiling | Discovery 130 |
| 257 | Barbara's Carol | Discovery 129 |
| 258 | You Stepped Out of a Dream | - |
| 259 | The Puppet That Dances<br>  Bop | Discovery 130 |

1949

BARBARA CARROLL TRIO:    Barbara Carroll (p,vo); Joe Schulman (b); Herbie
Wasserman (d).

| | |
|---|---|
| Morocco, I | Discovery 160 |
| Morocco, II | - |

March 10, 1949 - New York City

SERGE CHALOFF AND THE HERDSMEN:    Red Rodney (tp); Earl Swope (tb); Al
Cohn (ts); Serge Chaloff (bars); Barbara Carroll (p); Oscar Pettiford
(b); Denzil Best (d); Terry Gibbs (vib); Shorty Rogers (arr).

| MS704 | Chickasaw | Futurama 3003, Mercer LP1003, Esq 10-074, EP023, JS 591 |
| MS705 | Bop Scotch | Futurama 3003, Mercer LP1003, Esq 10-074, EP023, JS 591 |
| MS706 | The Most | Futurama 3004, Mercer LP1003, Esq 10-073, EP023,20-094 |
| MS707 | Chasin' the Bass | Futurama 3004, Mercer LP1003 Esq 10-073, EP023,20-094 |

April 1949 - New York City

EDDIE SHU QUINTET: Eddie Shu (tp,cl,as,ts,hca); Barbara Carroll (p); John Levy (b); Denzil Best (d).

| Flamingo | Rainbow 10072, Mercer LP 1002 |
| Two Pair O'Shu's | - - |
| Waltzin' the Blues | - |

November 9, 1951 - New York City

BARBARA CARROLL TRIO: Barbara Carroll (p,vo); Joe Schulman (b); Herbie Wasserman (d).

| Love of My Life | Atlantic EP 503,LP 132,LP 1271 |
| You Took Advantage of Me | - - - |
| Takin' A Chance on Love | - - - |
| My Funny Valentine | - - - |
| They Can't Take That Away From Me | - |
| The Lady's In Love With Me | - |
| Autumn in New York | - |
| 'Tis Autumn | - |

September 27, 1953 - New York City

same personnel.

| E3VB1992 | I Want a Little Girl | Victor LJM 1001 |
| E3VB1993 | What's the Use of Wonderin' | - |
| E3VB1994 | Serenade For a Wealthy Widow | - |
| E3VB1996 | From This Moment On | - |
| E3VB1997 | Cabin in the Sky | - |
| E3VB1998 | Mountain Greenery | - |
| E3VB1999 | Good Bait | - |
| E3VB2402 | The Folks Who Live on the Hill | - |
| E3VB2403 | Give Me the Simple Life | - |

October 26, 1953 - New York City

same personnel.

| E3VB1995 | Goodbye | Victor LJM 1001,LEJ-2,LPM1296 |
| E3VB2470 | Lullaby of Broadway | - |
| E3VB2471 | Let's Fall in Love | - |

October 13, 1954 - New York City

Ralph Pollack (d) replaces Wasserman.

| | | |
|---|---|---|
| E4VB5778 | Garrow's Way | Victor LJM 1023 |
| E4VB5779 | If I Had You | - |
| E4VB5780 | Sweet Georgia Brown | - |
| E4VB5781 | You'd Be So Nice to Come Home To | -, HMV 7EG 8138 |

October 15, 1954 - New York City

same personnel.

| | | |
|---|---|---|
| E4VB5791 | By Myself | Victor LJM 1023 |
| E4VB5792 | I Saw Starts | - |
| E4VB5793 | Come Rain or Come Shine | - |

October 20, 1954 - New York City

same personnel.

| | | |
|---|---|---|
| E4VB5809 | I Love a Piano | Victor LJM 1023, HMV 7EG8138 |
| E4VB5810 | The Lady is a Tramp | - |
| E4VB5811 | I've Got the World on a String | - |
| E4VB5812 | But Not For Me | - - |
| E4VB5813 | As Long As I Live | - - |

October 21, 1954 - New York City

same personnel.

| | | |
|---|---|---|
| E4VB5815 | Blue and Sentimental | Victor EPA 604 |
| E4VB5816 | Am I Blue | - |
| E4VB5817 | Blue Moon | - |
| E4VB5818 | Just Plain Blue | - |
| | Lullaby of Birdland | Victor EPA 673, LPM 146 |

June 3, 1955 - New York City

same personnel.

| | | |
|---|---|---|
| F2JB4535 | Two Ladies in De Shade | Victor LPM 1137 |
| F2JB4536 | I'm Glad There Is You | - |
| F2JB4537 | Love Is a Simple Thing | - |
| F2JB4538 | Get Happy | - |

June 4, 1955 - New York City

same personnel.

| | | |
|---|---|---|
| F2JB4539 | It's All Right With Me | Victor LPM 1137 |
| F2JB4540 | Almost Like Being in Love | - |

| | | |
|---|---|---|
| F2JB4541 | You're Mine You | - |
| F2JB4542 | Everything I've Got | - |
| F2JB4543 | Barbara's Carroll | - |
| F2JB4544 | Have You Met Miss Jones | - |

June 6, 1955 - New York City

same personnel.

| | | |
|---|---|---|
| F2JB4545 | Happiness Is Just A Thing Called Joe | Victor EPA 656 |
| F2JB4546 | You Stepped Out of a Dream | - |
| F2JB4547 | Dream a Little Dream of Me | - |
| F2JB4548 | I Had the Craziest Dream | - |
| F2JB4549 | Did You Ever See a Dream Walking | - |

1956 - New York City

BARBARA CARROLL TRIO: Barbara Carroll (p,vo); Joe Schulman (b); Phil Faite (d).

| | |
|---|---|
| The Trolley Song | Verve MGV 2095 |
| I've Grown Accustomed To Her Face | - |
| Life Is Just a Bowl of Cherries | - |
| It Might As Well Be Spring | - |
| Will You Still Be Mine | - |
| Love Is Just Around the Corner | - |
| Happy To Make Your Acquaintance | - |
| Blues for Blue Eyes | - |
| Easy Living | - |

1956 - New York City

details unknown.

| | | |
|---|---|---|
| Satin Doll | Kapp KL 1193, | K53143 |
| Lonely Night | - | - |
| Surrey With the Fringe on Top | - | - |
| Not Now | - | - |
| Ev'ry Time We Say Goodbye | - | - |
| For All We Know | - | - |
| Sleepin' Bee | - | - |
| Barbara's Carol | - | - |
| Midnight Sun | - | - |

1956 - New York City

Barbara Carroll (p,vo) acc. by unknown orchestra.

| | |
|---|---|
| Grant Avenue | Kapp KL (S) 1113 |
| Chop Suey | - |
| I Enjoy Being a Girl | - |

Like a God                      -
Selections from the Musical     -
"Flower Drum Song"

1956 - New York City

BARBARA CARROLL TRIO:   Barbara Carroll (p,vo); Joe Schulman (b); Joe
Petti (d).

All of You                  Victor EPA 839, LPM 1296
Lost in a Crowded Place         -               -
You Make Me Feel So Young        -               -
We Just Couldn't Say Goodbye    -
Today                                           -
Cherry Point                                    -
Goodnight My Love                               -
You Do Something To Me                          -
Just One of Those Things                        -
Royal Garden Blues                              -

1956 - New York City

same personnel.

Funny Face                  Verve MGV 2063, MGV 2092
Let's Kiss and Make Up           -               -
He Loves and She Loves           -               -
'S Wonderful                     -               -
How Long Has This Been           -               -
  Going On
Clap Your Hands                  -               -
Someone To Watch Over Me         -               -
Our Love is Here to Stay         -               -
They All Laughed                 -               -
Let's Call the Whole Thing Off   -               -

May 22-23, 1956 - New York City

Barbara Carroll (p,vo); Joe Schulman (b); Al Munroe (d).

G2JB4421   No Moon At All            Victor LPM 1396
G2JB4422   It Never Entered My Mind       -
G2JB4425   At Long Last Love              -
G2JB4427   It's a Wonderful World         -
G2JB4428   The Girl Friend                -
           Struttin' With Some Barbecue   -
           The Most Beautiful Girl..       -
           One Life to Live               -
           Fancy Pants                    -
           Spring is Here                 -
G2JB4431   Paris Without You        Victor LPM 1325
G2JB4432   California Here I Come          -

July 24, 1959 - New York

BARBARA CARROLL TRIO: Barbara Carroll (p); Alan Mack (b); Joe Boppo (d).

| | |
|---|---|
| Why Not | Sesac N3201/3202 |
| Would It Be the Same | - |
| Dark Moon | - |
| Later | - |
| You're Here Again | - |
| The Black Cat | - |
| Theme for a Starlet | - |
| Champagne Velvet | - |
| B's Flat Blues | - |
| Misty Morning | - |
| Lonely Night | - |
| Chevy's Chase | - |

January, 1964 - New York City

details unknown.

| | |
|---|---|
| What Makes Sammy Run | Warner Brothers WM(S)1543 |
| Friendliest Thing | - |
| A Pair of Shoes | - |
| Something to Live For | - |
| Room Without Windows | - |
| My Home Town | - |
| Maybe Some Other Time | - |
| Hello Dolly | - |
| Dancing Ribbons Down My Back | - |
| It Only Takes a Moment | - |
| Put On Your Sunday Clothes | - |

## CARSON, NORMA (trumpet)

See Collective Section.

## CHARTERS, ANN (piano)

December, 1958 - New York

A JOPLIN BOUQUET: Ann Charters (p).

| | |
|---|---|
| Fig Leaf Rag | Sonet SNTF 631 |
| Rose Leaf Rag | - |
| The Sycamore | - |
| Sunflower Slow Drag | - |
| Euphonic Sounds | - |
| Heliotrope Bouquet | - |
| Gladiolus Rag | - |

Palm Leaf Rag                              –
Pleasant Moment                            –
Weeping Willow                             –
The Chrysanthemum                          –

c. 1960 – New York

Cataract Rag                    Folkways FG 3563
Wall Street Rag                            –
Solace                                     –
Magnetic Rag                               –
Victory Rag                                –
Ethiopia Rag                               –
Pastime Rag No. 3                          –
Echoes From the Snowballs Club             –
Harlem Rag                                 –
Rag Sentimental                            –


## CHATMAN, CHRISTINE (piano)

April 6, 1944 – New York City

Christine Chatman (p) acc. by Mabel Smith (vo) and unknown others.

| 71948 | Napoleon Boogie | Decca 8660 |
| 71949 | Boogin' the Boogie | Decca 48035 |
| 71950 | Boogie Woogie Girl | – |
| 71951 | Hurry Hurry | Decca 8660 |

1948 – Chicago

GENE AMMONS BAND:  Gene Ammons (ts); Christine Chatman (p,vo); others unknown.

| CR1903 | Chabootie | Chess 1429, LP1445, VgV3009 |

1948 – Chicago

Andrew Tibbs (vo) acc. by TOM ARCHIA'S ALL STARS:  (prob.) Tom Archia (ts); Christine Chatman (p); Leo Blevins (g); Leroy Jackson (b); Wes Landers (d).

| U7074 | I Feel Like Crying | Aristocrat 1103 |
| U7077 | Married Man Blues | – |
| U7139 | McKie's Jam Boppers | Aristocrat 605 |
| U7140 | Swinging for Christmas | Aristocrat 606 |
| U7142 | Talk of the Town | – |

1948–1949 – Chicago

GENE AMMONS SEXTET:  Gene Ammons (ts); Christine Chatman (p,vo); Leo Blevins (g); Lowell Pointer (b); Ike Day (d); Mary Graham (vo).

| U7175 | Do You Really Mean It | Chess 1428 |
|---|---|---|
| U7179 | Bless You (vMG) | Chess 1425 |
| U7180 | Stuffy | Aristocrat 711 |
| U7181 | Once in a While | - |

## 1948-1949 - Chicago

Matthew Gee (tb); Gene Ammons (ts); Christine Chatman (p); Leo Blevin (g); LeRoy Jackson (b); Wes Landers (d).

| U7231 | Pennies From Heaven | Aristocrat 411, Chess 1431, LP1442,,VgV3152,LD140,LD151 |
|---|---|---|
| U7232 | The Last Chance | Aristocrat 411, - |
| U7233 | The Last Mile | -, Chess 1431,LP1445, Vg3049, LD151 |
| U7234 | Full Moon | Chess 1429,VgV2235,748, -, Vg3049 |
| U7248 | Goodbye | Chess 1428,LP1442 |
| U7249 | It's You or No One | LP1442 |
| U7250 | My Foolish Heart | Chess 1428, -,Vg3009, 45-23, LD151 |
| U7265 | Jug Head Ramble | Chess 1433,VgV2235,748,VgV3049, LD151 |
| U7266 | Don't Do Me Wrong | Chess 1450, LP1445 |
| U7268 | Prelude to a Kiss | - , LP1442 |
| U7337 | Baby, Won't You Please.. | Chess 1464, LP1445 |
| U7338 | Happiness is Just a Thing.. | - , LP1442 |

## CLARK, CORTELIA (guitar)

1966 - Live, Street in Nashville, Tennessee

Cortelia Clark (g,vo)

| Blues in the Street | RCA LSP-3568 |
|---|---|
| Felton Davis Interviews Cortelia | - |
| Baby, What Have I Done | - |
| Never Be Sad No Mo' | - |
| Watcha Gonna Do | - |
| Love Blues | - |
| Love, Oh Love | - |
| Ever'day Blues | - |
| Bye Bye, Love | - |
| Walk Right In | - |
| Baby Don't Belong to You | - |
| Trouble in Mind | - |
| Be My Darlin' | - |

## COATES, DOROTHY LOVE (piano)

1957

Dorothy Love Coates (p,vo) and the Original Gospel Harmonettes.

|  |  |
|---|---|
| That's Enough | CBS M67280 |

Summer 1968

Dorothy Love Coates (p,vo) acc. by u (org,g,b,d).

|  |  |
|---|---|
| Strange Man | CBS M67234 |

1968

details unknown.

| | |
|---|---|
| I Won't Let Go | Nashboro 947 |
| Heaven I've Heard So Much | - |
| Stop, Take Time to Pray | Nashboro 958 |
| Place of Rest | - |
| To My Father's House | - |
| They Don't Believe | - |
| I've Got to Make It | - |
| My Soul Needs Resting | - |

date unknown.

Dorothy Love Coates and the Harmonettes.

| | |
|---|---|
| That's Allright with Me | Nashboro 988 |
| Does Jesus Care | - |

## COLBERT, EMMA (violin)

See Collective Section.

## COLE, HELEN (drums)

See Collective Section.

## COLEMAN, GLORIA (organ)

May 21, 1963 - New York City

Leo Wright (as); Gloria Coleman (org); Grant Green (g); Pola Roberts (d).

| | Que Baby | Impulse A (S)-47 |
|---|---|---|
| | Sadie Green | - |
| | Hey Sonny Red | - |
| | Melba's Minor | - |
| | Funky Bob | - |
| | My Lady's Waltz | - |

**November 1, 1963 - New York**

Leo Wright (as,fl); Gloria Coleman (org); Kenny Burrell (g); Frankie Dunlap (d).

| 7362 | Soul Talk | Vortex 2011 |
|---|---|---|
| 7363 | Poopsie's Minor | - |
| 7364 | Skylark | - |
| 7365 | Blues Fanfare | - |
| 7366 | State Trooper | - |
| 7367 | Sometimes I Feel Like a Motherless Child | - |
| 7368 | Blue Leo | - |

**1965 - New York**

GLORIA COLEMAN SINGS & SWINGS ORGAN:  Ray Copeland (flhn); Dick Griffith (tb); James Anderson (ts); Gloria Coleman (org,vo); Earl Dunbar (g); Charlie Davis (d).

| | Bugaloo for Ernie | Mainstream MRL872 |
|---|---|---|
| | Sunday | - |
| | Monday as Always | - |
| | Fungi Momma | - |
| | You Better Go Now | - |
| | Blues for Youse | - |
| | Blue Bossa | - |
| | Love Nest | - |
| | Fly Me to the Moon | - |

## CONLEY, ALTHEA (trombone)

See Collective Section.

## COLLINS, JOYCE (piano)

**June 1-2, 1960 - Los Angeles**

Joyce Collins (p); Roy Green (Ray Brown) (b); Frank Butler (d).

| | Walkin' | Jazzland JLP-24 |
|---|---|---|
| | I Let a Song Go Out of My Heart | - |
| | Just in Time | - |

> I Get Along With You Very
>   Well                -
> The End of a Love Affair     -
> Day In, Day Out            -
> Something's Gotta Give      -
> Ah, Moore                  -
> Blue Jay                    -

## CRAWFORD, LILLIAN (piano)

February 7, 1934 - Richmond, Indiana

Lillian Crawford (p) solo.

| 19488 | In a Mist (Bixology) | Champ 16817 |

## CREATH, MARGE (piano)

Note: According to Phil Schaap, Ms. Creath recorded on many dates in St. Louis between 1920 and 1925 where the piano part had to be read, as the regular pianist could not read music.

## DABNEY, ELISHA "BARTLEY" (trombone)

February 4, 1949 - St. Louis

GEORGE HUDSON AND HIS ORCHESTRA: George Hudson, Tommy Turrentine, Sykes Smith, Cyrus L. Stone, Paul Gydner Campbell (tp); William Seals, Robert Horne, Elisha "Bartley" Dabney (tb); Frank Domageux, Cyrus L. Stoner (as); Ernie Milkins, William Adkins (ts); Wallace Brodis (bars); Robert Parker (p); James Royal (b); Earl Martin (d); Danny Knight (vo).

| K5674 | It's Love | King 4300 |
| K5675 | No One Sweeter Than You | King 4285 |
| K5676 | Applejack Boogie | - |
| K5677 | Put It On the Cuff | King 4300 |

## DANE, BARBARA (guitar)

1964 - New York

> You Don't Know Me        Folkways FA2471
> I Just Want to Make Love
>   to You                -
> Come Back Baby          -
> Strangers' Blues         -
> Victim to the Blues      -
> 'Way Behind the Sun      -

```
        Special Delivery Blues              -
        It Hurts Me                         -
        Come On In                          -
        Hard, oh Lord                       -
        Working People's Blues              -
        Dink's Blues                        -
```

June 18, 1964 - "The Cabale" - Berkely, California

Lightnin' Hopkins (g,vo) acc. by Barbara Dane (g,vo).

```
        Sometimes She Loves Me     Arhoolie F1022
        You Got Another Man               -, RCA LPM 10304
        I'm Going Back Baby               -
        Mother Earth                      -
```


## DAVIES, DESDEMONA (piano)

See Collective Section.


## DAVIES, RAMONA (piano)

November 25, 1932 - New York City

PAUL WHITEMAN AND HIS ORCHESTRA: Paul Whiteman (dir); Nat Natoli, Harry
Goldfield (tp); Andy Secrest (c); Jack Fulton (tb); Fritz Hummel, Bill
Rank (tb); Chester Hazlett (cl,b-cl,as); Charles Strickfaden (as,bars);
Frank Trumbauer (c-mel-sax,as,bassoon); Ray McDermott (cl,ts); Kurt
Dieterle, Mischa Russell, Matt Malneck, John Bowman (vn); Ramona Davies
(p,vo); Fritz Cicconi (g); Mike Pingitore (bj); Pierre Olker (b); George
Marsh (d).

```
74610-1    Rise 'N Shine              Victor 24197
```


December 14, 1932 - New York City

PAUL WHITEMAN AND HIS ORCHESTRA: Paul Whiteman (dir); Eddie Wade, Bunny
Berigan, Harry Goldfield (tp); Bill Rank, Vincent Grande (tb); Jack
Fulton (tb); Bennie Bovacio (cl,b-cl,as); John Cordaro (cl,as,c-mel
sax); Mischa Russell, Matt Malneck, Harry Stuble, Kurt Dieterle (vn);
Roy Borgy (p,arr); Ramona Davies (p,vo); Mike Pingitore (bj,g); Norman
McPherson (tuba); Art Miller (b); Casper Reardon (h); Chet Martin,
Herman Fink (d).

```
86459-1    Deep Forest                Victor 24852, HMV B-8318
86460-1    Serenade for a Wealthy Widow      -            -
```


March 1, 1933 - New York

Ramona Davies (p,vo) acc. by Nat Natoli (tp); Benny Bovacio (cl); Roy
Borgy (p,celeste).

| 75341 | What Have We Got to Lose | Victor 24268 |
|--------|--------------------------|--------------|
| 75342-1 | A Penny for Your Thoughts | Victor 24260 |
| 75343-1 | My Cousin in Milwaukee | - |

**April 4, 1933 - New York City**

PAUL WHITEMAN AND HIS ORCHESTRA: Paul Whiteman (dir); Nat Natoli, Harry Goldfield (tp); Andy Secrest (c); Jack Fulton (tb); Fritz Hummel, Bill Rank (tb); Chester Hazlett (cl,b-cl,as); Charles Strickfaden (as,bars); Frank Trumbauer (c-mel sax,as,bassoon); Ray McDermott (cl,ts); Kurt Dieterle, Mischa Russell, Matt Malneck, John Bowman (vn); Ramona Davies (p,vo); Fritz Cicconi (g); Mike Pingitore (bj); Norman McPherson (tuba) Pierre Olker (b); George Marsh (d); Peggy Healy (vo).

| 75713-1 | Look What I've Got | Victor 24285 |
|---------|--------------------|--------------|

**April 20, 1933 - Camden, New Jersey**

Ramona Davies (p,vo) acc. by Nat Natoli (tp); Benny Bovacio (cl); Roy Borgy (p,celeste).

| 75671-1 | Raisin' the Rent | Victor 24316 |
|---------|------------------|--------------|
| 75672-1 | Was My Face Red | Victor 24310 |
| 75673-1 | I've Got to Sing a Torch Song | Victor 23304 |

**July 20, 1933 - New York City**

same personnel.

| 76673-1 | Are You Makin' Any Money | Victor 24365 |
|---------|--------------------------|--------------|

**August 16, 1933 - New York**

Borgy out. Herb Quigley (d) added.

| 77498-1 | You Excite Me | Victor 24389 |
|---------|---------------|--------------|
| 77503-1 | Ah! The Moon is Here | - |

**September 11, 1933 - New York City**

PAUL WHITEMAN AND HIS ORCHESTRA: Paul Whiteman (dir); Nat Natoli, Harry Goldfield, Bunny Berigan (tp); Vincent Grande (tb); Fritz Hummel, Bill Rank (tb); Chester Hazlett (cl,b-cl,as); Charles Strickfaden (as,bars); Frank Trumbauer (c-mel sax,as,bassoon); Ray McDermott (cl,ts); Kurt Dieterle, Mischa Russell, Matt Malneck, John Bowman (vn); Ramona Davies (p,vo); Fritz Cicconi (g); Mike Pingitore (bj); Norman McPherson (tuba) Pierre Olker (b); George Marsh (d); Peggy Healy (vo).

| 76645-1 | It's Only a Paper Moon | Victor 24400, HMV B-6427, El EG-2903 |
|---------|------------------------|--------------------------------------|

```
76647-1    Sittin' on a Backyard        Victor 24403, HMV B-6434
           Fence
```

Ramona Davies (p,vo) acc. by Nat Natoli (tp); Benny Bovacio (cl); Roy
Borgy (p); Dick McDonough (g).

```
78264-1    I Found a New Way to         Victor 24440
           Go to Town
78265-1    I'm No Angel                      -
78265-1    Not for All the Rice in      Victor 24445
           China
```

November 3, 1933 - New York City

PAUL WHITEMAN AND HIS ORCHESTRA: Paul Whiteman (dir); Nat Natoli, Bunny
Berigan, Harry Goldfield (tp); Bill Rank, Vincent Grande (tb); Jack
Fulton (tb); Bennie Bovacio (cl,b-cl,as); John Cordaro (cl,as, c-mel
sax); Mischa Russell, Matt Malneck, Harry Stuble, Kurt Dieterle (vn);
Roy Borgy (p,arr); Ramona Davies (p,vo); Mike Pingitore (bj,g); Norman
McPherson (tuba); Art Miller (b); Herb Quigley (d).

```
78513-1    Something Had to Happen      Victor 24455
```

Rank and Fulton out.

```
81714-1    True                         Victor 24566,HMV B06481,
                                        EA1414, EI EG-3053
```

February 16, 1934 - New York City

Johnny Mercer (vo) added.  Jack Teagarden (tp) replaces Grande; Charlie
Teagarden (tp) replaces Berigan.

```
81715-1    Fare-Thee-Well to Harlem     Victor 24571,Bluebird B010969,
                                        HMV EA-3408
81716-1    Sun Spots                    Victor 24574,HMV EA-7344,
                                        RE-4382
81717-1    The Bouncing Ball                 -        -,RE-4382,
                                        BD-187
```

April 17, 1934 - New York City

same personnel.

```
81061-2    G Blues                      Victor 24668,HMV EA-1407,
                                        HMV X-4431
82319-1    Tail Spin                    Victor 24668,    -,HMV X-4431
82320-1    Christmas Night in Harlem*   Victor 24615,HMV B-6549,
                                        EA-3408,Bluebird B-10969
```

* Jack Teagarden and Johnny Mercer (vo).

June 29, 1934 - New York City

   same personnel. Ramona Davies (vo).

   83352-1    Born to Be Kissed             Victor 24670

August 18, 1934 - New York City

   same personnel. Peggy Healy, Johnny Mercer (vo).

   84010      Pardon My Southern Accent   Victor 24704
   84014-1    I Saw Stars                Victor 24705, HMV B-6532,
                                          EA-1416

   violins and tuba out.

   84012-1    Itchola                   Victor 24885, HMV NE-255

December 17, 1934 - New York City

   PAUL WHITEMAN AND HIS ORCHESTRA: Paul Whiteman (dir); Eddie Wade, Bunny
   Berigan, Harry Goldfield (tp); Bill Rank, Vincent Grande (tb); Jack
   Fulton (tb); Bennie Bovacio (cl,b-cl,as); John Cordaro (cl,as,c-mel
   sax); Mischa Russell, Matt Malneck, Harry Stuble (vn); Bob Lawrence
   (vn,vo); Roy Borgy (p,arr); Ramona Davies (p,vo); Mike Pingitore (bj,g);
   Norman McPherson (tuba); Art Miller (b); Chet Martin, Herman Fink (d).

   86470-1    The Night is Young        Victor 24844, HMV BD-130

July 9, 1935 - New York City

   PAUL WHITEMAN AND HIS ORCHESTRA: Paul Whiteman (dir); Eddie Wade,
   Charlie Teagarden, Harry Goldfield (tp); Bill Rank (tb); Jack Fulton
   (tb); Jack Teagarden (tb,vo); Benny Bonacio (cl,b-cl,as); John Cordaro
   (cl,b-cl,as,bars); Charles Strickfaden (cl,as,ts,bars,oboe); Frank
   Trumbauer (cl,as,c-mel sax); Kurt Dieterle, Mischa Russell, Matt
   Malneck, Harry Struble (vn); Roy Bargy, Ramona Davies (p); Mike
   Pingitore (g); Norman McPherson (tuba); Art Miller (b); Larry Gomar
   (d,vib); Casper Reardon (h); Durell Alexander (vo).

   92576-1    Dodging a Divorcee      Victor 25086, HMV B-8641
   92577-1    The Duke Insists        Victor 25113
   92579-1    Nobody's Sweetheart Now   Victor 25319, Bluebird B-10957
   92580-1    Ain't Misbehavin' (vJT)   Victor 25086, HMV EA-1560
   92581-1    Sugar Plum (vDA)        Victor 25150, HMV EA-1594,
                                      BD-5001
   92582-1    New O'leans (vJT)        Victor 25150,       -

September 7, 1935 - New York City

   PAUL WHITEMAN AND HIS ORCHESTRA: Paul Whiteman (dir); Eddie Wade,
   Charlie Teagarden, Harry Goldfield (tp); Bill Rank (tb); Jack Fulton,
   Jack Teagarden (tb); Benny Bonacio (cl,b-cl,as); John Cordaro (cl,

b-cl,as,bars); Charles Strickfaden (cl,as,ts,bars,oboe); Frank Trumbauer (cl,as,c-mel sax); Kurt Dieterle, Mischa Russell, Matt Malneck, Harry Struble (vn); Roy Bargy, Ramona Davies (p); Mike Pingitore (g); Norman McPherson (tuba); Art Miller (b); Larry Gomar (d,vib).

| 94192-1 | Farewell Blues | Victor 25192, HMV EA-1628 |
| 94197-1 | Announcer's Blues | Victor 25404, Jazz Archives 821 |

Fulton out. Bob Lawrence (vn,vo) replaces Dieterle and Malneck; Bob White (d) replaces Gomar. King's Men (vocal group) added.

| 99060-1 | Saddle Your Blues to a<br>Wild Mustang | Victor 25251, HMV EA-1676 |

September 13, 1935 - New York

RAMONA AND HER GANG: Ramona Davies (p,vo) acc. by Charlie Teagarden (tp); Jack Teagarden (tb); Ben Bonacio (cl,bars); Dick McDonough (g); Art Miller (b); Larry Gomer (d).

| 95024-1 | Every Now and Then | Victor 25138 |
| 95025-2 | No Strings | - |
| 95026-2 | I Can't Give You Anything<br>But Love | Victor 25156 |
| 95027-1 | Barrel-House Music | - |

December 2, 1935 - New York City

George Bamford (cl,ts,fl) added; King's Men (vocal group).

| 98181-1 | I'm the Echo (vKM) | Victor 25198,HMV EA-1633,<br>NE-278, JA 646 |
| 98184-1 | I Got Love | Victor 25198, -,NE-278,<br>JA 646 |

## DAVIS, BIRDIE (alto sax)

See Collective Section.

## DAVIS, MARTHA (piano)

August, 1946 - New York City

Martha Davis (p,vo)

| Martha's Boogie | Urban 120 |
| Why Am I | - |
| Be-Bop Bounce | Urban 121 |
| I'm Fer It | - |

August, 1946 - New York City

Martha Davis (p,vo) acc. by unknown orchestra.

| | | |
|---|---|---|
| | Lovin' Blues | Urban 126 |
| | Can't Be Bothered | - |
| | The Same Old Boogie | Urban 127 |
| | Time for the Postman's Ring | - |

1948

Martha Davis (p,vo) with unknown accompaniment.

| L4738 | I Ain't Getting Any Younger | Decca 48174 |
|---|---|---|
| | Kitchen Blues | - |
| | Cincinnati | Decca 24335 |
| | Honey Honey Honey | - |
| | Ooh Wee | Decca 24383 |
| | Trouble is a Man | - |

1948

Martha Davis (p,vo); Ralph William (g); Calvin Ponder (b); Lee Young (d).

| JRC262 | Bread and Gravy | Jewell ON-2002 |
|---|---|---|
| JRC263-1 | Little White Lies | - |
| JRC264 | When I Say Goodbye | Jewell ON-2003 |
| JRC265 | Sarah, Sarah | - |

May 10, 1951 - New York City

Martha Davis (p,vo); John Collins (g); Calvin Ponder (b); Art Blakey (d).

| | | |
|---|---|---|
| | Experience | Coral (# unknown) |
| | Piano Player Boogie | - |
| | How Could Anything Be So Bad | - |
| | You're the Doctor | - |

details unknown

| | | |
|---|---|---|
| | Get Out Those Old Records | Coral 65048 |
| | Would I Love You Love You | - |
| | No Deposit, No Return | Coral 60890 |
| | What Became of You | - |

<u>DAVIS, TINY</u> (trumpet)

See Collective Section.

## DEARIE, BLOSSOM (piano)

April 1, 1952 - New York City

Annie Ross (vo) acc. by Milt Jackson (vib); Blossom Dearie (p); Percy
Heath (b); Kenny Clarke (d).

| | | |
|---|---|---|
| Everytime | DeeGee EP-4010, Savoy MG12060, Regent MG6031 | |
| The Way You Look Tonight | DeeGee EP-4010, Regent MG6031 | -, |
| I'm Beginning to Think You Care | DeeGee EP-4010, Regent MG6031 | - |
| Between the Devil and the Deep Blue Sea | DeeGee EP-4010, Regent MG6031 | - |

1955 - Paris

Blossom Dearie (p,vo); Herman Garst (b); Bernard Planchenault (d).

| | |
|---|---|
| The Continental | Felsted (E) SDL 86034 |
| The Boy Next Door | - |
| They Can't Take That Away From Me | - |
| Moonlight Saving Time | - |
| The Surrey With the Fringe on Top | - |
| April in Paris | - |
| Blue Moon | - |
| Down in the Depths | - |

January 16, 1956 - Paris

Bobby Jaspar (fl); Blossom Dearie (p,vo); Benoit Quersin (b); Christian
Garros (d).

| | |
|---|---|
| Old Devil Moon | Barclay EP 74017 |
| Autumn in New York | - |
| Flamingo | - |
| There Will Never Be Another You | - |

1956 - New York City

Blossom Dearie (p,vo); Herb Ellis (g); Ray Brown (b); Jo Jones (d).

| | | | |
|---|---|---|---|
| 20277 | You For Me | Verve 10109, MGV 2037 | |
| | A Fine Spring Morning | | - |
| | Comment Allez Vous | | - |
| | 'Deed I Do | | - |
| | Everything I've Got | HMV 7EG8539, | - |
| | Tout Doucement | | - |
| | It Might As Well Be Spring | | - |
| | I Hear Music | - | - |
| | I Won't Dance | | - |
| | Lover Man | | - |
| | More Than You Kow | | - |

Now At Last                                          -
Thou Swell                               -           -
Wait Till You See Him                                -


August, 1957 - New York City

Blossom Dearie (p,vo); Herb Ellis (g); Ray Brown (b); Jo Jones (d).

21402       The Middle of Love              Verve 10109, MGV 2081
            Between the Devil and the                -
               Deep Blue Sea
            Bang Goes the Drums                       -
            Give 'Em Ooh La La                        -
            I Walked a Little Faster                  -
            Just One of Those Things                  -
            Let's                                     -
            Like Someone in Love                      -
            Plus Je Tie Brasse                        -
            They Say It's Spring                      -
            The Riviera                               -
            Try Your Wings                            -


1959 - New York City

Blossom Dearie (p,vo); Mundell Lowe (g); Ray Brown (b); Ed Thigpen (d).

            It Amazes Me                    Verve 10151, MGV 2111
            Doop-Dee-De-Doop                 -        -
            Tea for Two                               -
            The Surrey With the Fringe on Top         -
            Moonlight Savings Time                    -
            If I Were a Bell                          -
            We're Together                            -
            Teach Me Tonight                          -
            Once Upon a Summertime                    -
            Down With Love                            -
            Our Love is Here to Stay                  -


1959 - New York City

Blossom Dearie (p,vo); Kenny Burrell (g); Ray Brown (b); Ed Thigpen (d).

            Guys and Dolls                  Verve MGV 2133
            Confession                                -
            Rhode Island is Famous for You            -
            To Keep My Love Alive                     -
            Too Good for the Average Man              -
            The Gentleman is a Dope                   -
            I'm Always True to You                    -
               In My Fashion
            Napoleon                                  -
            Life Upon the Wicked Stage                -
            Love is the Reason                        -

```
           The Physician                      -
           Buckle Down                        -
```

1959 - New York City

Bobby Jaspar (fl); Blossom Dearie (p,vo); Kenny Burrell (g); Ray Brown
(b); Ed Thigpen (d).

```
           Chez Moi                 Verve MGV 2125
           Boum                               -
           L'Etang                            -
```

Jaspar out.

```
           Little Jazz Bird                   -
           My Gentleman Friend                -
           It's Too Good to Talk About Now    -
           You Fascinate Me So                -
           You've Got Something I Want         -
           Hello Love                         -
           Someone to Watch Over Me           -
           Lucky To Be Me          Verve MGV 2109
           Just in Time                       -
           Some Other Time                    -
           Dance Only With Me                 -
           I Like Myself                      -
           The Party's Over                   -
           How Will He Know                   -
           It's Love                          -
           Hold Me, Hold Me, Hold Me          -
           Lonely Town                        -
```

c. 1963

Blossom Dearie (p,vo) acc. by the Capitol Orchestra; Jack Marshall
(arr).

```
           I Wish You Love         Capitol 72086
           Charade                            -
           May I Come In                      -
           I'm Old Fashioned                  -
           Love is a Necessary Evil           -
           The Best is Yet to Come            -
           Put On a Happy Face                -
           Something Happens to Me            -
           I'm in Love Again                  -
           When Sonny Gets Blue               -
           Quiet Nights                       -
           Don't Twist Too Long               -
```

March, 1966 - Ronnie Scott's Club, London

```
           On Broadway             Fontana(E)(S)TL5352,(Am)MGF27562,
                                   SRF 67562
```

When the World Was Young     -     -     -
When in Rome     -     -     -
The Shadow of Your Smile     -     -     -
Everything I've Got     -     -     -
Once Upon a Summertime     -     -     -
I'm Hip     -     -     -
Mad About the Boy     -     -     -
The Shape of Things     -     -     -
Satin Doll     -     -     -

Summer, 1966 - London

Blossom Dearie (p,vo); Freddie Logan (b); Alan Ganley (d).

Let's Go Where the Grass    Fontana TL5399
    is Greener
You Turn Me On Baby     -
Sleepin' Bee     -
Sweet Lover No More     -
Sweet Georgie Fame     -
That's No Joke     -
Peel Me a Grape     -
One Note Samba     -
On a Clear Day You Can See Forever     -
I'll Only Miss Him When I     -
    Think of Him
Big City's For Me     -
You're Gonna Hear From Me     -

c. 1967

Blossom Dearie (p,vo) acc. by large band directed by Reg Guest.

A Wonderful Guy    Fontana TL5454
Trains and Boats and Planes     -
Alfie     -
Meditation     -
How Insensitive     -
Soon It's Gonna Rain     -
Watch What Happens     -
I Was Looking For You     -
   indi     -
Once I Loved     -
The Folks Who Live on the Hill     -

## DICKERSON, ALETHA (piano)

June 21, 1926 - Chicago

Marie Grinter (vo) acc. by Aletha Dickerson (p).

9761-A    East and West Blues     Okeh 8384
9762-A    M.C. Blues     -

May 4, 1937 - Aurora, Illinois

Billy and Mary Mack (vocal duets) acc. by Aletha Dickerson (p); Big Bill
Broonzy (g); u (b).

| 07622-1 | Stingaree Man | Bluebird B-8131 |
| 07623-1 | Every Night | Bluebird B-7097 |
| 07624-1 | Get Going | - |
| 07625-1 | I Vouch For My Man | Bluebird B-8131 |

October 11, 1937 - Aurora, Illinois

Sweet Peas Spivey (vo) acc. by Aletha Dickerson (p); u (d).

| 014348-1 | I Got a Man in the 'Bama Mines | Bluebird B-7224 |
| 014349-1 | Cold in Hand | - |
| 014350-1 | Ramblin' Blues | Bluebird B-8146 |
| 014351-1 | Disgusted Blues | - |
| 014352-1 | Blood Drippin' Blues | Bluebird B-8114 |
| 014353-1 | Road of Stone | - |

## DIEMAN, FLORENCE (trumpet)

See Collective Section.

## DIXON, LUCILLE (bass)

December 29, 1947 - New York

Tiny Grimes Quintet:  John Hardee (ts); George Kelly (p); Tiny Grimes
(g); Lucille Dixon (b); Sonny Payne (d).

| A111 | Profoundly Blue | Atlantic 858 |
| A112 | Blue Harlem | Atlantic 854 |
| A113 | That Old Black Magic | Atlantic 858 |
| A114 | Boogie Woogie Barbecue | Atlantic 854 |

## DONAHUE, JUEL (trumpet)

See Collective Section.

## DONALD, BARBARA (trumpet)

August, 1966 - New York

SONNY SIMMONS QUINTET:  Barbara Donald (tp); Sonny Simmons (as); John
Hicks (p); Teddy Smith (b); Marvin Patillo (perc).

| | |
|---|---|
| Metamorphasis | ESP 1030 |
| City of David | - |

Hicks out.

| | |
|---|---|
| Interplanetary Travelers | ESP 1030 |

Autumn, 1968 - New York

Barbara Donald (tp); Sonny Simmons (as); Mike Cohen (p); Juney Booth (b); Jim Zitro (d).

| | |
|---|---|
| Resolutions | ESP 1043 |
| Zarak's Symphony | - |
| Balladia | - |

Burt Wilson (ts) added.

| | |
|---|---|
| Dolphy's Days | - |

Note: Additional recordings by Ms. Donald lie outside the temporal scope of this discography.


## DONEGAN, DOROTHY (piano)

January 23, 1942 - Chicago

Dorothy Donegan (p) solo.

| | | |
|---|---|---|
| 070687-1 | Piano Boogie | Bluebird B-8979 |
| 070688-1 | Everyday Blues | - |

September, 1946 - New York

Dorothy Donegan (p) acc. by Carl "Flattop" Wilson (b); Oliver Coleman (d).

| | | |
|---|---|---|
| CU3553 | Limehouse Blues | Continental 6034 |
| CU3556 | Dorothy's Boogie Woogie | Continental 6033,Swingfare 1021 |
| CU3559 | Tiger Rag | Continental 6034 |
| | Yesterdays | Continental 6033 |
| | Jumpin' Jack Boogie | Continental 6051 |
| | Little Girl From St. Louis | - |

1946-1947 - New York

Dorethy Donegan (p) solo.

| | |
|---|---|
| Some of These Days | Continental 6056 |
| Kilroy Was Here | - |
| Schubert's Boogie Woogie | Continental 6057 |
| How High the Moon | - |

```
            The Man I Love              Continental 6058
            Two Loves Wuz One Too Many         -
              For Me
```

1959 - Los Angeles

  Dorothy Donegan (p) acc. by u (b,d).

```
            A Foggy Day                 Capitol T1226
            September in the Rain             -
            I've Got You Under My Skin       -
            The D.D.T. Blues                 -
            Day In, Day Out                  -
            Lover                            -
            Tea For Two                      -
            Moonlight in Vermont             -
            Thou Swell                       -
            I Only Have Eyes for You         -
            I'll Remember April              -
            Bye Bye Blackbird                -
```

c. 1960 - Live at the Roundtable - New York

  Dorothy Donegan (p) acc. by u (b,d).

```
            Take the A Train            Roulette R25514
            Lazy River                       -
            Moanin'                          -
            There's No Greater Love          -
            September Song                   -
            Just in Time                     -
            My Blue Heaven                   -
            A Foggy Day                      -
            Boogie in Nursery                -
            April in Paris                   -
            Limehouse Blues                  -
            Sweet Georgia Brown              -
```

date unknown.

  Dorothy Donegan (p) acc. by Tiny Webb (g) and others.

```
M542-2    D.D.T. Blues                Miltone S269
M545-1    Old Man River                    -
```

details unknown.

```
            Up a Lazy River             Jubilee LP11
            I Can't Give You Anything        -
              But Love
            Dancing on the Ceiling           -
            Happiness is a Thing Called Joe  -
            September Song                   -
```

St. Louis Blues                         -
I Get a Kick Out of You                 -


date unknown.

Dorothy Donegan (p) acc. by unknown rhythm.

        D.D.T.                  Roulette R25010
        Donegan Walk                    -
        Humoresque                      -
        Just in Time                    -
        Sweet Georgia Brown             -
        That Old Black Magic            -
        This Can't Be Love              -


## DRANES, JUANITA "ARIZONA" (piano)

June 17, 1926 - Chicago

Arizona Dranes (p,vo) acc. by Sara Martin, Richard M. Jones (vo).

9737-A    In that Day             Okeh 8320, Herwin LP210,
                                  Roots RL328
9738-A    It's All Right Now      Okeh 8353,    -, Roots RL304
9739-A    John Said He Saw the    Okeh 8352, Herwin LP210
            Number
9740-A    My Soul Is a Witness         -        -, Col G31086
            For the Lord


June 17, 1926 - Chicago

Arizona Dranes (p) solo.

9741-A    Crucifixion             Okeh 8380, Herwin LP210,
                                  Par PMC1174
9742-A    Sweet Heaven Is My Home


November 15, 1926 - Chicago

Arizona Dranes (p) acc. by the Rev. F.W. McGee and Jubilee Singers.

9877-A    Bye and Bye We're Going Okeh 8438, Herwin LP210
            To See the Lord
9878-A    I'm Going Home on the   Okeh 8419,       -
            Morning Train
9879-A    Lamb's Blood Has Washed      -           -
            Me Clean
9880-A    I'm Glad My Lord Saved Me  Okeh 8438,    -

July 3, 1928 - Chicago

Arizona Dranes (p) acc. by unknown choir and mandolin.

| | | |
|---|---|---|
| 400980-A | I Shall Never Wear a Crown | Okeh 8600, Hist HLP34, Herwin LP210 |
| 400981-A | God's Got a Crown | - |
| 400982-A | He Is My Story | -     - |
| 400983-B | Just Look | -  , Okeh 8646, Blues Cl BC18, |
| 400984-A | I'll Go Where You Want Me To Go | Okeh 8600,    - |
| 400985-B | Don't You Want To Go? | Okeh 8646,    - |

## DREVNAK, ANNE (bass)

See Collective Section.

## DUKES, AGGIE (piano)

c. 1957 - Los Angeles

Aggie Dukes (p,vo) acc. by Buddy Collette (fl) and others.

| | |
|---|---|
| Swing Low Sweet Cadillac.I | Aladdin 3364 |
| Swing Low Sweet Cadillac.II | - |
| Come Back Baby | -, 3588 |
| John John | - |
| Well of Lonliness | - |

## EDWARDS, BERNICE (piano)

February, 1928 - Chicago

"Moanin'" Bernice Edwards (p,vo).

| | | |
|---|---|---|
| 20359-2 | Sunshine Blues | Paramount 12653 |
| 20360-2 | Lonesome Longing Blues | - |
| 20361-1 | Mean Man Blues | Paramount 12633,Magpie 4404, Matchbox SDR182 |
| 20362-1 | Long Tall Mama | Paramount 12633,    -, Matchbox SDR182 |
| 20371-1 | Moaning Blues | Paramount 12620 |
| 20372-1 | Southbound Blues | - |

November, 1928 - Chicago

Bernice Edwards (p,vo).

| 21000-4 | Hard Hustlin' Blues | Paramount 12766, Magpie 4404 |
| 21001-5 | High Powered Mama Blues | - | - |
| 21010-4 | Low Down Dirty Shame Blue | Paramount 12741, | - |
| 21011-4 | Born to Die Blues | - | - |

Ramblin Thomas (g) added.

| 21023-2 | Two-Way Mind Blues* | Paramount 12713 |
| 21024-1 | Jack of All Trades* | - | - |

April 20, 1935 - Forth Worth

Bernice Edwards (p,vo) acc. by Black Boy Shine (p,vo); Howling Smith (g).

| FW-1163 | Bantam Rooster Blues | Vocalion 03036 |
| FW-1172-3 | Hot Mattress Stomp | Vocalion 03168,Roots RL312, Magpie 4411 |
| FW-1173-3 | 9th Street Stomp | Vocalion 03168 | - |

April 21, 1935 - Fort Worth

Bernice Edwards (p,vo).

| FW-1174-1 | Butcher Shop Blues | Vocalion 03036, Magpie 4411 |

## ELLIOTT, ELAINE (piano)

January 31, 1928 - Memphis, Tennessee

Alfoncy and Bethenea Harris (vocal duets) acc. by DOUG WILLIAMS' TRIO: Doug Williams (cl); Elaine Elliott or Edgar Brown (p); Sam Sims (d).

| 41811-2 | I Don't Care What You Say | Victor 21285 |
| 41812-1 | That Same Cat | - |

Doug Williams (cl) acc. by Elaine Elliott (p); Sam Sims (d).

| 41813-2 | Slow Death | Victor 21269,Bluebird B-6151 |
| 41814-2 | Roadhouse Stomp | - | - |
| 41815-1 | Far Away Texas Blues | Victor 21413 |
| 41816-2 | One Hour Tonight | -,V-38607,Creole 7* |

* listed as Johnny Dodds (cl).

## ELZEA, MARION (trumpet)

See Collective Section.

## ERSHOFF, ELIZABETH (harp)

October 31, 1958 - Los Angeles

JACK KANE & HIS ORCHESTRA: Don Fagerquist, Conrad Gozzo, Van Rasey, Don Paladino (tp); John Grass, Jules Jacobs (FrH); Gene Cipriano, Jules Kinsler (fl); Fred Fallensby (cl); Lloyd Hildebrand (bassoon); Jack Dumont, Phil Sobel (as); George Auld, Justin Gordon (ts); Bob Lawson (bars); Elizabeth Ershoff (h); Paul Smith (p); Howard Roberts (g); Red Mitchell (b); Alvin Stoller (d); Larry Binker (vib); Jack Kane (arr,cond).

| L10809 | Carioca | Coral CRL 57219 |
|--------|---------|------------------|
| L10810 | Some of These Days | - |
| L10811 | I'm Getting Sentimental Over You | - |
| L10812 | Poor Butterfly | - |


## FRANKLIN, ARETHA (piano, organ)

January 10, 1961 - New York City

Al Sears (ts,tamb); Aretha Franklin (p,vo); Lord Westbrook (g); Milt Hinton (b); Sticks Evans (d).

| CO-65795 | Who Needs You | Columbia CL 1612,C58412, Fontana TFL 5173 |
|----------|---------------|--------------------------------------------|
| CO-65796 | Are You Sure | Columbia 41985, CL 1612, C58412, Fontana TFL 5173 |
| CO-65797 | Maybe I'm a Fool | Columbia 41985, CL 1612, C58412, Fontana TFL 5173 |


April 24 & 25, 1963 - Nashville, Tennessee

THE COUNTRY'S BEST:  Aretha Franklin (p,vo); acc. by unknown group.

| Bonaparte's Retreat | Columbia CL2069, CS8869 | |
|---------------------|--------------------------|---|
| Pride | - | - |
| I Can't Stop Loving You | - | - |
| Hey, Good Lookin' | - | - |
| I Fall to Pieces | - | - |
| You're the Only Star | - | - |
| Walking the Floors Over You | - | - |
| I Can't Help It | - | - |
| Send Me a Pillow You Dream On | - | - |
| A Wound Time Can't Erase | - | - |
| The End of the World | - | - |
| Walk on By | - | - |


June 12, 1963 - New York

Aretha Franklin (p,vo) acc. by unknown group.

| C078821 | Skylark | Columbia CL2079, CS8879 |
| C078822 | Laughing on the Outside | – | – |
| C078823 | Where Are You | – | – |
| C078824 | Ol' Man River | – | – |

January, 1967 – Muscle Shoals, Alabama

Aretha Franklin (p,vo) acc. by Melvin Lastie (tp); King Curtis, Charlie Chalmera (ts); Willie Bridges (bars); Dewey "Spooner" Oldham (p); Jimmy Johnson (g); Tommy Cogbill (b); Roger Hawkins (d).

| 11575 | I Never Loved a Man the Way I Love You | Atlantic SD8139, SD8227 |

January, 1967 – New York

Aretha Franklin (p,org,vo); Tommy Cogbill (b); Roger Hawkins (d); Carolyn Franklin (background vo).

| 11576 | Do Right Woman, Do Right Man | Atlantic SD8139 |

January, 1967 – New York

Aretha Franklin (p,vo) acc. by unknown band.

| 11602 | Save Me | Atlantic SD8139 |

December 16 & 17, 1967 – New York

Aretha Franklin (p,vo) acc. by Melvin Lastie, Joe Newman, Bernie Glow (tp); Tony Studd (b-tb); King Curtis, Seldon Powell (ts); Frank Wess (ts,fl) Haywood Henry (bars); Spooner Oldham (el-p,org); Jimmy Johnson (g); Joe South, Bobby Womack, Eric Clapton (rhythm-g); Warren Smith (vib); Tommy Cogbill (b); Roger Hawkins (d); Carolyn Franklin & the Sweet Inspirations (background vo).

| 13635 | Since You've Been Gone | Atlantic SD8176 |
| 13636 | Be As Good to Me (As I Am to You) | – |
| 13637 | Niki Hokey | – |
| 13638 | Groovin' | – |
| 13639 | Sweet Sweet Man | Atlantic SD8186 |
| 13640 | A Change | – |

December 19 & 20, 1967 – New York

same personnel.

| 13653 | People Get Ready | Atlantic SD8176 |
| 13654 | Hello Sunshine | – |
| 13655 | Money Won't Change You | – |

| 13656 | Come Back Baby | - |
| 13657 | Ain't No Way | - |

**April, 1968 - New York**

probably similar personnel.

| 14318 | My Song | Atlantic 2574, (E)2091008 |
| 14319 | Think | Atlantic 2518, SD8186 |

**1968 - New York**

Aretha Franklin (p,vo) acc. by Ernie Royal, Snooky Young or Bernie Glow, Richard Williams, Joe Newman (tp); Jimmy Cleveland, Benny Powell, Urbie Green or Thomas Mitchell (tb); George Dorsey, Frank Wess (as); Seldon Powell, King Curtis (ts); David Newman (ts,fl); Pepper Adams (bars); Junior Mance (p); Kenny Burrell (g); Ron Carter (b); Bruno Carr (d).

| 14329 | You Send Me | Atlantic SD8186 |
| 14330 | See Saw | - |
| 14331 | Today, I Sing the Blues | Atlantic SD8212 |
| 14332 | The House That Jack Built | Atlantic 8227 |
| 14333 | I Say a Little Prayer | Atlantic 8186 |
| 14334 | Night Time is the Right Time | - |
| 14335 | Track of My Tears | Atlantic 8212 |
| 14336 | I Take What I Want | Atlantic 8186 |
| 14337 | I Can't See Myself Leaving You | - |

**May 7, 1968 - "Theatre Olympia" - Paris**

ARETHA IN PARIS: Aretha Franklin (p,vo); Donald Towns (cond); Little John Wilson, Ron Jackson, Russell Conway (tp); Rene Pitts (tb); Miller Brisker, Conald "Buck" Waldon (ts); David Squire (bars); Jerry Weaver (g); Roderick Hicks (b); George Davidson (d); Carolyn Franklin, Charness Butts-Jones, Wyline Ivey (background vo).

| | Dr. Feelgood | Atlantic SD8207 |
| | Since You've Been Gone | - |

### FREEMAN, SHARON (French Horn)

Note: Ms. Freeman began a recording session called "Escalator Over the Hill" under Carla Bley's direction in November, 1968. This issue was recorded over a period of several years and it is unknown which titles were recorded on which date.

### GANGE, MARION (guitar)

See Collective Section.

## GARRY, VIVIAN (bass)

**1945 - Los Angeles**

George Handy (p,vo); Arv Garrison (g); Vivian Garry (b); Roy Hall (d).

|      | Altitude                | Guild 124        |
|------|-------------------------|------------------|
|      | Relax Jack              | -                |
|      | Where You At            | V-Disc 690       |
|      | Baby I'm Gone           | -                |
| M101 | Hop Scotch (vGH)        | Sarco 101, 1002  |
| M102 | Where You At            | -                |
|      | I've Got To, That's All | Sarco 102, 1004  |
|      | I Surrender Dear        | -                |
|      | Tonsilectomy            | Sarco 103        |
|      | These Foolish Things    | -                |

**1945 - Los Angeles**

George Handy and THE VIVIAN GARRY TRIO: (prob.) George Handy (p); Arv Garrison (g); Vivian Garry (b); Roy Hall (d).

|  | Perdido               | Studio & Art 105 |
|--|-----------------------|------------------|
|  | Handy Man             | -                |
|  | Stick With a Sticker  | Exclusive 11     |
|  | Sleepy Time Down South | -               |

**1946 - Los Angeles**

Leo Watson (vo) acc. by Vic Dickenson (tb); Leonard Feather (listed as "Jelly Roll Lipschitz") (p); Arv Garrison (g); Vivian Garry (b); Hal "Doc" West (d).

| RT101 | Sunny Boy     | Signature 1007      |
|-------|---------------|---------------------|
| RT102 | Tight and Gay | -                   |
| RT103 | Snake Pit     | Signature 1004      |
| RT104 | Jingle Bells  | -, Folkways FP59    |

**October, 1946 - Los Angeles**

Rickey Jordon (vo) acc. by John Buckner (tp); Les Robinson (ts); Lucky Thompson (ts); Teddy Kaye (p); Arv Garrison (g); Vivian Garry (b); Roy Hall (d).

| 1076 | ABC Blues      | Exclusive 235 |
|------|----------------|---------------|
|      | Rickey's Blues | Exclusive 237 |
|      | Night and Day  | -             |

Buckner, Robinson and Thompson out.

|  | Blues in the Storm | Exclusive 235 |
|--|--------------------|---------------|

date unknown.

VIVIAN GARRY WITH THE NIGHTINGALES & DICK TAYLOR:  no details.

    Popcorn Man     Skylark 521
    The Old Carousel     -


## GELLER, LORRAINE (piano)

July 4, 1954 - Los Angeles

HERB GELLER QUARTET:  Herb Geller (as); Lorraine Geller (p); Curtis
Counce (b); Roy Harte (d).

    It's Swell of You    Imperial EP0121,London(E)RE-U1067
    Mad About the Boy     -       -
    Everything I Have Belongs to You -      -
    Feather in the Breeze     -       -


August 6, 1954 - Los Angeles

| 10874 | You Stepped Out of a Dream | EmArcyEP1-6079,MG26045,MG36040, EJL 1268, Merc MEP 14124 |
| 10875 | Kahagoon | EmArcyEP1-6079,MG26045,MG36040, EJL 1268, Merc MEP 14124 |
| 10876 | Breaking the Sound Barrier | EmArcyEP1-6079,MG26045,MG36040, EJL 1268, Merc MEP 14124 |
| 10877 | Happy Go Lucky | EmArcyEP1-6078,MG26045,MG36040, Merc MEP 14123 |


August 9, 1954 - Los Angeles

same personnel.

| 10881 | A Room With a View | EmArcyEP1-6079,MG26045,MG36040, EJL 1268, Merc MEP 14123 |
| 10882 | Sleigh Ride | EmArcyEP1-6078,MG26045,MG36040, Merc MEP 14123 |
| 10883 | Silver Rain | EmArcyEP1-6078,MG26045,MG36040, Merc MEP 14123 |
| 10884 | Alone Together | EmArcyEP1-6078,MG26045,MG36040, Merc MEP 14123 |


December 31, 1954 - Los Angeles

LEONARD FEATHER AND BEST FROM THE WEST:  Harry Edison (tp); Bob
Enevoldson (v-tb,ts); Herb Geller (as); Lorraine Geller (p); Joe
Mondragon (b); Larry Bunker (d).

    Santa Anita     Blue Note BLP 5059
    Hooray for Hollywood    -

```
          Blindfold Test No. 3        Blue Note BLP 5060
          Arcadia                     -
```

May, 155 - Los Angeles

HERB GELLER QUARTET:   Herb Geller (as); Lorraine Geller (p); Red
Mitchell (b); Mel Lewis (d).

```
          Aprojo                      EmArcy MG 36034
          Bewitched                   -
          Blues in the Night          -
          Come Rain or Come Shine     -
          Heather on the Hill         -
          I've Got a Feeling I'm Falling  -
          If I Were a Bell            -
          Patterns                    -
          Suppertime                  -
          The Answer Man              -
          Two of a Kind               -
          Love Your Magic Spell       -
```

August 14, 1955 - Los Angeles

HERB GELLER QUARTET:   Herb Geller (as); Lorraine Geller (p); Leroy
Vinnegar (b); Eldridge "Buzz" Freeman (d).

```
          Days I Never Knew           EmArcy MG 36040
          Domestic Harmony            -
          Love is Like a Turtle       -
          Sweet Vinnegar              -
```

August 19, 1955 - Los Angeles

HERB GELLER SEXTET:   Conte Condoli (tp); Herb Geller (as); Ziggy Vines
(ts); Lorraine Geller (p); Red Mitchell (b); Lawrence Marabe (d).

```
          Outpost                     EmArcy MG36045
          Rockin' Chair               -
          You'd Be So Nice To Come Home To  -, EP-6142
          Crazy She Calls Me          -
          Voya Mae                    -
```

August 22, 1955 - Los Angeles

Leroy Vinnegar (b) replaces Mitchell.

```
          Owl Eyes                    EmArcy MG36045, EP1-6142
          Gin for Flugelhorns         -         -
          Tardi at Zardi's            -         -
```

1956 - Los Angeles

Lorraine Geller (p); Leroy Vinnegar (b); Buzz Freeman or Lawrence
Marable (d).

| Madame X | Dot DLP 3174, S25174 | |
|---|---|---|
| Gee Baby Ain't I Good To You | - | - |
| Poinciana | - | - |
| What a Diff'rence a Day Made | - | - |
| Clash By Night | - | - |
| Close Your Eyes | - | - |
| Mystery Theater | - | - |
| Blue Room | - | - |
| Everybody's Blues | - | - |

March, 1957 - Los Angeles

HERB GELLER SEXTET: Kenny Durham (tp); Herb Geller (as); Harold Land (ts); Lou Levy (p); Ray Brown (b); Lawrence Marable (d).

| Jitterbug Waltz | Jubilee JLP(S)1044, Josie JS3502 | |
|---|---|---|
| An Air for an Heir | - | - |
| Here's What I'm Here For | - | - |
| Marble Eyes | - | - |
| Melrose and Same | - | - |
| Specific View | - | - |
| The Fruit | - | - |

## GETZ, JANE (piano)

June 2 & 3, 1964 - San Francisco

Clifford Jordan (ts); Jane Getz (p); Charlie Mingus (b); Danny Archmond (d).

| Meditations for a Pair of Wire Cutters | Fantasy 6017/86017 |
|---|---|

John Handy (as) added.

| New Fables | - |
|---|---|

September 10, 1964 - New York

PHAROAH SANDERS QUINTET: Stan Foster (tp); Pharoah Sanders (ts); Jane Getz (p); William Bennett (b); Marvin Patillo (perc).

| 7 by 7 | ESP-Disk 1003 |
|---|---|
| Bethera | - |

November 21, 1966 - New York

George Braith (c-mel sax); Jane Getz (p); Jay Carter (g); Victor Davis (org,b,b-g); Ben Dixon (d); Victor Allende (cga); Ellen Shashozan, Bunny Foy, Adrienne Barbeau (vo).

| Our Blessing | Prestige PRLP 7515 |
|---|---|
| You Keep Me Hanging On | - |

January 3, 1967 - New York

George Braith (ts); Jane Getz (p); Eddie Diehl (g); Bill Salter (b); Popito Allende, Angel Allende (d); Bunny Foy, Juanita Williams, Evelyn Blakey (vo).

| Laura | Prestige PRLP 7515 |
|---|---|
| Evelyn Anita | - |
| Dee Do | - |
| Embraceable You | - |

## GIBSON, MARGE (bass)

February 26, 1958 - Los Angeles

EARL BOSTIC AND HIS ORCHESTRA: Earl Bostic (as); Elmer Schmidt (vib); Fletcher Smith (p); Marge Gibson (b); Earl Palmer (d).

| K4180 | Two O'Clock Jump | King | EP418, | LP583,Par | PMD1071 |
|---|---|---|---|---|---|
| K4181 | Indian Boogie Woogie | King | 5152, | EP419, | LP583, - |
| K4182 | Anvile Chorus | King | EP417, | LP583, | LP 786,- |
| K4183 | Royal Garden Blues | King | EP418, | | - |
| K4184 | Fur Trapper's Ball | King | EP419, | | - |
| K4185 | Back Beat Boogie | King | EP418, EP419, | | - |

May 8 & 9, 1958 - Los Angeles

Earl Bostic (as); Gene Redd (vib); Fletcher Smith (p,org); Allan Seltzer (g); Marge Gibson (b); Charles Walton (d).

| K10072 | Over the Waves Rock | King 5136,EP421,LP597,Par(E)R4460 |
|---|---|---|
| K10073 | Goodnight Sweetheart | King 5152, - - ,Par GEP8741 |
| K10074 | Stairway to the Stars | King EP420, -, Par GEP8754 |
| K10075 | Be My Love | - - |
| K10076 | C Jam Blues | King EP422, - |
| K10077 | Home Sweet Rock | King 5144, -, Par GEP8741 |
| K10078 | Pinkie | - - - |
| K10079 | Rockin' With Richard | King 5161,EP420, -, Par GEP8754 |
| K10080 | Jer-On-Imo (Redskin Chacha) | - ,EP421, - |
| K10081 | The Wreckin Rock | King EP422, - |
| K10082 | Twighlight Time | King 5136,EP420, -, Par(E)R4460 |
| K10083 | Wee-Gee Board | King EP422, -, Par GEP8741 |

## GIRARD, ADELE (harp)

April 21, 1937 - New York City

JOE MARSALA'S CHICAGOANS: Marty Marsala (tp); Joe Marsala (cl); Ray

Biondi (vn); Adele Girard (h); Joe Bushkin (p); Eddie Condon (g); Artie
Shapiro (b); Danny Alvin (d).

| M-412-1 | Wolverine Blues | Variety 565 |
| M-413-1 | Chimes Blues | Epic LN-24029 |
| M-414-2 | Jazz Me Blues | Variety 565 |

March 16, 1938 - New York City

Jack McLaire (g) replaces Condon, Buddy Rich (d) replaces Alvin.

| M-779-1 | Mighty Like the Blues | Vocalion 4168 |
| M-780-1 | Woo-Woo | Vocalion 4116 |
| M-781-1 | Hot String Beans | Vocalion 4168 |
| M-782-1 | Jim Jam Stomp | Vocalion 4116 |

February 17, 1941 - New York

Joe Marsala (cl); Adele Girard (h); Carmen Mastren (g); unknown others.

| With a Twist of the Wrist | Joker (It) SM3115 |
| Lower Register | - |

March 21, 1941

JOE MARSALA AND HIS ORCHESTRA: Marty Marsala (tp); Joe Marsala (cl);
Ben Glassman (as); John Smith (ts); Adele Girard (h); Dave Bowman (p);
Carmen Mastren (g); Jack Kelleher (b); Shelley Manne (d).

| 68854-A | Bull's Eye | Decca 3715, M-30212 |
| 68855-A | Lower Register | Decca 3764, Br (E) 03245 |
| 68856-A | I Know That You Know | - - |
| 68857-A | Slow Down | Decca 3715, M-30212 |

October 23, 1942 - "Log Cabin Restaurant" - New York

JOE MARSALA AND HIS ORCHESTRA FEATURING ADELE GIRARD: Max Kaminsky,
Marty Marsala (tp); Joe Marsala (cl); Dave Tough (d); Al Jennings (tb);
Adele Girard (h) and unknown others.

| I've Got a Gal in | Aircheck 14 |
| Kalamazoo | |
| Lullaby in the Rain | - |
| Can't Get Out of This Mood | - |
| Blue Skies | - |
| There Are Such Things | - |
| Solid Geometry for Squares | - |

October 30, 1942

same personnel.

|            |                |
|------------|----------------|
| Barrell Roll   | Aircheck 14 |
| So Nobody Cares | −          |
| Mr. 5 By 5     | −           |
| Lover          | −           |
| Be Careful     | −           |
| It's My Heart  | −           |
| Topsy          | −           |

## November 29, 1944 – New York City

JOE MARSALA AND HIS ORCHESTRA:  Joe Thomas (tp); Joe Marsala (cl); Adele Girard (h); Charlie Queener (p); Chuck Wayne (g); Irving Lang (b); Buddy Christian (d).

| BW37 | Romance       | Black & White 1201 |
|------|---------------|--------------------|
| BW38 | Zero Hour     | −                  |
| BW39 | Joe Joe Jump  | Black & White 1202 |

## May 4, 1945

JOE MARSALA SEPTET:  Joe Thomas (tp); Joe Marsala (cl); Adele Girard (h); Charlie Queener (p); Chuck Wayne (g); Sid Weiss (b); Buddy Christian (d).

| 5284 | Southern Comfort      | Musicraft 328 |
|------|-----------------------|---------------|
| 5285 | Lover                 | Musicraft 329 |
| 5286 | Don't Let It End      | −             |
| 5287 | Gotta Be This or That | Musicraft 328 |

## November 30, 1945 – New York City

Marty Marsala (tp) replaces Thomas; Gene Di Novi (p) replaces Queener.

| 5346 | East of the Sun              | Musicraft 344   |
|------|------------------------------|-----------------|
|      | I Would Do Anything For You  | Allegro LP 3104 |
| 5348 | Slightly Dizzy               | Musicraft 344   |

## January 10-11, 1963 – Chicago

Bobby Gordon (cl); Adele Girard (h); u (strings); Eddie Higgins (p); Ray Biondi (g); Cleveland Eaton (b); Marshall Thompson (d).

| All Alone                          | Decca DLP 4394,DLP74394,BR(S)LAT8584 |   |   |
|------------------------------------|------------------|---|---|
| You're Nobody Till Somebody Loves You | −             | − | − |
| I Can't Give You Anything But Love | −                | − | − |
| You're Not the One and Only        | −                | − | − |
| Singing the Blues                  | −                | − | − |
| After You've Gone                  | −                | − | − |
| I Get the Blues When it Rains      | −                | − | − |
| I Cried For You                    | −                | − | − |

```
I'll Be Seeing You          -        -        -
Remembering                 -        -        -
I Must Be Dreaming          -        -        -
Bobby's Blues               -        -        -
```

### GLAMANN, BETTY (harp)

March 24, 1948 - Town Hall, Sydney, Australia

Nellie Small (vo) acc. by Ken Flannery (tp); Bob Rowan (tb); Bob Cruick-shanks (cl); James Somerville (p); Ray Price (g); Bruce Higginbotham (b); Clive Whitcombe (d); Betty Glamann (h).

A9537     Dinah                     Ellerston Jones A9537/A9536

1955 - New York City

SMITH-GLAMANN QUINTET:   Betty Glamann (h); Nick Perito (acc); Barry Galbraith (g); Rufus Smith (b).

```
        Poinciana               Bethlehem BCP 22
        Liza                         -
        Laura                        -
        Harp Capers                  -
        Lotus Land                   -
        Now Get Out                  -
        The Boy Next Door            -
        Stompin' at the Savoy        -
        September Song               -
        Ragtime Mambo                -
        That's All                   -
        Pulling Strings              -, BCP 84
```

September 17,24,25,28; October 22,23; December 6, 1956 - New York City

DUKE ELLINGTON AND HIS ORCHESTRA:   Cat Anderson, Willie Cook, Clark Terry (tp); Ray Nance (tp,vn,vo); Britt Woodman, John Sanders, Quentin Jackson (tb); Jimmy Hamilton (cl,ts); Russell Procope (as,cl); Johnny Hodges (as); Paul Gonsalves (ts); Harry Carney (bars); Duke Ellington (p); Jimmy Woode (b); Rick Henderson (as); Sam Woodyard (d); Betty Glamann (h); Tom Whaley, Louis Bellson, Terry Snyder, Candido Camero (perc); Margaret Tynes, Ozzie Baily, Joya Sherrill (vo).

```
        A Drum is a Woman (vMT)      Columbia CL 951
        Rhythm Pum Te Drum (vMT,OBMJS)    -
        Carribee Joe (vJS)                -
        What Else Can You Do With a Drum  -
        New Orleans                       -
        Hey Buddy Bolden (vJS)            -
        Congo Square                      -
        You Better Know It (vOB)          -
        Madam Zajj                        -
        Ballet of Flying Saucers          -
```

            Zajj's Dream (vJS)              -
            Rhumbop (vJS)                   -
            Finale (vOB)                    -


January 15, 1960 - New York

   Bill McColl (cl); Bob di Domenica (fl); Manny Ziegler (bassoon); Paul
   Ingraham (FrH); Jed Tekula (cello); Betty Glamann (h); Gunther Schueller
   (cond).

   4053      Exposure               Atlantic LP1245
   4054      Vendome                Atlantic LP1325
   4055      How High the Moon             -


                    GOOSSENS, MARIE (harp)

December 20, 1934 - London

   ARTHUR YOUNG AND HIS YOUNGSTERS:   Max Goldbert (tp); Freddy Gardner,
   Ernest Ritte (cl,as); Harry Berly (ts,viola); Jean Pougnet (vn); Marie
   Goossens (h); Arthur Young (p); Albert Harris (g); Don Stutely (b); Max
   Bacon (d); Helen Howard (vo).

   CAR-3128-1 A Bouquet for George      Regal Zonophone MR-1568
              Gershwin, Part I (in-
              cluding:  Intro, Rhapsody
              in Blue, Lady Be Good,
              Fascinating Rhythm, Do-Do-Do)
   CAR-3129-1 A Bouquet for George            -
              Gershwin, Part II (in-
              cluding:  Intro, 'S Wonderful,
              That Certain Feeling, Looking
              For a Boy, I'd Rather Charleston


                    GOTTESMAN, ROSE (drums)

See Collective Section.


                    GRAY, KITTY (piano)

October 30, 1937 - San Antonio

   Kitty Gray (vo,p) acc. by her WAMPUS CATS: u (b,d).

   SA-2838-1  I Can't Dance (Got Ants    Vocalion 03992
              in My Pants)
   SA-2839-1  Round and Round                  -
   SA-2840    You're Standing on the     Vocalion 04014
              Outside Now
   SA-2841    Swingology                 Vocalion 03869
   SA-2843    My Baby's Ways             Vocalion 04121

| SA-2847 | Weeping Willow Swing | Vocalion 04104 |
| SA-2848 | Gettin' Away | Vocalion 04121 |

October 31, 1937 - San Antonio

same personnel.

| SA-2853 | Posin' | Vocalion 03869 |

December 4, 1938 - Dallas

same personnel.

| DAL-700 | Doin' the Dooga | Vocalion 04629 |
| DAL-705 | I'm Yours to Command | - |

December 4, 1938 - Dallas

Oscar Woods (g,vo) acc. by u (2nd g); Herb Morand (tp); Kitty Gray (p); u (b,d).

| DAL702-1 | Jam Session Blues | Vocalion 04604 |
| DAL703-1 | Low Life Blues | Vocalion 04745 |

## GREEN, VIVIAN (piano)

1947-1948 - San Francisco

Vivian Greene (p,vo); Nick Esposito (g); Commodore Lark (b); Chuck Walker (d).

| Honey Honey Honey | Trilon 190 |
| Unfinished Boogie | - |
| Two Loves I Have | Trilon 202 |
| Lil's Laments | - |
| Love Me, Love Me, Love Me | Trilon 203 |
| Jades of Green | - |

Vivian Greene (p,vo); Trefoni Rizzi (g); Red Callender (b); Christopher Columbus (d).

| Honey Can't We Steal Away | Trilon 210 |
| Claire de Lune | - |

## GREENFIELD, MIRRIAM (piano)

See Collective Section.

## GRIFFITH, SHIRLEY (guitar)

September, 1960 - Indianapolis

Shirley Griffith (g,vo) acc. by J.T. Adams (g).

| | |
|---|---|
| Maggie Campbell | Flyright LP523 |
| Saturday Blues | - |
| Indiana Jump | - |
| Big Road Blues | - |

1961 - Indianapolis

THE BLUES OF SHIRLEY GRIFFITH: Shirley Griffith (g,vo).

| | |
|---|---|
| Meet Me in the Bottom | Bluesville BVLP 1087 |
| River Line Blues | - |
| Shirley's Jump (instrumental) | - |
| Take Me Back to Mama | - |
| Saturday Blues | - |
| Left Alone Blues | - |
| Big Road Blues | - |
| Bye Bye Blues | - |
| Hard Pill to Swallow | - |
| Maggie Campbell Blues | - |
| My Baby's Gone | - |

## HALE, CORKY
### (piano, harp, flute)

(also known as Merrilyn Cecelia Hecht)

c. 1955-1956

Corky Hale (harp,p,fl); Buddy Colette (fl,ts); Larry Bunker (vib);
Howard Roberts (g); Red Mitchell (b); Chico Hamilton (d).

| | |
|---|---|
| What is There to Say | Gene Norman Presents GNP17 |
| There's an Island in the West Indies | - |
| I Can't Get Started | - |
| Autumn in New York | - |
| Taking a Chance on Love | - |
| April in Paris | - |
| Cabin in the Sky | - |
| London in July | - |

c. 1955-1956

Corky Hale (h,p,celeste); Howard Roberts (g); Bob Enevoldsen (b); Don
Heath (d).

|                  |                             |
|------------------|-----------------------------|
| A Foggy Day      | Gene Norman Presents GNP17  |
| Soon             | -                           |
| Somebody Loves Me | -                          |
| But Not For Me   | -                           |

October 14, 1966 or November 1, 1966 - New York

Joe Firrantello, Don Ashworth, Irving Horowitz, Gerald Sanfino (wood-winds); Steve Kuhn (p); Corky Hecht Hale (h); Ron Carter (b); Marty Morell (d).

|                  |                |
|------------------|----------------|
| Traffic Patterns | Impulse AS9136 |
| Childhood Dreams | -              |
| Open Highway     | -              |

## HALL, AUDREY (reeds)

See Collective Section.

## HAMPTON, CARMELITA (baritone sax)

April 7, 1953 - Cincinnati

DUKE HAMPTON AND HIS ORCHESTRA: Billy Brooks, Leo Cornett, Russell Hampton, Ild Ferguson (tp); Slide Hampton, Harry Bell (tb); Thomas Badger, Aletra Kerley (as); Marcus Lucky Hampton (ts); Carmelita Hampton (bars); Virtus Whitted (p); Dawn Hampton (b); Calvin Shields (d); Duke Hampton (arr,cond).

| K9262 | The Push              | King 4625, Od (F) XOC 146 |   |
|-------|-----------------------|---------------------------|---|
| K9265 | Please Be Good To Me  | -                         | - |

## HANDY, KATHERINE (piano)

January, 1922 - New York City

Katherine Handy (p,vo).

| B-103-1 | Early Every Morning, Year After Year | Paramount 12011 |
|---------|--------------------------------------|-----------------|

## HARDAWAY, LIL (piano)

October, 1923 - Chicago

YOUNG'S CREOLE JAZZ BAND: Bernie Young (c); Preston Jackson (tb); Philmore Holly (cl); Lil Hardaway (p); Mike McKendrick (bj); Eddie Temple (d); Anna Oliver, Ollie Powers (vo).

| 1535-1-2 | Tin Roof Blues | Paramount 20272, 14023, Clx 40272, Har863, Puritan 11272, Century 3027, VJR 9 |
|---|---|---|
| 1536-1-2 | Every Saturday Night | Paramount 12060 |
| 1537-1-2 | What's the Use of Lovin' (vAO) | - |
| 1538-1-2 | Jazzbo Jenkins (vOP) | Paramount 12059, Har 874 |

**August 1, 1928 - Chicago**

Luella Miller (vo) acc. by LIL HARDAWAY'S ORCHESTRA:  Lil Hardaway (p); others unknown.

| C-2174 | Chicago Blues | Vocalion 1234 |
|---|---|---|

Luella Miller (vo) acc. by Lil Hardaway (p).

| C-2175 | Wee Wee Daddy Blues | Vocalion 1234 |
|---|---|---|

**September 22, 1928 - Chicago**

LIL HARDAWAY'S ORCHESTRA:  Lil Hardaway (p,dir); u (c,tb,as,bj,d). Vocal may be Cedric Odom, who may also be the drummer.

| C-2336 | Milenberg Joys | Vocalion 1252 |
|---|---|---|

**March 20, 1936 - Chicago**

DIAMOND LIL HARDAWAY AND HER GEMS OF RHYTHM:  u (tp,as); Lil Hardaway (p); u (g,b); Cedric Odom (d,vo).

| 90660-D | Back in the Country (Where They Ask for You) | Decca 7193 |
|---|---|---|
| 90661-D | You Know I Know (That I Love You So) | - |

**September 30 or October 1, 1936 - Chicago**

same personnel.

| 90905-A | Derbytown | Decca 7241 |
|---|---|---|
| 90906-A | Hotter Than Fire | - |
| 90907-A | Break 'Er Down | Decca 7247 |
| 90908-A | It's Your Yas Yas Yas | - |
| 90910 | What You Gonna Do | Decca 7276 |
| 90911 | 'Fore Day in the Morning | - |

See Collective Section for Additional Recordings

## HARRIS, NANCY (piano)

February 1, 1950 - New Zealand

Mavis Rivers (vo) acc. by Rex Stewart (c); Nancy Harris (p); George Campbell (b); Phil Maguire (d).

| 10668 | Small Hotel | Tanza Z91 |
|-------|-------------|-----------|
| 10669 | I'm in the Mood for Love | - |


## HEMINGWAY, JANE (piano)

October, 1926 - Chicago

WILSON'S T.O.B.A. BAND: Emmet Matthews or Andrew Webb (c); Sidney Costello (as); Jane Hemingway (p); Beverly Saxton (d); Willie Lewis (vo).

| 3023-1-3 | Steady Roll | Paramount 12408 |
|----------|-------------|-----------------|
| 3024-1 | Backyard Blues | - |


## HENDERSON, LEORA (trumpet)

March 11, 1932 - New York City

FLETCHER HENDERSON AND HIS ORCHESTRA: Fletcher Henderson (p,dir); Russell Smith, Leora Henderson, Rex Stewart, Bobby Stark (tp); Sandy Williams, J.C. Higginbotham (tb); Russell Procope (cl,as); Edgar Sampson (cl,as); Coleman Hawkins (cl,ts); Clarence Holliday (g,bj); John Kirby (b); Walter Johnson (d); Gene Gifford (arr); Harlan Lattimore (vo).

| B-11445-A | Casa Loma Stomp | Banner 32701, Domino 113, Melotone M-12340, M-12632, Perfect 15738, Br 01319, A-500191 |
|-----------|-----------------|------------------------------------|
| B-11446-B | Blue Moments (arrFH) | Melotone M-12368, Co CLO1685, BPG-62004, PMS-107 |
| B-11447-A-B | How Am I Don'-Hey Hey (vHL) | Banner 32440, Melotone M-12368 Perfect 15603, Romeo 1839 |
| B-11448-A | Goodbye Blues (vHL) | Melotone M-12340, Br 01319 |


## HENDERSON, LIL (piano)

March, 1926 - Chicago

Ma Rainey (vo) acc. by her GEORGIA BAND: Dave Nelson (c); Albert Wynn (tb); Artie Starks or Stomp Evans (sop,as); Lil Henderson (p); Cedric Odom (d).

| 2448-1-2 | Broken Hearted Blues | Paramount 12364 |
| 2451-3-4 | Jealousy Blues | - |
| 2452-1-2 | Seeking Blues | Paramount 12352 |

See Collective Section for Additional Recordings

## HENDERSON, ROSA (piano)

April, 1923 - New York City

Rosa Henderson (p,vo).

| 1376-1 | I'm Broke Fooling With You | Paramount 12058 |
| 1377-1-2 | I Ain't No Man's Slave | - |

## HESSER, FY (trombone)

See Collective Section.

## HEUMANN, ALTHEA (trombone)

See Collective Section.

## HILL, ROSA LEE (guitar)

1959 - Senatobia, Mississippi

Rosa Lee Hill, (g,vo).

| | Bullyin' Well | SD1352,(E)590025, London (E)K15215 |

October, 1968

"Rosalie Hill" (g,vo).

| | Pork and Beans | Arhoolie F1042 |

## HILL, RUTH (harp)

May 18, 1942 - New York City

Ziggy Elman, Chuck Peterson, James Blake, James Zito (tp); Tommy Dorsey, George Arus, James Skiles, Dave Jacobs (tb); Bruce Snyder, Heimie Beau, Harry Schuchman, Don Lodice, Fred Stulce (s); Leonard Atkins, Irving

Raymond, Bernard Tinterow, Leonard Posner, Sam Ross, William Ehren-
krantz, Alex Beller (vn); Harold Benko (cello); Ruth Hill (h); Milton
Raskin (p); Clark Yocum (g); Phil Stevens (b); Buddy Rich (d); Jo
Stafford, Frank Sinatra (vo).

| BS075204 | Just As Though You Were Here | Victor 27903 |
| BS075205 | Street of Dreams | - |

June 9, 1942 - New York City

Raul Pliakine (vn) replaces Raymond; Miroff and Stafford out.

| BS075264 | Take Me | Victor 27923 |
| BS075265 | Be Careful, It's My Heart | - |

June 17, 1942 - New York City

Tommy Dorsey out.

| 075282 | In the Blue of the Evening (vFS) | Victor 27947, 20-1530, V-Disc 18 |
| 075283-1 | Sleepy Lagoon | Bluebird 10-1045 |
| 075284-1 | Melody | - |

July 1-2, 1942 - New York City

add Tommy Dorsey (tb).

| BS075400 | There Are Such Things (vFS) | Victor 27974 |
| BS075401 | He's My Guy (vJS) | Victor 27941 |
| BS075402 | Daybreak (vFS) | Victor 27974 |
| BS075403 | It Started All Over Again | Victor 20-1522 |
| BS075404 | Mandy, Make Up Your Mind | - |
| BS075405 | Manhattan Serenade (vJS) | Victor 27962 |
| BS075406 | Blue Blazes | - |

Danny Vanelli (sax) added.

| BS075407 | Light a Candle in the Chapel (vFS) | Victor 27941 |

Vanelli out.

| BS075408 | A Boy in Khaki (vJS) | Victor 27947 |
| BS075409 | You Took My Love (vJS) | Victor 20-1539 |

HINTON, ALGIA MAE (guitar)

date unknown - Johnston County, North Carolina

Algia Mae Hinton (g,vo).

| | | |
|---|---|---|
| Buckdance (instrumental) | Crossroads C-101 | |
| Honeybabe | - | |
| Chicken, Lord, Lord | - | |
| Sweet Home | - | |

## HIPP, JUTTA (piano)

May 20, 1962 - Munich

HANS KOLLER QUARTET:  Hans Koller (ts); Jutta Hipp (p); Shorty Rogers (b); Karl Sanner (d).

| D6072 | Hans is Hip | Discovery DL2005, 1742 | |
|---|---|---|---|
| D6073 | I Cover the Waterfront | - | - |
| | Up from Munich | | - |
| | Beat | | - |
| | Stompin' at the Savoy | | - |
| | Jutta is Hip | | - |
| | All the Things You Are | | - |
| | My Melancholy Baby | | - |

May, 1953 - Baden-Baden

HANS KOLLER'S NEW JAZZ STARS:  Albert Mangelsdorff (tb); Hans Koller (ts); Jutta Hipp (p); Shorty Rogers (b); Karl Sanner (d).

| | | | |
|---|---|---|---|
| You Go to My Head | Vogue (F) LD144, (E) LDE 057 | |
| The Way You Look Tonight | - | - |
| Flamingo | - | - |
| Four Roses in an Icebox | - | - |
| Unter Den Linden | - | - |
| All the Things You Are | - | - |
| What's New | - | - |
| Indian Summer | - | - |

June 21, 1953 - Baden-Baden

HANS KOLLER QUINTET:  Albert Mangelsdorff (tb); Hans Koller (ts); Jutta Hipp (p); Shorty Rogers (b); Rudi Schring (d).

| 4940SM | Honeysuckle Rose | Brunswick(G)82769, DeDL8229 |
|---|---|---|
| 4941SM | 'S Wonderful | - - |
| 4947SM | Moonlight in Vermont | Brunswick(G)82778,     -,<br>Polydor 49133 |
| 4948SM | Stompin' At the Savoy | - - |
| 4949SM | Sound Koller | Brunswick(G)82777,86025LPB,<br>Polydor 45008LPH, De DL8229 |
| 4950SM | Come Back to Sorrento | Brunswick(G)82777,     - |

January, 1954 - Frankfurt

JUTTA HIPP AND HER GERMAN JAZZMEN: Emil Mangelsdorff (as); Joke Freund (ts); Jutta Hipp (p); Hans Kresse (b); Karl Sanner (d).

| | | |
|---|---|---|
| Simone | MGM E3157, | (E) EP535 |
| Lover Man | - | - |
| Anything Goes | - | - |
| Diagram | - | - |

April 24, 1954 - Frankfurt

JUTTA HIPP AND HER QUINTET: same personnel.

| | |
|---|---|
| Cleopatra | Blue Note BLP 5056 |
| Mon Petit | - |
| Blue Skies | - |
| Variations | - |
| Ghost of a Chance (no ts) | - |
| Laura (no as) | - |
| Don't Worry 'Bout Me (no as,ts) | - |
| What's New | - |

June 6, 1954 - Deutsche Jazz Festival - Frankfurt

same personnel.

| | |
|---|---|
| I Never Knew | Brunswick (G)86031LPB, Polydor LPH4551, De DL 8229 |

July 28, 1954 - Cologne, Germany

same personnel.

| | |
|---|---|
| Frankfurt Special | Mod BMLP 06015 |
| Simone | - |
| Morning Fun | - |
| Don't Worry 'Bout Me (no as,ts) | - |

January 31, 1955 - Stockholm, Sweden

JUTTA HIPP-LARS GULLIN: Lars Gullin (bars); Jutta Hipp (p); Simon Brehm (b); Boss Stoor (d).

| | |
|---|---|
| Always | Karusell KSEP 3018 |
| Man Lover | - |
| All the Things You Are | - |
| Yesterdays | - |

May 28, 1955 - Deutsche Jazz Festival - Frankfurt

JUTTA HIPP QUINTET:   Joke Freund (ts); Jutta Hipp (p); Attila Zoller (g); Branko Pejakovic (b); Karl Sanner (d).

Hipp-Noses                    Brunswick (G) LO022 EPB


April 5, 1956 - New York City

JUTTA HIPP TRIO:  Jutta Hipp (p); Peter Ind (b); Ed Thigpen (d).

Take Me In Your Arms        Blue Note BLP 1515
Dear Old Stockholm            -
Billie's Bounce               -
I'll Remember April           -
Lady Bird                     -
Mad About the Boy             -
Ain't Misbehavin'             -
These Foolish Things          -
Jeepers Creepers              -
The Moon Was Yellow           -
Gone With the Wind          Blue Note BLP 1516
After Hours                   -
The Squirrel                  -
We'll Be Together Again       -
Horatio                       -
I Married An Angel            -
Moonlight in Vermont          -
Star Eyes                     -
If I Had You                  -
My Heart Stood Still          -


July 29, 1956 - New York City

JUTTA HIPP-ZOOT SIMS:  Jerry Lloy (tp); Zoot Sims (ts); Jutta Hipp (p);
Ahmed Abdul-Malik (b); Ed Thigpen (d).

Just Blues                  Blue Note BLP 1530
Violets for Your Furs         -
Down Home                     -
Almost Like Being in Love     -
Wee-Dot                       -
Too Close for Comfort         -


HOFFMAN, JEAN (piano)

November 10, 1957 - San Francisco

Jean Hoffman (p,vo); Jack Weeks or Dean Reilly (b); Bill Young (d).

What Is There to Say        Fantasy LP 3260
Makin' Whoopee                -
Bewitched, Bothered and       -
  Bewildered
Time Was                      -
My Buddy                      -

November 11, 1957 - San Francisco

    same personnel.

|  |  |
|---|---|
| Sometimes I'm Happy | Fantasy LP 3260 |
| The World is Waiting for the Sunrise | - |
| I've Got it Bad | - |
| Sometimes I'm Happy | - |
| Yes Sir That's My Baby | - |
| Dancing on the Ceiling | - |
| Bluebird of Happiness | - |
| Street of Dreams | - |


## HOPE, MARY (piano)

April, 1950 - Chicago

LYNN HOPE QUINTET:  Lynn Hope (ts); Robert "Fox" Martin (vib); Mary Hope (p); Billy Davis (g); Ray Caulter (b); Billy Hope (d).

| UB50-226 | Song of the Wanderer | Premium 851 |
|---|---|---|
| UB50-227 | Tenderly | - |
| UB50-824 | Mona Lisa | Premium 862 |
| UB50-825 | Poinciana | Premium 861 |
| UB50-826 | She's Funny That Way | - |
| UB50-827 | Bonga Boogie | Premium 862 |
| U7419 | Stardust | Chess 1499 |
| U7420 | More Bounce to the Ounce | - |

c. 1950

    same personnel.

| UN1689 | Free and Easy | Aladdin 3103 |
|---|---|---|
| UN1690 | Jet/The Way You Look Tonight | Aladdin 3185 |
| UN1691 | Blow Lynn Blow | Aladdin 3095, EP505, LP707 |
| UN1692 | Blue Moon | -        -        - |

August 20, 1951 - New York City

    same personnel.

| NY1733 | Blues for Anna Bacoa | Aladdin 3165 |
|---|---|---|
| NY1734 | Eleven Till Two | Aladdin 3109 |
| NY1735 | She's Funny That Way | - |
| NY1738 | Too Young | Aladdin 3103 |

March 11, 1952 - New York City

    same personnel.

| | | |
|---|---|---|
| NY1886 | Hope Skip and Jump | Aladdin 3128, EP512, LP707 |
| NY1887 | Please Mr. Sun | – |
| NY1888 | Driftin' | Aladdin 3134,   –      – |
| NY1889 | Sentimental Journey | – |

June 13, 1952 - New York City

same personnel.

| | | |
|---|---|---|
| RCA5007 | Don't Worry About Me | Aladdin 3155 |
| RCA5008 | Move It | –, EP512, LP707 |
| RCA5009 | Tenderly | Aladdin 3185 |
| RCA5010 | September Song | – |

March 13, 1953 - New York City

same personnel.

| | | |
|---|---|---|
| RCA2105 | Morocco | Aladdin 3178 |
| RCA2106 | Swing Train | Aladdin 3208 |
| RCA2107 | Broken Hearted | Aladdin 3178 |
| RCA2108 | Rose Room | Aladdin 3208 |

## HORN, SHIRLEY (piano)

1963 - New York

Shirley Horn (p,vo) acc. by THE QUINCY JONES ORCHESTRA:    personnel unknown.

| | |
|---|---|
| Mack the Knife | Merc MG20835 |
| On the Streets Where You Live | – |
| Let Me Love You | – |
| After You've Gone | – |
| I'm in the Mood for Love | – |
| The Good Life | – |
| In the Wee Small Hours | – |
| Wouldn't It Be Loverly | – |
| The Great City | – |
| Come Dance With Me | – |
| That Old Black Magic | – |
| Go Away Little Boy | – |

1965 - New York

Shirley Horn (p,vo) acc. by Joe Newman (tp); Frank Wess, Jerome Richardson (fl,ts); Marshall Hawkins (b); Bernard Sweetney (d).

| | |
|---|---|
| Travelin' Light | ABC-Paramount ABC(S)538 |
| Sunday in New York | – |
| I Could Have Told You | – |

```
Big City                              -
I Want to Be With You                 -
Some of My Best Frriends              -
  Are the Blues
Have You Tried to Forget              -
Don't Be on the Outside              - ·
You're Blase                          -
Confessin'                            -
Yes I Know When I've Had It           -
And I Love Him                        -
```

## HORSEY, MABEL (piano)

September 28, 1928 - New York City

HORSEY'S HOT FIVE:  Walter Bennet (cl); J.C. Higginbotham (tb); Mabel Horsey (p); u (bj); Alberta Jones (vo).

| | | |
|---|---|---|
| GEX-2085 | Wild Geese Blues (no tb); | Gennett  6642,  Champion  15613 |
| GEX-2086 | Red Beans and Rice | -   , Champion 15635 |

Ruby Gowdy (vo) replaces Jones.  Darnell Howard (cl,vn) added.

| | | |
|---|---|---|
| GEX-2087 | Florida Flood Blues | Gennett 6708, Champion 15613, Cq 7265 |
| GEX-2088 | Breath and Britches Blues | -    - , Champion 15635 |

September 29, 1928 - New York City

same personnel.

| | | |
|---|---|---|
| GEX-2089-A | Weeping Blues | Gennett 6722 |
| GEX-2090 | Waiting For You Blues | - |

February, 1929 - Long Island City

J.C. JOHNSON AND HIS FIVE HOT SPARKS:  (Poss.) Walter Bennett (c); J.C. Higginbotham (tb); Darnell Howard (cl,as); Mabel Horsey (p); Ikey Robinson (bj).

| | | |
|---|---|---|
| 347 | Crying for You | QRS R-7064 |
| 348 | Red Hot Hottentot | -, Century 3011, Gz 1014 |

Alberta Jones (vo) acc. by MABEL HORSEY AND HER RED PEPPERS:  u (as); Mabel Horsey (p); u (b).

| | | |
|---|---|---|
| GEX-2731 | On Revival Day | Gennett 7252 |
| GEX-2732 | I Lost My Man | Gennett 7272, Champion 16058* |

GEX-2733   River Bottom              Gennett 7252
GEX-2734-A Bring it Back Daddy    Gennett 7274, Champion 16216*

* vocal listed as Bessie Sanders.

## HOWARD, CAMILLE (piano)

September, 1945

| | | |
|---|---|---|
| HJ005-5 | I'll Always Be in Love With You | Hamp-Tone 101 |
| HJ006 | Burma Road, Part I | Hamp-Tone 104 |
| HJ007 | Burma Road, Part II | - |
| HJ08-4 | To Be Alone Blues | Hamp-Tone 101 |

1945 - Los Angeles

CAMILLE HOWARD TRIO:  Camille Howard (p,vo); Dallas Bartley (b); Roy Milton (d).

| | |
|---|---|
| You Don't Love Me | Specialty 307 |
| X-Temporaneous Boogie | - |
| Miraculous Boogie | Specialty 332 |
| Fiesta in Old Mexico | - |
| Song of India Boogie | Specialty 433 |
| Old Baldy Boogie | - |
| Fire-Ball Boogie | Specialty 370 |
| I'm Blue | - |
| Ferocious Boogie | Specialty 359 |
| Maybe It's Best After All | - |
| O Sole Mio Boogie | Specialty 352 |
| Within This Heart of Mine | - |
| Instantaneous Boogie | Specialty 325 |
| The Mood That I'm In | - |
| Bump in the Road Boogie | Specialty 318 |
| Sundays With You | - |
| Barcarolle Boogie | Specialty 309 |
| Going Home Blues | - |

January 30, 1946 - Los Angeles

Joe Turner (vo) acc. by BILL MOORE'S LUCKY SEVEN BAND:  Russell Jacquet (tp); Lou Simon, Bill Moore (ts); Camille Howard (p); Teddy Bunn (g); Shifty Henry (b); Walter Murden (d).

| | | |
|---|---|---|
| | Sunday Morning Blues | National 4009, Savoy MG 14016 |
| | Mad Blues | -            - |
| NSC147 | It's a Low Down Dirty Shame | National 9099 |

1946 - Los Angeles

CLIFFORD LANG'S ALL STAR ORCHESTRA: including Ray Linn (tp); Gene Foster (tb); Chuck Gentry (bars); Barney Kessell (g); Camille Howard (p,vo).

| 80 | Widow Jenkins Blues | Pan American 141 |
|----|---------------------|------------------|
| 81 | Let's Try Again | - |
| | These Foolish Things | Pan American 142 |
| | Exactly Like You | - |


1946 - Los Angeles

ROY MILTON AND HIS SOLID SENDERS: Hosea Sapp (tp); Earl Sims (as); Buddy Floyd (ts); Camille Howard (p); Dave Robinson (b); Roy Milton (d,vo).

| | | |
|---|---|---|
| It Never Should Have Been | Roy Milton 101, Specialty 511 |
| Red Light | Roy Milton 102, -, 107 |
| Milton's Boogie (vRM) | Roy Milton 103, Juke Box/ Specialty 503 |
| Mr. Fine | Roy Milton 103, Specialty 515 |
| Groovy Blues | Roy Milton 105, DeLuxe3188, Specialty 503 |
| R.M. Blues (vRM) | Roy Milton 105, -, Juke Box/ Specialty 504 |
| Rainy Day Confession Blues, Part I | Roy Milton 110, Specialty 515 |
| Rainy Day... Part II | - - |
| Groovin' With Joe | Roy Milton 111, Specialty 514 |
| Blues in My Heart | - |
| Rhythm Cocktail | Juke Box/Specialty 504 |
| True Blues | Specialty 510 |
| Camille's Boogie | - |
| On the Sunny Side of the Street | Specialty 513 |
| I'll Always Be in Love With You | - |


Early 1947 - Los Angeles

ROY MILTON AND HIS SOLID SENDERS: Hosea Sapp (tp); Couchie Roberts (as); Buddy Floyd (ts); Camille Howard (p,vo); Dave Robinson (b); Roy Milton (d,vo).

| | | |
|---|---|---|
| Them There Eyes | Roy Milton 207, Specialty 516 |
| Little Boy Blues | - - |
| When I Grow Too Old to Dream | Specialty 107 |
| Pack Your Sack, Jack (vCH) | Miltone 219, Specialty 517 |
| Roy Rides | Specialty 519 |
| What's the Use (vRM) | - |
| Big Fat Mama | Specialty 518 |
| Thrill Me | - |

1947 - Los Angeles

ROY MILTON AND HIS SOLID SENDERS: Hosea Sapp (tp); Earl Sims (as); Bill Gaither (ts); Camille Howard (p,vo); Clarence Jones (b); Roy Milton (d,vo).

| | |
|---|---|
| Keep a Dollar in Your Pocket | Specialty 522 |
| My Blue Heaven | - |
| I've Had My Moments | Specialty 524 |
| Train Blues | - |

December, 1947 - Los Angeles

ROY MILTON AND HIS SOLID SENDERS: Hosea Sapp (tp); Cliff Noels (as); Bill Gaither (ts); Camille Howard (p); Jonny Rogers (g); Dallas Bartley (b); Roy Milton (d).

| | |
|---|---|
| Everything I Do is Wrong | Specialty 314 |
| Hop Skip and Jump | - |
| New Year's Resolution | Specialty 317 |
| Porter's Love Song | - |

1949 - Los Angeles

ROY MILTON AND HIS BAND: u (tp); Jackie Kelson (as); Benny Walters (ts); Camille Howard (p); Johnny Rogers (g); u (b); Roy Milton (d).

| | |
|---|---|
| The Hucklebuck | Specialty 328 |
| Sympathetic Blues | - |
| Playboy Blues | Specialty 366 |
| Cryin' and Singin' the Blues | - |
| Junior Jives | Specialty 358 |
| Where There is No Love | - |
| Bartender | Specialty ? |
| Sad Feeling | - |
| Walkin' Up Baby | Specialty 341 |
| Tain't Me | - |
| Junior Jump | Specialty 330 |
| There is Something Missing | - |
| Information Blues | Specialty 349 |
| My Sweetheart | - |

1950 - Los Angeles

Jimmy Witherspoon (vo) acc. by ROY MILTON'S BAND: Charles Gillum (tp); Jackie Kelson (as); Jimmy Jackson (ts); Camille Howard (p); Lawrence Kato (b); Roy Milton (d).

| | | |
|---|---|---|
| MM1479 | I Gotta Gal Lives Upon a Hill | Modern 20-808 |
| MM1480 | Ain't Nobody's Business | - , Crown CLP5156, GNP156X |

c. 1950 - Los Angeles

Lil Greenwood (vo) acc. by ROY MILTON AND HIS BAND:    Charles Gillum
(tp); Jackie Kelson (as); Eddie Taylor (ts); Camille Howard (p); Johnny
Rogers (g); Lawrence Kato (b); Roy Milton (d).

| | | |
|---|---|---|
| MM1344 | Boogie All Night Long | Modern 20-751 |
| MM1346 | Heart Full of Pain | - |
| | Ain't Gonna Cry | Modern 20-757 |
| | Come Back Baby | - |
| MM1400 | Young Blood | Modern 20-811 |
| MM1401 | Sittin' and Wonderin' | - |
| MM1402 | I'm Going Crazy | Modern 20-771 |
| MM1403 | Dissatisfied Blues | - |
| MM1471 | No More Heart Full of Pain | Modern 20-803 |
| MM1472 | Open Your Eyes | - |

1950-1951 - Los Angeles

u (tp); (prob.) Jackie Kelson (as); Benny Walters (ts); Camille Howard
(p); Johnny Rogers (g); u (b); Roy Milton (d).

| | |
|---|---|
| Oh Babe | Specialty 381 |
| Christmas Time Blues | - |
| Bye Bye Baby Blues | Specialty 386 |
| That's the One for Me | - |
| It's Later Than You Think | Specialty 403 |
| Numbers Blue | - |
| I Have News for You | Specialty 407 |
| T-Town Twist | - |
| Short, Sweet and Snappy | Specialty 414 |
| Best Wishes | - |

1951 - Los Angeles

ROY MILTON AND HIS BAND:    (prob.) Charles Gillum (tp); Jackie Kelson
(as); Eddie Taylor (ts); Camille Howard (p); Johnny Rogers (g); Johnny
Parker (b); Roy Milton (d).

| | |
|---|---|
| So Tired | Specialty 429 |
| Thelma Lou | - |
| As Time Goes By | Specialty 436 |

1952 - Los Angeles

Clifford Scott (ts) replaces Taylor; Claude Williams (g) replaces
Rogers.

| | |
|---|---|
| Night and Day | Specialty 438 |
| Am I Wasting My Time | - |
| Flying Saucer | Specialty 436 |
| Believe Me Baby | Specialty 446 |
| Blue Turning Grey Over You | - |

      Same Day                    Specialty 458
      Don't You Remember Baby       -

**March 5, 1953 - Los Angeles**

CAMILLE HOWARD AND HER ORCHESTRA: Charles Gillum (tp); Jackie Kelson
(as); Ewell "Bo" Rhambo (ts); Camille Howard (p); Harold Grant (g);
Dallas Bartley (b); Nat "Monk" Fay (d).

| F312 | I'm So Confused | Federal 12125 |
|------|-----------------|---------------|
| F313 | Excite Me Daddy | - |
| F314 | Hurry Back Baby | Federal 12134 |
| F315 | Losing Your Mind | Federal 12147 |

**May 13, 1953 - Los Angeles**

James Jackson (ts) replaces Rhambo.

|      | You're Lower Than a Mole | Federal 12147 |
|------|--------------------------|---------------|
| F329 | I Tried to Tell You | Federal 12134 |

**May 20, 1953 - Los Angelels**

Fred Clark (vo) added.

| F331 | Walkin' and Wonderin' | Federal 12136 |
|------|-----------------------|---------------|
| F332 | Grand Hog Snooper | - |

**1953-1954 - Los Angeles**

ROY MILTON AND HIS BAND:  (prob.) Charles Gillum (tp); Jackie Kelson
(as); Eddie Taylor (ts); u (bars); Camille Howard (p); Johnny Rogers
(g); Lawrence Kato (b); Roy Milton (d).

| Let Me Give You All My Love | Specialty 464 |
|-----------------------------|---------------|
| Early in the Morning | - |
| It's Too Late | Specialty 526 |
| Gonna Leave You Baby | - |
| Tell It Like It Is | Specialty 538 |
| How Can I Live Without You | - |
| What Can I Do | Specialty 545 |
| Baby, Don't Do That to Me | - |
| I Stood By | Specialty 480 |
| Baby Don't You Know | - |
| Bird in Hand | Specialty 489 |
| Make Me Know It | - |

**October 31, 1955 - Los Angeles**

Clifford Scott (ts) replaces Taylor; Floyd Turnham (bars); Jimmy Davis
(g) replaces Rogers.

|  |  |  |  |
|---|---|---|---|
| Fools Are Getting Scarcer | Dootone 363, LP 223 | |  |
| I Can't Go On | - | - |  |
| Reeling and Rocking | Dootone 369 | - |  |
| Nothing Left | - | - |  |
| I Never Would Have Made It | Dootone 377 | |  |
| I Want To Go Home | - | |  |
| I'm a Woman | Dootone 378 | |  |
| Cry Some Baby | Dootone 398, | - |  |
| Baby I'm Gone | - | - |  |

May 5, 1956 - Chicago

Leon Washington (ts); McKinely Easton (bars); Camille Howard (p,vo);
Lefty Bates (g); Al Smith (b); Al Duncan (d).

| 56-451 | Business Woman | Vee-Jay 198 |
| 56-452 | Rock 'N Roll Woman | - |

## HOWARD, LOUELLA (flute)

November 25, 1947 - Los Angeles

BENNY GOODMAN AND HIS ORCHESTRA: John Best (tp); Ed Kusby (tb); Benny
Goodman (cl); Jack Cane (FrH); Louella Howard (fl); George Smith, Nick
Mumolo (as); Bumpo Meyers (ts); Chuck Gentry (bars); Red Norvo (vib);
Mel Powell (p); Al Hendrickson (g); Artie Shapiro (b); Dick Cornell (d);
Emma Lou Welsch (vo).

|  |  |  |
|---|---|---|
| You Turned the Tables on Me | Capitol 15044 | |

## HUTTON, INA RAY (leader)

See Collective Section.

## HYAMS, MORJORIE (vibes)

October 2, 1944 - New York City

FLIP PHILLIPS FLIPTET: Neal Hefti (tp); Bill Harris (tb); Aaron Sacks
(cl); Flip Phillips (ts); Marjorie Hyams (vib); Ralph Burns (p); Billy
Bauer (g); Chubby Jackson (b); Dave Tough (d).

| BTS1 | Skyscraper | Signature 28106, Br BL58032 |
| BTS2 | Pappiloma | - -,(G)94040EPC |
| BTS3 | A Melody From the Sky | Signature 28119, Br80175, BL58032, Jazz 75117 |

December 11-12, 1944 - Los Angeles

WOODY HERMAN AND HIS ORCHESTTRA: Neal Hefti, Chuck Frankhauser, Roy
Wetzel, Pete Condoli, Carl Warwick (tp); Ralph Pfeffner, Bill Harris, Ed
Kiefer (tb); Woody Herman (cl,as,vo); Sam Marowitz, John La Porta (as);
Flip Phillips, Pete Mondello (ts); Skippy DeSair (bars); Ralph Burns
(p); Billy Bauer (g); Chubby Jackson (b); Dave Tough (d); Marjorie Hyams
(vib); Frances Wayne (vo).

| L3690A | As Long As I Live | Brunswick BL54024,Decca DL(7)9229 |
| L3691 | Saturday Night | Decca 18641 |
| L3695A | Please Don't Say No (vWH) | Coral 60001 |
| L3696A | I Ain't Got Nothin' But the Blues (vWH) | Coral EC81010,CRL56010,    -, Br BL54024 |
| L3696B | I Ain't Got Nothin' But the Blues (vWH) | Coral 60066 |

January 24, 1945 - New York City

VANDERBILT ALL-STARS: Neal Hefti (tp); Bill Harris (tb); Woody Herman
(cl,vo); Flip Phillips (ts); Ralph Burns (p); Chubby Jackson (b); Dave
Tough (d); Marjorie Hyams (vib).

Billy Bauer's Tune          V-Disc 925

Feburary 19, 1945 - New York City

Hefti out. Johnny Blowers (d) replaces Tough. Ben Webster (ts); Billy
Bauer (g) added.

Somebody Loves Me (vWH)     V-Disc 411

February 19, 1945 - New York City

WOODY HERMAN AND HIS SEMESTER: Sonny Berman, Chuck Frankhauser, Ray
Wetzel, Pete Condoli, Carl Warwick (tp); Ralph Pfeffner, Bill Harris, Ed
Kiefer (tb); Woody Herman (cl,as,vo); Sam Marowitz, John La Porta
(as,cl); Flip Phillips, Pete Mondello (ts); Skippy DeSair (bars);
Marjorie Hyams (vib); Ralph Burns (p); Billy Bauer (g); Chubby Jackson
(b); Dave Tough (d); Frances Wayne (vo).

| CO34288-2 | Laura (vWH) | Columbia 36785, CL6254, CL609, CL1959, V-Disc438, Par(E)R2987, Od(G)028358, Philips(C)507646R, CBS-BPG 62158 |
| CO34289-1 | Apple Honey | Columbia 36803,4-39411,4-33095, B2098,CL2509,CL6049,CL1959, CL2491,CS9291, Ha HL7013, Par(E)R2991, Co(E) 33S1060, Fnt(E)TFE17127,Od(G)028307, CBS-BPG62158 |
| CO34290-1 | I Wonder (vWH) | Columbia 36785,CL1959,V-Disc438 |

February 26, 1945 - New York City

same personnel.

| | | |
|---|---|---|
| CO34355-1 | Out of This World (vFW) | Columbia 36803, V-Disc 493 |
| CO34356-2 | June Comes Around Every Year (vWH) | Columbia 36835 |
| CO34357-1 | Caldonia (vWH) | Columbia 36789,4-39409,4-50074, B2521,CL6049,CL1959,CL2491, Par(E)R2990,Co(E)33S1060, V-Disc 458, Od (G)028102, CBS-BPG52158 |
| CO34357-2 | Caldonia (vWH) | Columbia CL592, Ha HL7093, Philips(E)BBE12286,BLL7123, Fnt(E)TFR6015,Philips(C)B07177L |

March 1, 1945 - New York City

same personnel.

| | | |
|---|---|---|
| CO34369-1 | Goosey Gander | Columbia 36815,4-39412,CL6049, CL533,B1746,CL1959, Ha HL7013, V-Disc 493, Par(E)R2990, Co(E)33S1060, Od(G)028102, CBS-BPG62158 |
| CO34371-1 | Northwest Passage | Columbia 36835,4-39412,4-50021, B2521,CL6059,CL2509,CL611, CL1959,CL2491,CS9291, V-Disc 504, Par(E)R2996, Co(E)33S1060,Fnt(E)TFE17137, Od(G)028107 |
| CO34371-2 | Northwest Passage | Columbia B2098, Ha H17013, Fnt(E)TFE17217 |
| CO34372-1 | A Kiss Goodnight (vWH) | Columbia 36815, CL1959, V-Disc 504, CBS-BPG62158 |
| CO34373-1 | I've Got the World On a String | Columbia 36897, CL1959, Par(E)R3017,Od(G)28258, CBS-BPG52158 |

Spring, 1945 - Los Angeles

same personnel.

| | |
|---|---|
| The Golden Wedding (La Cinquantaine) | First Heard FH36 |
| Perdido | - |

June 23, 1945 - New York

same personnel.

| | |
|---|---|
| Blue Flame | Fanfare 22-122 |
| Katushya (vWH) | -, FH2 |
| And There Are You (vFW) | - |

| | |
|---|---|
| Bijou | – |
| June Comes Around Every Year (vWH) | – |
| Goosey Gander | –  – |
| I Don't Care Who Knows It (vFW) | – |
| A Kiss Goodnight (vWH) | – |
| Apple Honey | – |

July, 1945 – Ritz Ballroom – Bridgeport, Connecticut

| | |
|---|---|
| Katushya | First Heard FH2 |

September 6, 1946 – New York City

CHARLIE VENTURA AND HIS NEW ORCHESTRA: Neal Hefti, Stan Fishelson, Jack Palmer, Al Stearns (tp); Bob Ascher, Leo Checci, Saul Kaye (tb); Charlie Ventura (as,to,sop); Tony Scott (cl,as); Ed Scalzi (as); Nick Jerrett, Barney Marino (ts); Tony Ferina (bars); Tony Aless (p); Billy Bauer (g); Clyde Lombardi (b); Ellis Tolin (d); Marjorie Hyams (vib); Lilyann Caron (vo).

| | | |
|---|---|---|
| NSC160 | Either It's Love Or It Isn't | National 7013 |
| NSC161 | Please Be Kind (vLC) | National 7015 |
| NSC162 | Misirlou | National 7013, ReEP103,EP7017, EmArcy-MG36015 |
| NSC163 | How High the Moon | National 7015    –    – EmArcy-MG36015 |

See Collective Section for Additional Recordings

## HYDE, JERRINE (piano)

See Collective Section.

## JACOBS, JULIE
(oboe/English Horn)

1946

Dale Pierce, Ray Linn, Frank Beach, Nelson Shelladay (tp); Ollie Wilson, Fred Zito, Hal Smith (tb); Harry Klee (as,fl); Wilbur Schwartz (as,cl); Ralph Lee (ts,bassoon); Gus McReynolds (ts); Hy Mandel (bass-sax); Boyd Raeburn (bass-sax, ts); Hal Schaefer (p); Tony Rizzi (g); Harry Babsin (b); Jackie Mills (d); Julie Jacobs (oboe,EngH); Gale Laughton (h); Ed Finckel (arr).

| | | |
|---|---|---|
| JRC-146 | Over the Rainbow | Jewel D1-2 |
| JRC-147 | Body and Soul | Jewel D1-3 |

| JRC-148 | Blue Echoes | Jewel D1-4 |
|---------|-------------|------------|
| JRC-149 | Little Boyd Blue | Jewel D1-6 |

## JENKINS, ANN (piano)

1952

Ann Jenkins (p); u others.

| Ann's Boogie Woogie | Br (E) LA8634 |
|---------------------|---------------|
| Le Secret | - |

## JENKINS, MYRTLE (piano)

November 19, 1936 - Chicago

STATE STREET SWINGERS: Herb Morand (tp); Arnett Nelson (cl); Myrtle Jenkins (p); Big Bill Broonzy (g); u (b); Mary Mack (vo).

| C-1686-2 | Rattlesnakin' Daddy | Vocalion 03395 |
|----------|---------------------|----------------|
| C-1687-1 | You Can't Do That To Me | Vocalion 03572 |

## JESHKE, DODY (drums)

See Collective Section.

## JOHNK, KATHERINE (harp)

October, 1955 - Los Angeles

Betty Bennett (vo) acc. by Shorty Rogers (tp,flhn); Frank Rosalino (tb); Harry Klee (as,fl); Gus Binova (cl); Dove Pejl (b-cl); John Cave (FrH); Arthur Gleghorn (fl); Philip Memoli (oboe); Bob Cooper (ts); Jimmy Giuffre (bars); Katherine Johnk (h); Andre Previn (p); Barney Kessel (g); Ralph Pena (b); Shelly Manne, Irv Cottler (d).

| Nobody Else But Me | Atlantic EP 572, LP 1226 | |
|--------------------|--------------------------|---|
| The Next Time I Care | - | - |
| Have Yourself a Merry Little Christmas | - | - |
| This is the Moment | - | - |
| Treat Me Rough | Atlantic EP 573 | - |
| Sidewalks of Cuba | - | - |
| You're Driving Me Crazy | - | - |
| Islands in the West Indies | - | - |
| Tomorrow Mountain | | - |
| Mountain Greenery | | - |
| You Took Advantage of Me | | - |
| My Man's Gone Now | | - |

### JOHNSON, EDITH NORTH (piano)

August 15, 1929 - Chicago

OLIVER COBB AND HIS RHYTHM KINGS: Oliver Cobb (c,dir,vo); Freddie Martin (cl,as); Walter Martin (as); Ernest Franklin (ts); Edith Johnson (p); Benny Jackson (bj); Singleton Palmer (tuba); Lester Nicholas (d).

| C-4088 | The Duck's Yas Yas Yas | Brunswick 7107 |
| C-4089 | Hot Stuff | - |

September 7, 1929 - Richmond, Indiana

Edith Johnson (p,vo) acc. by Baby James (c); Ike Rodgers (tb).

| 15558-A | Nickel's Worth of Liver Blues | Paramount 12823, Century 3108, Broadway 5093 |

### JOHNSON, LOUISE (piano)

May 28, 1930 - Grafton, Wisconsin

Louise Johnson (p,vo).

| L-398-1 | All Night Long Blues | Paramount 12992, Roots RSE5, Magpie P44401, Origin 11 |
| L-399-2 | Long Way From Home | Paramount 12292, -, Milestone MLP2018 |
| L-419-1 | On the Wall | Paramount 13008, Yazoo 1028, Riverside RLP12-153, RM8809, London 3544, RBF-RF12, Roots RSE5, Milstone MLP2009, Cardin (F) 93518 |
| L-420-2 | By the Moon and Stars | Paramount 13008, Roots RSE5, Magpie P44401, Milestone MLP2018, Cardin (F) 93518 |

### JOHNSON, MARGARET "QUEENIE" (piano)

September 15, 1938

Buck Clayton (tp); Dicky Wells (tb); Lester Young (cl,ts); Margaret "Queenie" Johnson (p); Freddy Green (g); Walter Page (b); Jo Jones (d); Billie Holiday (vo).

| 23467-1 | The Very Thought of You* | Vocalion 4457, PmR-2621, Od A-2359 |
| 23468-1 | I Can't Get Started** | Vocalion 4457, Co 37494, DS-1993, Pm R-2609 |
| 23469-2 | I've Got a Date With a Dream | Vocalion 4396, BrA-81918, Pm R-2609 |

23470-2    You Can't Be Mine              Vocalion 3496,    -,Pm A-7484

 * Young plays (cl).
** Young plays (ts).


JONES, BERTHA LEE (guitar)

June 17, 1961 - Indianapolis, Indiana

Bertha Lee Jones (g) solo.

              Spanish Blues              Flyright LP523


JONES, BETTY HALL (piano)

c. 1947 - Los Angeles

Betty Hall Jones (p,vo) acc. by Maxwell Davis (ts); Buddy Harper (g);
Ralph Hamilton (b);

              Learn to Boogie           Atomic 260
              Fine and Mellow Blues        -
              The Same Old Boogie        Atomic 261
              Make Me Know It              -


February 11, 1949 - Hollywood

Betty Hall Jones (p,vo) acc. by Henry Coker (tb); Bumpo Myers, Dave
Cavanaugh (ts); Mitchell Webb (g); Ralph Hamilton (b); Jesse Price (d).

3960-2A    Why Can't You Love That       Capitol 15422
              Way
3961-4A    This Joint's Too Hip for Me      -
3962-2A    If I Ever Cry                 Capitol 70011
3963-3A    You've Got to Have What it      -
              Takes


August 2, 1949 - Hollywood

Betty Hall Jones (p,vo) ac. by Forrest Powell (tp); Maxwell Davis (ts);
Mitchell Webb (g); Ralph Hamilton (b); Bob Harvey (d).

4757-2     I Never Miss the Sunshine     Capitol 832
4758-2     That's a Man for You             -
4759-2     Thrill Me                     Capitol 70046
4760-1     Buddy, Stay Off That Wine        -

c. 1952

Betty Hall Jones (p,vo) with unknown accompaniment.

      Richmond Blues            Dootone 305

date unknown.

Betty Hall Jones (p,vo) acc. by u (ts,g,b,d)

| Goin' Back to Town | Combo 10 |
| Way After Hours | -, Chicago LP202 |
| Poor Spending Daddy | Combo 15 |
| Frustration Frustration | - |

date unknown.

Betty Hall Jones (p,vo).

| I'm Leaving You | Coronet 5002 |
| Linda Brown | - |

## JONES, BRENDA (bass)

Late 1963 - New York

Tommy Tucker (p,org,vo); acc. by Dean "Sugar" Young (g); Brenda Jones (b); Johnny Williams (d).

| U12833 | Hi-Heel Sneakers | Checker 1067,LP2990,6445203 |
| U12833-2 | Hi-Heel Sneakers | Red Lightnin' 0022 |
| U12834 | I Don't Want 'Cha | Checker 1067,LP2990 |

March 18, 1964 - New York

Tommy Tucker (p,org,vo) acc. by Eddie Williams, Hal Mitchell (tp); Solomon Hall (ts); Paul Williams (bars) Dean Young, Mickey Baker (g); Jimmy Oliver (rhythm-g); Brenda Jones, James Smith (b); Johnny Williams, Shep Shepard (d).

| Just for a Day | Checker LP2990 |
| Trouble in Mind | - |
| Walking the Dog | - |
| Hard Luck Blues | - |
| It's a Mighty Hard Way | - |
| Come Rain or Come Shine | - |
| I Warned Him About You | - |
| I Can't Believe It | - |
| Suffering With the Blues | - |

April 24, 1965 - New York

Tommy Tucker (p,org,vo); Dean Young (g); Brenda Jones (b); Benny Jones (d).

| U13876 | Alimony | Checker 1112 |

Jimmy Oliver (g) replaces Young.

| U13877 | All About Melanie | Checker 1112 |


## JONES, DOLLY (cornet)

June 25, 1926 - Chicago

ALBERT WYNN'S GUT BUCKET FIVE: Dolly Jones (c); Albert Wynn (tb); Barney Bigard (sop,ts); Jimmy Flowers (p); Rip Bassett (bj); Lilli Delk Christian (vo).

| 9789-A | When (vLDC) | Okeh 8350 |
| 9790-A | That Creole Band | - , Stash ST 109 |


## JULYE, KATHRYNE (harp)

1959 - Los Angeles

June Christy (vo) acc. by THE BOB COOPER ORCHESTRA: Frank Rosalino (tb); Jim Decker (FrH); Buddy Collette, Bob Cooper, Bud Shank, Norman Beno, Chuck Gentry (reeds); Joe Castro (p); Red Callender (b); Mel Lewis, Stan Levy (d); Kathryne Julye (h).

| 32266  | My Ship                         | Capitol (S) T1308 |
| 322767 | I'm In Love                     | -                 |
| 32268  | Shadow Woman                    | -                 |
| 32269  | Night People                    | -                 |
| 32274  | Don't Get Around Much Anymore   | -                 |
| 32275  | Kissin' Bug                     | -                 |
| 32276  | Do Nothin' Till You Hear From Me | -                |
| 32277  | Bewitched                       | - , (S)T1693      |
| 32386  | I Had a Little Sorrow           | -                 |
| 32387  | Make Love to Me                 | -                 |


1959 - Los Angeles

June Christy (vo) acc. by THE BOB COOPER ORCHESTRA: Joe Gordon (tp); Vince DeRosa (FrH); Norman Beno (oboe); Bud Shank (fl); Bob Cooper (ts,b-cl); Buddy Collette (bars); Kathryne Julye (h); Al Viola (g); Monte Budwig (b); Shelly Manne (d).

| 35305 | I Know About Love | Capitol (S) 1586 |
| 35306 | Cry Like the Wind | -                |

```
35307      All You Need is a Quarter        -
35308      Make Someone Happy               -
```

Buddy Clark (b) replaces Budwig.

```
35313      Asking For You                   -
           One Note Samba        Capitol 4864
           The Bossa Nova                   -
```


## KELLY, JO ANN (guitar)

May, 1968 - London

Jo Ann Kelly (g,vo)

        Nothin' in Ramblin       Saydisc/Matchbox SDM142, Sire
                                  SAS-3701, Village Thing VT-SAM16


1966 - London

Jo Ann Kelly (g,vo) acc. by (prob) Steve Rye (hca); Dave Kelly (g).

        Ain't Seen No Whiskey      Immeidate IMLP014


September 7, 17-18, 1968 - London

Jo Ann Kelly (g,vo) acc. by Bob Hall (p).

        Make Me a Pollet on the    Liberty (E)LBS 83190
           Floor

Jo Ann Kelly (g,vo) acc. by Dave Kelly (g,vo).

        (Buy You a) Diamond Ring    Liberty (E)LBS 83190

Jo Ann Kelly (g,vo) acc. by Tony T.S. McPhee (g).

        Rollin' and Tumblin'       Liberty (E)LBS 83190


## KIMBALL, JEANETTE (SALVANT) (piano)

April 13, 1926 - New Orleans

CELESTIN'S ORIGINAL TUXEDO JAZZ ORCHESTRA:  Oscar Clestin (c,dir);
August Rousseau (tb); Paul Barnes (cl,as); Earl Pierson (t); Jeanette
Salvant (p); John Marrero (bj); Abby Foster (d); Charles Gills (vo).

```
142014-2   I'm Satisfied You Love Me   Columbia 14200-D
142015-2   My Josephine (vCG)          Columbia 636-D
142016-1-2 Station Calls                     -
142017-2   Give Me Some More           Columbia 14200-D
```

April 11, 1927 - New Orleans

Oscar Celestin (c,dir); Richard Alexis (c); August Rousseau (tb); Paul Barnes (cl,as); Sid Carriere (sop,ts); Simon Marrero (tuba); Earl Preison (ts); Jeanette Salvant (p); John Marrero (bj); Abby Foster (d,vo).

| 143953-1 | Dear Almanzoer | Columbia 14220-D |
| 143954-2 | Papa's Got the Jim-Jams (vAF) | - |
| 143955-1 | As You Like It | Columbia 14259-D |

Ferdinand Joseph (vo) added.

| 143956-1-3 | Just For You, Dear, I'm Crying | Columbia 14259-D |

October 25, 1927 - New Orleans

Oscar Celestin (c,dir); Richard Alexis or George McCullum (c); August Rousseau or William Matthews (tb); Clarence Hall (cl,sop,as); Oliver Alcorn (cl,ts); Jeanette Salvant (p); John Marrero (bj); Simon Marrero (tuba); Jonah Frazier (d).

| 145018-3 | When I'm With You | Columbia 14323-D |
| 145019-2 | It's Jam Up | - |

December 13, 1928 - New Orleans

CELESTIN'S ORIGINAL TUXEDO JAZZ ORCHESTRA: Oscar Celestin (c,dir); Guy Kelly (c); Ernest Kelly (tb); Earl Pierson (cl,as); Sid Carriere (cl,ts); Jeanette Salvant (p); Marvin Kimball (bj); Simon Marrero (tuba); Abby Foster (d,vo).

| 147632-2 | The Sweetheart of T.K.O. (vAF) | Columbia 14396-D |
| 147633-2 | Ta Ta Daddy | - |

1953 - New Orleans

PAPA CELESTIN AND HIS TUXEDO DIXIELAND BAND: Papa Celestin (tp); Richard Alexis (tp); Ed Pierson (tb); Joseph Thomas (d); Adolphe Alexander (as); Manuel Paul (ts); Jeanette Kimball (p); Albert French (bj); Sidney Brown (b); Louis Barbarin (d).

| C052652 | Tiger Rag | Columbia 48009 |
| C052626 | At the Darktown Strutter's Ball | - |

April 24, 1954 - New Orleans

Alexis and Paul out.

Do You Know What it Means    Southland SLP 206
Down By the Riverside                - , SEP 801, Stv(D)SLP310
When the Saints Go Marcing In   -                  -
Marie La Veau                   -        -        -
Oh Didn't He Ramble           -


May 13, 1954 - New Orleans

JOHNNY ST. CYR AND HIS HOT FIVE:  Thomas Jefferson (tp,vo); Joe Avery (tb); Willie Humphrey (cl); Jeanette Kimball (p); Johnny St. Cyr (bj).

| | |
|---|---|
| Bill Bailey (vTJ) | Southland SLP 212, Stv(D)SLP103 |
| Careless Love | - , Tempo(E)EXA99, Stv(D)SEP-354 |
| Bye and Bye | Southland SLP 212,   - , Stv(D)SEP-354 |
| Sister Kate | Southland SLP 212,   - , Stv(D)SEP-354 |

Paul Barbarin (d) added.

| | |
|---|---|
| Darktown Strutters' Ball | Southland SLP 212 |
| Down By The Riverside (vTJ) | - |

Sister Elizabeth Eustis (vo) added.

| | |
|---|---|
| Walk Through the Streets | - |


June 17, 1954 - New Orleans

GEORGE LEWIS AND HIS RAGTIME BAND:  Percy Humphrey (tp); Jim Robinson (tb); George Lewis (cl); Jeanette Kimball (p,vo); Johnny St. Cyr (bj); Stewart Davis or Frank Fields (b); Paul Barbarin (d).

| | |
|---|---|
| Someday | Storyville (D)SLP 195 |
| Come Back Sweet Papa | - |
| Savoy Blues | - |
| Somebody Else Is Taking My Place (vJK) | - |


July 25, 1954 - New Orleans

Sister Elizabeth Eustis (vo) added.

| | |
|---|---|
| Just a Closer Walk With Thee | Storyville (D)SLP 195 |


March 17, 1956 - New Orleans

EDDIE PIERSON'S BAND:  Albert Walters (tp); Eddie Pierson (tb); Joseph Thomas (c); Jeanette Kimball (p); Albert French (bj); Sidney Brown (b); Louis Barbarin, Sr. (d).

```
          Gettysburg March, In      Good Time Jazz L12020,Vg(E)LAG1214
          Gloryland
          Bill Bailey                      -                    -
```

August 31, 1956 - New Orleans

PAUL BARBARIN AND HIS JAZZ BAND:  Alvin Alcorn (tp); Jim Robinson (tb);
Willie Humphrey (cl); Jeanette Kimball (p); Lawrence Marrero (bj); Paul
Barbarin (d).

```
          Weary Blues               Southland SLP212,Tempo(E)EXA98,
                                     Stv(D)SEP350
          Sister Kate                      -          -          -
          You'll Tell Me Your Dreams       -          -          -
          Tipperary                        -          -          -
```

1961 - New Orleans

PUNCH MILLER'S HONGO FONGO PLAYERS:  Punch Miller (tp); Wendell Eugene
(tb); Joseph Thomas (cl); Jeanette Kimball (p); Albert French (bj);
Frank Fields or Stewart Davis (b); Louis Barbarin (d).

```
          Milenberg Joys            Imperial LP9160
          Alexander's Ragtime Band         -
             (tp and rhythm only)
          Ice Cream                        -
          Punch Miller Blues               -
          I Ain't Got Nobody (vPM)         -
          Hongo Fongo                      -
          Back in the Old Days in          -
             New Orleans (vPM)
          I've Been Mistreated (vPM)       -
          Nellie Gray (vPM)                -
          Somebody Stole My Gal (vPM)      -
          I Wish I Could Shimmy Like        
             My Sister Kate (vPM)
          Lady Be Good                     -
```

September, 1962 - New Orleans

Don Albert (tp); Frog Joseph (tb); Louis Cottrell (cl); Jeanette Kimball
(p); Placide Adams (b); Paul Barbarin (d).

```
          Roses of Picardy          Southland SLP-239
          Lily of the Valley               -
          Holding My Saviour's Hand        -
          After the Ball is Over           -
```

date unknown - New Orleans

THE DOC AND HIS PATIENTS:  Harry Shields (cl); Raymond Burke (cl,sop);
Jeanette Kimball (p,vo); Edmond "Doc" Soucher" (bj,g); Danny Barker

(g,vo); Johnny St. Cyr (g); Chink Martin (tuba); Sherwood Mangiapane (b); Monk Hazel (d); Blue Lu Barker (vo).

| | |
|---|---|
| Southland Blues (vBLB) | Southland SLP 218 |
| Sister Kate (vBLB) | - |
| All the Wrongs You've Done | - |
| Somebody Else is Taking My Place (vJK) | - |
| Rose Room | - |
| Shine | - |

date unknown - Dixieland Hall - New Orleans

PAPA FRENCH AND HIS NEW ORLEANS JAZZ BAND: Alvin Alcorn (tp); Waldren Joseph (tb); Joseph Thomas (cl); Jeanette Kimball (p,vo); Albert French (bj); Stewart Davis (b); Louis Barbarin (d).

| | |
|---|---|
| Bourbon Street Blues | Nobility LP 702 |
| Savoy Blues | - |
| Rampart Street Parade | - |
| Way Down Yonder in New Orleans | - |
| Marie Lafeau | - |
| Shine | - |
| Darktown Strutter's Ball | - |
| Mack the Knife | - |
| Alabama Jubilee | - |
| St. James Infirmary | - |
| Twelfth Street Rag | - |

date unknown - New Orleans

FRED JOSEPH'S OLD NEW ORLEANS DIXIELAND: Jack Willis (tp); Waldren "Frog" Joseph (tb); Louis Cottrell (cl); Jeanette Kimball (p); Placide Adams (b); Louis Barbarin (d).

| | |
|---|---|
| If Ever I Cease to Love | Dulai LP-800 |
| We Danced at the Mardi Gras | - |
| When the Saints Go Marchng In | - |
| 2189 Rag | - |
| Tishomingo Blues | - |
| Petite Fleur | - |
| Ory's Creole Trombone | - |
| Dippermouth Blues | - |

<u>KIRK, MARY E.</u> (piano)

See Collective Section.

## KOEHLER, CARMELITA (cello)

1963 - New York City

BOB BROOKMEYER AND HIS ORCHESTRA:  Bob Brookmeyer (v-tb); Frank Rehak
(tb); Leo Wright (as,fl); Phil Woods, Jerome Richardson (as); Zoot Sims,
Al Cohn (ts); Romeo Penque (reeds); Danny Bank (bars); Lalo Schiffrin
(p); Jimmy Raney (g); Ben Tucker (b); Dave Bailey (d); Carmelita Koehler
(cello); Jose Paul (perc).

|  |  |
|---|---|
| Samba Para Dos | Verve MGV (S6) 8543 |
| What Kind of Fool Am I | - |
| I Get a Kick Out of You | - |
| Just One of Those Things | - |
| Time After Time | - |
| It's All Right With Me | - |
| My Funny Valentine | - |
| But Not For Me | - |

## KORCHINSKA, MARIA (harp)

March 20, 1957 - London

Cleo Laine (vo) acc. by THE DAVID LEE QUINTET:  Bert Courtley (tp); Ken
Wray (tb); Ronnie Ross (bars,cl,as); Maria Korchinska (h); David Lee
(p); Eric Dawson (b); Kenny Clark (d), u (strings).

|  |  |  |
|---|---|---|
| The Lady Sings the Blues | MGM (E) C765, | E3593 |
| I'll Get By | - | - |
| Our Love is Here to Stay | - | - |
| Hit the Road to Dreamland | - | - |

October 24, 1957 - London

Cleo Laine (vo) acc. by the DAVID LINDRUP ORCHESTRA:  Derrick Abbott,
Stan Palmer, Bob Carson, Colin Wright, Dickie Hawdon (tp); Tony Russell,
Danny Alwood, Jack Botterell, Garry Brown, Laurie Monk (tb); Roy Wilcox
(cl); Danny Moss (ts,cl,b-cl); Alex Leslie (har,cl,fl); Ronnie Ross
(as,cl); David McCullum, David Katz, Jack Rothstein (vn); Patric Ireland
(viola); Bram Martin (cello); Maria Korchinska (h); Johnny Scott (fl);
Dave Lee (p); Eric Dawson (b); Kenny Clark (d); David Linlup (arr,dir).

|  |  |
|---|---|
| Teach Me Tonight | Nixa (E) NPT 19024 |
| He Needs Me | - |
| Something's Got to Give | - |
| All of You | - |

December 9, 1957 - London

Cleo Laine (vo) acc. by the DAVID LINDRUP ORCHSTRA:  including Johnny
Scott (fl); u (tp,strings); Maria Korchinska (h); (prob) David Lee (p);
Eric Dawson (b); Kenny Clark (d).

| Unforgettable | Nixa 7N35020, Marble Arch MAL1185 |
|---|---|
| Too Late Now | − − |
| Young at Heart | − − |
| Summer Is A'Coming In | − − |

March 10-13 and 18, 1964 - London

JOHNNY DANKWORTH AND HIS ORCHESTRA: Ken Wheeler, Leon Calvert (tp); Tony Russell (tb); Johnny Dankworth (cl,as); Vic Ash (cl,ts); Al Newmann (cl,fl,bars); Alan Branscombe (p,vib); Kenny Napper (b); Jonny Butts (d); Ron Snyder (tuba); Maria Korchinska (h); Cleo Laine (vo).

| My Love is a Fever | Fontana(E)TL5209,(Am)MGF27531 |
|---|---|
| If Music Be the Food of Love | − − |
| It Was a Lover and His Lass | − − |
| Blow, Blow Thou Winter Wind | − − |
| Shall I Compare Thee | − − |
| Fear No More | − − |
| Sigh No More Ladies | − − |
| The Compleat Works | − − |

## LAMB, LOIS (trumpet)

See Collective Section.

## LEE, BARBARA (alto sax)

1946 - Los Angeles

EARLE SPENCER AND HIS ORCHESTRA: Frank Beach, Al Killian, Ray Linn, Paul Lopez (tp); Ollie Wilson, Tom Pederson, Hal Smith (tb); Barbara Lee, Willie Schwartz (as); Ralph Lee, Lucky Thompson (ts); Hy Mandel (bars); Paul Polena (p); Arv Garrison (g); Harry Babasin (b); Jackie Mills (d).

| BW384 | E.S. Boogie, II | Black & White 800, Tops LP 948 |
|---|---|---|
| BW385 | E.S. Boogie, I | Black & White 799 |
| BW387 | Rhapsody in Boogie, I | Black & White 801 |
| BW389 | Spencerian Theory, II | Black & White 799 |
| BW390 | Rhapsody in Boogie, II | Black & White 801 |
| BW391 | Spencerian Theory, I | Black & White 800 − |

## LEE, CARROLL (piano)

date unknown - Northfield, Minnesota

DOC EVAN'S DIXIELAND BAND: Doc Evans (c); Al Jenkins (tb); John MacDonald (cl); Carroll Lee (p); Willy Sutton (b); Doc Cernardo (d).

| RL14770 | Milenberg Joys | Joco 107, TempoTR474*, MT2066, Oriole (E)1034*, EP7034 |
| RL14771 | Memphis Blues | Joco 107, TempoTR474,   -, Oriole(E)1034 |
| RL14772 | Walkin' the Dog | Joco 108, TempoTR476,   -, Oriole(E)1045 |
| RL14773 | Blues Doctor | Joco 105, TempoTR476,   -, Oriole (E)1044 |
| RL14774 | Ostrich Walk | Joco 108,   -   -, Oriole (E)1044 |
| RL14775 | Willie the Weeper | Joco 106, TempoTR478,   -, Oriole (E)1045, EP7034 |
| RL14776 | Doctor Joy | Joco 105, TempoTR480,   -, Oriole EP7034 |
| RL14777 | Play that Barbershop Chord | Joco 106,   -   -   -, |

* Tempo and Oriole(E) reissues list group as "Six Alarm Six."


## LEE, JULIA (piano)

1945 - Kansas City

Julia Lee (vo) acc. by TOMMY DOUGLAS' ORCHESTRA:  Clarence Davis (tp); Tommy Douglas (cl,as); Freddie Gulliver, Harry Ferguson (ts); Julia Lee (p); Efferge Ware (g); Ben Curtis (b); Sam "Baby" Lovett (d).

| 20237 | If It's Good | Premium 29012, Mercury 8005 |
| 20238 | Show Me Missouri Blue | - | - |
| 20239 | Lotus Blossom | Premium 29013, Mercury 8013 |
| 20240 | Dream Lucky Blues* | - | - |

* (p,b, and d) only.


September, 1946 - Los Angeles

JULIA LEE AND HER BOYFRIENDS:  Geechie Smith (tp); Henry Bridges (ts); Julia Lee (p,vo); Nappy Lamare (g); Billy Hadnott (b); Sam "Baby" Lovett (d).

| 1369 | Julia's Blues | Capitol 320 |
| 1370 | Lies | Capitol 308 |
| 1371 | Gotta Gimme Watcha Got | - |
| 1372 | When a Woman Loves a Man | Capitol 320 |

Lucky Ennois (g) added.

| 1376 | Oh Marie | Capitol 340 |
| 1377 | I'll Get Along Somehow | Capitol 379, 380 |
| 1378 | A Porter's Love Song | Capitol 40008 |


September, 1946 - Los Angeles

Karl George (tp); Dave Cavanaugh (ts); Julia Lee (p,vo); Lucky Ennois (g); Red Callender (b); Sam "Baby" Lovett (d).

| 1391 | Since I've Been With You | Capitol 40008 |
| 1393 | Young Girl's Blues | Capitol 390 |
| 1394 | On My Way Out | Capitol 340 |

June 11, 1947 - Los Angeles

JULIA LEE AND HER BOY FRIENDS:  Ernie Royal (tp); Dave Cavanaugh (ts); Julia Lee (p,vo); Jack Marshall (g); Harry Babasin (b); Sam "Baby" Lovett (d).

| 2042 | There Goes My Heart | Capitol 1009, T2038 |
| 2045 | Nobody Knows You When You're Down and Out | -, (E)CL13321 |
| 2043 | Snatch and Grab It | Capitol 40028, F15589, 6033, T2038, CL13323 |

June 13, 1947 - Los Angeles

Vic Dickenson (tb) added.  Red Callender (b) replaces Babasin.

| 2058 | Bleeding Hearted Blues | Capitol 1252 |
| 2059 | Back Street | Capitol 15300 |
| 2060 | Wise Guys | Capitol 15106, (E)CL13055 |

June 16, 1947 - Los Angeles

JULIA LEE AND HER BOYFRIENDS:  Red Nichols (c); Vic Dickenson (tb); Benny Carter (as); Dave Cavanaugh (ts); Red Norvo (xylophone); Julia Lee (p,vo); Jack Marshall (g); Red Callender (b); Sam "Baby" Lovett (d).

| 2061 | Mama Don't Allow It | Capitol 1589,H322,F15838,(D)LC6563 |
| 2062 | Doubtful Blues | Capitol 40056 |
| 2063 | Ain't It a Crime | Capitol 838,H228,F15589,(E)LC6535 |
| 2065 | Cold Hearted Daddy | Capitol 15300,(E)CL13323 |
| 2066 | My Sin | Capitol 40056, T1057 |

June 18, 1947 - Los Angeles

same personnel.

| 2067 | When You're Smiling | Capitol 40082, T1057 |
| 2068 | I Was Wrong | Capitol 40028,  -, T2038 |

November 11, 1947

Geechie Smith (tp) replaces Nichols, Norvo out.

| 2441 | Pagan Love Song | Capitol 1149 |
| 2442 | All I Ever Do is Worry | Capitol 15106 |
| 2443 | Take It or Leave It | capitol 57-70006 |
| 2444 | That's What I Like | Capitol 15060 |

| 2445 | King Size Papa | Capitol 40082,F15588,H228,T2038, LC6535, (E)CL13055 |
| 2446 | Blues for Someone | Capitol 57-70051 |
| 2447 | I'm Forever Blowing Bubbles | Capitol 1149 |
| 2448 | Breeze | Capitol 1589,H322,F15838, (D)LC6563 |

**November 13, 1947 - Los Angeles**

same personnel.

| 2458 | I Didn't Like It the First Time | Capitol 15367,F15590,H228, LC6535 |
| 2460 | Crazy World (no saxes) | Capitol 15060, T2038 |
| 2461 | Tell Me Daddy | Capitol 15144 |
| 2462 | Christmas Spirit | Capitol 15203 |
| 2463 | Until the Real Thing Comes Along | Capitol 15144 |

**November 14, 1947 - Los Angeles**

JULIA LEE AND HER BOYFRIENDS: Dave Cavanaugh (cl,ts); Julia Lee (p,vo); Jack Marshall (g); Charles Drayton (b); Sam "Baby" Lovett (d).

| 2479 | Charmaine | Capitol 15203 |
| 2480-3 | Lotus Blossom | Capitol 1376 |
| 2481 | Sit and Drink it Over | Capitol 15367 |
| 2483 | The Glory of Love | Capitol 57-70006 |

**April, 1949 - Kansas City**

JULIA LEE AND HER BOYFRIENDS: Tommy Douglas (ts); Julia Lee (p,vo); Jim "Daddy" Walker (g); Clint Weaver (b); Sam "Baby" Lovett (d).

| 4138 | Tonight's the Night | Capitol 57-70013,T2038,LC6535 |
| 4139 | My Man Stands Out | Capitol 1111 |
| 4140 | Do You Want It | Capitol 956 |
| 4146 | Don't Come Too Soon | Capitol 1111 |
| 4147 | Ugly Papa | Capitol 1432 |
| 4148 | Don't Save It Too Long | Capitol 838,F15588,H228, (E)LC6535 |
| 4149 | After Hours Waltz | Capitol 57-70013, T2038 |
| | Decent Woman Blues | Capitol 956, (E)CL13321 |
| 4166 | You Ain't Got It No More | Capitol 57-70031,F15590,H228, T2038,LC6535 |
| 4168 | Chuck It In a Bucket | Capitol 57-70031 |
| 4170 | Dragging My Heart Around | Capitol 57-70051,T1057,T2083 |

**July 21, 1950 - Kansas City**

JULIA LEE AND HER BOYFRIENDS:  Tommy Douglas (as); Gene Carter (ts); Julia Lee (p,vo); Leonard Johnson (b); William Nolan (d).

| 6330 | It Won't Be Long Now | Capitol 1252 |

July 22, 1950 - Kansas City

same personnel.

| 6334 | Scream in the Night | Capitol 1798 |
| 6335 | I Know It's Wrong | Capitol 1432 |
| 6337 | Pipe Dreams | Capitol 1376 |

July 2, 1952 - Kansas City

JULIA LEE AND HER BOYFRIENDS: Bob Dougherty (ts); Julia Lee (p,vo); James Scott (g); Clint Weaver (b); Robert Jordan (d).

| 10303 | Goin' to Chicago Blues | Capitol 2203 |
| 10304 | Last Call for Alcohol | - , 6033, T2038 |

c. 1956-1957

details unknown.

| King Size Papa | Foremost 104 |
| Bop and Rock Lullaby | - |
| Trouble in Mind | Foremost 105 |
| Saturday Night | - |

## LEE, PERRI (organ)

October 20, 1960 - "Count Basie Bar" - New York City

PERRI LEE TRIO: Eddie Chamblee (ts); Perri Lee (o); John Kriegh (d).

| Blues in the Closet | Roulette (S) R52080 |
| Duet | - |
| Doodlin' | - |
| Just the Blues | - |
| Red Sails in the Sunset | - |
| Mr. Lucky | - |
| Ummm | - |
| June Night | - |
| Land of Dreams | - |
| What's New | - |
| Loose Walk | - |
| A 'Hallelujah | - |

## LEIGHTON, ELAINE (drums)

January, 1954 - Live Concert, Germany (prob. Cologne)

Billie Holiday (vo) acc. by Carl Drinkard (p); Red Mitchell (b); Elaine
Leighton (d).

| | | | | | |
|---|---|---|---|---|---|
| Blue Moon | United Artists UAJ 14014, 15014, AE(E)ULP 1026,(G)69013 | | | | |
| All of Me | - | | - | - | - |
| My Man | - | | - | - | - |
| Them There Eyes | - | | - | - | - |
| I Cried For You | - | | - | - | - |
| What a Little Moonlight Can Do | - | | - | - | - |
| I Cover the Waterfront | - | | - | - | - |

See Collective Section for Additional Recordings


## LENS, MARIA (bass)

See Collective Section.


## LEWIS, CLARA (piano)

1945 - Los Angeles

Ernie Andrews (vo) acc. by CLARA LEWIS TRIO:  Clara Lewis (p); Leonard
Enois (g); Red Callender (b).

| | |
|---|---|
| Soothe Me | Gem 1, G&G 1 |
| Wrap It Up and Put It Away | -    - |
| Green Gin | Gem 2, Exclusive 55X |
| Dream Awhile | -    - |


## LEWIS, HELEN (piano)

1949 - Tulsa, Oklahoma

ERNIE FIELDS AND HIS ORCHESTRA:  Artis Paul, Harold Bruce, Walter Miller
(tp); Parker Berry (tb); Luther West, Harold "Geezel" Minerva (as); Elon
Watkins (ts); Oscar Estelle (bars); Helen Lewis (p); Ernest "Butch"
Lockett (g); Brooks Lewis (b); Al Duncan (d).

| | | |
|---|---|---|
| F123 | Long Lost Love | Gotham 273 |
| F124 | Butch's Blues | - |
| | Frustrated Woman | Gotham 281 |
| | My Prince | - |

c. 1949

same personnel.

T-Town Blues                     Bullet 302
E.F. Boogie                          -


## LEWIS, MILDRED (piano)

July 23, 1960 - Clarksdale, Mississippi

Kathryn Pitman (vo) acc. by Mildred Lewis (p) and the Centennial Baptist
Church Youth Choir (vo).

Save a Seat for Me               Arhoolie F1005


## LISTON, MELBA
### (trombone, conductor, arranger)

May 6, 1945

GERALD WILSON AND HIS ORCHESTRA:  Gerald Wilson, Emmett Berry, Hobart
Dotson (tp); Vic Dickenson, Robert Sanchez Huerta, Melba Liston, Isaac
Livingston (tb); Floyd Turnham, Vernon Slater (saxes); James Bunn (p);
Henry Green (d); William Edwards, Edward Hale, Olif West, James Hender-
son, Charles Waller, Fred Trainor (unknown instruments); Pat Kaye, Dick
Grey, Bette Roche (vo).

Moon Rise (vPK)           Excelsior 122
Synthetic Joe                 -
Top of the Hill           Excelsior 123
Puerto Rican Breakdown        -

May 21, 1945

same personnel.

Just One of Those Things   Excelsior 126
(vDG)
Give Me a Man (vBR)           -


1946 - Los Angeles

Dinah Washington (vo) acc. by GERALD WILSON'S ORCHESTRA:  including
Gerald Wilson, Snookie Young (tp); Melba Liston (tb); Jimmy Bunn (p);
James Robinson (tb); Clyde Dunn, Vernon Slater (ts); Maurice Simon
(bars); Henry Green (d).

Ooh-Wee-Walkie Talkie      Mercury 8010

June 5, 1947 - Los Angeles

DEXTER GORDON QUINTET:  Melba Liston (tb); Dexter Gordon (ts); Charles
Fox (p); Red Callender (b); Chuck Thompson (d).

| D1081D | Mischievous Lady | Dial 1018, LP204, Jzt J1005, J1235 |
| D1082C | Lullaby in Rhythm | Dial 1038,  -         -, Design DLP183 |

**April 11, 1949 - Los Angeles**

COUNT BASIE AND HIS ORCHESTRA: Harry Edison, Emmett Berry, Clark Terry, Jimmy Nottingham, Gerald Wilson (tp); Ted Donelly, Dickie Wells, George Matthews, Melba Liston (tb); Earl Warren, Charles Price (as); Paul Gonsalves, Bill "Wessel" Parker (ts); Jack Washington (bars); Count Basie (p); Freddy Green (g); Singleton Palmer (b); George "Butch" Ballard (d); Bobby Troup (vo).

| D9VB600 | Brand New Wall (vBT) | Victor 20-3449 |
| D9VB601 | Cheek to Cheek | -,Camden CAL395,Jzt J1245 |
| D9VB602 | An Old Manuscript | Victor LPM 1112, RCA(F)430, (F)575 |
| D9VB603 | Katy | -  , HMV 7EG 8221 |

**November 8, 1955 - Los Angeles**

DIZZY GILLESPIE AND HIS ORCHESTRA: Harry Edison (tp); Melba Liston (tb); Willie Smith (as); Ed Beel, Curtis Amy (ts); Clyde Dunn (bars); Carl Perkins (p); George Bledsoe (b); Albert Bartee (d); Toni Harper (vo).

| 2551 | Taking a Chance on Love | Norgran MGN1083, Verve MGV8173 |
| 2553 | Play Me Some Blues | Norgran 151, -          -, Co(E)LB10043 |
|  | Oasis | American Record Society G423, Pby PB1958 |
|  | Flamingo | American Record Society G405 |

**1955-1956 - New York City**

Frank Rehak, Melba Liston (tb); Marty Flax (bars); Walter Davis, Jr. (p); Nelson Boyd (b); Charlie Persip (d).

| Insomnia | Down DLP 1107 |
| Very Syrian Business | - |
| Never Do an Abadanian In | - |
| Zagreb This | - |

**May 18-19, June 6, 1956 - New York City**

DIZZY GILLESPIE AND HIS ORCHESTRA: Dizzy Gillespie, Ermet Perry, Carl Warwick, Quincy Jones (tp); Melba Liston, Frank Rehak, Rod Levitt (tb); Jimmy Powell, Phil Woods (as); Billy Mitchell, Ernie Wilkins (ts); Marty Flax (bars); Walter Davis, Jr. (p); Nelson Boyd (b); Charlie Persip (d).

| | | |
|---|---|---|
| 2828 | Hey Pete | Verve MGV 8017, ARS G423 |
| 2831 | Dizzy's Business | Norgran MGN 1084, Verve MGV 8174, (E)VLP90 |
| 2832 | A Night in Tunisia | Norgran MGN 1084, Verve MGV 8174, (E)VLP90, VSP-7 |
| 2833 | Jessica's Day | Norgran MGN 1084, Verve MMGV 8174, (E)VLP90, MGV 8230, MGV 8566 |
| 2834 | Tour de Force | Norgran MGN 1084, Verve MGV 8174, VLP 90 |
| 2835 | I Can't Get Started | Norgran 152, MGN 1084, Verve MGV 8174, Co(E)LB 10037 |
| 2836 | Stella By Starlight | Norgran MGN 1084, Verve MGV 8174 |
| 2837 | Doodlin' | Norgran 154, MGN 1084, Verve MGV 8174, 118, 10265, EPV5047 |
| 2839 | The Champ | Norgran MG 1084, Verve MGV 8174 |
| 2840 | Yesterdays | Verve MGV 8017, ARS G423 |
| 2841 | Tin Tin Deo | - |
| 2842 | Groovin' for Nat | Norgran 152, MGN 1084 |
| 2843 | My Reverie | -, Stash ST 109 |
| 2844 | Dizzy's Blues | Norgran 154, -, 8174, Verve (E)VLP 9076 |
| 2845 | Annie's Dance | Verve MGV 8017, ARS G423 |
| 2846 | Cool Breeze | - -, Verve VSP-7 |
| 2847 | School Days (vDG) | - - |

March 23 & April 7-8, 1957 - Los Angeles

DIZZY GILLESPIE AND HIS ORCHESTRA: Dizzy Gillespie, Lee Morgan, Ermet Perry, Carl Warwick, Talib Daawud (tp); Melba Liston, Al Grey, Rod Levitt (tb); Jimmy Powell, Ernie Henry (as); Billy Mitchell, Ben Golson (ts); Billy Root (bars); Wynton Kelly (p); Paul West (b); Charlie Persip (d); Austin Cromer (vo).

| | | |
|---|---|---|
| 20828 | Jordu | Verve MGV8207, MGV8222, VSP-7, VLP 9076 |
| 20829 | Birks Works | - -, MGV 8566, |
| 20830 | Umbrella Man (vDG) | - |
| 20831 | Autumn Leaves | -,Co(E)SEB 10046 |
| 20832 | Tangerine | Verve 89173, -, VSP-7 Co(E)SEB 10096, 33CX 10144 |
| 20833 | Over the Rainbow (vAC) | - -, LB 10079 |
| 20834 | Yo No Quiovre Bailar (vAC) | - |
| 29835 | If You Could See Me Now (vAC) | - |
| 20836 | Left Hand Corner | - - |
| 20837 | Whisper Not | Verve VLP9076, -, VSP-7, Co 33CX, 10144 |
| 20838 | Stablemates | -, MGV 8207 |
| 20839 | That's All | - - |
| 20840 | Groovin' High | - |
| | Mayflower Rock | Verve 89173 |

July 6, 1957 - Newport Jazz Festival

DIZZY GILLESPIE AND HIS ORCHESTRA: Dizzy Gillespie, Ermet Perry, Carl Warwick, Talib Daawud (tp); Melba Liston, Al Grey, Ray Connor (tb);

Jimmy Powell, Ernie Henry (as); Billy Mitchell, Benny Golson (ts); Pee
Wee Moore (bars); Wynton Kelly (p); Paul West (b); Charlie Persip (d).

|       | Dizzy's Blues         | Verve MGV 8242, MGV 8560       |          |
|-------|-----------------------|--------------------------------|----------|
|       | Doodlin'              | -                              | -        |
|       | School Days           | -                              | -        |
|       | I Remember Clifford   | -, VSP-7                       |          |
|       | Manteca               | -                              |          |
|       | Cool Breeze           | -                              |          |
|       | Night in Tunisia      | Verve MGV 8244                 |          |
| 21092 | Joogie Boogie         | Verve 89193, Pby PB1957,       |          |
|       |                       | Co(E) 33CX, 1570               |          |
| 20192-2 | Joogie Boogie       | Verve 118, 10265, Co(E)LB10079 |          |


September, 1957 - New York City

ERNIE HENRY ALL STARS: Lee Morgan (tp); Melba Liston (tb); Ernie Henry
(as); Benny Golson (ts); Cecil Payne (bars); Wynton Kelly (p); Paul
Chambers (b); Philly Joe Jones (d).

|   | Autumn Leaves          | Riverside RLP 12-266 |
|---|------------------------|----------------------|
|   | Beauty and the Blues   | -                    |
|   | All the Things You Are | -                    |
|   | Melba's Tune           | -                    |


December, 1957 - New York City

ART BLAKEY BIG BAND: Donald Byrd, Idrees Sulieman, Bill Hardman, Ray
Copeland (tp); Melba Liston, Frank Rehak, Jimmy Cleveland (tb); Sahib
Shihab, Bill Graham (as); John Coltrane, Al Cohn (ts); Bill Slapin
(bars); Walter Bishop (p); Wendell (b); Art Blakey (d).

|   | Ain't Life Grand        | Bethlehem 11086, BCP 6027 |   |
|---|-------------------------|---------------------------|---|
|   | El Toro Valiente        | -                         | - |
|   | Midriff                 |                           | - |
|   | The Kiss of No Return   |                           | - |
|   | Late Date               |                           | - |
|   | The Outer World         |                           | - |


c. 1958 - New York City

Betty Carter (vo) acc. by Kenny Dorham, Ray Copeland (tp); Melba Liston
(tb); Tommy Gryce, Jimmy Powell (as); Benn Golson (ts); Sahib Shihab
(bars); Wynton Kelly (p); Sam Jones (b); Specs Wright (d).

|   | You're Driving Me Crazy       | Progressive Jazz PLP90 |
|---|-------------------------------|------------------------|
|   | I Can't Help It               | -, PJ801               |
|   | By the Bend of the River      | -                      |
|   | Babe's Blues                  | -                      |
|   | Foul Play                     | -                      |
|   | You're Getting to Be a Habit  | -                      |

c. 1958 - New York City

Betty Carter (vo) acc. by Ray Copeland (tp); Melba Liston (tb); Jerome
Richardson (ts); Wynton Kelly (p); Peck Morrison (b); Specs Wright (d).

| | | | |
|---|---|---|---|
| On the Isle of May | Progressive Jazz PJ 801, PLP90 | | |
| But Beautiful | - | - | |
| All I've Got | | - | |
| Make It Last | | - | |
| Blue Bird of Happiness | | - | |
| Something Wonderful | | - | |

July 6, 1958 - Newport Jazz Festival

Dinah Washington (vo) acc. by Blue Mitchell (tp); Melba Liston (tb);
Harold Ousley (ts); Sahib Shihab (bars); Wynton Kelly (p); Paul West
(b); Max Roach (d).

| | | | |
|---|---|---|---|
| 17638 | Lover Come Back to Me | EmArcy MG36141, Merc(E)YEP 9501 | |
| 17639 | Crazy Love | - | - |
| 17640 | Back Water Blues | - | - |

October, 1958 - New York City

Ray Copeland (tp); Melba Liston (tb); Johnny Griffin (ts); Randy Weston
(p); Jamil Nasser (b) Charlie Persip (d).

| | | | |
|---|---|---|---|
| Early Birth | United Artists UAL 4011, UAS5011 | | |
| Little Susan | - | - | |
| Nice Ice | - | - | |
| Little Niles | - | - | |
| Pam's Waltz | - | -, | |
| | MX21, SX71 | | |
| Let's Climb a Hill | - | - | |

Idrees Sulieman (tp) replaces Copeland.

| | | |
|---|---|---|
| Babe's Blues | - | - |

December 22, 1958 - New York City

Melba Liston, Benny Green, Al Grey, Benny Powell (tb); Kenny Burrell
(g); Jamil Nasser (b); Charlie Persip (d).

| | |
|---|---|
| The Trolley Song | Metrojazz (S)E 1013 |
| Blues Melba | - |
| You Don't Say | - |

Jimmy Cleveland, Frank Rehak, Slide Hampton (tb) replace Green, Grey and
Powell.

| | |
|---|---|
| Pow | Metrojazz (S)E 1013 |
| Wonder Why | - |
| Christmas Eve | - |

What's My Line Theme        –

Dark Before Dawn            –

December 26, 1958 – New York City

TROMBONES, INC.: Eddie Bert, Jimmy Cleveland, Henry Coker, Benny Green, Melba Liston, Benny Powell, Frank Rehak (tb); Bob Brookmeyer (v-tb); Dick Hixon, Bart Varsalona (b-tb); Hank Jones (p); Wendell Marshall (b); Osie Johnson (d).

| | |
|---|---|
| Neck Bones | Warner Brothers WB(WS)1272, (E)WM4023, WS8023 |
| I've Found a New Baby | Warner Brothers WB(WS)1281, (E)WM4015, WS8015 |

December 29, 1958 – New York City

same personnel.

| | |
|---|---|
| Soft Winds | Warner Brothers WB(WS)1272, (E)WM4023, WS8023 |
| Dues Blues | Warner Brothers WB(WS)1272, (E)WM4023, WS8023, (E)WM4005, WS8005. |

December 31, 1958 – New York City

same personnel.

| | |
|---|---|
| Long Before I Knew You | Warner Brothers WB(WS)1272, WM4023, WS8023 |
| Tee Jay | –    –    – |

June 23, 1959 – New York City

Ray Charles with QUINCY JONES' ORCHESTRA: Marcus Behgrave, John Hunt, Clark Terry, Ernie Royal, Joe Newman, Snookie Young (tp); Melba Liston, Al Grey, Quentin Jackson, Tom Mitchell (tb); Marshall Royal, Frank Wess (as); Dave Newman, Paul Gonsalves, Zoot Sims (ts); Bennie Crawford, Charlie Fowlkes (bars); Ray Charles (o,vo); Freddie Green (g); Edgar Willis, Eddie Willies, Eddie Jones (b); Teagle Felming, Charlie Persip (d).

| A3953 | Let the Good Times Roll | Atlantic 2047, LP1312, LP8064, (F) 212038, Lnd(E)HLE9058, |
|---|---|---|
| | Deed I Do | Atlantic LP 1312, LP8094 |
| | Alexander's Ragtime Band | –      –,(F)212038 |

Billy Mitchell (ts) replaces Sims.

| | | |
|---|---|---|
| | It Had to Be You | Atlantic LP 1312, LP8094 |
| | When Your Lover Has Gone | –      – |
| | Two Years of Torture | –      –,(F)212038 |

September 8, 11 and 17, 1959 - New York City

Gloria Lynne (vo) acc. by MELBA LISTON'S ORCHESTRA:   including Melba
Liston (arr,cond,tb).

| | | |
|---|---|---|
| Love I've Found You | Everest 19390, LPB R5063 | |
| Am I Blue | - | |
| 'Tis Autumn | - | |
| For All We Know | Everest LPB R5226, - ,SDB R5226 | |
| Hands Across the Table | - | |
| Blue and Sentimental | Everest LPB R5203, -,SDB R1203 | |
| Little Girl Blue | - | -,5226,1226 |
| Men of Mind | - | |
| Then I'll Be Tired of You | - | |
| We Never Kissed | - | |
| Fly Me to the Moon | - | |
| Sentimental Melody | - | |

1959 - New York

Babs Gonzales (vo) acc. by Les Spann (fl); Johnny Griffin (ts); Kenny
Burrell (g); Peck Morrison (b); Roy Haynes (d); Melba Liston (arr).

| | |
|---|---|
| The Hat Box Chicks | Jaro JAM5000 |
| Broadway 4 a.m. | - |
| You Need Connections | - |
| Dem Resolution-Liars | - |
| Manhattan Fable | - |
| Dem Jive New Yorkers | - |
| The Squares | - |
| A Dollar is Your Only Friend | - |

September 20, 1960 - New York City

EDDIE DAVIS BIG BAND:   Clark Terry, Richard Williams, Bob Bryant (tp);
Jimmy Cleveland, Melba Liston (tb); Oliver Nelson, Eric Dolphy (as);
Eddie Davis (ts); Jerome Richardson, George Barrows (ts,fl); Bob Ashton
(bars); Richard Wyands (p); Wendell Marshall (b); Roy Haynes (d).

| 2498 | Walk Away | Prestige LP7206, Esq32-174, | | |
|---|---|---|---|---|
| | | X-traXTRA5019 | | |
| 2499 | Trane Whistle | - | - | - |
| 2500 | Whole Nelson | - | - | - |
| 2501 | The Stolen Moment | - | - | - |
| 2502 | Jaws | - | - | - |
| 2503 | You Are Too Beautiful | - | - | - |

1961 - New York

RIVERSIDE JAZZ STARS:   Blue Mitchell, Ernie Royal (tp); Clark Terry
(flhn); Melba Liston (tb,arr); Julius Watkins (FrH); George Dorsey (as);
Jimmy Heath (ts,arr); Arthur Clarke (bars); Bobby Timmons (p); Ron
Carter (b); Al Heath (d); Ernie Wilkins (arr)

| Sweet Danger | Riverside RLP(S9) 397 |
|---|---|
| Chime In | - |
| Penny Plain | - |
| To Look Upon My Love | - |
| The Fog and the Grog | - |
| Elena | - |
| Inevitable | - |
| Willow, Willow, Willow | - |

January 13, 1961 - New York City

SAM JONES PLUS TEN: Nat Adderley (c); Blue Mitchell (tp); Melba Liston (tb); Julian Cannonball Adderley (as); Jimmy Heath (ts); Tate Houston (bars); Vic Feldman (p); Les Spann (g); Sam Jones (b); Louis Hayes (d).

| The Chant | Riverside RLP(S9) 358 |
|---|---|
| Four | -, RM(S)3504 |
| Blues on Down | -, RM(S)3505 |
| Off Color | - |

January 26, 1961 - New York City

Nat Adderley (c); Blue Mitchell (tp); Melba Liston (tb); Julian Cannonball Adderley (as); Jimmy Heath (ts); Tate Houston (bars); Vic Feldman (vib); Sam Jones (cello); Wynton Kelly (p); Keeter Beets (b); Louis Hayes (d).

| Sonny Boy | Riverside RLP(S9)358 |
|---|---|
| In Walked Ray | - |
| Blue Bird | -, RM(S)3506 |
| Over the Rainbow | - |

May 9 & 15, 1961 - New York City

CANNONBALL ADDERLEY AND HIS ORCHESTRA: Nat Adderley (c); Clark Terry, Ernie Royal, Nick Travis (tp); Bob Brookmeyer (v-tb); Melba Liston, Jimmy Cleveland, Paul Faulise (tb); Julian Adderley (as); George Dorsey (as,fl); Jerome Richardson, Oliver Nelson (ts,fl); Arthur Clarke (bars); Wynton Kelly (p); Sam Jones (b); Don Butterfield (tuba); Louis Hayes (d); Olatunji (cga); Charlie Persip (bgs); Ernie Wilkins (arr).

| The Uptown | Riverside 4501,EP3210,LP377 |
|---|---|
| Something Different | - - - |
| West Coast Blues | - |
| Letter From Home | - |
| Blue Brass Groove | Riverside 4528, - |
| I'll Close My Eyes | - |
| Stockholm Sweetnin' | - |
| Smoke Gets In Your Eyes | - |
| This Here | - |

November 10, 1961 - New York City

OLIVER NELSON ORCHESTA: Clyde Ressinger, Ernie Royal, Joe Newman (tp);
Melba Liston, Billy Byers, Paul Faulise (tb); Oliver Nelson (as,ts);
Ernie Dixon (ts,fl); Don Butterfield (tuba); Art Davis (b); Ed Shaugh-
nessy (d); Ray Baretto (cga,bgs).

        Jungleaire                    Prestige PR (S) 7225c
        Goin' Up North              -

November 29, 1961 - New York City

QUINCY JONES AND HIS ORCHESTRA: Jerry Kail, Clyde Ressinger, Clark
Terry, Joe Newman (tp); Billy Byers, Melba Liston, Paul Faulise (tb);
Julius Watkins (FrH); Phil Woods (as); Eric Dixon, Jerome Richardson
(ts); Bobby Scott (p); Buddy Catlett (b); Stu Martin (d); Quincy Jones
(arr,cond).

        For Lena and Lennie       Impulse 206, A(S)11, HMV CLP1581,
                                    SCD 1462
        The Twitch                  -      -      -

September or November, 1961 - New York

Mark Murphy (vo) acc. by Clark Terry, Blue Mitchell, Joe Wilder, Bernie
Glow, Ernie Royal (tp); Jimmy Cleveland, Urbie Green, Melba Liston (tb);
Wynton Kelly, Bill Evans (p); Barry Galbraith, Sam Herman (g); George
Duvivier, Art Davis (b); Jimmy Cobb (d); Ray Baretto (cga); Ernie
Wilkins (dir,arr).

        Angel Eyes                 Riverside RLP 395
        Green Dolphin Street     -
        Stoppin' the Clock       -
        Spring Can Really Hang   -
           You Up the Most
        No Tears for Me           -
        Out of This World        -
        My Favorite Things      -
        L'il Darlin'             -
        I'll Be Seeing You        -

1962-1963 - New York

  similar personnel.

        My Favorite Things      Riverside RLP 395
        Like Love               -
        Fly Away My Love        -

February 22, 1962 - New York City

RAY BROWN AND HIS ALL STAR BIG BAND: Ernie Royal, Joe Newman, Nat
Adderley, Clark Terry (tp); Jimmy Cleveland, Melba Liston, Britt

Woodman, Paul Faulise (tb); Cannonball Adderley, Earl Warren (as); Budd
Johnson, Seldon Powell (ts); Yusef Lateef (fl); Jerome Richardson
(bars,fl); Ray Brown (cello); Hank Jones (p); Sam Jones (b); Osie
Johnson (d).

| | |
|---|---|
| My One and Only Love | Verve MGV(S6)8444, (E)(S)VLP9011, Barclay GLP3628 |
| Two for the Blues | - - - |
| Baubles Bangles and Beads | - - - |

February 23, 1962 - New York City

Tommy Flanagan (p); replaces Jones; Ray Brown (B) replaces Jones.

| | |
|---|---|
| Work Song | Verve MGV(S6)8444, (E)(S)VLP9011, Barclay GLP3628 |
| It Happened in Monterey | - - - |
| Tricotism | - - - |
| Thumbstung | - - - |
| Cannon Bilt | - - - |
| Day In, Day Out | - - - |

June 13-15, 26 and 28, 1962 - New York

Clark Terry (flhn,tp); Ernie Royal, Roy Elder, Snooky Young, Jimmy
Nottingham (tp); Nat Adderley (listed as "Pat Brotherly") (c); Jimmy
Cleveland, Melba Liston, Paul Faulise, Slide Hampton, Britt Woodman
(tb); Willie Ruff, Ray Alonge, Julius Watkins, Morris Secon, Jimmy
Buffington (FrH); Don Butterfield (tuba); Julius "Cannonball" Adderley
(as); Jad Brotherly, Norris Turney (as); Jerome Richardson, James Moody
(ts); Seldon Powell, George Dorsey (bars); Oscar Peterson (p); Ray Brown
(b); Ed Thigpen (d).

| | |
|---|---|
| Blues for Big Scotia | Verve MGV 8476, V6-8480 |
| West Coast Blues | - - |
| Here's That Rainy Day | - - |
| I Love You | - - |
| Daawud | - - |
| Tricotism | - - |
| I'm Old Fashioned | - - |
| Young and Foolish | - - |
| Manteca | - - |

late June, 1962 - New York City

| | | |
|---|---|---|
| XY176 | Round Midnight | Riverside 45479,RLP(S9)429 |
| | The Dream is You | Riverside R(S)3511, - |
| | If You Could See Me Now | - |

July 5, 1962 - New York City

Clark Terry, Nat Adderley, Bernie Glow, Ernie Royal (tp); Jimmy Cleveland, Melba Liston, Paul Faulise (tb); Jerome Richardson, George Dorsey

(as); James Moody (ts,fl); Jimmy Heath (ts); Arthur Clarke (bars); Hank
Jones (p); Ron Carter (b); Philly Joe Jones (d); Milt Jackson (vib).

| | | |
|---|---|---|
| Old Devil Moon | Riverside RLP(S9)429 | |
| You'd Be So Nice to Come Home To | - | |
| Later Than You Think | - | |

July 5, 1962 - New York City

Clark Terry, Snooky Young, Ernie Royal (tp); Tom McIntosh, Melba Liston,
(tb); Earl Warren (as); James Moody (ts); Jerome Richardson (ts,fl);
Tate Houston (bars); Willie Ruff (FrH); Milt Jackson (vib); Hank Jones
(p); Ron Carter (b); Connie Kaye (d); Ernie Wilkins, Tadd Dameron
(arr,cond).

| XY194 | Namesake | Riverside 45479,RLP(S9)429, Fontana(E)SET505B | |
|---|---|---|---|
| | Echoes | Riverside RLS(S9)429, Fontana(E)SET505B | |
| | Star Eyes | - | - |
| | If I Should Lose You | - | - |

March 8, 1963 - New York City

FREDDIE HUBBARD AND HIS ORCHESTRA: Freddie Hubbard, Ed Armour, Richard
Williams (tp); Melba Liston, Curtis Fuller (tb); Bob Northern, Julius
Watkins (FrH); Eric Dolphy (as,fl); Jerome Richardson (bars); Cedar
Walton (p); Reggie Workman (b); Philly Joe Jones (d); u (strings).

| | | |
|---|---|---|
| Chocolate Shake | Impulse (S) A-38 | |
| Skylark | - | |
| I Got It Bad and That Ain't Good | - | |

March 11, 1963 - New York City

FREDDIE HUBBARD AND HIS ORCHESTRA: Al DeRisi, Freddie Hubbard, Ernie
Royal, Clark Terry (tp); Melba Liston, Curtis Fuller (tb); Eric Dolphy
(as,fl); Seldon Powell, Wayne Shorter (ts); Charles Davis, Jerome
Richardson (bars); Bob Northern (FrH); Robert Powell (tuba); Cedar
Walton (p); Reggie Workman (b); Philly Joe Jones (d).

| | | |
|---|---|---|
| Carnival | Impulse (S) A-38 | |
| Arico | - | |
| Thermo | - | |

July, 1963 - New York City

Jimmy Maxwell, Joe Newman, Charlie Shavers (tp); Kai Winding, Jimmy
Cleveland, Melba Liston, Paul Faulise (tb); Phil Woods, Jerry Dodgion
(as); Budd Johnson, Seldon Powell (ts); Marvin Halladay (bars); Jimmy
Smith (o); Kenny Burrell (g); Art Davis (b); Herbie Lovelle (d).

```
          Tubs                      Verve MGV (V6) 8552
          You Came A Long Way From            -
            St. Louis
          G'won Train                         -
```

Snooky Young (tp) replaces Shavers.  Bob Bushness (el-b) added.

```
          The Ape Woman             Verve MGV (V6) 8552
          Blues for C.A.                      -
```

December 20, 1964 - New York City

QUINCY JONES AND HIS ORCHESTRA:  Dizzy Gillespie, Nat Adderley, Freddie
Hubbard, Jimmy Maxwell, Jimmy Nottingham, Joe Newman (tp); Curtis
Fuller, J.J. Johnson, Kai Winding, Melba Liston (tb); Jerry Dodgion,
Phil Woods (as); James Moody (fl,as,ts); Roland Kirk, Benny Golson,
Lucky Thompson (ts); Pepper Adams (bars); Milt Jackson (vib); Bobby
Scott (p); Bob Cranshaw (b); Art Blakey (d); Quincy Jones (arr,cond).

```
34247    I Had a Ball              Limelight LM82002,LS86002,22012LMY
34248    Almost                             -          -         -
34249    Addie's At It Again                -          -         -
```

February 16, 1965 - New York

AND THEN AGAIN:  Hunt Peters (tb);  Frank Wess (ts,fl); Charles Davis
(bars); Don Friedman (p); Paul Chambers (b); Elvin Jones (d); Melba
Liston (arr).

```
8631     Again                     Atlantic LP1443
8632     Len Sirrah                         -
8633     Soon After                         -
```

March 18, 1965 - New York

AND THEN AGAIN:  Thad Jones (c); Hurt Peters (tb); Charlie Davis (bars);
Hank Jones (p); Art Davis (b); Elvin Jones (d); Melba Liston (arr).

```
8758     Elvin Elpus               Atlantic LP1443
8759     Forever Summer                     -
8760     All Deliberate Speed               -
```

May 27, 1966 - New York

HOLD ON, I'M COMING:  Chuck Mangione (tp); Melba Liston, Garnett Brown
(tb); Frank Mitibele (ts); Malcolm Bass (o); Grant Green (g); Reggie
Johnson (b); Art Blakey (d); John Rodriguez (cga).

```
          She Blew a Good Thing     Limelight LML4023, 82038
          Day Dream                          -        -
          Mame                               -        -
```

Brown out.

|  | Got My Mojo Working | - | - |
|  | Secret Agent Man | - | - |
|  | Monday, Monday | - | - |

June 14, 1966 - New York

Snooky Young, Joe Newman, Ernie Royal, Richard Williams (tp); Phil Woods, Jerome Richardson, Bob Ashton, Jack Agee, Jerry Dodgion (reeds); Donald Corrado, Willie Buff (FrH); Don Butterfield (tuba); Jimmy Smith (org); Kenny Burrell, Billy Butler, Billy Suyker, Barry Galbraith (g); Bob Crenshaw (b-cl); Richard Davis (b); Grady Tate (d); Bobby Rosengarden (perc); Buddy Lucas (hca); Oliver Nelson (arr,cond).

| 100438 | I'm Your Hoochie Koochie Man | Verve V(6)8667, V(6)8721 |  |
| 110439 | One Mint Julep | - | - |
| 100440 | Ain't That Just Like a Woman | - | - |
| 100441 | Boom Boom | - | - |
| 100442 | Blues and the Abstract Truth | - | - |

July, 1966 - New York

similar personnel.

| 100657 | TNT | Verve V(6)8667 |
| 100662 | I'm Your Hoochie Koochie Man Pt. 1 | Verve VK 10426 |
| 100663 | I'm Your Hoochie Koochie Man Pt. 2 | - |

September, 1966 - New York

similar personnel.

| 101130 | Jimmy and the Duck | Verve V(6)8652 |
| 101131 | Meal Time | - |

September 21, 1966 - New York

JIMMY SMITH-WES MONTGOMERY: Jimmy Maxwell, Joe Newman, Ernie Roayl (tp); Clark Terry (tp,flhn); Jimmy Cleveland, Richard Hixson, Quincy Jones, Melba Liston (tb); Jerry Dodgion (as,cl,fl); Jerome Richardson (fl,cl); Phil Woods (cl,as); Bob Ashton (ts,fl,cl); Danny Bank (bars,b-cl,fl); Jimmy Smith (org); Wes Montgomery (g); Richard Davis (b); Grady Tate (d); Ray Baretto (perc); Oliver Nelson (arr,cond).

| 101192 | 13 (Death March) | Verve V(6)8678 |
| 101193 | Milestones | Verve V(6)8766 |

September 23, 1966 - New York

Tony Studd (b-tb) replaces Hixson; Baretto out.

| 101191 | Down By the Riverside | Verve V(6)8678 |
|--------|----------------------|----------------|
| 101194 | Night Train | - |

date unknown.

(prob) Gerald Wilson, Snooky Young, Hobard Dotson, J. Kelly, J. Anderson (tp); Melba Liston, Robert Sanchez Huerta, Isaac Livingston, B. Bledsoe (tb); Floyd Turnham, L. Trommel, Vernon Salter, E. Davis, M. Simon (saxes); Jimmy Bunn (p); B. Sexton (g); H. Rudd (b); Henry Green (d).

| Yenta | Excelsior 149 |
|-------|---------------|
| Come Sunday | - |
| Love Me a Long Long Time | Excelsior 150 |
| I Don't Know What That Is | - |
| Groovin' High | Excelsior 159 |
| I've Got a Right to Sing the Blues | - |
| You Better Change Your Way of Lovin' | Excelsior 160 |
| Skip the Gutter | - |
| Ain't It a Drag | Excelsior 161 |
| I'll String Along With You | - |

See Collective Section for Additional Recordings

## LUTCHER, NELLIE (piano)

April 10, 1947 - Los Angeles

NELLIE LUTCHER AND HER RHYTHM: Nellie Lutcher (p,vo); Ulysses Livingston (g); Billy Hadnot (b); Lee Young (d).

| 1823 | The One I Love | Capitol 10108 |
|------|----------------|---------------|
| 1824 | Hurry On Down | Capitol 40002,1604,H/T232, Cap(E)CL13013, LC6506, Music for Pleasure MFP 1038 |
| 1825 | The Lady's In Love With You | Capitol 4002, H/T232, Cap(E)13049,LC6506, Music For Pleasure MFP 1038 |
| 1826 | You Better Watch Yourself, Bub | Capitol 40042,(E)CL13053 |

April 30, 1947 - Los Angeles

Nappy Lamare (g) replaces Livingston.

| | | |
|---|---|---|
| 1876 | Sleepy Lagoon | Capitol 9004 |
| 1877 | My Mother's Eyes | Capitol 40042, H/T232, (E)CL13070, LC6506, Music for Pleasure MFP 1038 |
| 1878 | He's a Real Gone Guy | Capitol 40017, H/T232, (E)CL13053, LC6506, Music for Pleasure MFP 1038 |
| 1879 | Let Me Love you Tonight | Capitol 40017, H/T232, (E)CL13053, LC6506, Music for Pleasure MFP 1038 |

**August 19, 1947 - Los Angeles**

NELLIE LUTCHER AND HER RHYTHM: Nellie Lutcher (p,vo); Ulysses Livingston (g); Billy Hadnott (b).

| | | |
|---|---|---|
| 2176 | Pig Latin Song | Capitol 15032, (E)CL13049 |
| 2177 | Do You or Don't You Love Me | Capitol 40063, H/T232, (E)LC506, Music for Pleasure MFP 1038 |
| 2178 | Chi-Chi-Chicago | Capitol 10108 |
| 2179 | Lovable | Capitol 1026,(E)CL13366 |
| 2180 | Fine and Mellow | Capitol 57-70026,(E)CL13234 |
| 2181 | There's Another Mule in Your Stall | Capitol 10109, (E)CL13254 |
| 2182 | I Thought About You | Capitol 15112 |
| 2183 | Kinda Blue and Low | Capitol 1026 |

**August 26, 1947 - Los Angeles**

Nellie Lutcher (p,vo); Irving Ashby (b); Billy Hadnott (b); Sidney Catlett (d).

| | | |
|---|---|---|
| 2199 | Reaching for the Moon | Capitol 10109 |
| 2200 | The Song is Ended | Capitol 40063, 1728, (E)CL13026 |
| 2201 | So Nice to See You Baby | Capitol T232, Music for Pleasure MFP 1038 |
| 2207 | Lake Charles Boogie | Capitol 10110,15148,(E)CL13234 |

**December 27-29, 1947 - Chicago**

Nellie Lutcher (p,vo); Hurley Ramey (g); Charles "Truck" Parham (b); Alvin Burroughs (d).

| | | |
|---|---|---|
| 3034 | Fine Brown Frame | Capitol 15032,H/T232,(E)CL15053, LC6506, Music for PleasureMFP1038 |
| 3035 | Humoresque | Capitol 1728 |
| 3036 | Imagine You Having Eyes For Me | Capitol 15112 |
| 3037 | Alexander's Ragtime Band | Capitol 15180,T232,(E)CL13087, Music for Pleasure MFP1038 |
| 3039 | Wish I Was in Walla Walla | Capitol 15279,(E)CL13070 |
| 3041 | A Maid's Prayer | Capitol 15279 |

| | | |
|---|---|---|
| 3042 | Ditto From Me to You | Capitol 57-70001 |
| 3046 | Lutcher's Leap | Capitol 57-70044 |
| 3047 | Say a Little Prayer For Me | Capitol 15352 |
| 3048 | Cool Water | Capitol 15148,(E)CL13018 |
| 3049 | A Chicken Ain't Nothin' But a Bird | Capitol 57-70001 |
| 3050 | Princess Poo-Loo-Ly | Capitol 57-70026,(E)CL13274 |
| 3051 | He Sends Me | Capitol 15064,(E)CL13087 |
| 3052 | My Little Boy | Capitol 15180,T232,(E)CL13018, Music for Pleasure MFP1038 |
| 3053 | My New Papa Got to Have Everything | Capitol 15352 |
| 4000 | Come and Get it Honey | Capitol 15064,H/T232,(E)CL13049, CL6506,Music for Pleasure MFP1038 |
| 4001 | Little Sally Walker | Capitol 798 |
| 4002 | To Be Forgotten | Capitol 1217 |

February 4, 1949 - Los Angeles

NELLIE LUTCHER AND HER RHYTHM: Nellie Lutcher (p,vo); Ulysses Livingston (g); Benny Booker (b); Lee Young (d).

| | | |
|---|---|---|
| 3949 | That Will Just About Knock Me Out | Capitol 1217,(E)CL13502 |
| 3950 | Glad Rag Doll | Capitol 57-70044,(E)CL13254 |
| 3952 | Only You | Capitol 798 |

April 27, 1949 - Los Angeles

Nellie Lutcher (p,vo); John Collins (g); Benny Booker (b); Early Hyde (d).

| | | |
|---|---|---|
| 3774 | Kiss Me Sweet | Capitol 57-70009,(E)CL13223 |
| 3775 | Baby, Please Stop and Think About Me | - |

January 4, 1950 - Los Angeles

Stanley Morgan (g) replaces Collins.

| | | |
|---|---|---|
| 5361 | That's a Plenty | Capitol 878,T232,(E)CL13274, Music for Pleasure MFP1038 |
| 5363 | I'll Never Get Tired | Capitol 878 |
| 7058 | Pa's Not Home - Ma Upstairs | Capitol 1420,(E)CL13509 |
| 7059 | I Really Couldn't Love You | - - |

c. February, 1952 - Los Angeles

Nellie Lutcher (p,vo) acc. by HAROLD MOONEY'S ORCHESTRA: personnel unknown.

| 9639 | That's How it Goes | Capitol 2038 |
| 9641 | Keepin' Out of Mischief Now | - |

December 1, 1952 - New York City

Nellie Lutcher (p,vo); Jimmy Canady, Sal Salvatore (g); George Duvivier (b); Marty Wilson (d).

| C048580 | How Many More | Okeh 6935,Epic LN1108, Philips |
| | | (E)BBE12045,(G)B12012H |
| C048581 | Muchly Verily | Okeh 6935,Epic LN1108,   -, |
| | | (G)B12012H |
| | Blues for Bill Bailey | Epic 9005,            - |

August 25, 1953 - Los Angeles

Harry Edison (tp); Marshall Royal (as); Nellie Lutcher (p,vo); Ulysses Livingston (g); Lee Young (d).

| RHC010589 | Whee Baby | Epic 9005,LN1108,Philips(E)BBE12045 |
| RHC010590 | Taking a Chance on Love | Okeh 7030,  - |
| RC010591 | The St. Louis Blues | -        -        - |

March 15, 1956 - Los Angeles

Nellie Lutcher (p,vo) acc. by Lloyd Ulyate, Dick Nash, Milt Bernhart, Murray McEahern (tb); Buddy Collette (fl,as); Red Norvo (vib); Ulysses Livingston (g); Red Mitchell (b); Bill Richmond (d).

| | Blue Skies | Liberty LRP3014,Sunset SUM1124, |
| | | SUS5124, London (E) HA-U2036 |
| | Three Little Words | Liberty LRP3014,Sunset SUM1124, |
| | | SUS5124, London (E)HA-U2036 |
| | You Made Me Love You | Liberty LRP3014,Sunset SUM1124, |
| | | SUS5124, London (E)HA-U2036 |

April 12, 1956 - Los Angeles

Nellie Lutcher (p,vo) acc. by Buddy Childers, Bob Fowler, Frank Beach (tp); Lloyd Ulyate, Dick Nash, Sy Zentner, Murray McEahern (tb); Ryland Weston (bars,bass-sax); Howard Roberts, Ulysses LIvingston (g); Mike Rubin (b); Bill Richmond (d).

| | My Heart Sings | Liberty LRP3014,SunsetSUM1124, |
| | | SUS5124,London(E)HA-U2036 |
| | Rose Coloured Glasses | Liberty LRP3014,SunsetSUM1124, |
| | | SUS5124,London(E)HA-U2036 |
| | Ole Buttermilk Sky | Liberty LRP3014, London(E) |
| | | HA-U2036 |
| | Have You Ever Been Lonely | Liberty LRP3014,SunsetSUM1124, |
| | | SUS5124,London(E)HA-U2036 |

April, 1957 - Los Angeles

    details unknown.

| | | |
|---|---|---|
| IM1268 | Hurry On Down | Imperial 5436 |
| IM1273 | I Never Get Tired | - |

January, 1963 - Los Angeles

| | |
|---|---|
| Heart of a Clown | Melic 4131 |
| Reaching for the Moon | - |

details unknown.

| | |
|---|---|
| I Want to Be Near You | Capitol 1789 |
| The Birth of the Blues | - |
| What a Difference a Day Made | Capitol 1978 |
| The Heart of a Clown | - |

## McDONALD, JOYCE (piano)

February 15, 1949 - Chicago

DOC EVANS' DIXIELAND FIVE: Doc Evans (c); Don Thompson (tb); Johnny McDonald (cl,ts); Joyce McDonald (p); Doc Cernardo (d); Willie Sutton (b).

| | | |
|---|---|---|
| AFRS491 | High Society | Art Floral 102 |
| AFRS492 | Shim-Me-Sha-Wabble | Art Floral 104 |
| AFRS493 | Georgia Cakewalk | Art Floral 101, Tempo MT2066 |
| AFRS494 | Ballin' the Jack | Art Floral 103, - |
| AFRS495 | Stru Miss Lizzie | Art Floral 104, -,TR486 |
| AFRS496 | Basin Street Blues | Art Floral 103, - - |
| AFRS497 | That Eccentric Rag | Art Floral 102, Tempo TR488 |
| AFRS498 | When the Saints Go Marcing In | Art Floral 101, - |

## McFARLAND, ELAINE (piano)

September 6, 1961 - Chicago

LITTLE BROTHER MONTGOMERY AND HIS FRIENDS: Ted Butterman (c); Bob Gordon (cl); Bob Shriver (ts); Little Brother Montgomery (p,vo); Mike McKendrick (bj); Elaine McFarland (p,vo).

| | | |
|---|---|---|
| 243 | Saturday Night Function | Riverside RLP390 |
| 344 | Satellite Blues | - |
| 344-1 | New Satellite Blues | Riverside RLP403 |

| 346 | Cooter Crawl | Riverside RLP390 |
| 353 | Something Keeps On Worryin' Me | Riverside RLP389 |


## McFARLAND, LORETTA (harp)

August 27, 1934 - New York City

TED LEWIS AND HIS BAND: Ted Lewis (cl,dir); Bob Clitherow, Muggsy Spanier, Carl Agee (tp); Sam Blank, Nat Lobovsky (tb); Harold Diamond, Al Padova, Ben Glassman, Moe Dale (cl,as,ts); Sol Klein, Sam Shapiro (vn); Jack Aaronson or Vic Artese (p); Loretta McFarland (h); Jimmy Moore (b); Rudy van Gelder (d).

| 38349-A-C | Jazznocracy | Decca 107, Br 01966 |
| 38440-A-B | White Heat | -      - |


October 1, 1934 - New York City

same personnel. Ted Lewis (vo).

| 38764-A | Pop Goes Your Heart | Decca 239, Br RL-208 |


## McLAWLER, SARAH (organ)

1950 - Chicago

Sarah McLawler (org,vo).

| UB50-690 | My Whole Life Through | Premium/Chess 857 |
| UB50-708 | It's the Truth So Help Me | - |


March, 1953 - New York

Sarah McLawler (org,vo) acc. by u (ts,g,b,d).

| 84190 | Your Fool Again | Br 84018 |
| 84191 | I'm Tired Cryin' Over You | Br 84009 |
| 84193 | Foolin' Myself | - |
| 84197 | Blues for Rex | Br 84018 |


August, 1953 - New York

Sarah McLawler (org,vo) acc by Richard Otto (vn); u (b,d).

| 85052 | You're Gone | Br 84026 |
| 85053 | Yesterdays | Br 84024 |
| 85054 | Body & Soul | - |
| 85055 | Somehow | Br 84026 |

May 26, 1956 - Chicago

Richard Otto (vn); Sarah McLawler (org,vo); Lefty Bates (g); Quinn
Wilson (b); John Cooper (d).

| 56-473 | Molly and Me | Vee Jay 239 |
|---|---|---|
| 56-477 | Flamingo | Vee Jay 199 |
| 56-685 | What's New | Vee Jay 239 |

March 14, 1957 - Chicago

Thomas Hunter (d) replaces Cooper.

| 57-644 | Stella by Starlight | Vee Jay LP1003 |
|---|---|---|

March 15, 1957 - Chicago

same personnel.

| 57-645 | Babe in the Woods | Vee Jay LP1003 |
|---|---|---|
| 57-646 | Laura | - |
| 57-649 | Love for Sale | - |
| 57-650 | Temptation | - |

October 24, 1958 - Chicago

Richard Otto (vn); Sarah McLawler (org,vo); L.D. Young (g); Isaac Holt
(d).

| 58-1011 | Robin's Nest | Vee Jay LP1006 |
|---|---|---|
| 58-1012 | Lullaby of Birdland | - |
| 58-1014 | When the Lilacs Bloom Again | - |
| 58-1015 | Midnight Sun | - |

October 26, 1958 - Chicago

same personnel.

| 58-1016 | Love Walked In | Vee Jay LP1006 |
|---|---|---|
| 58-1017 | Slow Boat to China | - |
| 58-1018 | A Foggy Day | - |
| 58-1019 | My Reverie | - |
| 58-1020 | The High and the Mighty | - |
| 58-1022 | Canadian Sunset | - |
| 58-1023 | Rainbow Over the River | - |
| 58-1024 | Caravan | - |

September 13, 1960 - Chicago

Richard Otto (vn); Sarah McLawler (org,vo); Dino Walton (g); Robert
Brooks (d).

| 60-1597 | Drum's Boogie | Vee Jay LP1030 |
|---|---|---|
| 60-1598 | Get It | - |

Walton out.

| 60-1602 | The Midnight Sun Will<br>Never Set | - |
|---|---|---|
| 60-1604 | Well, Love is Here to Stay | - |
| 60-1608 | September Song | - |
| 60-1609 | Swingin The Bow | - |
| 60-1610 | Man With a Horn | - |
| 60-1611 | I Could Write a Book | - |
| 60-1613 | I Gotta Have You | - |
| 60-1614 | Take the A Train | - |

## McLEOD, ALICE (COLTRANE)
### (piano,organ,vibes,harp)

1963 - New York City

TERRY GIBBS SEXTET: Al Epstein (Young) (ts,cga); Terry Gibbs (vib); Alice McLeod (p); Jimmy Raney (g); William Wood (b); Al Belding (d).

| | | |
|---|---|---|
| Joshua | Time 52105 | |
| John Henry | - | |
| When Johnny Comes Marching Home | - | |
| Michael | - | |
| Polly Wolly Doodle All the Day | - | |
| Tom Dooley | - | |
| Greensleeves | - | |
| Boll Weevil | - | |
| Down By the Riverside | - | |
| Sam Hall | - | |

January 11, 1963 - New York City

Sam Kutcher (tb); Ray Musiker (cl); Terry Gibbs (vib,marimba); Alice McLeod Coltrane, Alan Logan (p); Herman Wright (b); Bobby Pike, Sol Gaye (d).

| 22686 | Papirossen | Mercury MG20812, SR 60812 | |
|---|---|---|---|
| 22687 | Shaine Une Zees | - | - |
| 22688 | My Yiddishe Momme | - | - |
| 22690 | And the Angels Sing | - | - |

March 11, 1963 - New York City

same personnel.

| 22824 | S and S | Mercury MG20812, SR 60812 | |
|---|---|---|---|
| 22825 | Kazochock | - | - |
| 22826 | Bei Mir Bist Du Schoen | - | - |

| 22827 | Nyah Shore | - | - |
| 22829 | Veiloch | - | - |

February 2, 1966 - San Francisco

JOHN COLTRANE SEXTET:  John Coltrane (ts,b-cl); Pharoah Sanders (ts,fl,pic); Alice Coltrane (p); Jimmy Garrison (b); Ray Appleton (d,perc).

| Manifestation | Imperial AS9223-2,CRC AU4950 |
| Reverend King | CRC AU4950 |
| Peace on Earth | Imperial AS9225 |
| Leo | - |

* Note:  this recording was later overdubbed by Ms. Coltrane (org,vib) and bass parts were substituted by Charlie Haden.

May 28, 1966 - Village Vanguard - New York City

JOHN COLTRANE QUINTET:  John Coltrane (ts); Pharoah Sanders (fl,ts); Alice Coltrane (p); Jimmy Garrison (b); Ray Appleton (d); Emanual Rahim (perc).

| My Favorite Things | Imperial AS9124 |
| Naima | - |

July 11, 1966 - "Sankei Hall" - Tokyo

JOHN COLTRANE QUINTET:  John Coltrane (sop,ts); Pharoah Sanders (ts); Alice Coltrane (p); Jimmy Garrison (b); Ray Appleton (d); Hisato Aikura (announcer).

| Afro-Blue | Imperial (Jap)YB 8508/09/10 |
| Peace on Earth | - |
| Bass Introduction | - |
| Crescent | - |
| Leo | - |

July 22, 1966 - "Koseinenkin Hall" - Tokyo

same personnel.

| Meditation/Leo | Imperial A9246, AS9266 |
| Peace on Earth | - | - |
| My Favorite Things | - | - |

February 15, 1967 - Englewood Cliffs, New Jersey

JOHN COLTRANE QUINTET:  John Coltrane (ts); Alice Coltrane (p); Jimmy Garrison (b); Ray Appleton (d).

To Be                Imperial AS9120
Offering            -,AS9253-3

March 7, 1967 - Englewood Cliffs, New Jersey

  same personnel.

Number One           Imperial IA9360
Ogunde Varer        Imperial AS9120, AS9223-2

Spring, 1967 - Englewood Cliffs, New Jersey

  same personnel.

Expression            Imperial AS9120, AS9278-2

1968 - New York

ROLAND KIRK AND HIS ORCHESTRA - EXPANSIONS: Richard Williams (tp); Dick Griffin (tb); Benny Powell (b-tb); Roland Kirk (ts,manzello,stritch,fl, siren, celeste, African thumb piano & various other small instruments); David Jones (bassoon); Pepper Adams (bars); Alice Coltrane (h); Ron Burton (p); Vernon Martin (b); Jimmy Hopps (d); Sonny Brown, Warren Smith (perc); Joe Texidor (sound coloring). Mixed by Roland Kirk.

Kirkquest               Atlantic SD1518
Kingus Mingus             -
Celestialness             -
A Doom of Beauty Re-incarnated    -
Frisco Vibrations          -
Classical Jazzical         -
Ellington Psalms           -
Haynes' Brain's Sayin's      -
What's Next - Overture        -

January 29, 1968 - New York

Pharoah Sanders (ts,fl,b-cl); Alice McLeod Coltrane (p); Jimmy Garrison (b); Ben Riley (d).

Ohnedaruth             Imperial A(S)9156

Jimmy Garrison (b-vn); Ben Riley (perc) added.

Lord Help Me to Be      Imperial A(S)9148
The Sun                 -

* Note: John Coltrane (speaking) recorded at an earlier date and dubbed in.

June 6, 1968 - New York

Alice Coltrane (p); Jimmy Garrison (b); Rashied Ali (d).

        Gospel Trane               Imperial A(S)9156
        I Want to See You           -

Alice Coltrane (h); others the same.

        Lovely Sky Boat          Imperial A(S)9156
        Oceanic Beloved          -
        Atomic Peace              -

* Note: John Coltrane (speaking) recorded at an earlier date and
  dubbed in.


## McMANUS, SUE (banjo)

July 1, 1956 - London

Desmond "Dizzy" Burton (tp); Roy Williams (tb); Tom Alker (cl); Jim
Smith (p); Sue McManus (bj); Eric Batty (b); Ron Peach (d).

| 870 | Sing On | Esquire 10-488,32-015 |
|-----|---------|----------------------|
| 871 | Last Mile of the Way | Esquire EP-123,   - |
| 872 | Keep Cool | Esquire 10-488,   - |
| 874 | Nobody Knows the Way.. | Esquire EP-123 |
| 875 | Madame Beccasine | -       - |
| 876 | One Sweet Letter From You | Esquire 10-493 |

January 27, 1957 - London

same personnel.

| 912 | Cindy, Ooh Cindy | Esquire 10-506,32-022 |
|-----|------------------|----------------------|
| 913 | College Rag | -       - |
| 914 | East Coast Trot | - |
| 915 | Deep Bayou Blues | - |
| 916 | Marching Through Georgia | - |
| 917 | Sarais Marias | - |


## McMURRAY, RUTH (trombone)

See Collective Section.

## McPARTLAND, MARIAN (piano)

March, 1949 - Chicago

Jimmy McPartland (c); Harry Lepp (tb); Jack O'Connel (cl,as); Marian
McPartland (p); Ben Carlton (b); Mousie Alexander (d).

| | | |
|---|---|---|
| UR8815 | Royal Garden Blues | Unison MCP501, Prest 302, Harmony (E)A1007 |
| UR8816 | Daughter of Sister Kate | Unison MCP501, -, Harmony(E)A1002 |
| UR8817 | Singin' the Blues | Unison MCP501, -, Harmony (E)A1007 |
| UR8818 | In a Mist | Unison MCP500, -, Harmony (E)A1002 |

December 21, 1950 - Chicago

JIMMY McPARTLAND ALL STARS: Jimmy McPartland (c); Vic Dickenson (tb); Gene Sedric (cl,ts); Marian McPartland (p); Max Wayne (b); Bob Varney (d).

| | | |
|---|---|---|
| MCP600 | Use Your Imagination | Prestige 304 |
| MCP602 | Come Back Sweet Papa | Prestige 303 |
| MCP603 | Manhattan | Prestige 303 |
| MCP605 | Davenport Blues | Prestige 304 |

March 15, 1951 - New York City

Marian McPartland (p); Reinhardt Elster (h); Barnard Greenhouse (cello); Bob Carter (b); Don Lamon (d).

| | | |
|---|---|---|
| F132 | Flamingo | Federal 12029, KingLP540, Par(E)GEP8677,Swing 371 |
| F133 | It's Delovely | Federal 12029, KingLP540, Par(E)GEP8677,Swing 371 |
| F134 | Liebestraum No.3 | Federal 1203, King LP540, Par(E)GEP8677 |
| F135 | Four Brothers | Federal 1203, -, Par(E)GEP8677 |

June 2, 1951 - New York City

Marian McPartland (p); Eddie Safranski (b); Don Lamon (d).

| | | |
|---|---|---|
| | Gypsy in My Soul | Savoy XP8104,MG15019,MG12004 |
| | Strike Up the Band | - - - |
| | These Foolish Things | Savoy XP8105, - - |
| | Get Happy | - - - |

June 4, 1951 - New York City

same personnel.

| | | |
|---|---|---|
| | Yesterdays | Savoy XP8034,MG15027,MG12016 |
| | Love for Sale | - - - |
| | All the Things You Are | Savoy XP8108, - - |
| | Moonlight in Vermont | - - |

April 21, 1952 - New York City

Marian McPartland (p); Max Wayne (b); Mel Zelnick (d).

| SMM4185 | It Might As Well Be Spring | Savoy 856,XP8106,MG15027,MG12016 |
| SMM4186 | The Gypsy in My Soul | - | - | - | - |
| SMM4187 | Strike Up the Band | Savoy 846, | - | - | - |
| SMM4188 | Our Love Is Here to Stay | - | - | - | - |

1952 - New York City

Mousie Alexander (d) replaces Zelnick.

| SMM4282 | Lullaby of Birdland | Savoy 879,XP8033,MG15021,MG12005 |
| SMM4283 | Nightingale Sang in Berkeley Square | - | - | - | - |
| SM4284 | Paper Moon | Savoy 880,XP8034, - | - |
| SMM4285 | Moonlight in Vermont | - | - | - | - |
| | Hallelujah | Savoy XP8034,MG15021,MG12005 |
| | Limehouse Blues | Savoy XP8033, | - | - |

1952-1953 - New York City

Marian McPartland (p); Bob Carter (b); Joe Morello (d).

| | A Fine Romance | Savoy XP8032,MG15022,MG12005 |
| | All My Life | - | - | - |
| | What Is This Thing Called Love | - | - | - |
| | Willow Weep for Me | - | - | - |
| | Lullaby in Rhythm | Savoy XP108, | - | - |
| | There'll Never Be Another You | - | - | - |

1953 - New York City

Vinnie Burke (b) replaces Carter.

| | Manhattan | Savoy MG15032,MG12004 |
| | A Foggy Day | - | - |
| | Four Brothers | - | - |
| | Aunt Hagar's Blues | - | - |
| | The Lady is a Tramp | - | - |
| | I've Got the World on a String | - | - |
| | Once in a While | - |
| | Squeeze Me | Savoy MG12043 |
| | Liza | - |
| | September Song | Savoy MG12097 |
| | Embraceable You | - |
| | Laura | - |

May 24, 1953 - Port Monmouth

HOT LIPS PAGE WITH MARIAN McPARTLAND TRIO: Hot Lips Page (tp,vo); Marian McPartland (p); Walter Yost (b); Mousie Alexander (d).

| 84618 | St. Louis Blues | BrBL54002,Coral LVA9017,CV80017, LP96011 |
|---|---|---|
| 84619 | Sunny Side of the Street | BrBl54002 |
| 84620 | St. James Infirmary | -    -|
| 84621 | The Sheik of Araby | - |

September, 1954 - New York City

Marian McPartland (p); Bill Crow (b); Joe Morello (d).

| 20398 | Lush Life | Capitol EAP3-574,T574,(E)LCT6017 |
|---|---|---|
| 20399 | Moon Song | Capitol EAP1-574,  -    - |
| 20400 | Love You Mad | Capitol EAP3-574,  -    - |
| 20401 | How Long Has This Been Going On | Capitol EAP2-574,  -    - |
| 20402 | Tickle-Toe | Capitol EAP1-574,  -    - |
| 20415 | Ja-Da | Capitol EAP2-574,  -    - |
| 20416 | Skylark | Capitol EAP1-574,  -    - |
|  | I Hear Music | -    -    - |

February, 1956 - New York City

JIMMY McPARTLAND QUINTET: Jimmy McPartland (tp); Marian McPartland (p); Jimmy Raney (g); Trigger Alpert (b); Joe Morello (d).

| Stardust | Grand Award 33-334, Audition 33-5943, Top Rank (E) SKP2037 |
|---|---|
| Rockin' Chair | Grand Award 33-334, Top Rank (E)SKP2037 |
| Georgia on My Mind | -    - |
| New Orleans | -    - |
| Blue Orchids | -, Audition 33-5943 |

1956 - New York City

JIMMY McPARTLAND'S CHICAGO ROMPERS: Jimmy McPartland (tp); Vic Dickenson (tb); Bill Stegmeyer (cl); Bud Freeman (ts); Marian McPartland (p); Milt Hinton (b); Joe Morello (d).

| My Gal Sue | Jazztone J1034,J1227,J1241 |
|---|---|
| McBlues | -    -    - |
| Sweet Adeline | -    -    - |
| Shine on Harvest Moon | -    -    - |
| Slic Vic | -    -    - |
| Stranger in the Night | -    -, J1282 |
| Donna | -    - |
| Decidedly Blues | Jazztone J735,   -, J1241 |
| Swanee River | -    - |
| Kerry Dancers | -    - |
| Baby-O | -    - |
| Blues for David | Jazztone J1034 |

July 25-30, 1956 - New York City

| 21187 | Stompin' at the Savoy | Capitol T785, T1034 |
| 21188 | There'll Be Other Times | - |
| 21189 | The Baron | - |
| 21190 | Bohemia After Dark | - |
| 21192 | This Love of Mine | - |
| 21193 | The Things We Did Last Summer | - |
| 21195 | Carioca | - |
| 21196 | Dream a Little Dream of Me | - |
| 21197 | Hallelujah | - |
| 21198 | Symphony | - |

1957 - New York City

Helen Merrill (vo) with HAROLD MOONEY'S ORCHESTRA:  u (strings, harp);
Marian McPartland (p); Milt Hinton (b) and others.

| Soft as Spring | EmArcy MG36107 |
| Black is the Color | - |
| The Things We Did Last Summer | - |
| Lazy Afternoon | - |
| After You | - |
| If I Go | - |
| If I Forget You | - |
| If Love Were All | - |
| Easy Come Easy Go | - |
| I'll Be Around | - |
| Blue Guitar | Mercury 71166 |
| Listen | - |

January 2, 1958 - New York City

JIMMY McPARTLAND'S ALL STARS:  Jimmy McPartland, Dick Cary, Max
Kaminsky, Johnny Glasel (tp); Frank Rehak, Lou McGarity, Cutty Cutshall
(tb); William Stanley (tuba); Sol Yaged (cl); Bud Freeman (ts); Marian
McPartland (p); Sal Salvador (g); Bill Crow (b); George Wettling (d).

| C059279 | Till There Was You | Epic LN3463, BN506 |
| C059280 | It's You | - | - |
| C059281 | Iowa Stubborn | - | - |

January 3, 1958 - New York City

Jimmy McPartland, Dick Cary, Max Kaminsky, Johnny Glasel (tp); Al
Gusikoff, Lou McGarity, Cutty Cutshall (tb); William Stanley (tuba); Pee
Wee Russell, Bob Wilber (cl); Bud Freeman (ts); Marian McPartland (p);
Eddie Condon (g); Bill Crow (b); George Wettling (d).

| C060300 | Gary, Indiana | Epic LN3463, BN506 |
| C060301 | The Wells Fargo Wagon | - | - |

September 24, 1958 - London House - Chicago

  Marian McPartland (p); William Britto (b); Joe Cusatis (d).

| | |
|---|---|
| Play Fiddle Play | Argo LP(S)640 |
| Easy Blues | - |
| Like Someone in Love | - |
| Tune for Tex | - |
| Signature Blues | - |
| Blues Intro | - |
| Steeplechase | - |
| Give Me the Simple Life | - |
| Sweet and Lovely | - |
| So Many Things | - |

c. 1960

  Jimmy McPartland (listed as "Manhattan Red") (tp); Urbie Green (tb); Andy Fitzgerald (cl); Dick Cary (c-mel sax); Marian McPartland (p); Ben Tucker (b); Mousie Alexander (d); u (fl).

| | |
|---|---|
| Mystery March | Design DLP144 |
| Sentimental Journey | - |
| I-M-4-U | - |
| Mr. Lucky | - |
| Peter Gunn | - |
| Londonderry Air | - |
| Thanks for Dropping In | - |
| Bat Masterson | - |

September 28, 1960 - Chicago

  Marian McPartland (p); Ben Tucker (b); Jack Hanna (d).

| | | |
|---|---|---|
| It's Love | Time LP52013, | LPS2013 |
| Cool | - | - |
| Lonely Town | - | - |
| Somewhere | - | - |
| Ya Got Me | - | - |
| A Little Bit in Love | - | - |
| Lucky To Be Me | - | - |
| Some Other Time | - | - |
| I Feel Pretty | - | - |
| Maria | - | - |

1963

  Marian McPartland (p); Ben Tucker (b); Dave Bailey (d); Ralph Dorsey (cga); Bob Crowden (tamb).

| | |
|---|---|
| Love for Sale | Time LP52073 |
| With You in Mind | - |
| Stranger in a Dream | - |
| Sweet and Lovely | - |

```
        Coming Home, Baby              -
        Tell Me                        -
        Green Dolphin Street           -
        Baby, You Should Know It       -
```

January, 1964 - New York

Phil Bodner (fl); Leo Krusczek, Harry Lookofsky (vn); Harold Coletta
(viola); Alan Shulman (cello); Marian McPartland (p); Barry Galbraith
(g); George Duvivier (b); Dave Bailey (d); Frank Hunter (arr,cond).

```
        Warmin' Up              Sesac N6501/2
        Y'Know What I Mean             -
        Don't Panic                    -
        The Magpie                     -
        Ida                            -
        Lonely                         -
        A Secret                       -
        Easy Like                      -
        Hawk Talk                      -
        Deep River                     -
        So Little Time                 -
        Blues for Indian Jim           -
```

May 29, 1966 - Manassas Jazz Festival - Virginia

Maxine Sullivan (vo) acc. by Tom Gwaltney (cl); Marian McPartland (p);
Keter Betts (b); Jake Hanna (d).

```
        Surprise Party          Jazzology J-17
        If I Had a Ribbon Bow          -
        I Thought About You            -
        Loch Lamond                    -
        I'm Coming Virginia            -
```

June, 1968 - New York

```
        Thanks                  Dot DLP25907
        Moon Song                      -
        My Old Flame                   -
        Je Vous Adore                  -
        Beware My Heart                -
        Cocktails for Two              -
        Sing You Sinners               -
        The Day You Come               -
        Little White Gardenia          -
        Just One More Chance           -
        In the Middle of a Kiss        -
        I'm in Love with the           -
          Honorable Mr. So and So
```

*  Note:  The  remainder  of  Ms.  McPartland's  extensive  recording  career
   lies outside the temporal scope of this discography.

MARCUS, MARIE (piano)

January 16, 1951 - Miami

Preacher Rollo (Rollo Laylan) and the Five Saints: Tommy Justice (c);
Jerry Gorman (tb,b); Tony Parenti (cl); Marie Marcus (p); Rollo Laylan
(d,vo); Ralph Rischer (vo).

| 51S65004 | When the Saints Go Marching In | Lion L70073, MGM 10950 |
| 51S6005 | Do You Know What it Means To Miss New Orleans | - |

April 18, 1951 - Miami

Tommy Justice (c); Jerry Gorman (tb); Ernie Goodson (cl); Marie Marcus
(p); Al Mattucci (b); Rolly Laylan (d).

| 51S6051 | Tiger Rag | MGM 30445, Lion L70073 |
| 51S6052 | Sweet Georgia Brown | MGM 30447 |
| 51S6053 | Ballin' the Jack | MGM 30446 |
| 51S6054 | Darktown Strutters Ball | MGM 30448, - |

April 19, 1951 - Miami

Tommy Parenti (cl) replaces Goodson.

| 51S6048 | Original Dixieland One-Step | MGM 30448 |
| 51S6049 | Ostrich Walk | MGM 30446, Lion L70073 |
| 51S6050 | High Society | MGM 30447, - |
| 51S6055 | Trombonium | MGM 30445 |

June, 1951 - Miami

Mattucci out.  Marie Marcus (vo) added.

| 51S6042 | South | MGM 11047 |
| 51S6043 | What You're Going to Do When the Rent Comes Around (vMM) | - |

April 19, 1952

Tommy Justice (c); Jerry Gorman (tb); Tony Parenti (cl); Marie Marcus
(p); Al Mattucci (b); Rollo Laylan (d); Dolly Cooper (vo).

| Sweet Georgia Brown (vDC) | Florida 1001 |
| Heart of My Heart (vDC) | - |

May 28, 1952 - Miami

Mary Peck (vo) added.

| ART-7 | Waiting (vMP) | Florida 2003 |
| ART-8 | Dee Doo | - |
| ART-9 | The Old Spinning Wheel | Florida 2002 |
| ART-10 | Rose of the Rio Grande | - |

May 30, 1952 - Miami

| Sensation | MGM 30690, EP606 |
| Pralines | MGM 30692, - |
| Bill Bailey | MGM 30693, - |
| Jelly Roll | MGM 30691, EP644 |

June 2, 1952 - Miami

same personnel.

| Who Walks In When I Walk Out | MGM 30693, EP644 |
| Blue Danube in Dixieland | MGM 30690, - |
| Save Your Confederate Money, Boys, the South Will Rise Again | MGM 30692, - |
| Blues My Naughtie Sweetie Gave to Me | MGM 30691, EP606 |

March 19, 1953 - Miami

same personnel.

| Tin Roof Blues | MGM E3259, EP682 |
| Fidgety Feet | - EP566 |
| Panama | - |
| At the Jazz Band Ball | - |
| Memphis Blues | MGM EPX217 |
| A Good Man is Hard to Find | MGM E3259 |
| Wolverine Blues | - |
| That Da Da Strain | - |

March, 1953 - Miami

same personnel.

| Riverboat Shuffle | MGM X1050 |
| Livery Stable Blues | - |
| Muskrat Ramble | - |
| Royal Garden Blues | MGM E220 |
| Chimes Blues | MGM X1050 |
| Tap Room Blues | MGM E220 |
| Jazz Me Blues | - |

```
            That's A Plenty            -
            That Da Da Strain          -
```

**1955 - Miami**

Tommy Justice (c); Jerry Gorman (tb); Ernie Goodson (cl); Bobby Rosen
(p); Al Mattucci (b); Rollo Laylan (d).

```
            I've Found a New Baby      MGM E3403, Lion 70073
            Struttin' With Some        -            -
              Barbecue
            I'm Gonna Sit Right Down    -
            South Rampart Street        -
              Parade
            Who's Sorry Now             -
            Big Butter and Egg Man      -
            Carolina in the Morning     -
            Indiana                     -
```

**1955 - Miami**

Bobby Krapf (c) replaces Justice; Paul Yelvington (cl) replaces Goodson.

```
            Black and Blue             MGM E3403
            Rose Room                   -
            How Come You Do Me Like     -
              You Do
            Sister Kate                 -
```


## MARSHALL, BESSIE (piano)

Henryette Davis (vo) accc. by Clarence Black (vn); Bessie Marshall (p).

```
9755-A    Another Sweet Daddy      Okeh 8371
9756-A    My Man Jean              Okeh 8395
9756-A    Jazzophobia Blues        Okeh 8371
9758-A    Mail Box Blues           Okeh 8395
```


## MARTIN, MADONNA (piano)

**1949 - Los Angeles**

Madonna Martin (p,vo) with unknown accompaniment.

```
SE13      We've Come a Long Way     Selective 117
            Together
SE14      Rattlesnakin' Papa        Selective 104
SE15      Madonna's Boogie          Selective 117
SE16      I'm the Same Old Fool     Selective 104
```

## MINNIE, MEMPHIS (guitar)

June 18, 1929 - New York

Joe McCoy (g,vo) acc. by Memphis Minnie (g).

| 148707-2 | I Want That | Columbia 14542-D |
|----------|-------------|------------------|
| 148708-3 | That Will Be Alright | Columbia 14439-D, Yazoo 1021, Origin 21 |
| 148711-1 | When the Levee Breaks | Columbia 14542-D |

June, 1930 - Chicago

Joe McCoy (vo) acc. by Memphis Minnie (g).

| C-5819 | Botherin' That Thing | Hist Rec 32, Paltram 101 |
|--------|----------------------|--------------------------|
| C-5820-A | I'm Wild About My Stuff | - , Vo 1570, - |
| C-5864-A | Cherry Ball Blues | Vocalion 1535, - |
| C-5865-A | Botherin' That Thing | Vocalion 1570 |
| C-6012 | Pile Drivin' Blues | Vocalion 1612, Yazoo 1002 |

June 1, 1930 - Chicago

Memphis Minnie (g,vo) acc. by Joe McCoy (g,vo)

| C-5817 | I Don't Want No Woman | Vocalion 1535 |
|--------|------------------------|---------------|
| C-5822 | Memphis Minnie Jities Blues | Vocalion 1588, Blue CL13 |
| C-5823 | Good Girl Blues | Vocalion 1603 |
| C-5831 | Plymouth Rock Blues | Vocalion 1631, - |

July, 1930 - Chicago

| C-5866-A | Bumble Bee No. 2 | Vocalion 1588 |
|----------|-------------------|---------------|
| C-5867 | Georgia Skin Blues | Vocalion 1603 |
| C-5894 | New Dirty Dozen | Vocalion 1618, Blues CL13 |
| C-5895 | New Bumble Bee | - |

July 14, 1930 - Chicago

| C-6009 | Frankie Jean | Vocalion 1588, Blues CL13 |
|--------|--------------|---------------------------|
| C-6010-A | I'm Talking 'Bout You #2 | Vocalion 1556 |
| C-6011 | She Put Me Outdoors | Vocalion 1612 - |
| C-6013 | I Called You This Morning | Vocalion 1631 - |

August, 1930 - Chicago

Memphis Minnie (g,vo) acc. by JED DAVENPORT JUG BAND: u (hca,g,jug).

| C-6082 | Grandpa and Grandma Blues | Vocalion 1601, Origin LP4 |
|--------|----------------------------|---------------------------|
| C-6083 | Garage Fire Blues | - - |

October 9, 1930 - Chicago

Memphis Minnie (g,vo) acc. by Kansas Joe (McCoy) (g).

| C-6433-A | Dirt Double Blues | Vocalion 1638 |
|----------|-------------------|---------------|
| C-6434-A | You Dirty Mistreatin' | - |

June 18, 1929 - New York

same personnel.

| 148709-2 | Goin' Back to Texas | Columbia 14455-D, Paltram 101 |
|----------|---------------------|-------------------------------|
| 148710-2 | Frisco Town | - |
| 148711-2 | Where the Levee Breaks | Philips BBL7369, Blues CL1 |
| 148712-2 | Bumble Bee | Columbia 14542-D, Blues CL7 |

February, 1930 - Memphis, Tennessee

Memphis Minnie (g,vo) acc. by Joe McCoy (g).

| MEM-730 | I'm Gonna Bake My Biscuits | Vocalion 1512 |
|---------|----------------------------|---------------|
| MEM-731 | Mr. Tango Blues | - |
| MEM-732 | She Wouldn't Give Me None | Vocalion 1576 |
| MEM-765 | What Fault You Find of Me | Vocalion 1500 |
| MEM-766 | What Fault You Find of Me Part 2. | - |
| MEM-772-A | I'm Talking About You | Vocalion 1476, His Rec 2, Paltram 101 |
| MEM-773 | Bumble Bee | Vocalion 1476,   -,Paltram 101 |
| MEM-790 | Can I Do It for You Pt. 1 | Vocalion 1523 |
| MEM-791 | Can I Do It for You Pt. 2 | - |

May 26, 1930 - Chicago

McCOY & JOHNSON: Memphis Minnie and Joe Johnson (vocal duet) acc. by (prob) Memphis Minnie (g).

| 59992 | I'm Goin' Back Home | Victor 23352, Paltram 101 |
|-------|---------------------|---------------------------|

May 29, 1930 - Chicago

same personnel.

| 62538 | I Never Told a Lie | Victor 23313 |
|-------|--------------------|--------------|
| 62539 | Don't Want No Woman | - |
| 62540 | Georgia Skin Bules | Victor 23352, Paltram 101 |

October 15,1930 - Chicago

Memphis Minnie (g,vo) acc. by Joe McCoy (g,vo).

```
C-6442      What's the Matter With       Vocalion 1550, Blues CL13
              the Mill
C-6443      North Memphis Blues                -             -
```

January 30, 1931 - Chicago

```
VO-111      I Don't Want That Junk       Vocalion 1678, Yazoo 1008
              Outa You
VO-112      Crazy Cryin' Blues                     -, Blues CL13
VO-113-A    Tricks Ain't Working No      Vocalion 1653
              More
```

February, 1931 - Chicago

same personnel.

```
VO-118      Don't Bother It              Vocalion 1673
VO-119      Today's Today Blues          -
            Preacher's Blues             Blues CL1
```

March, 1931 - Chicago

same personnel.

```
VO-135-A    Lay My Money Down            Vocalion 1665
              (If You Run Around)
VO-136-A    Hard Down Lie                -
VO-137-A    Somebody's Got to Help You   Vocalion 1653
```

April or May, 1931 - Chicago

Memphis Minnie, Kansas Joe McCoy (guitar duets).

```
VO-151-A    Soo Cow Soo                  Vocalion 1658, Yazoo 1021
VO-152-A    After Awhile Blues                     -, Blues CL13
```

February 3, 1932 - New York

same personnel.

```
11213-A     Fishin' Blues                Vocalion 1711
11214-A     Jailhouse Trouble Blues      Vocalion 1718
11215-A     Outdoor Blues                Vocalion 1698
11216-A     Where is My Good Man              - or LP6
11217-A     You Stole My Cake            Vocalion 1688
11218-A     Kind Treatment Blues         Vocalion 1711
```

February 4, 1932 - New York

same personnel.

11231-A     Socket Blues            Vocalion 1688

Georgia Tom Dorsey (p,vo); Tampa Red (g,vo) added.

11232-A     Minnie Minnie Bumble Bee     Vocalion 1682

October 27, 1933 - New York

Dorsey and Red out.

| | | |
|---|---|---|
| 152534-B | By Butcher Man | Okeh 8948 |
| 152535-B | Too Late | - |
| 152537-B | Ain't No Use Trying<br>To Tell On Me | Yazoo 1021 |

March 24, 1934 - New York

| | | |
|---|---|---|
| CP-1069-1 | Stinging Snake Blues | Vocalion 02711, Paltram 101 |
| CP-1070-1 | Drunken Barrell House Blues | -, Yazoo 1021 |

August 24, 1934 - 1934 - New York

| | | |
|---|---|---|
| C-9380 | You Got to Move Pt. 1 | Decca 7038, Blues CL1 |
| C-9381 | Keep It To Yourself | Decca 7037, Mamlish 3801 |

August 31, 1934 - New York

Memphis Minnie (g,vo) acc. by Kansas Joe McCoy (g).

C-9389     You Got to Move Pt. 2       Decca 7038

September 3, 1934 - New York

same personnel.

| | | |
|---|---|---|
| C-9382 | Chickasaw Train Blues | Decca 7019, A/H AH72, Paltram 101 |
| C-9383 | Banana Man Blues | -   , Yazoo 1043 |

September 6, 1934

same personnel.

| | | |
|---|---|---|
| C-9402 | Hole in the Wall | Decca 7023 |
| C-9407 | Give It To Me in My Hand | -, Sunflower 1403,<br>Flyright 108 |

September 10, 1934 - New York

| | | |
|---|---|---|
| C-9426-A | Squat It | Decca 7146, Roots 329 |
| C-9427 | Moaning the Blues | Decca 7037 |

January 10, 1935 - New York

Memphis Minnie (g,vo) acc. by (prob) Charlie Segar (p).

| C-9641-A | Dirty Mother For You | Decca 7048, Paltram 101 |
| C-9642-A | Sylvester and His Male Blues | Decca 7084 |
| C-9643-A | When You're Asleep | - |
| C-9644-A | You Can't Give It Away | Decca 7048, - |


January 15, 1935 - Chicago

"Gospel Minnie" (g,vo) acc. by u (p).

| C-9657 | Let Me Ride | Decca 7063 |
| C-9658 | When the Saints Go Marching In | - |


May 27, 1935 - Chicago

| 90016 | Jockey Man Blues | Decca 7125 |
| 90017 | Weary Woman's Blues | - |
| 90018 | Reachin' Pete | Decca 7107, Mamlish 3803 |
| 90019 | Down in New Orleans | - |


July 27, 1935 - Chicago

Texas Tessie (prob. Memphis Minnie) (g,vo) and u (g).

| 91420 | You Wrecked My Happy Home | Bluebird B6429 |
| 91421 | I'm Waiting for You | Bluebird B6141 |
| 91422 | Keep on Goin' | - |


August 22, 1935 - Chicago

Memphis Minnie (g,vo) acc. by Black Bob (p); Bill Settles (b).

| C-1098-B | Ball and Chain Blues | Vocalion 03541 |
| C-1099-B | He's in the Old Ring (Doin' the Same Old Thing) | Vocalion 03046, Paltram 101, CBS 63288 |
| C-1100-A | Joe Louis Strut (spoken) | Vocalion 03046, Blues CL1 |


October 31, 1935 - Chicago

Memphis Minnie (g,vo) acc. by (prob) Black Bob (p); Casey Bill Weldon (steel-g); Bill Settles (b).

| 96226 | After the Sun Goes Down Pt. 2 | Bluebird B6187 |
| 96227 | Hustlin' Woman Blues | Bluebird B6202,Sunflower 1403, Flyright 108 |

| 96228 | Swing My Pork Chops | Bluebird B6199 |
| 96229 | Doctor, Doctor Blues | - |

December 16, 1935 - Chicago

Memphis Minnie (g,vo) acc. by (prob) Black Bob (p); u (b).

| C-1183-2 | Biting Bug Blues | Vocalion 03144 |
| C-1184-1-3 | Minnie's Lonesome Song | Vocalion 03187 |
| C-1185-1 | You Ain't Done Nothing To Me | Vocalion 03144 |
| C-1186-2 | Ain't Nobody Home But Me | Vocalion 03187 |

February 18, 1936 - Chicago

Black Bob out.

| C-1263-1 | Ice Man | Vocalion 3222, Sunflower 1403, Flyright 108 |
| C-1264-1 | Hoodoo Lady | Vocalion 3222, -,Flyright 108 |
| C-1265-1 | My Strange Man | Vocalion 3285, - - |
| C-1266-1 | I'm a Gamblin' Woman | Vocalion 3258, - - |

May 27, 1936 - Chicago

Memphis Minnie (g,vo) acc. by u (b, woodblocks, p).

| C-1384-1 | I'm a Bad Luck Woman | Vocalion 3541 |
| C-1385 | Caught Me Wrong Again | Vocalion 3258 |
| C-1386 | Black Cat Blues | Vocalion 3581, Paltram 101 |
| C-1387 | Good Morning | Vocalion 3436 |
| C-1388 | Man You Won't Give Me No Money | Vocalion 3474, Blues CL1 |
| C-1389 | If You See My Rooster | Vocalion 3285, Sunflower 403, Flyright 108 |

November 12, 1936 - Chicago

| C-1667-2 | I Don't Want You No More | Vocalion 3436, Sunflower 1403, Flyright 108 |
| C-1558-1 | Out in the Cold | Vocalion 3398 |
| C-1669-2 | Dragging My Heart Around | - |
| C-1670-1 | Moonshine | Vocalion 3894, Blues CL1 |
| C-1671-1 | It's Hard to be Misunderstood | Vocalion 3474, - |
| C-1172-2 | Haunted House | Vocalion 3581 |

June 9, 1937 - Chicago

Memphis Minnie (g,vo) acc. by (prob) Alfred Bell (tp); Blind John Davis (p); Fred Williams (d).

| | | |
|---|---|---|
| C-1925 | Hot Stuff | Vocalion 3651 |
| C-1926-1 | Living the Best I Can | Vocalion 3768 |
| C-1927-1 | You Can't Make Me | Vocalion 3697 |
| C-1928-1 | No Need You Doggin' Me | - |
| C-1929 | Look What You Got | Vocalion 3612 |

June 17, 1937 - Chicago

Bell out.

| | | |
|---|---|---|
| C-1936-1 | My Baby Don't Want Me No More | Vocalion 3894, Blues CL1 |
| C-1937-2 | Wants Cake When I'm Hungry | Vocalion 3768 |
| C-1938 | Down in the Alley | Vocalion 3612 |

June 22, 1937 - Chicago

same personnel.

| | | |
|---|---|---|
| C-1942 | Keep on Sailing | Vocalion 3651 |

December 15, 1937 - Chicago

Memphis Minnie (g,vo) acc. by (prob) Arnett Nelson (cl); Blind John Davis (p); u (b).

| | | |
|---|---|---|
| C-2053-1 | Walking and Crying Blues | Vocalion 3966 |

Nelson out.

| | | |
|---|---|---|
| C-2056-1 | New Caught Me Wrong Again | Vocalion 3966 |

June 23, 1938 - Chicago

Memphis Minnie (g,vo) acc. by u (p, b); Charlie McCoy (mand).

| | | |
|---|---|---|
| C-2280-1 | I Hate to See the Sun Go Down | Vocalion 4356 |
| C-2281-1 | Long As I Can See You Smile | Vocalion 4506 |
| C-2282-1 | Has Anyone Seen My Man | Vocalion 4250 |
| C-2283-1 | Good Biscuits | Vocalion 4295 |
| C-2284-1 | I've Been Treated Wrong | Vocalion 4250 |
| C-2285-1 | Keep on Walking | Vocalion 4356 |
| C-2286-1 | Keep on Eating | Vocalion 4295 |
| C-2287-1 | I'd Rather See Him Dead | Vocalion 4506 |

February 3, 1939 - Chicago

Memphis Minnie (g,vo) acc. by Little Son Joe (Ernest Lawler) (g); u (d).

| | | |
|---|---|---|
| C-2452-1 | Black Widow Stinger | Vocalion 4694 |
| C-2453-1 | Good Spoonin' | - |
| C-2456-1 | Poor and Wandering Woman Blues | Vocalion 5004 |
| C-2457-1 | Bad Outside Friends | Vocalion 4797, Sunflower 1403, Flyright 108 |

**February 6, 1939 - Chicago**

same personnel.

| | | |
|---|---|---|
| C-2454-1 | Worried Baby Blues | Vocalion 4898 |
| C-2455-1 | Call the Fire Wagon | Vocalion 4858 |
| C-2458-1 | Low Down Man Blues | Vocalion 4797, Sunflower 1403, Flyright 108 |
| C-2459-1 | Don't Lead My Baby Wrong | Vocalion 4898 |
| C-2460-1 | Keep Your Big Mouth Closed | Vocalion 4858 |

**May 21, 1941 - Chicago**

Memphis Minnie (g,vo) acc. by Little Son Joe (g); u (b).

| | | |
|---|---|---|
| C-3764-1 | In My Girlish Days | Okeh 6410, Blues CL1 |
| | Me and My Chauffer Blues | Okeh 6288      -, CBS 66218 |
| | Down by the Riverside | Conqueror 9936 |
| | I Got to Make a Change Blues | Conqueror 9935 |

**December 12, 1941 - Chicago**

| | | |
|---|---|---|
| C-4090-1 | I'm Not a Bad Girl | Okeh 6624, Matchbox 182 |
| C-4091-1 | You Got to Get Out of There | Columbia 30134, Sunflower 1403, Flyright 108 |
| C-4093-1 | Looking the World Over | Okeh 6707,                -, Flyright 109 |
| C-4094-1 | It Was You Baby | Okeh 6624, Matchbox 182 |

**December 19, 1944 - Chiago**

Memphis Minnie (g,vo); Little Sam Joe (Ernest Lawler) (g); u (d).

| | | |
|---|---|---|
| C4303 | When You Love Me | Okeh 06733, Columbia 37455, 30022, Sunflower 1400, Flyright 109 |
| C4304 | Please Set a Date | Columbia 36895,3003,-, Flyright 109 |
| C4305 | Mean Mistreatin' Blues | Columbia 37295, 30015 |
| C4306 | Love Come and Go | Okeh 06733, Co 37455, 3002, Sunflower 1400, Flyright 109 |
| C4307 | True Love | Columbia 36895, 3003, Sunflower 1400,        - |

February 26, 1946 - Chicago

  u (b) instead of (d).

CC041504    I'm So Glad               Columbia 37295, 30015


September 20, 1946 - Chicago

  u (b,d).

| CC04506 | Killer Diller Blues | Columbia 37977, 30102 |
| CC04628 | Hold Me Blues | - |
| CC04629 | Fish Man Blues | Columbia 37579, 30054 |
| CC04630 | Western Union | Columbia 30134 |
| CC04632 | Lean Meat Won't Fry | Columbia 37579 |


December 27, 1947 - Chicago

Blind Joe Davis (p); Memphis Minnie (g,vo); Little Son Joe (g); u (b,d).

| CC04968 | Three Times Seven Blues | Columbia 38099, 30111 |
| CC04971 | Shout the Boogie | -      - |


February, 1949 - Chicago

| CC05043 | Tears On My Pillow | Columbia 30176 |
| CC05044 | Sweet Man | - |
| CC04047 | Tonight I Smile With You | Columbia 30146, Sunflower 1400, Flyright 109 |
| CC05048 | Jump Little Rabbit | Columbia 30146, - , Flyright 109 |


1949 - Chicago

Memphis Minnie (g,vo) acc. by unkown others.

| | Night Watchman Blues | Biograph 12035 |
| | Down Home Girl | - |


1952 - Chicago

MEMPHIS MINNIE AND HER COMBO: Sunnland Slim (p); Memphis Minnie (g,vo); u (b,d).

| 2606 | Kissing in the Dark | J.O.B. 1101, B.D. 101/102 |
| 2607 | World of Trouble | -       - |


July 11, 1952 - Chicago

Memphis Minnie (g,vo) acc. by Joe Hill Lewis (hca,g); u (p,d).

| 1024 | Broken Heart | Checker 777 |
| 1027 | Me and My Chauffeur Blues | - |

c. 1962

Memphis Minnie (g,vo).

| | Hoodoo Lady | Heritage RE-103 |
| | Ice Cream | - |
| | Good Morning Blues | - |
| | Don't Want You No More | - |

date unknown.

Memphis Minnie (g,vo) acc. by Little Son Joe (g).

| WC-3166-A | Lonesome Shack Blues | Okeh 5728, Blues CL1 |
| WC-3167-A | Nothing in Rambling | Okeh 5670, - |
| WC-3168-A | Boy Friend Blues | - - |
| WC-3169-A | Finger Print Blues | Okeh 5811, Sunflower 1403, Flyright 108 |
| WC-3170-A | It's Hard to Please My Man | Okeh 5728, Blues CL1 |
| WC-3171-A | Ma Rainey | Okeh 5811, Sunflower 1408, Flyright 108 |

date unknown.

Memphis Minnie (g,vo) acc. by Little Son Joe (g); u (b).

| | Black Rat Swing | Flyright 109, Blues CL1, Sunflower 1400 |
| C-3768-1 | Pig Meat on the Line | Cq 9935, Flyright 108, Sunflower 1403 |
| C-3769-1 | My Gauge is Going Up | Okeh 6410, Flyright 109, Sunflower 1403 |
| C-3770-1 | This is Your Last Chance Blues | Okeh 6505, Flyright 108, Sunflower 1403 |
| C-3771-1 | Can't Afford to Lose My Man | Okeh 6288, Flyright 109, Sunflower 1403 |

Note:  see Dixon & Goodman, Blues Discography, for other blues recordings.


## MILLER, BETTY (piano)

date unknown.

BETTY MILLER TRIO: Betty Miller (p); u (b,d).

| | Mambo Inn | Foremost FML1001 |
| | Spring is Here | - |

```
        Speak Low                    -
        The Lady is a Tramp          -
        Out of Nowhere               -
        Let's Fall in Love           -
        Jet                          -
        Undecided                    -
        The Breeze and I             -
```

## MINGHETTI, LISA (violin)

January 19, 1961 - Los Angeles

Ben Webster (ts); Armand Kaproff, Cecil Figeloki (viola); Alfred Lust-garten, Lisa Minghetti (vn); Don Trenner (p); Don Bagley (b); Frank Capp (d); Johnny Richards (arr,cond).

```
        Accent on Youth        Reprise R2001
        But Beautiful                -
        It Was So Beautiful          -
        With Every Breath I Take     -
        It's Easy to Remember        -
```

## MOSIER, GLADYS (piano)

See Collective Section.

## MURPHY, ROSE (piano)

c. 1948

Rose Murphy (p,vo) acc. by u (b,d).

```
D8VB3453   Girls Were Made to Take    HMV (E) B9901
             Care of Boys
D8VB3454   Busy Line                        -
D8VB3456   Gee, I Wonder What the     HMV (E) B9884
             Trouble Can Be
D8VB3458   Rosetta                          -
```

late 1962 - New York

Charlie Shavers (tp); Seldon Powell (ts,fl); Rose Murphy (p,vo); Ernie Hayes (org); Carl Lynch (g); Slam Stewart (b); Specs Powell or Jo Jones (d); Julio Colozzo (cga).

```
        If You Were Mine       United Artists (E) ULP1046
        When Johnny Comes Marching     -
          Home
        You Made Me Love You             -
        I've Got Everything              -
```

All of Me                        -
You Go to My Head                -
Seasons Greeting                 -
Oh Lady Be Good                  -
Little Lamb                      -
Kids                             -
What Good                        -
Put On a Happy Face              -


## NEGRI, RUTH (harp)

See Collective Section.


## NEWELL, LAURA (harp)

May 24, 1940 - New York City

NEW FRIENDS OF RHYTHM: Buster Bailey (cl); Sylvan Shulman, Harry Glickman (vn); Louis Kievman (viola); Alan Shulman (cello); Tony Colucci (g); Laura Newell (h); Harry Patent (b).

| 050856-1 | Heavy Traffic on Canal Street | Victor 26647, 27927 |
| 050857-1 | Coo, Dinny, Coo | Victor 27412,   - |
| 050858-2 | The Mood in Question | Victor 26647 |

June 26, 1941

Henry Allen (tp); J.C. Higginbotham (tb); Artie Shaw (cl); Benny Carter (as); Sonny White (p); Jimmy Shirley (g); Billy Taylor (b); Shep Shepherd (d); Laura Newell (h); u (strings).

| 66147 | Love Me a Little | Victor 27509 |
| 66149 | Don't Take You Lover From Me | -, 20-1593 |

1946-1947 - New York City

Maxime Sullivan (vo) acc. by the NEW FRIENDS OF RHYTHM: Hank D'Amico (cl); Laura Newell (h); Tony Colucci (g); Harry Patent (b); u (strings).

| Mad About the Boy | International 210 |
| If I Had a Ribbon Bow | - |
| I Must Have That Man | International 211 |
| Lock Lamond | - |
| I Can't Get Started | International 213 |
| Jackie Boy | - |

See Collective Section for Additional Recordings

## NOEL, HATTIE (piano)

date unknown.

Hattie Noel (p,vo) with unknown accompaniment.

| | |
|---|---|
| Chattanooga | Blue 104 |
| Hot Nuts | - |
| Find Out What They Say | Blue 111 |
| If I Can't Sell It | - |
| Military Man | Blue 124 |
| Mama Like to Take Her Time | - |
| Thinkin' 'Bout My Baby | MGM 10275 |
| Put Some Glue on That Mule | - |
| Rockin' Jenny Jones | MGM 10355 |
| High Jivin' Papa | - |
| Grandma's Boogie | MGM 10752 |
| Evil Daddy Blues | - |

## NORRIS, CATHERINE (cello)

October 10, 1966 - New York

INTENTS & PURPOSES: THE JAZZ ARTISTRY OF BILL DIXON: Bill Dixon (tp,flhn); Jimmy Cheatham (b-tb); Robin Kenyatta (as); Byard Lancaster (as,b-cl); George Marge (EngH); Catherine Norris (cello); Jimmy Garrison, Reggie Workman (b); Robert Frank Pozar (d); Marc Levin (perc).

| | |
|---|---|
| Metamorphoses 1962-1966 | Victor LSP 3844, RCA(F)FXLI-7337 |

January 17, 1967 - New York

Bill Dixon (tp,flhn); Byard Lancaster (b-cl); Catherine Norris (cello); Jimmy Garrison (b); Robert Frank Pozar (d).

| | |
|---|---|
| Voices | Victor LSP 3844, RCA(F)FXLI-7337 |

## O'BRIEN, ELAINE (drums)

See Collective Section.

## ODETTA (guitar)

c. 1964

Odetta (g,vo) acc. by Bruce Lanhorne (g); Leslie Grinage (b).

| | |
|---|---|
| Troubled | Victor LPM 2923 |
| Katy Cruel | - |
| Anathea | - |

Sun's Comin' Up            -
Boy                        -
Looky Yonder               -
Froggy Went Acourtin'      -
Wayfarin' Stranger         -
Four Marys                 -
Paths of Victor            -
Sea Lion Woman             -
Deportee                   -


### O'HARA, BETTY (valve trombone)

December 28, 1968 - University Club - Pasadena, California

Ray Linn (tp); Dick Carey (peck horn,p); Moe Schneider (tb); Betty
O'Hara (v-tb); Matty Matlock (cl); Wayne Songer (as,bars); Jack Chaney
(ts); Stan Wrightsman (p); Nappy Lamare (g); Ira Westley, Ward Ervin
(b); Jack Spaling (d).

Blues My Naughty Sweetie    Blue Angel BAJC503
    Taught Me
Save It Pretty Mama                  -


### O'FLYNN, BRIDGET (drums)

See Collective Section.


### OSBORNE, MARY (guitar)

May 30, 1944 - Chicago

STUFF SMITH QUARTET: Stuff Smith (vn,vo); Jimmy Jones (p); Mary Osborne
(g); John Levy (b).

Blues in Mary's Flat         Selmer 7143
Blues in Stuff's Flat (vSS)        -
Sweet Lorraine               Selmer Y7144
I Got Rhythm                       -


January 17, 1945 - The Auditorium - New Orleans

ESQUIRE 2ND ANNUAL JAZZ CONCERT: Leon Prima (tp); Julian Lane (tb);
Irving Faxola (cl); Pete Lauderman, Frank Frederico, Mary Osborne
(g,vo); Bunny Franks (b); Charlie Drake (d).

Rose Room                    Saga(E)6924, FDC 1997
Embraceable You (vMO)              -

1946

MARY OSBORNE TRIO:  Sanford Gold (p); Mary Osborne (g); u (b).

| | | |
|---|---|---|
| The One I Love | Signature 15077 | |
| Mary's Guitar Boogie | - | |
| Oops My Lady | Signature 15087 | |
| Blues in Mary's Flat | - | |

February 27, 1946 - New York City

COLEMAN HAWKINS AND HIS 52ND STREET ALL STARS:  Charlie Shavers (tp);
Pete Brown (as); Coleman Hawkins (ts); Allen Eager (ts); Jimmy Jones
(p); Mary Osborne (g); Al McKibbon (b); Shelly Manne (d).

| | | |
|---|---|---|
| PD6VB1308 | Say It Isn't So | Victor 40-0131,LPV-501,HMV-B9605 |
| PD6VB1309 | Spotlite | -,LPV-544, HMV-DLP1055,  -, |
| | | RCA(E) RD7904 |

Shavers and Hawkins out.

| | | |
|---|---|---|
| PD6VB1311 | Allen's Alley | Victor 40-0133,LPV-519,HMV-B9639, |
| | | Victor LPM-2027, RCA(E)RD7909 |

March 18, 1946 - New York City

MERCER ELLINGTON OCTET WITH JACQUES BUTLER:  Jack Butler (tp,vo); Mercer
Ellington (tp); Lawrence Brown (tb); Al Sears (ts); Harry Carney (bars);
Leonard Feather (p); Mary Osborne (g); Bill Pemberton (b); Heyward
Jackson (d).

| | | |
|---|---|---|
| LGF1001 | She's Got the Blues for Sale | Aladdin 146 |
| LGF1002 | The Willies | Aladdin 145 |
| LGF1003 | Messy Bessie | Aladdin 146 |
| LGF1004 | Ditty A La Dizzy | Aladdin 145 |

April 16, 1946 - New York City

Ethel Waters (vo) acc. by J.C. HEARD'S ORCHESTRA:  George Treadwell
(tp); Dickie Harris (tb); Ray Perry (as,vn); Reggie Beane (p); Mary
Osborne (g); Al McKibbon (b); J.C. Heard (d).

| | | |
|---|---|---|
| 3525 | Taking a Chance on Love | Continental 1006,LP16008,RmgLP1025 |
| 3526 | Dinah | Continental 1007,  -  - |
| 3527 | Man Wanted | -  -  - |
| 3528 | You Took My Man | Continental 1008,  - |
| 3529 | Honey in a Hurry | Continental 1009 |
| 3530 | Cabin in the Sky | Continental 1006, -  - |
| 3531 | Am I Blue | Continental 1008, -  - |
| 3532 | I Shoulda Quit | Continental 1009 |

November 30, 1946 - New York City

WYNONIE HARRIS AND HIS ALL STARS:  Pat Jenkins, Joe Newman (tp); Tab
Smith (as); Allan Eager (ts); Larry Belton (bars); Bill Dogget, Leonard
Feather (p); Mary Osborne (g); Al McKibbon (b); Walter Jonson (d).

| | | |
|---|---|---|
| 75 | Mr. Blues Jumped a Rabbit | Aladdin 171 |
| 76 | Rugged Road | Aladdin 172 |
| 77 | Come Back Baby | - |
| 78 | Whiskey and Jelly Roll Blues | Aladdin 171 |

July, 1947 - New York City

same personnel.

| | | |
|---|---|---|
| A4025 | You Got to Get Yourself a Job Girl | Aladdin 208 |
| A4026 | Hard Ridin' Mama | - |
| A4027 | Big City Blues | Aladdin 196 |
| A4028 | Ghost of a Chance | - |
| A4077 | Battle of the Blues Pt. 1 | Aladdin 3036 |
| A4078 | Battle of the Blues Pt. 2 | - , Imperial LM84002 |

1947

MARY OSBORNE TRIO:  Hank Trueman (p); Mary Osborne (g,vo); Frenchy
Covette (b).

| | |
|---|---|
| Honey | Aladdin 530 |
| What Will I Tell My Heart | - |
| I Cover the Waterfront | Aladdin 3010 |
| You've Changed | - |

December, 1947

Jack Pleis (p); Mary Osborne (g,vo); Hy White (g); Burke Blake (b);
Cliff Leeman (d).

| | |
|---|---|
| Wonder Where's My Man Tonight | Decca 24308 |
| You're Gonna Get a Letter in the Morning | - |
| No Moon At All | Coral 60058 |
| Thank You Mother Nature | - |

September 13, 1956 - New York City

Charlie O'Kane (as,bars); Elliott Lawrence (p); Piano Red (p,vo); Mary
Osborne (g); Russ Saunders (b); Osie Johnson (d).

| | | |
|---|---|---|
| G5JB7262 | You Wee Mine for Awhile | Groove G0169 |
| G5JB7265 | Woo-ee | - |

March 28-29, 1957 - New York City

TYREE GLENN AND HIS ORCHESTRA: Harold Baker (tp); Tyree Glenn (tb,vib);
Hank Jones (p); Mary Osborne (g); Tommy Potter (b); Jo Jones (d).

| | | | |
|---|---|---|---|
| After the Rain | Roulette R25009,Esq 32-061,WRCT430 | | |
| What Can I Tell My Heart | - | - | - |
| Tyree's Tune | - | - | - |
| Until the Real Thing Comes Along | - | - | - |
| I Thought About You | - | - | - |
| I Wanna Be Loved | - | - | - |
| Too Marvelous for Words | - | - | - |
| Sinbad the Sailor | - | - | - |
| Lonely Moment | - | - | - |
| Without a Song | - | - | - |
| How High the Moon | - | - | - |

1958 - Roundhouse - New York City

Baker out.

| | | |
|---|---|---|
| Teach Me Tonight | Roulette 8002, (S)R25050 | |
| There Will Never Be Another You | - | - |
| All of Me | Roulette 8008, | - |
| Sweet and Lovely | - | - |
| Sunday | | - |
| Just a Wearyin' For You | | - |
| Royal Garden Blues | | - |
| Wonder Why | | - |
| Dear Old Southland | | - |
| Them There Eyese | | - |
| Marcheta | | - |
| Limehouse Blues | | - |

1958-1959 - New York City

ELLIOTT LAWRENCE AND HIS ORCHESTRA: Urbie Green (tb); Andy Fitzgerald
(cl); Hal McKusick (as); Zoot Sims (ts); Al Howard, Stan Webb (woodwinds); Elliott Lawrence (p); Mary Osborne (g); Russ Saunders, Buddy
Jones (b); Don Lamond, Sol Gerbin (d).

| | | |
|---|---|---|
| Azure Mist | Top Rank RM(S)304,Surrey SS1019 | |
| Design for Autumn | - | - |
| Enchanted Flute | - | - |
| Gypsy Love Song | - | - |
| Night Serenade | - | - |
| None But the Lonely Heart | - | - |
| Shrine of St. Cecilia | - | - |
| So Little Time | - | - |
| Trombolero | - | - |
| Wind on Velvet | - | - |
| You're Here Again | - | - |
| Macuma | - | - |

|                    |                  |
|--------------------|------------------|
| Blue Catch         | Sesac NA 51-52   |
| Groovin' in the A.M. | -              |
| In a Cloud of Dust | -                |
| We'll Shine Tonight | -               |

## 1959 - New York City

Tommy Flanagan (p,celeste); Mary Osborne (g); Danny Barker (g); Tommy Potter (b); Jo Jones (d).

|                              |                |
|------------------------------|----------------|
| I Love Paris                 | Warwick W2004  |
| I Let a Song Go Out of My Heart | -           |
| How High the Moon            | -              |
| When Your Lover Has Gone     | -              |
| Mary's Goodbye Blues         | -              |
| I Found a New Baby           | -              |
| Sophisticated Lady           | -              |
| I'm Beginning to See the Light | -            |
| Body and Soul                | -              |
| I Surrender Dear             | -              |
| These Foolish Things         | -              |

## November 28, 1960 - New York City

ELLIOTT LAWRENCE AND HIS ORCHESTRA: Urbie Green (tb); Andy Fitzgerald (cl); Hal McKusick (as); Zoot Sims (ts); Al Howard, Stan Webb (woodwinds); Elliott Lawrence (p); Mary Osborne (g); Russ Saunders, Buddy Jones (b); Don Lamond, Sol Gerbin (d).

|          |                            |                    |
|----------|----------------------------|--------------------|
| L3PB5229 | I Ain't Down Yet           | Camden CAL(S) 667  |
| L3PB5230 | Belly Up the Bar Boys      | -                  |
| L3PB5231 | I've Already Started In     | -                  |
| L3PB5232 | I'll Never Say No          | -                  |
| L3PB5233 | Beautiful People of Denver | -                  |
| L3PB5234 | Are You Sure               | -                  |
| L3PB5235 | Bon Jour                   | -                  |
| L3PB5235 | Bon Jour                   | -                  |
| L3PB5236 | Chick a Pen                | -                  |
| L3PB5237 | Keep a' Hoppin'            | -                  |
| L3PB5238 | Dolce Far Niente           | -                  |

## c. 1961 - London House - Chicago

Harold Baker (tp); Tyree Glenn (tb,vib); Hank Jones (p); Mary Osborne (g); Milt Hinton (b); Jo Jones (d).

|                      |                     |
|----------------------|---------------------|
| Bye and Bye          | Roulette (S) R25138 |
| On the Alamo         | -                   |
| Lonesome Road        | -                   |
| Stomping at the Savoy | -                  |
| Some Other Spring    | -                   |
| Waycross Walk        | -                   |
| Mack the Knife       | -                   |

| | |
|---|---|
| 'Til There Was You | - |
| Avalon | - |
| Learn to Croon | - |
| Blue Lou | - |
| Indiana | - |

c. April, 1963 - New York City

LOUIS BELSON AND GENE KRUPA:  Joe Wilder, Joe Newman (tp); Tyree Glenn (tb); Phil Woods (as); Seldon Powell (ts); Dick Kyman (p); Mary Osborne (g); Milt Hinton (b); Louis Belson, Gene Krupa (d).

| | |
|---|---|
| The Three Drags | Roulette (S)R52098 |
| Paradiddle Song | - |
| Accent on Flamboyance | - |
| Rolls Ala Bossa Nova | - |
| The Mighty Two Alone Together | - |
| Rolls Ala Bossa Nova No. 2 | - |
| More Flams | - |
| Swingin' the Rudiments | - |
| Cue Sticks | - |
| Two in One | |

See Collective Section for Additional Recordings

## PALMER, GLADYS (piano)

August 6, 1935 - New York City

Gladys Palmer (p,vo) acc. by (prob) Eddie Farley (tp); Mike Riley (tb); Slats Long (cl); Arthur Ens (g); Goerge Yorke (b); Vic Engle (d).

| | | |
|---|---|---|
| 39819-A | I'm Livin' in a Great Big Way | Decca 7106, Br 02089 |
| 39820-A | In the Middle of a Kiss | -         - |
| 39821-A | Get Behind Me, Satan | Decca 7107 |

August 7, 1935 - New York City

same personnel.

| | | |
|---|---|---|
| 39825-A | Trees | Decca 7107 |

## PEACOCK, MARY (bass)

July 10, 1964 - New York City

ALBERT AYLER TRIO:  Albert Ayler (ts); Mary Peacock (b); Sonny Murray (d).

|                          |                |
|--------------------------|----------------|
| Ghosts (1st variation)   | ESP-Disk 1002  |
| The Wizard               | -              |
| Spirits                  | -              |
| Ghosts (2nd variation)   | -              |

September 9, 1964 - Copenhagen

Don Cherry (tp) added.

|                          |                   |
|--------------------------|-------------------|
| Ghosts (theme)           | Debut (D) DEB-144 |
| Children                 | -                 |
| Holy Spirit              | -                 |
| Ghosts (long version)    | -                 |
| Vibrations               | -                 |
| Mothers                  | -                 |

## PENNAK, EVELYN (tenor sax)

See Collective Section.

## PIERCE, MAE (guitar)

April 25, 1961 - New York City

King Curtis (as,ts,g,vo); Paul Griffin (p); Al Casey, Mae Pierce (g); Jimmy Lewis (b); Belton Evans (d); The Cookies (vocal group).

| 2989 | Trouble in Mind            | Tru-Sound 401, (S)15001 |
|------|----------------------------|-------------------------|
| 2990 | Bad Bad Whiskey            | -                       |
| 2991 | Don't Deceive Me           | -                       |
| 2992 | But That's All Right       | -                       |
| 2993 | I Have to Worry            | Tru-Sound 406,     -    |
| 2994 | Nobody Wants You When      | -                       |
|      | You're Down and Out        |                         |
| 2995 | Woke Up This Morning       | -                       |
| 2996 | Ain't Nobody's Business    | -                       |
| 2997 | Deep Fry                   | -                       |
| 2998 | Jivin' Time                | -            -          |

## PITTS, TRUDY (organ)

February 15, 1967 - New York

Trudy Pitts (org,vo); Pat Martino (g); Bill Caney (d); Garnell Johnson (cga).

|                          |                |
|--------------------------|----------------|
| It Was a Very Good Year  | Prestige PR7523 |
| Siete                    | -              |
| Fiddlin'                 | -              |
| Steppin' in Minor        | -              |

       Something Wonderful               -
       Music for Girl Watchers        -

**February 21, 1967 - New York**

same personnel.

       Spanish                    Prestige PR7523
       Night Song                 -
       Take Five                 Prestige 45-443

**September 21, 1967 - New York**

Trudy Pitts (org,vo); Pat Martino (g); Bill Carney (d).

       The House of the Rising     Prestige PR7538
         Sun (vTP)
       Eleanor Rigby (vTP)        -
       Count 9                  -
       Man and a Woman         -
       A Whiter Shade of Pale (vTP)  -
       These Blues of Mine (vTP)   -

**September 25, 1967 - New York**

same personnel.

       Organology               Prestige PR7538
       Just Us Two              -
       Teddy Makes Three       -
       What the World Needs Now   -

**December 20, 1967 - New York**

Trudy Pitts (org); Wilbert Longmire (g); Bill Carney (d).

       Bucket Full of Soul       Prestige 45-461, PR7560
       Renaissance               -

**February 8, 1968 - New York**

same personnel.

       My Waltz                Prestige PR7560
       Come Down               -
       Love for Sale            -
       Satin Doll               -
       Please Keep My Dream      -
       The Shadow of Your Smile   -
       Lil' Darlin'             -

May 24, 1968 - Baron's - New York

  same personnel.

| | | |
|---|---|---|
| Never My Love | Prestige PR7583 | |
| Autumn Leaves | - | |
| W.T. Blues | - | |
| Trudy 'n Blues | - | |

## POLLARD, TERRY (piano, vibes)

January 10, 1955 - Los Angeles

  Don Fagerquist (tp); Terry Pollard (p); Howard Roberts (g); Herman
  Wright (b); Frank DiNito (d).

| | | |
|---|---|---|
| Freddi | Bethlehem BCP 1, | BCP 15 |
| Laura | - | - |
| Where or When | - | - |
| Autumn Serenade | - | - |
| The More I See You | - | - |
| Scrapple From the Apple | - | - |
| Almost Like Being in Love | - | - |
| Emaline | - | -,BCP 83 |

  See Collective Section for Additional Recordings

## POPE, MELBA (piano)

May, 1945 - Chicago

  Brother John Sellers (vo) acc. by the MELBA POPE TRIO: Melba Pope (p);
  Huey Long or Johnny Johns (g); Allan Lott (b).

| | | |
|---|---|---|
| | Shorty Came Out from Under My Bed | Southern 128 |
| | He Came All the Way Down Bye and Bye | Southern 132 |
| | | - |
| 75844 | When the Roll is Called | Decca 48144 |
| 75845 | I Started to Make Heaven My Home | - |
| UN23 | Mirror Blues | King 4114 |
| UN30 | Rocking Mama Blues | - |

1945-1946 - New York City

  Dossie "Georgia Boy" Terry (vo) acc. by MELBA POPE'S BLUE BOYS: Melba
  Pope (p); others unknown.

| | | |
|---|---|---|
| N15 | Furlough Blues | Chicago 117 |
| N16 | The O.P.A. Blues | - |

## PORTER, HELEN (drums)

March, 1931 - New York

EUBIE BLAKE AND HIS ORCHESTRA: Alfred Brown, Frank Belt, George Win-
field (tp); Calvin Jones (tb); Benjamin Whittet, Ralph Brown (cl,as);
Bob Robinson (ts,cl); Eubie Blake, George Rickson (p); Leroy Vanderveer
(bj); Frank Smith (tuba); Helen Porter (d); Dick Robertson (vo).

| 1234-4 | Please Don't Talk About Me When I'm Gone | Crown 3090 |
| 1239-1 | I'm No Account Anymore | - |
| 1240 | When You Lover Has Gone | Crown 3086 |
| 1241 | It Looks Like Love | Crown 3105 |

April, 1931 - New York

same personnel.

| 1295-1 | Two Little Blue Eyes | Crown 3111, Harrison LPG |
| 1296-2 | Nobody's Sweetheart | Crown 3130, - |
| 1297-1 | One More Time | Crown 3111, - |
| 1298-3-4 | St. Louis Blues | Crown 3130, - |

June 3, 1931 - New York

same personnel.

| 69683-1 | Thumpin' and Bumpin' | Victor 22737, Harrison LPG |
| 69684-1 | Little Girl | - - |
| 69685-2 | My Blue Days Blow Over | - - |

September, 1931 - New York

same personnel.

| 1476-3 | Blues in My Heart | Crown 3197, Harrison LPG |
| 1477-2,3 | Life is Just a Bowl of Cherries | Crown 3193 |
| 1478-2 | Sweet Georgia Brown | Crown 3197, - |
| 1479-1,2 | River Stay Away From My Door | Crown 3193 |

## POTTS, MARTHA (piano)

1946 - Los Angeles

MONTE EASTER AND HIS ORCHESTRA: Monte Easter (tp,vo); Earl Sims (as);
Hubert Allen (ts); Martha Potts (p); Addison Farmer (b); Charlie Blackwell (d); Judy Canova (vo).

| | |
|---|---|
| Ain't Cha Glad | Sterling 103 |
| Empty Bed Blues | - |
| Monte's Blues | Sterling 104 |
| She Knows What To Do | - |
| St. Louis Blues | Sterling 106 |
| Time for Jokin' | - |
| Evening Blues | Sterling 107 |
| I Need a Girl Like You | - |

## PUTMAN, JANET (harp)

March 14, 1955 - New York

MODERN JAZZ SOCIETY: Gunther Schuller (FrH); J.J. Johnson (tb); Jim Politis (fl); Manny Ziegler (bassoon); Tony Scott (cl); Stan Getz (ts); John Lewis (p); Percy Heath (b); Connie Kay (d); Janet Putman (h);

| | | |
|---|---|---|
| 5000-6 | The Queen's Fancy | Norgran MGN1040, MGV8131 |
| 5001-4 | Midsummer | - - |

Aaron Sacks (cl) replaces Scott; Lucky Thompson (ts) replaces Getz.

| | | |
|---|---|---|
| 5002 | Sun Dance | Norgran MGN1040, MGV8131 |
| 5003 | Django | - - |
| 5004 | Little David's Fugue | - - |

August 5, 1955 - New York City

Ella Fitzgerald (vo) acc. by TOOTS CAMARATA AND HIS ORCHESTRA: Jimmy Nottingham, Charlie Shavers, Dale McMickle (tp); Will Bradley, Frank Sarocco, Cutty Cutshall, Ward Silloway (tb); Al Howard, Hymie Schertzer (as); Al Kink, Hal Feldman (ts); Don Abney (p); Al Casementi (g); Eddie Safranski (b); Jimmy Crawford (d); Janet Putman (h); u (strings).

| | | |
|---|---|---|
| 88546 | My One and Only Love | Decca 29746,DL8156,DL8695, DX156(2), Br (E) 05584 |
| 88549 | The Tender Trap | Decca 29746, DX145(2) |

1956 - New York City

Beverly Kenney (vo) acc. by RALPH BURNS' ORCHESTRA: including Nick Travis (tp); Urbie Green (tb); Julius Watkins (FrH); Sam Marowitz (as); Janet Putman (h); Moe Welscher (p); Billy Bauer, Barry Galbraith (g); Milt Hinton (b); Don Lamond, Ted Sommer (d).

| | |
|---|---|
| Give Me the Simple Life | Roost RLP 2212 |
| Guess I'll Hang My Tears Out to Dry | - |
| The Trolley Song | - |
| Violets For Your Furs | - |
| This Can't Be Love | - |
| Scarlett Ribbons | - |
| If I Were a Bell | - |

                    Why Try to Change Me Now            -
                    Swingin' On a Star                  -
                    You Go To My Head                   -
                    It Ain't Necessarily So             -
                    You Make Me Feel So Young            -


June 12, 1956 - New York City

LES JAZZ MODES: Julius Watkins (FrH); Charlie Rouse (ts); Gildo Mahones
(p); Paul Chambers (b); Ron Jefferson (d); Janet Putman (h); Eileen
Gilbart (vo).

                    Idle Evening          Dawn DLP 1108
                    Strange Tale                  -
                    So Far                        -
                    Blue Modes                    -
                    Garden Delights               -
                    Town and Country              -
                    When the Blues Come On        -   , DLP 1123
                    You Are Too Beautiful         -
                    Two Songs                     -
                    Stallion              Jazztone J1245


September 9, 1956 - New York City

Lee Wiley (vo) acc. by RALPH BURNS' ORCHESTRA: Romeo Penque, Ray
Beckenstein (reeds); Janet Putman (h); u (strings); Moe Wechsler (p);
Barry Galbraith (g); Milt Hinton (b); Don Lamond (d).

G2JB7525   My Ideal               Victor LPM 1408
G2JB7526   Who Can I Turn To             -
G2JB7527   East of the Sun               -
G2JB7528   As Time Goes By               -


December 4, 1956 - New York City

Julius Watkins (FrH); Charlie Rouse (ts); Gildo Mahones (p); Martin
Rivera (b); Ron Jefferson (d); Janet Putman (h); Chino Pozo (cga,bgs);
Eileen Gilbart (vo).

                    Autumn Leaves         Dawn DLP 1117, Seeco CLP 468
                    Baubles Bangles and Beads     -             -
                    Golden Chariott               -             -
                    Let's Try                     -             -
                    Bohemia                       -             -
                    Mood in Scarlet               -             -
                    Linda Dalia                   -             -
                    Catch Her                     - ,DLP1124,   -
                    Hoo Tai                       -             -
                    We Can Talk It Over   Harmony HL 7196

February 10-11, 1958 - New York City

DON ELLIOT WITH BILLY BYERS' ORCHESTRA: Don Elliot (tp,vib,vo); Hal
McKusick (fl,cl,b-cl,as,ts); Bill Evans (p); Barry Galbraith (g); Ernie
Furtado (b); Paul Motian (d); Janet Putman (h); u (vocal group).

| | | | |
|---|---|---|---|
| 104322 | Summer Scene | Decca DL(7)9208, Br(E)LAT8263 | |
| 140323 | When the Sun Comes Out | - | - |
| 104324 | Blue Waltz | - | - |
| 140325 | A Million Dreams Ago | - | - |
| 104326 | The Story of a Starry Night | - | - |
| 104327 | Dinah | - | - |
| 104328 | A Waltz | - | - |
| 104329 | Poinciana | - | - |
| 104330 | Tired of Me | - | - |
| 104331 | Play Fiddle Play | - | - |
| 104332 | I Don't Want To Walk Without You | - | - |
| 104333 | It's Only a Paper Moon | - | - |

March 3, 1959 - New York City

BILLIE HOLIDAY WITH RAY ELLIS' ORCHESTRA: Jimmy Cleveland (tb); Romeo
Penque (ts); Hank Jones (p); Kenny Burrell (g); Joe Benjamin (b); Osie
Johnson (d); Janet Putman (h); u (strings); Billie Holiday (vo).

| | | | | | |
|---|---|---|---|---|---|
| 59XY435 | All the Way | MGM E(S)3764,(E)C792,(F)F2-109, WRC T530 | | | |
| 59XY436 | It's Not For Me to Say | - | - | - | - |
| 59XY437 | I'll Never Smile Again | - | - | - | - |
| 59XY438 | Just One More Chance | - | - | - | - |

March 4, 1959 - New York City

Harry Edison (tp); Jimmy Cleveland (tb); Gene Quill (as); Hank Jones
(p); Barry Galbraith (g); Milt Hinton (b); Janet Putman (h); u
(strings); Billie Holiday (vo).

| | | | | | |
|---|---|---|---|---|---|
| 59XY439 | When It's Sleepy Time Down South | MGM E(S)3764,(E)C792,(F)F2-109, WRC-T530 | | | |
| 59XY440 | Don't Worry 'Bout Me | - | - | - | - |
| 59XY441 | Sometimes I'm Happy | - | - | - | - |
| 59XY442 | You Took Advantage of Me | - | - | - | - |

March 11, 1959 - New York City

Harry Edison, Joe Wilder (tp); Billy Byers (tb); Al Cohn, Danny Banks
(ts); Hank Jones (p); Barry Galbraith (g); Milt Hinton (b); Osie Johnson
(d); Billie Holiday (vo).

| | | | | |
|---|---|---|---|---|
| 59XY455 | There'll Be Some Changes Made | MGM E(S)3764,(F)F2-109,WRC-T530 | | |
| 59XY456 | 'Deed I Do | - | - | - |
| 59XY457 | All of Me | - | - | - |
| 59XY458 | Baby Won't You Please Come Home | - | - | - |

November 20, 1959 - New York City

MILES DAVIS WITH GIL EVANS' ORCHESTRA: Miles Davis, Bernie Glow, Taft
Jordan, Louis Mucci, Ernie Royal (tp); Dick Hixon, Frank Rehak (tb);
Danny Banks (b-cl,fl); Albert Block, Eddie Caine (fl); Harold Feldman
(oboe, b-cl); John Barrows, Jimmy Buffington, Earl Chapin (FrH); James
McAllister (tuba); Janet Putman (h); Paul Chambers (b); Jimmy Cobb,
Elvin Jones (d); Gil Evans (arr,cond).

C063971    Concierto de Aranjuez       Columbia CL 1480


March 10, 1960 - New York City

Miles Davis, Ernie Royal, Bernie Glow, John Coles (tp); Dick Hixon,
Frank Rehak (tb); Danny Banks (b-cl,fl); Albert Block, Harold Feldman,
Eddie Caine (fl); Romeo Penque (oboe); Joe Singer, Tony Miranda, Jimmy
Buffington (FrH); Jack Knitzer (bassoon); Bill Barker (tuba); Janet
Putman (h); Paul Chambers (b); Jimmy Cobb, Elvin Jones (d); Elden C.
Bailey (perc); Gil Evans (arr,cond).

C064558    The Pan Pipier              Columbia CL 1480


March 11, 1960 - New York City

Louis Mucci (tp) added.

C064560    Solea                       Columbia 33037, CL1480
C064561    Will O' the Wisp                 -          -
C064562    Saeta                            -          -


May 16, 1960 - New York

Ann Williams (vo) acc. by Clark Terry (tp,flhn); Seldon Powell
(fl,cl,ts); Frank Williams (p); Joe Puma (g); George Duvivier (b); Bubby
Donaldson (d); Harry Lookofsky, George Ockner (vn); Dave Sawyer (viola);
Janet Putman (h).

           You and Your Lullaby        Charlie Parker CP807
           When a Woman is Blue              -
           Now You're Leaving Me            -
           Everything I've Got             -


November 17, 1961 - New York City

personnel unknown.

M2PB5475   This Time the Dream's       Victor LPM (S) 2508
             On Me
M2PB5476   Someone's Rocking My Dreamboat     -
M2PB5477   Dream                             -
M2PB5478   Wrap Your Troubles in Dreams      -

May 1, 1962 - New York City

Wild Bill Davis (org); Calvin Newborn (g); Les Spann (fl); Paul Gonsalves (ts); Janet Putman (h); Grady Tate (d).

| 112143 | On a Little Street in Singapore | Coral 57417,Vg(E)-Coral LVA9208 | |
|--------|--------------------------------|----------------------------------|---|
| 112144 | Manhattan | - | - |
| 112145 | African Waltz | - | - |
| 112145 | Midnight in Moscow | - | - |

## RAY, CARLINE (bass)

1968 - New York

Arnie Lawrence (as); Hal Gaylor, Richard Davis, Carline Ray (b); Larry Coryell (g); Roy Haynes (d).

| | |
|---|---|
| Contentment | Project 3 PR5028 |
| The Meeting of Two Worlds | Project 3 PR5028 |
| Seymour Chik-Chick | - |
| Feelin' Good | - |
| Look Forward the Day of Man's Awakening | - |
| I Wish I Knew How Itr Would Feel To Be Free | - |

## REDD, VI
### (alto and soprano saxes)

May 21, 1962 - Los Angeles

VI REDD SEXTET: Carmell Jones as "Kansas Lawrence" (tp); Vi Redd (as); Russ Freeman (p); Leroy Vinegar (b); Richie Goldberg (d); Roy Ayers (vib).

| | | |
|---|---|---|
| Now's the Time | United Artists VAL14016, UAS15016 | |
| Just Friends | - | - |
| Perhaps/Cool Blues | - | - |
| I Remember Bird | - | - |
| Old Folks (no tp) | - | - |

May 22, 1962 - Los Angeles

Vi Redd (as,vo); Russ Freeman (p); Herb Ellis (g); Bob Whitlock (b); Richie Goldberg (d).

| | | |
|---|---|---|
| If I Should Lose You (vVR) | United Artists VAL14016, UAS15016 | |
| Summertime (vVR) | - | - |
| Anthropology (vVR) | - | - |

|  | All the Things You Are | - | - |
|  | I'd Rather Have a Memory<br>Than a Dream | - | - |

**November 23, 1962 - New York**

Vi Redd (as,vo); Dick Hyman (org); Paul Griffin (p); Bucky Pizzarelli (g); Ben Tucker (b); Dave Bailey (d).

| 6651 | This Love of Mine | Atco 33-157 |
| 6652 | Oh, Sweet Mystery of Life | - |
| 6653 | We'll Be Together Again | - |
| 6654 | Evil Gal's Daughter Blues | - |
| 6655 | All I Need is You | - |
| 6656 | Yours | - |
| 6657 | That's All | - |
| 6658 | Next Time You See Me | - |

**January 30, 1963 - Los Angeles**

Vi Redd (as,vo); Bill Perkins (ts,fl); Jenwell Hawkins (org); Barney Kessel (g); Leroy Vinnegar (b); Leroy Harrison (d).

| 6763 | Lady Soul | Atco 33-157 |
| 6764 | Your Love is Like the Wind | - |
| 6765 | Salty Papa Blues | - |

<u>REMSEN, DOROTHY</u> (harp)

**c. 1960 - Los Angeles**

THE THRILLER - T.V. SERIES: Frank Beach, Don Fagerquist, Ollie Mitchell, Van Rosey (tp); Milt Bernhart, Dick Nash, Frank Rosolino (tb); George Roberts (b-tb); James Decher, Vince de Rosa, Dick Perissi (FrH); Red Callender (tuba); Bud Shank, Ronny Lang, Harry Klee, Gene Cipriano, Bob Cooper, Norman Herzberg (reeds); Jack Conherly (org); Caesar Giovanni, Jimmy Rowles (p); Laurindo Almeida, Bob Bain (g); Red Mitchell, Joe Mondragon (b); Dorothy Remsen (h); Larry Bunker, Frank Flynn, Milt Holland, Lou Singer, Alvin Stoller (d,tympany,perc); u (vn,cello); Pete Rugolo (comp,arr,cond).

|  | The Thriller | Time LP 52034 |
|  | The Hungry Glass | - |
|  | Voodoo Man | - |
|  | The Guilty Men | - |
|  | Girl With a Secret | - |
|  | The Purple Room | - |
|  | Twisted Image | - |
|  | Rose's Last Summer | - |
|  | Worse Than Murder | - |
|  | Child's Play | - |
|  | Finger or Fear | - |
|  | The Man in the Middle | - |

1967 - Los Angeles

THE VENEZUELO JOROPO: VIC FELDMAN & HIS ORCHESTRA: Bill Perkins
(fl,alto-fl); Vic Feldman (vib,marimba,el-harpsichard); Emil Richards
(vib,marimba); Al Hendrickson (g); Dorothy Remsen (h); Max Bennett
(b,el-b); Milt Holland (marraccas,perc); Larry Bunker (timbales).

| | |
|---|---|
| El Gavilan | Pacific Jazz PJ10128 |
| Obsession Waltz | - |
| Por El Camino Real | - |
| Frenesi | - |
| Passion | - |

See Collective Section for Additional Recordings


## RIVERS, MARYE (bass)

See Collective Section.


## ROBINSON, ALETHA (piano)

May 15, 1939 - Chicago

Ramona Hicks (vo) acc. by Joseph "Buster" Bennett (as); Aletha Robinson
(p); Leroy Brown (b); Jimmy Adams (vib).

| | | |
|---|---|---|
| 034800-1 | I Must Have It | Bluebird B-8173 |
| 034801-1 | Ramona Blues | - |
| 034802-1 | Where the Eagle Builds His Nest | Bluebird B-8200 |
| 034803-1 | Evil and Blue | Bluebird B-8233 |
| 034804-1 | Don't Be Like Me | - |
| 034805-1 | Tell My Mama On You | Bluebird B-8200 |


## ROGERS, BILLIE (trumpet)

November 13, 1941 - Chicago

WOODY HERMAN AND HIS ORCHESTRA: Woody Herman (cl,as,vo,dir); Georg
Seaburg, Billie Rogers, John Owens, Cappy Lewis (tp); Neal Reid, Jerry
Rosa, Vic Hamann (tb); Eddie Scalzi, Sam Rubinowich (as); Saxie Mansfield, Herbie Haymer (ts); Tommy Linehan (p); Hy White (g); Walter Yoder
(b); Frank Carlson (d); Jiggs Noble (arr).

| | | |
|---|---|---|
| 93766-A | Las Chiapanecas | Decca 4176,25300,BM-30819, FM-5453, Od 284967 |
| 93767-A | 'Tis Autumn | Decca 4095, Br 03306 |
| 93768-A | I Guess I'll Be.. | Decca 4253, BM-1230, Br 03342 |
| 93769 | Even Steven | - - - |

January 28, 1942 - New York City

Ray Linn (tp) replaces Owens.  Jimmy Horvath (as) replaces Scalzi.

| 70248-A | A String of Pearls | Decca 4176, Br 03331 |
| 70250-A | The Lamplighter's Serenade | Decca 4253, BM-1230, Br03342 |

December 18, 1941 - New York City

WOODY HERMAN AND HIS ORCHESTRA:  Woody Herman (vo,cl,as,dir);  Georg
Seaberg, Ray Linn, Cappy Lewis, Billie Rogers (tp); Neal Reid, Jerry
Rosa, Vic Hamarin (tb); Jimmy Horvath, Sam Rubinowich (as); Saxie
Mansfield, Herbie Haymer (ts); Tommy Linehan (p); Hy White (g); Walter
Yoder (b); Frank Carlson (d); Carolyn Grey (vo).

| 70079-A | Someone's Rocking My Dreamboat | Decca 4113, Br 03318 |
| 70080-A | Rose O'Day (Filla-Ga-Dusha Song) | -  , Br 03306 |
| 70081-A | Night of Nights (vWH) | Decca 4198 |
| 70082-A | I Think of You (vWH) | Decca 4135 |
| 70083-A | Fooled | Decca 4188 |

January 28, 1942 - New York City

same personnel.

| 70249-A | Skylark (vWH) | Decca 4198 |
| 70251-A | You Can't Hold a Memory In Your Arms | Decca 4188, Y-5805 |

April 2, 1942 - New York City

Woody Herman (cl,as,vo,dir); Georg Seaburg, Ray Linn, Cappy Lewis (tp);
Billie Rogers (tp,vo); Neal Reid, Jerry Rosa, Vic Hamann (tb); Edmund
Costanza, Sam Rubinowich (as); Saxie Mansfield, Herbie Haymer (ts);
Tommy Linehan (p); Hy White (g); Walter Yoder (b); Frank Carlson (d);
Carolyn Grey (vo).

| 70615-A | There Are Rivers to Cross (vWH) | Decca 18314 |
| 70616-A | We'll Meet Again (vBR) | - |
| 70617-A | She'll Always Remember (vCG) | Decca 18315 |
| 70618-A | A Solder Dreams of You Tonight (vWH) | - |
| 70619-A | Amen | Decca 18346,Y-5805,Coral 60019, Br 03380 |
| 70620-A | Whisper That You Love Me | Decca 18357, Br 03359 |
| 70621-A | Deliver Me to Tennessee (vWH) | Decca 18346, Br 03380 |

April 23, 1942 - New York City

same personnel.

| 70691-A | Don't Tell A Lie About Me Dear (and I Won't Tell the Truth About You) | Decca 18357 |
| 70692-A | The Story of a Starry Night (vWH) | Decca 18356,25351, Br A-82535 |
| 70693-A | Just Plain Lonesome (vWH) | - |
| 70694-A | Ooch Ooch a Goon Attach (vWH) | Decca 18364 |

July 24, 1942 - Los Angeles

WOODY HERMAN AND HIS ORCHESTRA: Woody Herman (cl,as,vo,dir); Charles Peterson, Billie Rogers (tp,vo); Georg Seaburg, Cappy Lewis (tp); Neal Reid, Tommy Farr, Walter Nims (tb); Edmund Costanza, Sam Rubinowich (as); Pete Mondello, Mickey Flous (ts); Tommy Linehan (p); Hy White (g); Walter Yoder (b); Frank Carlson (d).

| L-3123-A | Four or Five Times (vWH) | Decca 18526, Br 03522 |
| L-3124-A | There Will Never Be Another You | Decca 18469, BM-1239, Br-03394 |
| L-3125-A | Down Under* | Decca 18526 |
| L-3128-A | Gotta Get to St. Joe (vWH) | Decca 4372 |

* Dizzy Gillespie (arr).

July 29, 1942 - Los Angeles

same personnel.

| L-3148-A | Let Me Love You Tonight (vWH) | Decca 18619, 10192 |
| L-3149-A | The Singing Sands of Alamosa (vWH) | Decca 4372 |

July 31, 1942 - Los Angeles

Charles Peterson (vo) added.

| L-3166-A | Santa Claus is Coming To Town (vWH) | Decca 18512,Coral 60129,Br03481 |
| L-3167-A | Jingle Bells (vWH) | -    -    - |
| L-3168-A | I Dood It (vCP) | Decca 18506, Br 03454 |
| L-3169-A | Be Not Discouraged (vORCH) | -    - |

ROHL, ELVIRA (trumpet)

See Collective Section.

## ROSS, MARGARET (harp)

June 10, 1957 - New York City

BRANDEIS JAZZ FESTIVAL: Art Farmer, Louis Mucci (tp); Jimmy Knepper
(tb); Jimmy Buffington (FrH); John LaPorta (as); Robert DiDomenica (fl);
Manuael Zegler (bassoon); Hal McKusick (ts); Teddy Charles (vib);
Margaret Ross (h); Bill Evans (p); Barry Galbraith (g); Joe Benjamin
(b); Ted Sommer (d); Gunther Schuller, George Russell (arr,cond).

| CO58194 | All About Rose, I | Columbia WL 127 |
| CO58196 | Suspensions | -      , C2L31 |

June 18, 1957 - New York City

Fred Zimmerman (b) replaces Benjamin. Teo Macero (bars); Charlie Mingus
(vo).

| CO58202 | Revelations (1st movement) | Columbia WL 127 |
| CO58203 | All Set | - |

June 20, 1957 - New York City

same personnel.

| CO58204 | All About Rosie, II | Columbia WL 127 |
| CO58205 | Transformation | - |
| CO58206 | On Green Mountain | - |

February 14, 1962 - New York

JERRI WINTERS AGAIN: Jerri Winter (vo) acc. by Willie Thomas (tp);
Frank Rehak, Buster Cooper (ts); Ray Alonge (FrH); Phil Bodner
(cl,oboe); Hal McKusick (as,fl); Al Klink (ts,b-cl); Don Hammond
(ts,fl); Sol Schlinger (bars,b-cl); Mundell Lowe (g,arr,dir); George
Duvivier (b); Ed Shaughnessy (d); Margaret Ross (h).

| I'm Gonna Laugh You | Summit (E) AJS18, Charlie Parker |
| Out of My Life | PLP 808 |
| Through Again | -            - |
| In the Wee Small Hours | -            - |
| Did I Remember | -            - |

July 25-26, 1963 - New York

Dave Nadien, Gene Orloff, Raoul Paliakin, Emanuel Vardi, George Ricci
(strings); Margaret Ross (h); Charlie Mariano (as); Phil Bodner (reeds);
Jim Hall (g); Bob Phillips (p,vib,celeste); Richard Davis (b); Ed
Shaughnessy (d).

| The Wind | Regina R286 |
| Goodbye | - |
| Deep in a Dream | - |

September, 1963 - New York City

GIL EVANS AND HIS ORCHESTRA: Jimmy Cleveland, Gil Cohen (tb); Don
Corado, Julius Watkins (FrH); Steve Lacy (sop); Al Block (fl); Eric
Dolphy (cl,b-cl); Bob Trock (reeds); Margaret Ross (h); Gil Evans
(p,arr,cond); Barry Galbraith (g); Paul Chambers (b); Ben Tucker,
Richard Davis (b); Elvin Jones (d).

       Flute Song              Verve MGV (S6) 8555


February 5, 1964 - New York City

QUINCY JONES AND HIS ORCHESTRA: Clark Terry, Snooky Young, Jimmy
Maxwell, Ernie Royal (tp); Dick Hixon, Urbie Green, Billy Byers, Quentin
Jackson, Tony Studd (tb); Jimmy Buffington, Tony Miranda, Bob Northern,
Ray Alonge (FrH); Harvey Phillips (tuba); Jerome Richardson, Stan Webb,
Roland Kirk (saxes); Gary Burton (vib); Bobby Scott (p); Mundell Lowe
(g); Milt Hinton (b); Osie Johnson (d); Martin Groupp (perc); Margaret
Ross (h); Quincy Jones (arr,cond).

| 31078 | Days of Wine and Roses | Mercury MG20853, SR 60863 |
|-------|------------------------|---------------------------|
| 31079 | Moon River | -      - |
| 31080 | Dreamsville | -      - |
| 31081 | Don't You Forget It | -      - |


September 15, 1964 - New York City

QUINCY JONES AND HIS ORCHESTRA: Jimmy Buffington, Morris Secon (FrH);
Jerome Richardson, (ts,sop); Bill Slapin, George Dessinger, Stan Webb,
(reeds); Don Elliott (marimba, vib,vo); Bobby Scott (p); Jim Hall (g);
Milt Hinton, Art Davis (b); Ed Shaughnessy (d); u (strings); Margaret
Ross (h); Quincy Jones (arr,cond).

| 32405 | Golden Boy Theme | Mercury MG20938, SR60938 |
|-------|------------------|--------------------------|
| 32406 | Seaweed (vDE) | -      - |


September 29, 1964 - Englewood Cliffs, New Jersey

Ernie Royal, Bernie Glow, Danny Stiles, Joe Wilder (tp); Joe Newman
(flhn); Jimmy Cleveland, Chauncey Welsh (tb); Paul Faulise, Tommy
Mitchell (b-tb); Earl Chapin, Don Corrado, Morris Secon, Jim Buffington
(FrH); Harvey Phillips (tuba); Jimmy Smith (org); Kenny Burrell (g); Art
Davis (b); Grady Tate (d); George Devens (perc); Margaret Ross (h);
Billy Byers (arr).

| God Rest Ye Merry | Verve V(6) 8604, 8666 |
|-------------------|------------------------|
| The Three Kings | -      - |
| The Christmas Song | -      - |
| White Christmas | -      - |
| Silent Night | -      - |

December 1-11, 1964 - New York City

MAYNARD FERGUSON AND HIS ORCHESTRA: Maynard Ferguson, John Bello, Chet
Ferretti, Jimmy Nottingham, Don Rader (tp,flhn); Bernie Glow, Wayne
Andre, Urbie Green, John Messner, William Watrous (tb); Paul Faulise
(b-tb); Ray Alonge, Jimmy Buffington (FrH); Lanny Morgan (fl,cl,as);
Willie Maiden, Frank Vicari (ts); Roger Pemberton (bars); Romeo Penque,
Phil Bodner (reeds); Stan Webb (bars,b-cl,bassoon); Don Butterfield
(tuba); Mike Abene (p); Barry Galbraith (g); Richard Davis (b); Mel
Lewis (d); Margaret Ross (h).

| | |
|---|---|
| Night Train | Mainstream M56045 |
| Every Day I Have the Blues | - |
| Mary Ann | - |
| I Believe To My Soul | - |
| What'd I Say | - |
| Baltimore Oriole | - |
| Alright, Okay, You Win | - |
| I've Got a Woman | - |

May, 1965 - Englewood Cliffs, New Jersey

Roger Kellaway (p); West Mongtomery (g); Bob Crenshaw (b); Helcio
Mililito or Grady Tate (d); Candido Camero (cga,bgs); Arnold Eidus,
Lewis Eley, Paul Gershman, Louis Haber, Julius Held, Harry Lookofsky,
Joe Malignaggi, Gene Orloff, Sol Shapiro (vn); Harol Colletta, David
Schwartz (viola); George Ricci, Charles McCracken (cello); Margaret Ross
(h); Don Sebesky (arr,cond).

| | | |
|---|---|---|
| Bumpin' | Verve V(6)8625,(E)VLP9106 | |
| Tear It Down | - | - |
| A Quiet Thing | - | - |
| Con Alma | - | - |
| Love Theme from "The<br>    Sandpiper" | - | - |
| Mi Cosa | - | - |
| Here's That Rainy Day | - | - |
| Musty | - | - |

May 4, 1965 - Los Angeles

Freddie Hubbard, Ernie Royal, Snooky Young, Clark Terry (tp); Jimmy
Cleveland, J.J. Johnson, Tony Studd, Bob Brookmeyer (tb); Jim Buffing-
ton, Robert Northern, Willie Ruff (FrH); Jerome Richardson, James Moody
(ts,fl); Phil Woods (as,cl,fl); u (strings); Margaret Ross (h); Lalo
Schifrin (p); Kenny Burrell (g); Don Butterfield (tuba); Grady Tate,
Dave Bailey (d); Irene Reed (vo).

| | |
|---|---|
| Blues A Go Go | Verve 8624 |
| Once a Thief (vIR) | - |
| Insinuations | - |
| The Right to Love (vIR) | - |
| The Cat | - |
| The Man From Trush | - |
| Roulette Rhumba | - |

The Joint                              -
Once a Thief (instrumental)            -

May, 1967 - New York

Astrud Gilberto (vo) acc. by Bernie Glow, Jimmy Nottingham, Ernie Royal
(tp); Marvin Stamm (tp,flhn); Warren Covington, Wayne Andre, Urbie Green
(tb); Tony Studd (b-tb); Ray Alonge, Earl Chapin, Tony Miranda, Jimmy
Buffinton (FrH); John Barber (tuba); Seldon Powell, Hubert Laws (fl);
Stan Webb, Phil Bodner, Bill Hammond, Hubert Laws (woodwinds); George
Devens (vib); Benny Aranov, Warren Berhardt (p); Barry Galbraith, Marcos
Valle (g); Toots Thielemans (g,hca); Ron Carter, Jule Ruggiro (b);
Claudio Slon, Grady Tate (d); Alan Dangles, Jack Jennings, Bobby Rosen-
garden, Don Romano (perc); Margaret Ross (h); u (cellos,vns); Don
Sebesky, Eumir Deodato (arr,cond).

| 102885 | Stay                     | Verve V(6) 8708 |
|--------|--------------------------|-----------------|
| 102886 | Beach Samba              | -               |
| 102887 | A Banda (Parade)         | -               |
| 102888 | Oba Oba                  | -               |
| 102889 | My Foolish Heart         | -               |
| 102890 | Misty Roses              | -               |
| 102891 | I Had the Craziest Dream | -               |
| 102892 | The Face I Love          | -               |
| 102893 | Canoeiro                 | -               |
| 102894 | Dia Das Rosas            | -               |
| 102895 | Nao Bate O Coracao       | -               |

June 6-8, 1967 - Englewood Cliffs, New Jersey

A DAY IN THE LIFE:  Ray Alonge (FrH); George Marge, Romeo Penque, Joe
Soldo, (bass-fl); Stand Webb (b-fl); Phil Bodner (woodwinds); Herbie
Hancock (p); Wes Montgomery (g); Ron Carter (b); Grady Tate (d); Ray
Barretto, Jack Jennings, Joe Wohletz (perc); Julius Brand, Peter Buon-
sonsiglio, Mac Ceppos, Lewis Eley, Harry Glickman, Harry Katzman, Leo
Kruczek, Gene Orloff, Tosha Samaroff, Sylvar Shulman, Harry Urbout, Jack
Zayde (vn); Harold Colletta, Emanuel Vardi (viola); Charles McCracken,
Alan Shulman (cello); Margaret Ross (h); Don Sebesky (arr,cond).

| A Day in the Life          | A&M AML2001, SP3001 |   |
|----------------------------|---------------------|---|
| Watch What Happens         | -                   | - |
| When a Man Loves a Woman   | -                   | - |
| California Nites           | -                   | - |
| Angel                      | -                   | - |
| Eleanor Rigby              | -                   | - |
| Willow Weep for Me         | -                   | - |
| Windy                      | -                   | - |
| Trust in Me                | -                   | - |
| The Joker                  | -                   | - |

ROTENBERG, JUNE (bass)

See Collective Section.

## ROUDEBUSH, BETTY (piano)

See Collective Section.

## ROY, MATA (piano)

See Collective Section.

## RUBIN, QUEENIE ADA (piano)

August 21, 1936 - New York City

TEMPO KING AND HIS KINGS OF TEMPO:  Marty Marsala (tp); Joe Marsala (cl): Queenie Ada Rubin (p); Eddie Condon (g); Mort Stuhlmaker (b); Stan King (d); Tempo King (vo).

| 0229-1 | Bojangles of Harlem | Bluebird B-6533, RZ MR-2267 |
| 0230-1 | I'll Sing a Thousand Love Songs | Bluebird B-6535, RZ MR-2269 |
| 0231-1 | Organ Grinder's Swing | Bluebird B-6533, RZ MR-2267 |
| 0232-1 | Papa Tree Top Tall | Bluebird B-6535, RZ MR-2269 |
| 0233-1 | William Tell | Bluebird B-6534 |
| 0234-1 | I Would Do Anything for You | - |

September 11, 1936 - New York City

same personnel.

| 0420-1 | A High Hat, a Piccolo and a Cane | Bluebird B-6575, RZ MR-2303 |
| 0421-1 | We Can Huddle at Home | Bluebird B-6563 |
| 0422-1 | You're Giving Me a Song and a Dance | Bluebird B-6575, RZ MR-2302 |
| 0423-1 | Alabama Barbecue | Bluebird B-6560, RZ MR-2460 |
| 0424-1 | That's What You Mean to Me | - |
| 0425-1 | Sweet Adeline | Bluebird B-6563 |

October 15, 1936 - New York City

George Yorke (b) replaces Stuhlmaker.

| 0975-1 | You've Got Something There | Bluebird B-6642 |
| 0976-1 | Through the Courtesy of Love | Bluebird B-6637, RZ MR-2322 |
| 0977-1 | I Was Saying to the Moon | Bluebird B-6643 |
| 0978-1 | One Hour for Lunch | Bluebird B-6642 |
| 0979-1 | To Mary, With Love | Bluebird B-6637 |
| 0980-1 | Swingin' the Jinx Away | Bluebird B-6643 |

November 17, 1936 - New York City

same personnel.

| 03237-1 | Keepin' Out of Mishcief Now | Bluebird B-6684, Victor JR-76 |
| 03238-1 | Hallelujah! Things Look Rosy Now | Bluebird B-6687 |
| 03239-1 | You Turned the Tables on Me | Bluebird B-6684, RZ MR-2323 |
| 03240-1 | Hey! Hey! Hey! Hey! | Bluebird B-6687 |
| 03242-1 | The Boston Tea Party | Bluebird B-6690* |
| 03243-1 | Something Has Happened to Me | - |

* Note: listed as the CHICAGO RHYTHM KINGS.


December 10, 1936 - New York City

TEMPO KING AND HIS KINGS OF TEMPO: Marty Marsala (tp); Joe Marsala (cl); Queenie Ada Rubin (p); Ray Biondi (g); George Yorke (b); Stan King (d); Tempo King (vo).

| 03700-1 | Nero | Bluebird B-6721 |
| 03701-1 | Pennies From Heaven | - , Twin FT-8258 |
| 03702-1 | Someone To Care For Me | Bluebird B-6725, Regal Zonophone MR-2396 |
| 03703-1 | Timber | Bluebird B-6725 |
| 03704-1 | Slumming on Park Avenue | Bluebird B-6748,Twin FT-8275, RZ MR-2503 |
| 03705-1 | He Ain't Got Rhythm | Bluebird B-6758 |


January 14, 1937 - New York City

same personnel.

| 04171-1 | Swing High, Swing Low | Bluebird B-6880, RZ MR-2439 |
| 04172-1 | My Last Affair | Bluebird B-6770 |
| 04173-1 | Moonlight on the Prairie, Mary | Bluebird B-6768 • |
| 04174-1 | There's a Ranch in the Sky | - - |
| 04175-1 | Floating on a Bubble | Bluebird B-6880, - |
| 04176-1 | Gee, But You're Swell | Bluebird B-6770 |


## RUSSELL, NINA (organ)

See Collective Section.


## RUTH, HELEN (reeds)

See Collective Section.

## RYAN, BABS (piano)

July 11, 1935 - New York

Babs Ryan (p,vo) acc. by Russ Case (tp); Will Bradley (tb); Slats Long (cl); Dick McDonough (g); Delmar Kaplan (b); Stan King (d).

| | |
|---|---|
| Let's Swing It | Brunswick 02393 |
| You're So Darn Charming | - |
| My Very Good Friend the Milkman | Brunswick 02059 |
| Double Trouble | - |

December 4, 1935 - New York

same personnel.

| | |
|---|---|
| When a Great Love Come Along | Brunswick 2126 |
| Yankee Doodle Never Went To Town | - |
| No Other One | Brunswick 2116 |
| A Little Bit Independent | - |

## SATTLEY, BETTY (reeds)

See Collective Section.

## SAUNDERS, NETTIE (piano)

date unknown.

Nettie Saunders (p,vo); with unknown rhthym.

| | |
|---|---|
| Ain't No Place To Go | Universal 80 |
| Mercy, Mercy, Mercy | - |
| Sleeptyime Gal | Universal 38 |
| Eness Boogie | - |

## SCHWARTZ, JULIE (alto sax)

November 13, 1941 - New York City

BENNY GOODMAN AND HIS ORCHESTRA: Jimmy Maxwell, Billy Butterfield, Al Davis (tp); Lou McGarity, Bob Cutshall (tb); Benny Goodman (cl); Julie Schwartz, Clint Neagley, Vido Musso, Charles Gentry George Berg (saxes); Mel Powell (p); Tom Morganelli (g); Sid Weiss (b); Ralph Collier (d); Peggy Lee (vo).

| | | |
|---|---|---|
| C031741-1 | Somebody Else is Taking My Place | Okeh 6497,Co 37244,C-539,C-6323, 38198 |
| C031742-1 | Somebody Nobody Loves | Okeh 6562,Co 38283,291375, 291666, C-579, C-6402 |
| C031743-2 | How Long Has This Been Going On | Okeh 6544, Co 291405, C-566, Harmony HL-7005 |
| C031744-1 | That Did It, Marie | Okeh 6497, Co 37244, C-539, C-6323, 291375 |

## SCOTT, DOT (piano)

July 7, 1936 - Chicago

Victoria Spivey (vo) acc. by DOT SCOTT'S RHYTHM DUKES: Randolph Scott (tp); u (as); Dot Scott (p); u (g,b,d).

| | | |
|---|---|---|
| 90784-A | Sweet Pease | Decca 7222 |
| 90785-A | Black Snake Swing | Decca 7203 |
| 90786-A | Grievin' Me | Decca 7204 |
| 90787-C | Double Dozens (You Dirty No Gooder) | Decca 7204 |
| 90788-A | You Weren't True (But You're Still in My Heart) | Decca 7237 |
| 90789-A | I'll Never Fall in Love Again | Decca 7203 |
| 90790-A | T.B.'s Got Me Blues | Decca 7222 |
| 90791-C | 410 Blues | Decca 7237 |

September 15, 1936 - Chicago

Justine Lamar (vo) acc. by DOT SCOTT'S RHYTHM BOYS: Randolph Scott (tp); u (as); Dorothy Scott (p); u (g,d).

| | | |
|---|---|---|
| 90867 | That'll Never Work With Me | Decca 7238 |

Stella Johnson (vo) replaces Lamar.

| | | |
|---|---|---|
| 90868-A | Don't Come Over | Decca 7217 |
| 90869-A | Hot Nuts Swing | - |

September 29, 1936 - Chicago

Justine Lamar (vo) replaces Johnson.

| | | |
|---|---|---|
| 90901 | Always Mine | Decca 7238 |

October 13, 1936 - Chicago

same personnel.

```
90921-B      Mama Don't Want You        Decca 7284
             No More
```

## SCOTT, HAZEL (piano)

December 1, 1939

SEXTET OF THE RHYTHM CLUB OF LONDON: Danny Polo (cl); Pete Brown (as);
Hazel Scott (p,vo); Albert Harris (g); Pete Bargy (b); Arthur Herbert
(d).

```
043945-1    Calling All Bars           Bluebird B10529, HMV X7087
043946-1/2  Mighty Like the Blues              -              -
043947-1    You Gave Me the Go-By      Bluebird B10557, HMV B9062,
                                       EA-3117
043948-1    Why Didn't William Tell           -       -        -
```

December 11, 1940 - New York City

Hazel Scott (p) acc. by J.C. Heard (d).

```
68480-A     Valse in D$^b$ Major        Decca 18129, Br 03476, DL5130
            (Chopin, p.64, #1)
68481-A     Country Gardens            Decca 18128, Y-5828,    -
            (Paul Grainger)
68482-A     Ritual Fire Dance          Decca 18127,           -
            (Manuel de Falla)
68483-A     Prelude in C# Minor        Decca 18128,    -      -
            (Rachmaninoff)
68484-A     Two-Part Invention in      Decca 18127,           -
            A Minor (Bach)
68485-A     Hungarian Rhapsody No. 2   Decca 18129, Br 03476, -
            (Liszt)
```

February 27, 1942 - New York City

Hazell Scott (p); acc. by J.C. Heard (d).

```
70410-A     Embraceable You            Decca 18341, DL 5130
70411-A     Hazel's Boogie-Woogie      Decca 18340, Br 04799, DL 5130
70412-A     Blues in B Flat                   -       -        -
70413-A     Hallelujah                 Decca 18342,           -
70414-A     Dark Eyes                         -                -
70415-A     Three Little Words         Decca 18341,           -
```

August 27, 1943 - New York City

Hazel Scott (p,vo) acc. by Sid Catlett (d).

```
VP-107      Body and Soul              V-Disc 68
VP-108      People Will Say We're      V-Disc 30
            in Love
```

```
VP-109      Honeysuckle Rose             -
VP-110      C Jam Blues                  V-Disc 68
```

May 3, 1945 - New York

HAZEL SCOTT WITH TOOTS CAMARATA'S ORCHESTRA:  (prob) Hazel Scott (p,vo);
Nat Natoli, Yank Lawson, Pee Wee Irwin (tp); John Owens (tp,tb); Hymie
Schertzer (as,bars); u (strings); Joe Dixon (ts); Ellis Larkins (p);
Carl Kress (g); Leonard Gaskin (b); Johnny Blowers (d); Toots Camarata
(arr,cond).

```
72849       I'm Glad There is You        Decca 23551
72850       Fascinating Rhythm           Decca 23429
72851       The Man I Love               -
```

Spring, 1946 - New York City

Hazel Scott (p) solo.

```
196         Valse in C                   Signature 15023
197         How High the Moon            Signature 15025
198         Rainy Night in Georgia       -
199         I'll Have to Change          Signature 15023
              My Plans
200         Sonata in C Minor            Singature 15026
201         Fantasie                     Signature 10524
202         Nocturne in B♭ Minor         -
203         Idyll                        Signature 15026
```

Early 1947 - New York City

Hazel Scott (p,vo) with TOOTS CAMARATA'S ORCHESTRA:  Featuring Charlie
Shavers (tp); Ernie Caceras (bars).

```
            I've Got the World           Signature 15073
              On a String
            On the Sunny Side of the     -
              Street
            Butterfly Kick               Signature 15126
            Ich Will Sich Spielen        -
```

October, 1947 - New York City

Hazell Scott (p) with unknown rhythm.

```
38226       Emaline                      Columbia 37997, Co CL 6090
38227       Nightmare Blues              Columbia 37999,     -
38228       Mary Lou                     Columbia 37998,     -
38229       Soon                         Columbia 37996,     -
38238       Brown Bee Boogie             Columbia 37999,     -
38239       Love Me or Leave Me          Columbia 37996,     -
38240       Love Will Find a Way         Columbia 37997,     -
38241       Dancing on the Ceiling       Columbia 37998,     -
```

1951 - Paris

Hazel Scott (p,vo); Georges Hadjo (b); Dave Pochonet (d).

| P1118-2 | Body & Soul | Decca MF21594 |
| P1119 | Tea For Two | Decca (F) MF21595 |
| P1120 | La Ronde (vHS) | Decca (F) MF21596 |
| P1121 | The One I Love | - |
| P1122 | How Blue Can You Get | Decca (F) MF21595 |
| P1123 | St. Louis Blues | Decca (F) MF21596 |

1952 - Los Angeles

Hazel Scott (p); Red Callender (b); Lee Young (d).

| 10301 | The Girl Friend | Capitol H364, (E) LC6607 |
| 10313 | The Way You Look Tonight | - | - |
| 10314 | Thou Swell | - | - |
| 10316 | I Get a Kick Out of You | - | - |
| 10318 | S'Wonderful | - | - |
| 10319 | I'll Be Around | - | - |
| 10320 | I'm Yours | - | - |
| 10323 | That Old Black Magic | - | - |

September 28, 1953 - Paris

Hazel Scott (p,vo); Benny Banks (b); Gerard Pochonet (d).

| P1152 | For All We KNow | Decca (F) MF36243 |
| P1153 | Tinkle Bells Blow Again v(HS) | - |
| P1154 | Soothe Me | Decca (F) MF36244 |
| P1155-2 | Un Gaim de Paris | - |
| P1156 | Whatever Happened to Captain Cook | Decca (F) MF36245 |
| P1157 | J'Aime Bien Paris (vHS) | - |

January 21 1955 - New York City

Hazel Scott (p); Charles Mingus (b); Max Roach (d).

| | Like Someone in Love | Debut DLP 16 |
| | Peace of Mind | - |
| | Lament | - |
| | The Jeep Is Jumpin' | - |
| | Get Up From There | - |
| | A Foggy Day | - |

## SCOTT, RHODA (organ)

June 29, 1962 - New York

Joe Thomas (ts); Rhoda Scott (org); Carl Lynch (g); Herbie Lovell (d);

The Shouters (vocal group); Bill Elliot (d).

| SA166 | I Only Have Eyes for You | Trusound TR15013 |
|-------|--------------------------|------------------|

Herbie Lovell (d) replaces Elliot.

| SA167 | Stand By Me    | -                |
|-------|----------------|------------------|
| SA168 | If You're Lonely | Trusound 45-417 |
| SA169 | Hey Hey Hey    | -                |

October 24, 1962 - New York

Joe Thomas (ts); Rhoda Scott (org); Leonard Gaskin (b); Bill Elliot (d).

| SA184-6  | In My Little Corner of | Trusound 45-418 |
|----------|------------------------|-----------------|
|          | the World              |                 |
| SA185-7  | Endlessly              | Trusound TRU 15013 |
| SA186-10 | Sha-Bazz               | -               |
| SA187-4  | If This Isn't Love     | -               |
| SA188-2  | Ebb Tide               | -               |
| SA189-3  | Splanky                | -               |
| SA190-3  | Fly Me to the Moon     | -               |

March 23, 1963 - "Key Club" - New York

Gaskin out.

| Hey Hey Hey     | Trusound TRU ST 15014 |
|-----------------|-----------------------|
| Shab-bazz       | -                     |
| Work Song       | -                     |
| I-Yi-Yi-Yi      | -                     |
| Watermelon Man  | -                     |
| Midnite Sun     | -                     |
| Little Darlin'  | -                     |
| Danny Boy       | -                     |

## SCOTT, SHIRLEY (organ, piano)

December 17-19, 1957 - New York City

EDDIE DAVIS TRIO AND JOE NEWMAN: Joe Newman (tp); Eddie Davis (ts); Shirley Scott (org); Count Basie (p); George Duvivier (b); Butch Ballard (d).

| 12551 | Telegraph                | Roulette SR52007, Co (E)33SX 1117 |
|-------|--------------------------|-----------------------------------|
| 12552 | Frouk                    | -                | -              |
| 12554 | A Misty One              | -                | -              |
| 12555 | Swingin' Till the Girls  | -                | -              |
|       | Come Home                |                  |                |
| 12556 | Street of Dreams*        | -                | -              |
| 12557 | Save Your Love for Me    | -                | -              |
| 12558 | Lock-Up**                | -                | -              |
| 12559 | Braodway                 | -                | -              |

| 12560 | Marie | - | - |
| 12561 | Don't Blame Me*** | - | - |

| * | omit Newman and Davis. |
| ** | omit Newman. |
| *** | omit Basie. |

March, 1958 - New York City

EDDIE DAVIS TRIO: Eddie Davis (ts); Shirley Scott (org); George Duvivier (b); Arthur Edgehill (d).

|  | A Gal in Gallico | Roulette (S) R52019 |
|  | Close Your Eyes | - |
|  | Now That I Need You | - |
|  | Just One More Chance | - |
|  | Fine and Dandy | - |
|  | Canadian Sunset | - |
|  | Night and Day | - |
|  | Snowball | - |
|  | Afternoon in a Madhouse | - |
|  | This Time the Dream's On Me | - |
|  | There Is No Greater Love | - |
|  | What Is There To Say | - |

January 13, 1958 - New York City

JOE NEWMAN QUARTET: Joe Newman (tp,vo); Shirley Scott (org); Ernie Wilkins (p); Eddie Jones (b); Charlie Persip (d).

| 104005 | Save Your Love for Me | Coral CRL 57208, (E) LVA 9106 |

Wilkins out.

| 104006 | The Farmer's Daughter (vJN) | - | - |
| 104007 | Three Little Words | - | - |

January 15, 1958 - New York City

same personnel.

| 104008 | Too Marvelous For Words | Coral CRL 57208, (E) LVA 9106 |
| 104009 | Scotty | - | - |
| 104010 | Makin' Whoopee (vJN) | - | - |
| 104011 | Rosetta | - | - |

January 17, 1958 - New York City

same personnel.

| 104012 | Organ Grinder's Swing | Coral CRL 57208, (E) LVA 9106 |
| 104013 | I Let a Song Got Out Of My Heart (vJN) | - | - |

| 104014 | There's a Small Hotel (vJN) | - | - |
| 104015 | Moonglow | - | - |

May, 1958 - New York City

Eddie Davis (ts); Shirley Scott (org); George Duvivier (b); Arthur Edgehill (d).

| | Scotty | Roost RLP 2227, CID (F) 42003 | |
| | On the Street Where You Live | - | - |
| | Dee Dee's Dance | - | - |
| | Don't Get Around Much Anymore | - | - |
| | Everything I Have Is Yours | - | - |
| | Don't Worry 'Bout Me | - | - |
| | Day By Day | - | - |
| | Do Nothing Till You Hear From Me | - | - |
| | I Remember You | - | - |
| | Autumn in New York | - | - |
| | Penthouse Serenade | - | - |
| | Land of Dreams | - | - |

May 27, 1958 - New York City

SHIRLEY SCOTT TRIO:  Shirley Scott (org); George Duvivier (b); Arthur Edgehill (d).

| 1516 | It Could Happen To You | Prestige LP 7195 | | |
| 1517 | There'll Never Be Another You | - | | |
| 1518 | Summertime | Prestige 45-147, LP 7195 | | |
| 1519 | Brazil | Prestige LP-7143,Esq 32-086, Met J521 | | |
| 1520 | The Scott | Prestige 45-117, | - | |
| 1521 | Baby Won't You Please | Prestige 45-156, LP-7195 | | |
| 1522 | Indiana | - | - | |
| 1523 | Cherokee | Prestige LP-7143, Esq 32-086 | | |
| 1524 | Nothing Ever Changes | - | - | |
| 1525 | Trees | - | - | |
| 1526 | All of You | Prestige 45-117, LP-7143, | - | , |
| | | Met J521 | | |
| 1527 | Goodbye | Prestige 45-118, | - | |
| 1528 | Four | - | - | - |
| 1529 | S'Posin' | Prestige LP-7195 | | |
| 1530 | Ebb Tide | Prestige 45-167 | | |

November 23, 1958 - New York City

same personnel.

| 1625 | Mr. Wonderful | Prestige LP-7155 | |
| 1626 | How Deep Is the Ocean | - | |
| 1627 | Time On My Hands | Prestige 45-145, LP-7155 | |
| 1628 | Sweet Lorraine | Moodsville LP 5 | |
| 1630 | Hong Pong | Prestige 45-145, | - |

| 1631 | Can't See For Looking | Prestige LP-7195 |
| 1632 | Takin' Care of Business | Prestige 45-147, - |
| 1633 | Gee Baby, Ain't I Good To You | Prestige 45-179, Moodsville LP 5 |
| 1636 | Cherry | Prestige 45-136, LP-7155 |
| 1637 | Dianne | -   - |
| 1638 | I Should Care | Moodsville LP 5 |
| 1639 | Send Me Someone To Love | Prestige 45-135, - |
| 1640 | Until the Real Thing Comes Along | Moodsville LP 5 |

April 24, 1959 - New York City

same personnel.

| 1756 | Just Squeeze Me | Prestige 45-149, LP 7163 |
| 1757 | Just A Sittin | Prestige 45-154, - |
| 1758 | In A Mellotone | Prestige 45-149, - |
| 1759 | Prelude To A Kiss | Prestige 45-154, - |
| 1760 | C Jam Blues | - |
| 1762 | Caravan | - |
| 1763 | In a Sentimental Mood | - |

December 4, 1959 - New York City

SHIRLEY SCOTT TRIO: Shirley Scott (org); Wendell Marshall (b); Arthur Edgehill (d).

| 1935 | Duck and Rock | Prestige 45-167, LP 173 |
| 1936 | Boss | - |
| 1937 | You Won't Let Me Go | - |
| 1938 | Plunk, Plunk, Plunk | - |
| 1939 | Soul Searching | - |
| 1940 | Moanin' | - | - |
| 1941 | Gee Baby Ain't I Good To You | - |
| 1967 | Yes Indeed | - |

Late 1959 - New York City

Al Smith (vo) acc. by Eddie "Lockjaw" Davis (ts); Shirley Scott (p,org); Wendell Marshall (b); Arthur Edgehill (d).

| Tears In My Eyes | Bluesville 45-801, BVLP 1001 |
| Night Time is the Right Time | Bluesville 45-805 |

Davis out.

| Come On Pretty Baby | Bluesville 45-801, BVLP 1001 |
| Pledging My Love | Bluesville 45-805 |

1960 - New York City

Mildred Anderson (vo) acc. by Eddie Davis (ts); Shirley Scott (org); George Duvivier (b); Arthur Edgehill (d).

| | | |
|---|---|---|
| Connections | Bluesville 45-804, | BVLP-1004 |
| Person to Person | - | - |
| I'm Free | | - |
| Please Don't Go | | - |
| Hello Little Boy | | - |
| Good Kind Daddy | | - |
| Kidney Stew | | - |
| I Didn't Have a Chance | | - |

April 8, 1960 - New York City

SHIRLEY SCOTT TRIO: Shirely Scott (org); George Tucker (b); Arthur Edgehill (d).

| | | |
|---|---|---|
| 2152 | I Thought I'd Let You Know | Moodsville LP 5 |
| 2153 | Spring Is Here | - |
| 2154 | I Didn't Know What Time It Was | - |
| 2155 | Lover Man | - |
| 2160 | Bye Bye Blackbird | - |

June 23, 1960 - New York

Shirley Scott (org); Lem Winchester (vib); George Duvivier (b); Arthur Edgehill (d).

| | | |
|---|---|---|
| 2326 | Like Young | Prestige PR/ST 7392 |
| 2327 | Sonnymoon For Two | - |
| 2328 | On Green Dolphin Street | - |
| 2329 | Blues for Tyrone | - |
| 2330 | The More I See You | - |
| 2331 | Get Me To the Church On Time | - |
| 2332 | Now's the Time | - |

July 8, 1960 - New York City

Shirley Scott (org); Gene Casey (p); Bill Ellington (b); Manny Ramos (timbales); Phil Diaz (bgs); Juan Amalbert (cga).

| | | |
|---|---|---|
| 2358 | The Lady is a Tramp | Prestige LP 7182 |
| 2359 | Muy Azul | - |
| 2460 | I Get a Kick Out of You | - |
| 2461 | Walkin' | - |
| 2362 | Tell Me | - |
| 2363 | Mucho Mucho | - |

September 27, 1960 - New York City

Shirely Scott (org); George Duvivier (b); Arthur Edgehill (d).

| 2513 | You Do Something To Me | Moodsville LP 19 |
| 2514 | More Than You Know | - |
| 2515 | Once In Awhile | - |
| 2516 | Little Girl Blue | - |
| 2517 | Laura | -  , LP 37 |
| 2518 | Like Cozy | - |
| 2519 | My Heart Stood Still | - |
| 2520 | 'Deed I Do | - |

March 7, 1961 - New York

Shirley Scott (org); George Tucker (b); Jack Simpkins (d).

| 2905 | It Don't Mean a Thing.. | Prestige PR/ST 7283 |
| 2906 | Satin Doll | - |
| 2907 | C Jam Blues | - |
| 2908 | Perdido | - |
| 2909 | Mood Indigo | - |
| 2910 | Solitude | - |
| 2911 | Things Ain't What They Used To Be | - |

March 24, 1961 - New York

Shirley Scott (org); Ronnell Bright (p); Wally Richardson (g); Peck Morrison (b); Roy Haynes (d).

| 2943 | Travelin' Light | Prestige PRLP 7456 |
| 2944 | You're My Everything | - |
| 2945 | Stompin' at the Savoy | - |
| 2946 | Worksong | Prestige PRLP 7424 |
| 2947 | Down By the Riverside | Prestige PRLP 7456 |
| 2948 | Chapped Chops | Prestige PRLP 7424 |

June 2, 1961 - New York City

Stanley Turrentine (listed as "Stan Turner") (ts); Shirley Scott (org); Herb Lewis (b); Roy Brooks (d).

| 3069 | 411 West | Prestige LP 7205 |
| 3070 | Out of This World | - |
| 3071 | Stanley's Time | - |
| 3072 | By Myself | - |
| 3073 | Trane's Blues | - |
| 3074 | Hip Soul | -  , 45-200 |

June 8, 1961 - New York City

details unknown.

| Baia | Blue Note 45-1914, BLP 4081 |
| Wee Hour Theme | -     - |
| My Shining Hour | - |

226

Troubles of the World                                    -
Dearly Beloved                                           -
Nothing Ever changes My Love For You                     -


August 22, 1961 - New York

Joe Newman (tp); Oliver Nelson (ts); Shirley Scott (org); George Tucker
(b); Roy Brooks (d).

| 3177 | Blue Seven | Prestige PR/ST 7376 |
| 3178 | How Sweet | Prestige PR/ST 7440 |
| 3179 | Give Me the Simple Life | Prestige PR/ST 7376 |
| 3180 | Wagon Wheels | - |
| 3181 | Don't Worry About It | - |
| 3182 | Nancy | - |


November, 1961 - New York City

Shirley Scott (org); Henry Grimes (b); Otis Finch (d).

| 3269 | Moon Ray | Prestige LP 7240 |
| 3270 | Doodlin' | - |
| 3271 | The Preacher | - |
| 3272 | Senor Blues | - |
| 3273 | Sister Sadie | -,  45-230 |
| 3274 | Strollin' | - |


November 17, 1961 - New York City

Stanely Turrentine (ts); Shirley Scott (org); George Tucker (b); Otis
Finch (d).

| 3275 | Ridin' and Runnin' | Prestige LP 7226, Esq 32-186 |
| 3276 | At Last | - | - |
| 3277 | Violet Blues | - | - |
| 3278 | The Very Thought of You | - | - |
| 3279 | All Tore Down | - | - |
| 3280 | Hip Twist | - , Prestige 45-210, - |
| 3281 | That's All | - | - |


November, 1962 - New York City

Shirley Scott (org); Earl May (b); Roy Brooks (d).

| 3641 | Happy Talk | Prestige LP 7262 |
| 3642 | Jitterbug Waltz | - |
| 3646 | My Romance | - |


December 5, 1962 - New York City

same personnel.

| 3673 | Sweet Slumber | Prestige LP 7262 |
|---|---|---|
| 3674 | Where or When | - |
| 3675 | I Hear a Rhapsody | - |

**January 10, 1963 - Englewood Cliffs, New Jersey**

Stanley Turrentine (ts); Shirley Scott (org); Major Holley (b); Grasella Oliphant (d).

| | | |
|---|---|---|
| | The Soul is Willing | Prestige LP 7267 |
| | Yes Indeed | - , 45-259 |
| | Stolen Sweets | - |
| | I Feel All Right | - |
| | Secret Love | - |
| | Remember | - |

**February 13, 1963 - New York City**

STANLEY TURRENTINE QUINTET: Stanley Turrentine (ts); Shirley Scott (org); Major Holley, Sam Jones (b); Al Harewood, Clarence Johnston (d); Ray Baretto (cga).

| | | |
|---|---|---|
| Trouble | Blue Note 45-1893, BLP 4129 |
| Never Let Me Go | Blue Note 45-1894, - |
| Major's Minor | - - |
| God Bless the Child | - |
| Sera's Dance | - |
| Without a Song | - |
| You'll Never Get Away From Me | - |

**March 27, 1963 - New York**

Shirley Scott (org); Major Holley (b); Roy Brooks (d).

| 3790 | Drag 'Em Out | Prestige PR/ST 7305 |
|---|---|---|
| 3791 | The Song Is Ended | - |
| 3792 | The Second Time Around | - |
| 3793 | Out Of It | - |

**August 22, 1963 - New York City**

Shirley Scott (org); Earl May (b); Jimmy Cobb (d).

| | | |
|---|---|---|
| Blues For Members | Impulse A (S) 51 |
| I've Grown Accustomed To Her Face | - |
| Marchin' To Riverside | - , 219 |
| We're Goin' Home | - |
| Lisa and Pam | Impulse A (S) 59, HMV (E) CLP 1798 |

August 24, 1963

Thad Jones, Jimmy Nottingham, Ernie Royal, Jerome Kail (tp); Thomas
Mitchell, Quentin Jackson, Tom McIntosh, Jimmy Cleveland (tb); Shirley
Scott (org); Mundell Lowe (g); Art Davis (b); Ed Shaughnessy (d); Joe
Venuto (perc); Eddy Manson (hca).

| 11689 | Toys in the Attic | Impulse A (S) 51 |
|-------|-------------------|------------------|
| 11690 | Southern Comfort  | -                |
| 11691 | Blue Piano        | -                |
| 11692 | Freedom Dance     | -                |

October 15, 1963 - New York

Stanley Turrentine (ts); Shirley Scott (org); Earl May (b); Gresella
Oliphant (d).

|  |  |  |
|--|--|--|
| Gravy Waltz | Prestige PR/ST 7312 | |
| In the Still of the Night | - | , PR 7773 |
| Deeep Down Soul | - | , PR 7707 |
| Serenata | - | |
| Soul Shoutin' | - | - |

October 21, 1963 - New York City

STANLEY TURRENTINE QUINTET: Blue Mitchell (tp); Stanley Turrentine
(ts); Shirley Scott (org); Earl May (b); Al Harewood (d).

| One O'Clock Jump | Blue Note BLP 4150 |
|------------------|--------------------|
| Midnight Blue | - |
| Blues in Hoss' Flat | - |
| Spring Can Really Hang You Up | - |
| Cherry Point | - |

January 24, 1964 - Englewood Cliffs, New Jersey

HUSTLIN': Stanley Turrentine (ts); Shirley Scott (org); Kenny Burrell
(g); Bob Cranshaw (b); Otis Finch (d).

| Trouble (no. 2) | Blue Note BLP 4162 |
|-----------------|--------------------|
| Love Letters | - |
| The Hustler | - |
| Lady Fingers | - |
| Something Happens To Me | - |
| Goin' Home | - |

February 17, 1964 - Englewood Cliffs, New Jersey

Shirley Scott (org); Kenny Burrell (g); Eddie Kahn (b); Otis Finch (d).

| Travelin' Light | Prestige PRLP 7328 |
|-----------------|--------------------|
| Solar | - |
| Nice and Easy | - |

```
                  They Call It Stormy Monday        -
                  Baby It's Cold Outside            -
                  Kerry Dance                       -
```

March 31, 1964 - Englewood Cliffs, New Jersey

Shirley Scott (org); Stanley Turrentine (ts); Bob Cranshaw (b); Otis
Finch (d).

```
                  The Funky Box           Prestige PRLP 7338
                  Hip Knees an' Legs           -
                  Five Spot After Dark         -
                  Grand Street                 -
                  Flamingo                     -
                  As It Was                    -
```

May 14, 1964 - New York

Shirley Scott (org,vo); Bob Cranshaw (b); Otis Finch (d).

```
                  Five O'Clock Whistel    Impulse A(S)67, HMV (E)1,
                                          CLP 1822
                  The Blues Ain't Nothin'
                     But Some Pain (vSS)       -              -
                  I'm Getting Sentimental Over You      -     -
                  Make Someone Happy           -              -
                  The Blues Ain't Nothin' But
                     Some Pain (instrumental) Impulse A(S)100
```

May 20, 1964 - New York

Jerome Kail, Jimmy Nottingham, Snooky Young, Joe Wilder (tp); Urbie
Green, Quentin Jackson, Willie Dennis, Tony Struda (tb); Bob Ashton,
Romeo Penque (reeds); Shirley Scott (org); Barry Galbraith (g); George
Duvivier (b); Johnny Pacheco, Willie Rodriguez, Osie Johnson (perc);
Lillian Clark, Jerry Graff (vo); Oliver Nelson (arr,dir).

```
                  A Shot in the Dark      Impulse A(S)67, HMV(E)CLP1822
                  Great Scott                  -              -
                  The Seventh Down             -              -
                  Hoe Down                     -              -
                  Shadow of Paris (vLC,JG)     -              -
```

September 23, 1964 - New York

Stanley Turrentine (ts); Shirley Scott (o); Bob Cranshaw (b); Otis Finch
(d).

```
90165   The Feeling of Jazz     Impulse A (S) 73
90166   Sent For You Yesterday       -
90167   The Lamp is Low               -
90168   Everybody Loves a Lover       -
        Time After Time         Impulse A(S)101,HMV(E)CLP1931
```

Howard Collins, Barry Galbraith (g); Willie Rodriguez (perc) added.

|  |  |
|---|---|
| Little Miss Know It All | Impulse A(S)73 |

Turrentine out.

|  |  |
|---|---|
| Blue Bongo | - |

December 2, 1964 - "The Front Room" - Newark, New Jersey

Stanley Turrentine (ts); Shirley Scott (org); Bob Cranshaw (b); Otis Finch (d).

| | | |
|---|---|---|
| Just In Time | Impulse A(S)81,HMV(E)CLP3509 | |
| Just Squeeze Me | - | - |
| Rapid Shave | - | - |
| That's For Me | - | - |
| The Theme | - | - |

July 21, 1965 - New York

Shirley Scott (org); Gary McFarland (vib); Jimmy Raney (g); Bob Cranshaw (b); Mel Lewis (d); Willie Rodriguez (perc).

| | |
|---|---|
| Downtown | Impulse A(S)93 |
| Can't Get Over the Bossa Nova | - |
| This Love of Mine | - |
| Hanky Panky | - |
| Noche Azul | - |
| Dreamsville | - |

July 22, 1965 - New York

Richard Davis (b) replaces Crenshaw. Jerome Richardson (fl); Leo Kruczcek, Aaroz Rosand, Harry Cykman, Charles Libove, Arnold Eidus (vn); Joseph Telcula, Edgardo Sodero, Charles McCracken (cello) added.

| | |
|---|---|
| Latin Shadows | Impulse A(S)93 |
| Who Can I Turn To | - |
| Perhaps, Perhaps, Perhaps | - |
| Soul Sauce | - |
| Feeling Good | - |

1966 - New York

Shirley Scott (org); Ron Carter (b); Jimmy Cobb (d).

| | | |
|---|---|---|
| 90499 | Corcovado | Impulse A(S)9109 |
| 90450 | Cold Winter Blues | - |
| 90451 | The Days of Wine and Roses | - |
| 90452 | What the World Needs Now Is Love | - |

| 90453 | On a Clear Day You Can See Forever | - |
| 90454 | What'll I Do | - |
| 90455 | All Alone | - |
| 90456 | Instant Blues | - |

**April 15, 1966 - New York**

Shirley Scott (org); Richard Davis (b); Ed Shaughnessy (d).

| 90525 | Tippin' In | Impulse A(S)9119 |
| 90526 | Ain't Misbehavin' | - |
| 90527 | A Tisket a Tasket | - |
| 90528 | Things Ain't What They Used To Be | - |

**April 19, 1966 - New York**

Shirley Scott (org); George Duvivier (b); Grady Tate (d).

| 90534 | Stompin' at the Savoy | Impulse A(S)9119 |
| 90535 | Little Brown Jug | - |

**July, 1966 - New York**

LET IT GO: Stanley Turrentine (ts); Shirley Scott (org); Ron Carter (b); Mack Simpkins (d).

| | Let it Go | Impulse A(S)9115 |
| | On a Clear Day You Can See Forever | - |
| | Ciao, Ciao | - |
| | It Ain't What You Do | - |
| | Good Lookin Out | - |
| | Sure As You're Born | - |
| | Deep Purple | - |

**August 19, 1966 - New York**

Clark Terry (flhn); Shirley Scott (org); George Duvivier (b); Mickey Roker (d).

| 90613 | Until I Met You | Impulse A(S)9133 |
| 90614 | Clark Bars | - |
| 90615 | Heat Wave | - |
| 90616 | This Light of Mine | - |

**August 22, 1966 - New York**

Bob Cranshaw (b) replaces Duvivier.

| 90621 | Joonji | Impulse A(S)9133 |
| 90622 | Soul Duo | - |

```
90623      Up a Hair                              -
90624      Taj Mahal                              -
```

1967 - New York

no details.

```
           Come Back                    Impulse A(S)9141
           We'll Be Together Again            -
           Love Nest                          -
           Swingin' the Blues                 -
           Keep the Faith                     -
           Chicago                            -
           On the Train                       -
           You're a Sweetheart                -
           Girl Talk                          -
```

February 9-10, 1967 - New York

Jimmy Rushing (vo) acc. by OLIVER NELSON AND HIS ORCHESTRA: Clark Terry (tp); Dicky Wells (tb); Bob Ashton (ts); Hank Jones (p,org); Shirley Scott (org); George Duvivier (b); Grady Tate (d); Oliver Nelson (dir,arr); u (others).

```
           Evil Blues                    Bluesway BLS 6005
```

August 30, 1968 - Englewood Cliffs, New Jersey

COMMON TOUCH: Stanley Turrentine (ts); Shirley Scott (org); Jimmy Ponder (g); Bob Cranshaw (el-b); Leo Morris (d).

```
           Buster Brown                  Blue Note BST 84315
           Blowin' in the Wind                -
           Lonely Avenue                      -
           Boogaloo                           -
           Common Touch                       -
           Living Through It All              -
```

September 9, 1968 - New York

Stanley Turrentine (ts); Shirley Scott (org,vo); Roland Martinez (el-b); Bernard Purdie (d).

```
15209      Soul Song                     Atlantic SD 1515
```

September 10, 1968 - New York

Jerry Jemmott (b) replaces Martinez; Eric Gale (g) added. Turrentine out.

```
15213      I Wish I Knew How It          Atlantic SD 1532
           Would Feel to Be Free
```

Stanley Turrentine (ts) added.

| 15214 | When a Man Loves a Woman | Atlantic SD 1515 |

November 7, 1968 - New York

Turrentine out.

| 15629 | Think | Atlantic SD1515 |

Stanley Turrentine (ts) added.

| 15630 | Like a Lover (vSS) | - |

Note: Additional recordings by Ms. Scott lie outside the temporal scope of this discography.

## SHAW, SISTER ROSA (guitar)

c. 1951

Sister Rosa Shaw acc. by (prob) own (g).

| M5080 | Stop Playing the Numbers | Dot 1116 |
| M5081 | House of the Lord | - |
| | He Rolled the Stone Away | Dot 1134 |
| | On the Highway | - |

date unknown.

Sister Rosa Shaw (vo) acc. by (prob) own (g).

| | Do You Know Him | Coral 65033 |
| | The Old Ship of Zion | - |
| | I Can Feel His Power | Coral 65036 |
| | Divine | |
| | Just One Moment in My | - |
| | God's Kingdom | |

## SIMONE, NINA (piano)

1957 - New York

Nina Simone (p,vo) acc. by Jimmy Bond (b); Al Heath (d).

| 6491 | Plain Gold Ring | Bethlehem BCP6028 |
| 6499 | Central Park Blues | - |
| 6560 | For All We Know | Bethlehem BCP6041 |
| 6561 | Good Bait | Bethlehem BCP6028 |
| 6570 | You'll Never Walk Alone | - |

| 6571 | He's Got the Whole World<br>In His Hand | Bethlehem BCP6041 |
|---|---|---|
| | I Love You Porgy | Bethlehem BCP6028 |
| | Love Me or Leave Me | - |

Bond and Heath out.

| | Don't Smoke in Bed | - |
|---|---|---|

Jimmy Bond (b) added.

| | Little Girl Blue | - |
|---|---|---|

Al Heath (d) added.

| | My Baby Just Cares For Me | - |
|---|---|---|
| | He Needs Me | - |
| | Mood Indigo | - |
| | African Mailman | Bethlehem BCP6041 |


1959

Nina Simone (p,vo) acc. by unknown orchestra directed by Bob Mersey.

| | Tomorrow We Will Meet | Colpix CP (S) 407 |
|---|---|---|
| | Children Go When I Send You | - |
| | Blue Prelude | - |
| | Stompin' at the Savoy | - |
| | It Might As Well Be Spring | - |
| | You've Been Gone Too Long | - |
| | That's Him Over There | - |
| | Chilly Winds Don't Blow | - |
| | Theme From the Middle of the Night | - |
| | Can't Get Out of This Mood | - |
| | Willow Weep For Me | - |
| | Solitaire | Colpix CP (S) 116 |
| | Since My Love Has Gone | Colpix CP (S) 151 |
| | Nobody Knows You | Colpix CP (S) 158 |


September 12, 1959 - Town Hall - New York

Nina Simone (p,vo) solo.

| | Cotton-Eyed Joe | Colpix CP (S) 409 |
|---|---|---|

Jimmy Bond (b); Al Heath (d) added.

| | The Other Woman | - |
|---|---|---|
| | Fine and Mellow | - |
| | Exactly Like You | - |
| | Return Home | - |
| | Black is the Color of My<br>True Love's Hair | - |
| | Wild is the Wind | - |
| | Summertime | - |

```
                Under the Lowest               -
                You Can Love Him               -
```

June 30, 1960 - Newport

```
                Trouble in Mind          Colpix CP (S) 412
                Blues for Porgy                -
                Little Liza Jane               -
                You'd Be So Nice to Come Home To   -
                Flo Me La                      -
                Nina's Blues                   -
                In the Evening By the Moonlight    -
```

1961 - New York

same personnel.

```
                Rags and Old Iron        Colpix CP (S) 419
                Work Song                      -
                Just Say I Love Him            -
                Memphis in June                -
                Forbidden Fruit                -
                No Good Man                    -
                Gin House Blues                -
                I'll Look Around               -
                I Love to Hate (I Love to Love)    -
                Where Can I Go Without You     -
```

1961 - Village Gate - New York

(prob) same personnel.

```
                Just in Time             Colpix CP (S) 421
                He Was Too Good To Me          -
                House of the Rising Sun        -
                Bye Bye Blackbird              -
                Brown Baby                     -
                Zingo                          -
                If He Changed My Name          -
                Children Go Where I Send You   -
```

1963 - New York

Nina Simone (p,vo) acc. by big band including strings and the Malcolm
Dodds Singers (vocal choir).

```
                I Got It Bad and That    Colpix CP (S) 425
                  Ain't Good
                Do Nothin' Till You Hear       -
                  From Me
                Hey, Buddy Bolden              -
                Merry Mending                  -
                You Better Know It             -
```

I Like the Sunrise                    -
Solitude                              -
The Gal From Joe's                    -
Satin Doll                            -
It Don't Mean a Thing                 -
Something to Live For                 -


c. 1964

   same personnel.

I Loves You Porgy              Colpix CP (S) 495
Blackbird                             -
Falling in Love Again                 -
Baubles, Bangles and Beads            -
Spring is Here                        -
That's All                            -
Chain Gang                            -
Man With a Horn                       -
Porgy, I Is Your Woman Now            -
Pigs Foot                             -


March 21 and April 1 & 6, 1964 - New York

Nina Simone (p,vo) acc. by Al Shackman (hca,g); Rudy Stevenson (g,fl);
Lisle Atkinson (b); Bobby Hamilton (d).

| 31230 | I Loves You Porgy | Philips PHM 200-135 |
| 31231 | See-Line Woman | Philips PHM 200-148 |
| 31232 | Old Jim Crow | Philips PHM 200-135 |
| 31234 | Wild is the Wind | Philips PHM 200-207 |
| 31236 | The Other Woman | Philips PHM 200-202 |
| 31246 | Don't Smoke in Bed | Philips PHM 200-135 |
| 31250 | Images | Philips PHM 200-202 |
| 31257 | Pirate Jenny | Philips PHM 200-135 |
| 31258 | Mississippi Goddam | - |
| 31260 | Go Lim | - |
| 31267 | Little Girl Blue | Philips PHM 200-202 |
| 31268 | Chilly Winds Don't Blow | Philips PHM 200-187 |
| 31270 | Black is the Color of My | Philips PHM 200-207 |
|       | True Love's Hair | |
| 31272 | Plain Gold Ring | Philips PHM 200-135 |


January, 1965 - New York

Nina Simone (p,vo) acc. by u (fl,ts,tb); Rudy Stevenson (g); u
(b,d,strings,harp,vocal group).

| 34807 | Ne Me Quitte Pas | Philips PHM 200-172 |
| 34808 | July Tree | - |
| 34809 | Beautiful Land | - |
| 34810 | Take Care of Business | - |
| 34811 | You've Got to Learn | - |
| 34812 | Tomorrow is My Turn | - |

| 34813 | I Love Your Lovin' Ways | Philips PHM 200-207 |
|-------|-------------------------|---------------------|
| 34814 | Gimme Some (strings out) | Philips PHM 200-172 |
| 34815 | Feeling Good | Philips PHM 200-207 |
| 34816 | Marriage Is For Old Folks | - |
| 34817 | One September Day | - |
| 34818 | I Put a Spell On You | - |
|       | Blues on Purpose | - |

**May 19-20, 1965 - New York**

| 36164 | End of the Line | Philips PHM 200-187 |
|-------|-----------------|---------------------|
| 36165 | Nearer Blessed Lord | Philips PHM 200-202 |
| 36166 | Be My Husband | Philips PHM 200-187 |
| 36167 | Nobody Knows You When You're Down and Out | - |
| 36168 | Tell Me More and More and Then Some More | - |
| 36169 | Trouble in Mind | - |
| 36170 | Ain't No Use | - |
| 36174 | The Ballad of Hellis Brown | Philips PHM 200-202 |
| 36175 | Sinnerman | Philips PHM 200-187 |
| 36176 | Strange Fruit | - |
| 36177 | If I Should Lose You | Philips PHM 200-207 |

**September 30 - October 1, 1965 - New York**

Shackman out.

| 36967 | Mood Indigo | Philips PHM 200-202 |
|-------|-------------|---------------------|
| 36968 | Don't Explain | - |
| 36969 | This Year's Kisses | - |
| 36970 | Lilac Wine | Philips PHM 200-207 |
| 36971 | Four Women | - |
| 36972 | Love Me or Leave Me | Philips PHM 200-202 |
| 36973 | Chauffeur | - |
| 36974 | Either Way I Lose | Philips PHM 200-207 |
| 36975 | What More Can I Say | - |
| 36976 | For Myself | Philips PHM 200-202 |
| 36977 | Breakdown and Let it All Out | Philips PHM 200-207 |
| 36978 | That's All I Ask | - |

**1966**

Nina Simone (p,vo) acc by large orchestra with Hal Mooney (arr,cond).

| 38964 | Work Song | Philips PHM 200-219 |
|-------|-----------|---------------------|
| 38965 | The Gal From Joe's | - |
| 38966 | I'm Gonna Leave You | - |
| 38996 | Brown Eyed Handsome Man | - |
| 38997 | Take Me to the Water | - |
| 38998 | Come Ye | - |
| 39000 | Don't You Pay Them No Mind | - |
| 39001 | I Hold No Grudge | - |

| 39002 | He Ain't Commin' Home No More | - |
| 39003 | I Love My Baby | - |
| 39005 | I'm Going Back Home | - |
| 39009 | Keeper of the Flame | - |

**December 19, 1966 - New York**

Buddy Lucas (ts,hca); Nina Simone (p,vo); Ernie Hayes (org); Jose Bushnell (el-b); Bernard Purdie (d).

| TPA1-8536 | Day and Night | RCA LPM/LSP 3789 |
| TPA1-8537 | Do I Love You | - |

**December 22, 1966 - New York**

same personnel.

| TPA1-8540 | Blues for Mama | RCA LPM/LSP 3789 |
| TPA1-8541 | Real Real | - |

**January 5, 1967 - New York**

same personnel.

| UPA1-4201 | Since I Fell For You | RCA LPM/LSP 3789 |
| UPA1-4202 | My Man's Gone Now | - |
| UPA1-4203 | I Want a Little Sugar in My Bowl | - |
| UPA1-4204 | Backlash Blues | - |
| UPA1-4205 | The House of the Rising Sun | - |
| UPA1-4207 | In the Dark | - |
| UPA1-4208 | Buck | - |

**June 13, 1967 - New York**

Nina Simone (p,vo) acc. by large orchestra with Sammy Lowe (arr,cond).

| UPA1-4286 | Consummation | RCA LPM/LSP 3837 |
| UPA1-4287 | Turning Point | - |
| UPA1-4288 | Turn Me On | - |

**June 15, 1967 - New York**

same personnel.

| UPA1-4289 | It Be's That Way Sometimes | RCA LPM/LSP 3837 |
| UPA1-4290 | I Wish I Knew How It Would Feel to be Free | - |
| UPA1-4291 | The Look of Love | - |

June 21, 1967 - New York

  same personnel.

| | | |
|---|---|---|
| UPA1-4292 | Go to Hell | RCA LPM/LSP 3837 |
| UPA1-4293 | Some Day | - |
| UPA1-4294 | Cherish | - |

June 29, 1967 - New York

  same personnel.

| | | |
|---|---|---|
| UPA1-4295 | Love O' Love | RCA LPM/LSP 3837 |

December 20, 1967 - New York

  no details.

| | | |
|---|---|---|
| UPA1-6079 | I Can't See Nobody | RCA LPM/LSP 4152 |

April 7, 1968 - New York

  Nina Simone (p,vo) acc. by u (g); Gene Taylor (b); u (d).

| | | |
|---|---|---|
| WPA1-2821 | In the Morning | RCA LSP 4065 |
| WPA1-2822 | Sunday in Savannah | - |
| WPA1-2823 | Backlash Blues | - |
| WPA1-2824 | Please Read Me | - |
| WPA1-2825 | Gin House Blues | - |
| WPA1-2826 | Why (The King of Love is Dead) | - |
| WPA1-2827 | Peace of Mind | - |
| WPA1-2828 | Ain't Got No Money | - |
| WPA1-2829 | I Loves You Porgy | - |
| WPA1-2830 | Take My Hand | - |
| WPA1-3765 | Do What You Gotta Do | - |

September 16, 1968 - New York

  same personnel.

| | | |
|---|---|---|
| WPA1-6251 | Nobody's Fault But Mine | RCA LSP 4102 |
| WPA1-6252 | I Think It's Going to Rain Today | - |
| WPA1-6253 | Everyone's Gone to the Moon | - |
| WPA1-6255 | Who Am I | - |
| WPA1-6258 | I Get Along Without You Very Well | - |
| WPA1-6259 | The Desperate Ones | - |

October 1, 1968 - New York

| | | |
|---|---|---|
| WPA1-6250 | Seems I'm Never Tired Of You | RCA LSP 4102 |

    WPA1-6254  Compensation                -
    WPA1-6256  Another Spring              -
    WPA1-6257  The Human Touch            -

date unknown.

    Nina Simone (p,vo) acc. by unknown band.

            This Year's Kisses          Marble Arch (E) MAL(S)895

    Nina Simone (p,vo) acc. by unknown orchestra including strings.

            I Can't Stand You           Marble Arch (E) MAL(S)895


    Note:  Additional recordings by Ms. Simone lie outside the temporal
    scope of this discography.


                        SINGER, LIL (drums)

See Collective Section.


                        SKINNER, JEAN (drums)

See Collective Section.


                        SLAVIN, ESTELLA (trumpet)

See Collective Section.


                        SMITH, BETTY (tenor sax)

November 17, 1953 - London

    FREDDY RANDALL AND HIS BAND:  Freddie Randall (tp); Norman Cave (tb);
    Archie Semple (cl); Betty Smith (ts); Dave Fraser (p); Ken Englefield
    (b); Lennie Hastings (d).

    CE14789    Carolina in the Morning    Parlophone R3835, GEP 8715
    CE14790    Tin Roof Blues                    -
               Muskrat Ramble              Parlophone R3853,    -


October 5, 1955

    Freddy Randall (tp); Orme Stuart (tb); Al Gay (cl); Betty Smith (ts);
    Harry Smith (p); Jack Peberdy (b); Stan Bourke (d).

```
          Shine                   Parlophone R3853
          Tin Roof Blues                    -
CE15451   Ja Da                   Parlophone R4191, GEP 8611
```

c. 1953-1955 - London

(prob) Freddie Randall (tp); Norman Cave (tb); Archie Semple (cl); Betty
Smith (ts); Dave Fraser (p); Ken Englefield (b); Lennie Hastings (d).

```
          Black and Blue          Parlophone R4006, GEP 8533
          Farewell Blues                   -           -
          Riverboat Shuffle       Parlophone R4040, GEP 8557
          Washington and Lee Swing         -           -
          Hindustan               Parlophone R4093
          November Blues                   -
          Memphis Blues           Parlophone R4059,    -
          My Tiny Band is Chosen           -           -
          Hotter Than Than        Parlophone MSP 6137
          Someday Sweetheart               -
          Royal Garden Blues      Parlophone GEP 8533
```

February 26, 1956

(prob) Freddy Randall (tp); Orme Stuart (tb); Al Gay (cl); Betty Smith
(ts); Harry Smith (p); Jack Peberdy (b); Stan Bourke (d).

```
          Ain't Misbehavin'       Parlophone R4191, GEP 8611
```

July 4, 1957 - London

Betty Smith (ts,vo); Brian Lemon (p); Terry Walch, Barry Phillips (g);
Jack Peberty (b); Stan Bourke (d).

```
          Little White Lies (vBS)    Tempo (E) A167, EXA 74
          There'll Be Some Changs Made       -          -
```

Phillips out.

```
          Lulu's Back in Town             -           -
          Sweet Georgia Brown             -           -
```

## SMITH, DOROTHEA (guitar)

August 29, 1947 - New York City

Albinia Jones (vo) acc. by SAMMY PRICE AND HIS TRIO:  Sammy Price (p);
Dorothea Smith (g); Percy Joell (b); Bill Butler (d).

```
74027     Give It Up Daddy Blues  Decca 48069
74029     Papa Tree Top Blues             -
```

### SMITH, DOTTIE (drums)

November, 1947 - New York City

HARLEMAIRES: Chester Slater (p,vo); Billy Butler (g,vo); Percy Doll (b,vo); Dottie Smith (d,vo).

| A52 | If You Mean What You Say | Atlantic 856 |
|-----|--------------------------|--------------|
| A72 | Rose of the Rio Grande | - |

### SMITH, ELIZABETH (ukelele)

September 6, 1926 - New York City

Elizabeth Smith (uk,vo).

| 36097-2 | No Sooner Blues | Victor 20297 |
|---------|-----------------|--------------|

### SMITH, ETHEL (organ)

May 8, 1950 - New York

Ethel Smith (org); acc. by u (g,b,d).

| 76293 | Steamboat Rag | Brunswick 82641 |
|-------|---------------|-----------------|
| 76294 | Maple Leaf Rag | - |

### SMITH, LAVERNE (piano)

1954 - New Orleans

Laverne Smith (p,vo).

| Lover Man | Cook LP 1081 |
|-----------|--------------|
| One Scotch, One Bourbon, One Beer | - |
| Hurry on Down to My House | - |
| Blues in the Night | - |
| Straighten Up and Fly Right | - |
| The Nearness of You | Savoy MG 12031 |
| Basin Street Blues | - |
| Imagination | - |
| A Hundred Years From Today | - |
| No Greater Love | - |
| Am I Blue | - |
| I Got a Right to Cry | - |
| Fool That I Am | - |
| Mobile | - |
| Somehow | - |
| Careless | - |
| It's Over | - |

## SMOCK, EMMA GINGER (violin)

March 31, 1953 - Los Angeles

Cecil "Count" Carter (vo) acc. by Emma Ginger Smock (vn); Freddie Simon (ts); Gerald Wiggins (p); Red Callender (b); Rudy Pitts (d); George Collier (unknown instrument).

| F316 | What's Wrong With Me | Federal 12130 |
| F317 | Strange Blues | - |
| F318 | I Know I Know | Federal 12135 |
| F319 | Ginger Bread | - |


## SNOW, VALAIDA (trumpet)

October 5, 1932 - New York City

WASHBOARD RHYTHM KINGS: Valaida Snow (tp); Ben Smith (cl,as); Jerome Carrington (as); Carl Wade (ts); Eddie Miles (p); Steve Washington (bj,vo); Ghost Howell (b); H. Smith (wb).

| 12426-A | Sentimental Gentleman From Georgia | Vocalion 1724, Br A-86014 | |
| 12427-A | It Don't Mean a Thing (If It Ain't Got That Swing) | - | - |
| 12428-A | I Would Do Anything For You | Vocalion 1734 | |
| 12429-A | Somebody Stole Gabriel's Horn | Vocalion 1725 | |
| 12430-A | Spider Crawl* | Vocalion 1734 | |
| 12431-A | The Scat Song (vSW) | Vocalion 1725 | |

* Bella Benson (vo).


January 18, 1935 - London

Valaida Snow (tp,vo) acc. by BILLY MASON AND HIS ORCHESTRA: Billy Mason (p,dir); Duncan Whyte (tp); Harry Hayes (as); Buddy Featheronhaugh (ts); Alan Ferguson (g); Sam Molyneux (b); George Elrick (d).

| CE6800-1 | I Wish I Were Twins | Parlophone F-118, A-6116, Od 194309, A-221890, 031374 |


January 19, 1935 - London

same personnel.

| CE6802-1 | I Can't Dance (I Got Ants in My Pants) | Parlophone F-118, A-6116, Od 194309, A-221890, 031374 |

February 20, 1935 - London

same personnel.

| | | | | |
|---|---|---|---|---|
| CE686-1 | It Had To Be You | Parlophone<br>Od A-221911 | | F-140,A-6158, |
| CE6862-2 | You Bring Out the Savage<br>In Me | -<br>Stash ST109 | - | -, |

April 26, 1935 - London

same personnel.

| | | | | |
|---|---|---|---|---|
| CE6948 | Imagination | Parlophone<br>Od A-272045 | F-230, | A-6305, |
| CE6949-1-3 | Sing, You Sinners | - | - | - |
| CE6952-1 | Whisper Sweet | Parlophone F-165, Od 194433,<br>A-221942 | | |
| CE6953-1 | Singin' in the Rain | - | - | - |

September 6, 1936 - London

Valaida Snow (tp,vo) acc. by Harry Owen (tp); Freddy Garner (cl,as,ts);
George Scott Wood (p); Joe Young (g); Dick Escott (b); Max Bacon (d).

| | | |
|---|---|---|
| CE-7819-1 | Until the Real Thing<br>Comes Along | Parlophone F-559, Od OF-5260 |
| CE-7820-1 | High Hat, Trumpet and<br>Rhythm | - , A-6755, -, |

September 8, 1936 - London

Jack Jacobson (d) replaces Bacon. Jack Fleming (tb) added.

| | | |
|---|---|---|
| CE-7826-1 | I Want a Lot of Love | Parlophone F-575, A-6601,<br>Od OF-5274 |
| CE-7827-1 | Take Care of You For Me | Parlophone F-657, A-6649,<br>Od OF-5348 |

September 18, 1936 - London

same personnel.

| | | |
|---|---|---|
| CE-7834-1 | Lovable and Sweet | Parlophone F-657, A-6649,<br>Od OF-5348 |
| CE-7835-1 | I Must Have That Man | Parlophone F-575, A6601,<br>Od OF-5274 |
| CE-7836-1 | You're Not the Kind | Parlophone F-631, A-6623<br>Od OF-5328 |
| CE-7837-1 | You Let Me Down | Parlophone F-605, Od OF-5304,<br>Scala 330 |

September 25, 1936 - London

  same personnel.

  CE-7838-2  Mean to Me               Parlophone   F-631,    A-6623,
                                    Od OF-5328
  CE-7839-2  Dixie Lee                Parlophone F-605,  Od OF-5304,
                                    Scala 330

July 7, 1937 - London

  Valaida Snow (tp,vo) acc. by Johnny Claes (tp); Derek Neville (as,bars);
  Reg Dare (ts); Gunn Furley (p); Norman Brown (g); Louis Barreiro (b);
  Ken Stewart (d).

  CE-8479-1  The Mood That I'm In     Parlophone F-867, A-6764,
                                Od OF-5491
  CE-8480-1  Sweet Heartache        -      -     -
  CE-8481-1  Don't Know If I'm Comin' Parlophone F-868, A-6765,
              Or Goin'         Od OF-5492
  CE-8482-1  Where is the Sun      -      -     -

July 8, 1937 - London

  same personnel.

  CE-8486-1  Some of These Days   Parlophone F-952, Od OF-5558
  CE-8487-1  Chloe                Parlophone F-1048
  CE-8488-1  Swing is the Thing   Parlophone F-891, A-6790,
                                  Od OF-5514
  CE-8489-1  Nagasaki            Parlophone F-952, Od OF-5558

July 9, 1937 - London

  same personnel.

  CE-8490-1  I Wonder Who Made Rhythm Parlophone F-891, A-6790,
                                  Od OF-5514
  CE-8491-1  I Got Rhythm       Parlophone F-1048

July 14, 1937 - London

  same personnel.

  CE-8492-1  I Can't Believe That   Parlophone F-923, Od OF-5537
              You're In Love With Me
  CE-8493
  -1-3      Tiger Rag          -        -

August 28, 1939 - Stockholm

  Valaida Snow (tp,vo) acc. by LULLE ELLBOJ'S ORCHESTRA:  Lulle Ellboj

(as,dir); Engt Artander, Gunnar Green (tp); Sture Green (tb); Gunnar
Wallberg (as); Rudolf Eriksson (ts); Willard Ringstrand (p); Karl Lohr
(g); Roland Bengtsson (b); Olle Sahlin (d).

| | | |
|---|---|---|
| 4875-SEB | Minnie the Moocher | Sonora 3577, Tono M-11104 |
| 4876-SEC | Caravan | Sonora 3557, 511, De 9112, Jazz Club de Belgique 4225 |
| 4877-SEB | Swing Low, Sweet Chariot | Snora 3577, De 9112, -, Tono M11104 |
| 4878-SEB | My Heart Belongs to Daddy | Sonora 3557, 511,  -  - |

July 26, 1940 - Copenhagen

MISS VALAIDA MED WINSTRUP OLESENS SWINGBAND: Valaida Snow (tp,vo);
Winstrop Oleson (tp,cir); Kai Moeller (cl); Leo Mathiesen (p); Helge
Jacobsen (g); Christian Jensen (b); Kai Fischer (d).

| | | |
|---|---|---|
| 1062-B | You're Driving Me Crazy | Tono 21165, Ekko 280 |
| 1063-B | Take It Easy | -       - |
| 1064-A-B | I Can't Give You Anything But Love | Tono 21166, Ekko 281 |
| 1065-B | St. Louis Blues | -       - |

October, 1940 - Copenhagen

MISS VALAIDA MED MAT ADORERNE: Valaida Snow (tp,vo); Tage Rasmussen
(tp); Aage Voss (cl,as,bars); Henry Hageman-Larsen (ts,cl); Bertrand
Beck (p); Willy Sorenson (b); Eric Kragh (d,vib).

| | | |
|---|---|---|
| 1140-B | Some of These Days | Tono 21194, Ekko 309 |
| 1141-B | Carry Me Back to Old Virginny | -       - |

December, 1945 - Los Angeles

Valaida Snow (tp,vo) acc. by BUZZY ADLAM'S ORCHESTRA AND THE DAY-
DREAMERS: unknown big band with strings.

| | | |
|---|---|---|
| BT54 | Fool That I Am | Bel-Tone 7001 |
| BT56 | Lonesome Road | -  , Gold Star 5657 |
| | If I Only Had You | Bel-Tone ,7002   - |
| | Talk of the Town | - |

January, 1950 - New York City

Valaida Snow (tp,vo) acc. by JIMMY MUNDY'S ORCHESTRA: including Jonah
Jones (tp); Dave McRae (bars).

| | |
|---|---|
| Chloe | Halo LP 50280 |
| When a Woman Loves a Man | - |
| Tell Me How Long the Train's Been Gone | - |
| Coconut Head | - |

1953 - Chicago

    details unkown.

    4405        I Ain't Gonna Tell          Chess 1555
    4407        If You Don't Mean It        -

date unknown.

    details unknown.

                I Must Have That Man        Bel-Tone 7007
                Solitude                    -
                Caravan                     Bel-Tone 7008
                Frustration                 -


## SORTIER, AMANDA (washboard)

December 17, 1940 - Chicago

    Joe McCoy (vo) acc. by (prob) Lee McCoy (hca); Amanda Sortier (wbd,vo);
    u (b).

    3504-1      If You Take Me Back         Okeh 06141
    3505-1      I'm Through With You        Okeh 06175
    3506-1      When You Said Goodbye       -
    3507-1      I Love You Baby             Okeh 06141


July 23, 1941 - Chicago

    Big Joe (vo,g) acc. by Lee McCoy (hca); Charlie McCoy (mandolin); Alfred
    Elkins (imitation-b); Amanda Sortier (wbd).

    064723-1    What Will I Do              Bluebird B8864
    064724-1    Oh Red's Twin Brother       -
    064725-1    We Can't Agree              Bluebird B8814
    064726-1    Let's Try Again             -


## SOYER, JANET (harp)

April 19, 1960 - New York City

    Sarah Vaugh (vo) acc. by JIMMIE JONES' ORCHESTRA:  Harry Edison (tp);
    Gerald Sanfino (fl,ts); Ronnell Bright (p); Barry Galbraith (g); Richard
    Davis, George Duvivier (b); Percy Brice (d); Janet Soyer (h); u
    (strings).

    14956       The More I See You          Roulette REP1003, R(S) 52046
    14597       Star Eyes                   -               -
                Moon Over Miami             -               -,F(S)52053

| | |
|---|---|
| Hands Across the Table | Roulette R(S) 52046 |
| I'll Be Seeing You | - |
| You've Changed | -, R(S)52050,Forum F(S)9064 |
| Trees | -, R(S)52053,Forum F(S)9067 |
| Why Was I Born | -, R(S)52050,Forum F(S)9064 |
| My Ideal | - |
| Crazy He Calls Me | -, R(S)52057 |
| Stormy Weather | - |
| Dreamy | - |

January 24, 1962 - New York

Jackie Paris (vo) acc. by Clyde Raesinger, Irv Markowtiz, Al Derisi, Louis Gluckin (tp); Don Gravine, Paul Faulise, Bill Schaler, Phil Giacabbe (tb); Hal McKusick, Tom Alfano, John Murtaugh, Howard Rittner (reeds); Phil Bodner (fl); Janet Soyer (h); Barry Galbraith (g); George Duvivier (b); Maurice Mach (d); Willard Dillon (perc).

| | |
|---|---|
| Nobody Loves All the Time | Impulse A(S) 17 |

## SPIVEY, VICTORIA
(piano, organ, ukelele)

May 11, 1926 - St. Louis

| 9651-A | Black Snake Blues | Okeh 8338 |
|---|---|---|
| 9652-A | Dirty Woman's Blues | Okeh 8351 |

June 24, 1961 - New York City

Victoria Spivey (p).

| | |
|---|---|
| Brownskin Warmup | Queen Vee Souvenir 1 |

July 13, 1961 - New York City

| 281 | I Got the Blues So Bad | Bluesville BLP 1044 |
|---|---|---|

August 16, 1961 - New York City

Victoria Spivey (p,vo) acc. by BUSTER BAILEY'S BLUES BUSTERS: Sidney De Paris (tp,tuba); J.C. Higginbotham (tb); Buster Bailey (cl); Zutty Singleton (d).

| 304 | Black Snake Blues | Bluesville BVLP 1052 |
|---|---|---|
| 305 | Goin' Back Home | - |

September 21, 1961 - New York City

    Victoria Spivey (p,vo); Lonnie Johnson (g,vo).

| | |
|---|---|
| Grow Old Together | Bluesville BVLP 1054 |
| I'm a Red Hot Mama | -,  BVLP 1055 |
| Thursday Girl | - |
| Christmas Without Santa Claus | - |
| Let's Ride Together | - |
| Wake Up Daddy | - |

September 26, 1961 - New York City

    Victoria Spivey (p) solo.

| | |
|---|---|
| 1930 Blues | Queen Vee Souvenir 1 |

February 12, 1962 - New York City

    Eddie Barefield (as,cl); Victoria Spivey (p,org,uk,vo); Pat Jenkins (d).

| | | |
|---|---|---|
| 14 | Grant Spivey | Spivey LP 1002 |
| 15 | Cool Papa | - |
| 17 | New York Moan | - |
| 18 | Talk About Moanin' | - |
| 19 | Brooklyn Bridge | - |
| 20 | When I Was Seven | - |
| 21 | Thirty Years | - |
| 22 | Buddy Tate | - |
| 23 | Mr. Daddy | - |
| 24 | So Long Buddy | - |
| 25 | From Broadway to Seventh Avenue | - |
| 26 | New York Tombs | - |

February 21, 1962 - New York City

    Lucille Hegamin (vo) acc. by Eddie Barefield (cl,as); Victoria Spivey (p); Pat Wilson (d).

| | | |
|---|---|---|
| 33 | Brown Skin | Spivey LP 1001 |

March 14, 1962 - New York City

    Victoria Spivey (p,org,uk,vo).

| | | |
|---|---|---|
| 60 | Playing With the Keys | Spivey EP 101 |
| 69 | Got the Best of Me | Spivey LP 1001 |
| 73 | Turpentine | Spivey EP 101 |
| 76 | My Debts | Spivey LP 1001 |
| | Blues for Robert Calvin | - |

October 18, 1962 - New York City

Victoria Spivey (p,uk,vo); Pat Wilson (d).

| | |
|---|---|
| By Yourself | Folkways FS 3815 |
| My Head is Bad | - |
| Eagle and the Hawk | - |
| Can I Wash Your Clothes | - |
| Low Friends | - |
| Good Sissages | - |
| Don't Care | - |
| Don't Worry About It | - |
| Six Foot Daddy | - |
| Big Black Belt | - |
| You're My Man | - |

Kazoo Papa (Len Kunstadt) (kazoo) added.

| | |
|---|---|
| Won't Need Nobody | - |
| Kazoo Papa Blues | - |

October 13, 1963 - Bremen, Germany

Victoria Spivey (uke,vo) acc. by Willie Dixon (b); Bill Stepney (d).

| | |
|---|---|
| Grant Spivey | Fontana 6815102L |

August 9, 1964 - Meridien

| | |
|---|---|
| Sister Kate | G.H.B. GHB-17 |
| Careless Love | - |
| Four or Five Times | - |
| Shaky Babe From New Orleans | - |
| Mama's Gone Goodbye | - |
| See See Rider | - |

Note: Additional recordings by Ms. Spivey lie outside the temporal scope of this discography.

### STARR, JEAN (trumpet)

See Collective Section.

### STICHT, BETTY
(clarinet, alto sax, tenor sax)

See Collective Section.

STOBART, KATHY (tenor sax)

January 25, 1949 - London

VIC LEWIS AND HIS ORCHESTRA: Johnny Shakespeare, Bunny Lazell, Hank Shaw, Harold Duff (tp); Gordon Langhorn, Stan Smith, Jack Waters (tb); Ronnie Chamberlain, Peter Howe (cl,as,sop); Kathy Stobart, Vince Bovil (ts); Bill Collins (bars); Dill Jones (p); Al Ferman (g); John Honeyman (b); Peter Coleman (d); Vic Lewis (cond).

| CE12500 | West Indian Ritual | Parlophone (E) R3195 |
|---------|--------------------|----------------------|
| CE12501 | Sunday Girl        | -                    |
| CE12502 | High on a Windy Hill | Parlophone (E) R3208 |
| CE12503 | No Orchids         | -                    |

September-October, 1949 - London

Mickey Meene, Johnny Oldfield, Norman McCaskill (tp) replace Lazell, Shaw and Shakespeare; Mac Minshull (tb) replaces Waters; Jack Phillips (bars) replaces Collins. Ferdman out.

| | Harlem Holiday | Vic Lewis Society DR 1352 |
|---|----------------|---------------------------|
| | You Was | - |
| | Safranski | Vic Lewis Society DR 1353 |
| | Heir to a Chinese Maiden | - |
| | Inspiration | Vic Lewis Society DR 1351 |

May 7, 1951 - London

VIC LEWIS AND HIS ORCHESTRA: Ronnie Simmonds, Stan Reynolds, Bert Courtley (tp); Terry Lewis (tp); Johnny Keating, Ken Goldie (tb); Ronnie Chamberlain, Derek Humble (as,cl); Kathy Stobart, Peter Warner (ts); Jimmy Simmonds (bars); Arthur Greenslade (p); Pete Blanin (b); Peter Coleman (d); Marian Williams (vo).

| 174 | Vic's Riff | Esquire 10-134 |
|-----|------------|----------------|
| 175 | Everywhere | Esquire 10-144 |
| 176 | Be My Love | Esquire 5-024 |
| 177 | The Apple | Esquire 10-144, Discovery 1752, LP 2001 |
| 178 | Festival Riff | Esquire 10-134 |
| 179 | The Moon Was Yellow | Esquire 10-174 |
| 180 | Foggy Day | - |
| 181 | Tea for Two (vMW) | Esquire 5-024 |

October, 1951 - Manchester

KATHY STOBART AND HER ORCHESTRA: Bert Courtley (tp); Derek Humble (as); Kathy Stobart (ts,vo); u (p); Len Harrison (b); Pete Bray (d).

| M182 | He Was a Good Man | Decibel P2 |
|------|-------------------|------------|
| M183 | Idaho (vKS) | Decibel P3 |
| M184 | Old Black Magic | - |
| M185 | Lover Come Back to Me | Decibel P2 |

March 26, 1952 - London

VIC LEWIS AND HIS NEW MUSIC:  Bert Courtley (tp); Tommy Smith (FrH);
Ronnie Chamberlain (as,sop); Kathy Stobart (ts); Jimmy Simmonds
(bars,b-cl); Clive Chaplin (p); Martin Gilbay (b); Peter Coleman (d);
Vic Lewis (cond).

| 284 | Why Do I Love You | Esquire 10-222 |
| 285 | J.D. to V.L. | Esquire 10-232 |
| 286 | Street Scene | Esquire 10-222 |
| 287 | Haru | Esquire 10-232 |

January 9, 1955 - Royal Festival Hall - London

"IN TOWN" JAZZ GROUP:  Dizzy Reece (tp); Johnny Rogers (as); Kathy
Stobart (ts); Eddie Thompson (p); Jack Fallon (b); Don Lawson (d).

| DR20168 | I've Got You Under My Skin | Decca (E) LF 1217 |
| DR20169 | I Can't Get Started | - |
| DR20170 | Good Queen Bess | - |
| DR20171 | 52nd Street Theme | - |

November 25, 1957 - London

HUMPHREY LYTTLETON AND HIS BAND:  Humphrey Lyttleton (tp); Eddie Harvey
(tb); Tony Coe (as,cl); Kathy Stobart (ts); Ian Armit (p); Brian
Brockelhurst (b); Eddie Taylor (d).

| Gee Baby Ain't I Good to You | Parlophone (E)PMD1052, Stash ST109 |

John Picard (tb); replaces Harvey.

| Goin' Out the Back Way | Decca (D)LP4276, Eclipse ECM(S)2009, London (Am)LC3101 |

November 26, 1957 - London

same personnel.

| Pocket of Blues | Parlophone (E) PMD 1052 |
| Rain | - |

December 3, 1957 - London

same personnel.

| In a Mellotone | Parlophone (E) PMD 1052 |
| Kath Meets Humph | - |
| Moten Swing | - |

December 5, 1957 - London

   same personnel.

               Buona Sera                  Parlophone (E) R4392
               Blues in the Afternoon          -

February 16 ,1959 - London

HUMPHREY LYTTLETON AND HIS BAND: Humphrey Lyttleton, Eddie Blair, Bert
Courtley, Bobby Pratt (tp); John Picard, Eddie Harvey, Keith Christie
(tb); Tone Coe (as,cl); Ronnie Ross (as); Jimmy Skidmore, Kathy Stobart
(ts); Joe Temperley (bars); Ian Armit (p); Brian Brockelhurst (b); Eddie
Taylor (d).

               Swingtime in the Rockies     London (Am) LL3132,PS-178
               I Can't Get Started           -          -
               For Dancers Only              -          -
               Alligator Crawl               -          -

May 25, 1966 - Paris

Buck Clayton, Humphrey Littleton (tp); Chris Pyne (tb); Kathy Stobart
(ts); Eddie Harvey (p,tb); Dave Green (b); Tony Taylor (d).

               Say Forward, I'll March     "77" LEU 12/18
               Russian Lullaby               -
               Talkback                     -
               One for Buck                 -
               An Evening in Soho            -
               The Jumpin' Blues             -
               Blue Mist                    -
               The Swingin' Birds            -
               Poor Butterfly               -

<u>STOCKTON, ANN MASON</u> (harp)

1957 - Los Angeles

Paul Horn (cl,as,fl); Ann Mason Stockton (h); Fred Katz (cello); Calvin
Jackson (p); John Pisano (g); Harold Gaylor (b); Chico Hamilton (d).

               Satori                     Decca DL 9202
               Andante                    -
               Lament of the Oracles      -
               I'm Glad There is You      -
               The Toy That Never Was     -

               See Collective Section for Additional Recordings

### TEAGARDEN, NORMA (piano)

December 11, 1944 - New York City

JACK TEAGARDEN AND HIS SWINGIN' GATES:  Max Kaminsky (tp); Jack Teagarden (tb,vo); Ernie Cacecres (cl); Norma Teagarden (p); George "Pops" Foster (b); George Wettling (d); Wingy Mannone (vo).

| 4839 | Chinatown | Commodore 592, FL 20.015 |
| 4840 | Big "T" Blues (vJT) | - | - |
| 4841 | Rockin' Chair (vJT,WM) | Commodore 1521, | -, Jzt J1216 |
| 4842 | Pitchin' A Bit short | - | - | - |

March, 1945 - Los Angeles

JACK TEAGARDEN AND HIS ORCHESTRA: Jerry Redmond, Ray Borden, Tex Williamson, Jerry Rosen (tp); Jack Teagarden, Wally Wells, Jack Lantz, Palmer Combatelli (tb); Merton Smith, Bob Derry, Voc Rosi, Bert Noah, Dale Jolley (saxes); Norma Teagarden (p); Charles Gilruth (g); Lloyd Springer (b); Frank Horrington (d); Sally Lang (vo).

| | |
|---|---|
| Big "T" Jump | Standard Transcriptions Z201 |
| Little Rock Getaway | - |
| Out of Nowhere | - |
| Hundustan | -, Climax (G) EP109, Allegro LP1656, Rondolette A18, Royale LP 18135, LP 18156, Ember (E) CJS803 |
| King Porter Stomp | Standard Transcriptions Z201, Climax (G) EP109, Allegro LP 1656, Rondolette A18, Royale LP 18156, Ember (E) CJS 803 |
| Sweet Lorraine (vSL) | Standard Transcriptions Z201 |
| Somewhere a Voice is Calling | - |
| How Come (vSL) | - |
| The Mole | - |
| Hobson Street Blues | V-Disc 823 |

November 4, 1953 - New York City

JACK TEAGARDEN AND HIS BAND:  Charlie Teagarden (tp); Jack Teagarden (tb,vo); Jay St. John (cl); Norma Teagarden (p); Kass Malone (b); Ray Bauduc (d).

| 85474 | I Gotta Right to Sing the Blues | Decca 91832, DL8304, Br (E) LAT 8229, Ace of Hearts AH28 |
| 85475 | I'm Gonna Stomp Mr. Henry Lee | Decca 91833, DL8304, Br (E) LAT 8229, Ace of Hearts AH28 |
| 85476 | Love Me (vJT) | Decca 91833, DL8304, Br (E) LAT 8229, Ace of Hearts AH28 |
| 85477 | Body and Soul | Decca 91832, DL8304, Br (E) LAT 8229, Ace of Hearts AH28 |

November 12, 1954 - New York City

Fred Greenleaf (tp); Jack Teagarden (tb,vo); Kenny Davern (cl); Norma
Teagarden (p); Kass Malone (b); Ray Bauduc (d).

| | |
|---|---|
| Riverboat Shuffle | Period SPL1110,Jzt J1033,J1222, Bethlehem BCP32, London LTZ-N15077 |
| King Porter Stomp | Period SPL1110,Jzt J1033,J1222, Bethlehem BCP32, London LTZ-N15077, Par(E) GEP 8834 |
| Milenberg Joys | Period SPl1106, Jzt J1033,J122, Bethlehem BCP32, BCP 6042, London LTZ N-15077, Ember EMB3340 |

TERRELL, SISTER O.M. (guitar)

c. 1951 - Nashville, Tennesse

Sister O.M. Terrell (g,vo) acc. by u (g,b,d).

| | | |
|---|---|---|
| C049044 | The Bible's Right | Columbia (4) 21228-R |
| C049046-1A | The Gambling Man | Columbia (4) 21092-R, Blues Cl BC18 |
| C049047-1A | I'm Going To That City (To Die No More) | Blues Cl BC18 |
| C049048 | Lord, I Want You to Lead Me On | Columbia (4) 21228-R, Yazoo 1046 |
| | Swing Low Sweet Chariot | Columbia (4) 21139-R |
| | God's Little Birds | - |

TERRY, THELMA (bass)

March 29, 1928 - Chicago

THELMA TERRY AND HER PLAY BOYS: Thelma Terry (dir,b); Johnny Mendel,
Carl Rinker (tp); Floyd O'Brien (tb); Bud Jacobson (cl); Mike Platt
(cl,as); Phil Shukin (cl,ts); Bill Otto (p); Roy Campbell (bj); Gene
Krupa (d).

| | | |
|---|---|---|
| 145852-3 | Mama's Gone, Goodbye | Columbia 1706-D |
| 145853-3 | Lady of Havana | Columbia 1390-D, 5015 |
| 145854-3 | The Voice of the Southland | -           -, 01481 |
| 144855-4 | Starlight and Tulips | Columbia 1532-D |

September 27, 1928 - New York City

THELMA TERRY AND HER PLAY BOYS: Thelma Tery (dir,b); Dub Fleming (c);
Warren Smith (tb); Charles Dornberger (cl,as); Earl Gray (as); Pat
Davies (cl,ts); Bob Zurke (p); George Shirley (bj); Joe Davis (d).

| 146961-3 | When Sweet Susie Goes Steppin' By | Columbia 1588-D, 01403 |
|---|---|---|
| 146962-2 | Dusky Stevedore | -         -  , 5164 |

## THARPE, SISTER ROSETTA (guitar, piano)

October 31, 1938 - New York

Sister Rosetta Tharpe (g,vo).

| 64727-A | Rock Me | Decca 2243, MCA 510187, Jazz Society LP-20 |
|---|---|---|
| 64728-A | That's All | Decca 2503 |
| 64729-A | My Man and I | Decca 2243, MCA 510187, Jazz Society LP-20 |

January 10, 1939 - New YOrk

Sister Rosetta Tharpe (g,vo).

| 64881-A | Bring Back Those Happy Days | Decca 2558 |
|---|---|---|
| 64882-A | This Train | - |
| 64883-A | I Looked Down the Line (and I Wondered) | Decca 2328, MC 510187 |
| 64884-A | God Don't Like It | -         - |
| 64885-A | Beams of Heaven | Decca 3254 |
| 64886-A | Saviour, Don't Pass Me By | - |

March 13, 1941 - New York

Sistern Rosetta Tharpe (g,vo).

| 68815-A | End of My Journey | Decca 8538 |
|---|---|---|
| 68816-A | Sit Down | -  , Jazz Society LP-20 |
| 68817-A | There is Something Within Me | Decca 8548,         - |
| 68818-A | Stand By Me | -         - |

June 27, 1941 - New York City

LUCKY MILLINDER AND HIS ORCHESTRA: Lucky Millinder (dir); William Scott, Archie Johnson, Nelson Bryant (tp); George Stevenson, Donald Cole, Eli Robinson (tb); Billy Bowen, George James (as); Buster Bailey (cl,ts); Stafford Simon (ts); Ernest Purce (bars); Bill Doggett (p); Abe Bolar (b); Panama Francis (d); Sister Rosetta Tharpe (g,vo); Trevor Bacon (vo).

| 69437-A | Trouble in Mind (vSRT) | Decca 4041, 48053,Br 03295, V-Desc 129 |
|---|---|---|
| 60438-A | Slide, Mr. Trombone (vTB) | Decca 3956 |
| 60440-A | Rock, Daniel (vSRT) | Decca 3956 |

Floyd Brady, Edward Morant (tb) replace Cole and Robinson.

| 69709-A | Rock Me (vSRT) | Decca 18353 |

December 1, 1941 - New York

Sister Rosetta Tharpe (g,vo).

| 69980-A | Just a Closer Walk With Thee | Decca 8594 |
| 69981-A | Precious Lord Hold My Hand | Decca 8610 |
| 69982-A | I'm In His Care | Decca 8594 |
| 69983-A | Nobody's Fault But Mine | Decca 8610, Jazz Society LP-20 |

June 10, 1942 - New York

Sister Rosetta Tharpe (g,vo).

| 70852-A | What He Done For Me | Decca 8639 |
| 70853-A | I Want Jesus To Walk Around My Bedside | Decca 8634 |
| 70854-A | All Over This World | Decca 8639 |
| 70855-A | Pure Religion | Decca 8634 |

November 26, 1943 - New York

Sister Rosetta Tharpe (g,vo).

| 71523-AA | Let That Liar Alone | Decca 48023 |
| 71524-AA | The Devil Has Thrown Him Down | Decca 48024 |
| 71525-A | Sleep On Darling Mother | Decca 8657 |
| 71526 | God Don't Like It | Decca 48022 |

December 15, 1943 - New York

Sister Rosetta Tharpe (g,vo).

| 71570-A | I Want to Live So God Can Use Me | Decca 8657 |

April 21, 1944 - New York

Sister Rosetta Tharpe (g,vo).

| 72016-A | What's the News | Decca 48023 |

September 11, 1944 - New York

Sister Rosetta Tharpe (g,vo).

| 72377-A | Nobody Knows, Nobody Cares | Decca 48209 |
| 72378-A | Jesus Taught Me How to Smile | Decca 48021 |
| 72379-A | Forgive Me Lord and Try Me One More Time | - |
| 72380-A | What is the Soul of Man | Decca 48022 |

November 26, 1944 - New York

Sister Rosetta Tharpe (g,vo).

| 72396-A | Singing in My Soul | Decca 8672 |
| 72397-A | I Claim Jesus First | - |
| 72398-A | Strange Things Happening Every Day | Decca 8669, DL 8782 |
| 72399-A | Two Little Fishes and Five Loaves of Bread | - |

January 11, 1946

Sister Rosetta Tharpe (g,vo) and THE SAM PRICE TRIO: Sam Price (p); Billy Taylor (b); Wallace Bishop (d).

| 73274 | Don't Take Everybody To Be Your Friend | Decca 11022, 48025 |
| 73277 | When I Move to the Sky | -        - |

May 2, 1946

Ben Moten (b); replaces Taylor; Ed Bourne (d) replaces Bishop.

| 73548 | Jesus is Here Today | Decca 48013 |
| 73549 | Jonah | - |
| 73550 | God's Mighty Hand | MCA 510148 |
|       | The Lord Followed Me | Decca 48030 |

July 2, 1947 - New York

Sister Rosetta Tharpe (g,vo) acc. by THE SAM PRICE TRIO: Sam Price (p); George "Pops" Foster (b); Kenny Clark (d).

| 73987-A | This Train | Decca 48043, DL 8783 |

Marie Knight (vo) added.

| 73988-A | Oh, When I Come to the End of My Journey | -   , MCA 510148 |
| 73989-A | Didn't It Rain | Decca 48054, DL 8782 |
| 73990-A | Stretch Out | -   , MCA 510148 |

November 24, 1947 - New York

Sister Rosetta Tharpe (g,vo) acc. by THE SAM PRICE TRIO:  Sam Price (p);
George "Pops" Foster (b); Wallace Bishop (d).

| 74153-A | Beams of Heaven | Decca 48070, MCA 510148 | |
|---|---|---|---|
| 74154-A | Up Above My Head I Hear Music in the Air | Decca 48090, DL 8782 | |
| 74155-A | My Journey to the Sky | - | - |

November 25, 1947 - New York

same personnel.

| 74166-A | Teach Me To Be Right | Decca 48083, MCA 510148 | |
|---|---|---|---|
| 74167-A | I Heard My Mother Call My Name | Decca 48166 | |
| 74168-A | Heaven is Not My Home | Decca 48190, | - |
| 74169-A | The Natural Facts | Decca 48166 | |
| 741670-A | Cain't No Grave Hold My Body Down | Decca 48154 | |
| 741671-A | Lay Down Your Soul | Decca 48083, | - |

Marie Knight (vo) added.

| 741672-A | Precious Memories | Decca 48070, | - |
|---|---|---|---|

Knight out.

| 741673-A | Family Prayer | Decca 48190 |
|---|---|---|

December 30, 1947 - New YOrk

Sister Rosetta Tharpe (g,vo) acc. by the Dependable Boys (vocal trio).

| 74491-A | Everybody's Gonna Have a Wonderful Time Up There | Decca 48071, MCA 510148 | |
|---|---|---|---|
| 74492-A | My Lord and I | - | - |

c. 1948 - New York

Sister Katie Marie (Sister Rosetta Tharpe) (g,vo).

| I Don't Know Why | Downbeat/Swingtime 142 |
|---|---|
| It is Well With My Soul | - |
| On the Battle Field for My Lord | Downbeat/Swingtime 144 |
| Like a Ship Tossed at Sea | - |
| I Know It Was the Blood | Downbeat/Swingtime 156 |
| Does Anybody Here Know My Jesus | - |

u (p,b,d) added.

> If I Could Hear My Mother  Downbeat/Swingtime 143
> Pray Again
> What a Friend We Have in Jesus      -

December 2, 1948 - New York

Sister Rosetta Tharpe (g,vo) acc. by the SAM PRICE TRIO:  Sam Price (p);
Billy Taylor (b); u (d); Marie Knight (vo).

| 74637-A | He Watches Me | Decca 48098, MCA 510148 |
| 74638-A | He's All I Need | - |

The Dependable Boys (vocal trio) added.

| 74641 | Down By the Riverside | Decca 48106, DL 8782 |
| 74643 | My Lord's Gonna Move | -          - |

December 3, 1948 - New York

same.

| 74646-A | Ain't No Room in the | Decca 48154, MCA 510148 |
|         | Church for Liars |  |
| 74648 | Little Boy How Old Are You | Decca 48177 |
| 74649 | Going Back To Jesus | -          - |

December 12, 1949 - New York

Katie Bell Nubin (vo) acc. by Sister Rosetta Tharpe (g); James Roots
(p); Billy Taylor Sr. (b); Herbert Cowens (d).

| 75586-A | Pressing on the Upward Way | Decca 48132 |
| 75587-A | My Body Belongs to God | - |

May 3, 1950 - New York

same personnel.

| 76264-A | Run to Jesus Everyone | Decca (9) 48222 |
| 76265-A | Is Everybody Happy | - |

December 6, 1954 - New York

Marie Knight (vo) acc. by THE SAM PRICE TRIO:  Sam Price (p); Sister
Rosetta Tharpe (g); u (b, d).

| | Who Rolled the Stone Away | Decca 48333, MCA (F) 510129 |
| | A Traveler's Tune | Decca 48334,          - |
| | A Storm is Passing Over | Decca 48336,          - |
| | I Must Tell Jesus | -          - |

c. 1960 - New York

SOUL SEARCHIN': Katie Bell Nubin (vo) acc. by Dizzy Gillespie (tp); Leo Wright (as); Junior Mance, Sister Rosetta Tharpe (p); Les Spann (g); Art Davis (b); Lex Humphries (d).

| | |
|---|---|
| Pressin' On | Verve V (6) 3004 |
| I Shall Not Be Moved | - |
| Come Over Here | - |
| When the Bridegroom Comes | - |
| Angels Watchin' Over Me | - |
| Where's Adam | - |
| Sad to Think of My Saviour | - |

## THOMAS, LILETTE (piano)

1945 - Los Angeles

LILETTE THOMAS AND HER BOYS: Maxwell Davis (ts); Lilette Thomas (p,vo); Buddy Harper (g); Ralph Hamilton (b); Eddie Harris (d).

| | |
|---|---|
| Blues for My Daddy | Sterling 100 |
| Lilette's Boogie | - |
| Variety Boogie | Sterling 101 |
| That's What Happened to Me | - |

1946 - Los Angeles

LILETTE THOMAS AND HER ESCORTS: Lilette Thomas (p,vo); Hal Mitchell (g); Willie Davis (b); S. Joshua (d).

| | |
|---|---|
| Boogie Woogie Time Down South | Sterling/Sunshine 108 |
| Down It and Get From Around It | - |
| Riffs and Rhythm | Sterling/Sunshine 109 |
| Old Time Daddy Blues | - |

## THOMPSON, BARBARA
### (flute, piccolo, soprano sax)

June, 1967 - London

A SYMPHONY OF AMARANTHS: Derek Watkins, Henry Lowther, Nigel Carter (tp,flhn); Harry Beckett (tp,flghn); Derek Woodsworth (tb); Ray Premra (b-tb); Dick Hart (tuba); Barbara Thompson (fl,pic,sop); Don Kendell (fl,alto-fl,sop,ts); Dave Gelly (cl,b-cl,ts,glochenspiel); Dick Heckstall-Smith (sop,ts); John Clementson (oboe); Bunny Gould (bassoon); Neil Ardley (synthesizer); Stan Tracey (p); Frank Ricotti (vib); David Snell (h); Jack Rothenstein, Kelly Isaacs (vn); Kenneth Essex (viola); Charles Tunnell, Francis Gabaro (cello); Chris Lawrence (b); John Hiseman (d,per); Jack Rothstein (dir).

|                    |                         |
|--------------------|-------------------------|
| Carillon I         | Regal-Zonophone SLR 21028 |
| Nocturne II        | -                       |
| Entracte III       | -                       |
| Impromptu IV       | -                       |

### June 16-17, 1967 - London

Piano and strings out. Norma Winstone (vo); David Snell (h) added. Neil Ardley (dir) replaces Jack Rothstein.

|                              |                         |
|------------------------------|-------------------------|
| After Long Silence           | Regal-Zonophone SLR 21028 |
| She Weeps Over Raboon        | -                       |
| Will You Walk a Little Faster | -                      |

## THOMPSON, LORETTA (harp)

### 1946 - Los Angeles

BOYD RAEBURN AND HIS ORCHESTRA: Frank Beach, Ray Linn, Dale Pierce, Nelson Shelladay (tp); Tommy Pederson, Hal Smith, Fred Zito (tb); Lloyd Otto, Evan Vail (FrH); Bill Starkey (EngH); Willie Schwartz (cl,as); Ralph Lea, Guy McDonald (ts); Hy Mandel (bars); Boyd Raeburn (sop,bass-sax); Loretta Thompson (h); Hal Schaefer (p); Tony Rizzi (g); Harry Babsin (b); Jackie Mills (d); Ginnie Powell (vo).

| JRC230 | Hep Boyd's         | Jewell GN100003, Savoy 804, |
|        |                    | XP8041, MG15011, MG12025    |
| JRC231 | Man With the Horn  | Jewell GN100003, Savoy 800, |
|        |                    | XP8040, MG150110, MG12025   |
| JRC232 | Prelude to the Dawn | Jewell GN100004, Savoy 807, |
|        |                    | XP8043, MG15011, MG12025    |
| JRC233 | Duck Waddle        | Jewell GN100004, Savoy 806, |
|        |                    | XP8042, MG15012, MG12025    |

### Autumn, 1946 - Los Angeles

Bob Fowler (tp) replaces Shelladay; Burt Johnson, Ollie Wilson (tb); replace Smith and Zito; Max Albraight (d) replaces Mills. Ethmer Roden (fl,as) added.

| JRC238 | Love Talks          | Jewell GN10005, Savoy 808, |
|        |                     | XP8041, MG15011, MG12025   |
| JRD239 | Soft and Warm (vGP) | Jewell GN10005, Savoy 801, |
|        |                     | XP8041, MG15011, MG12025   |

## VAN DER HARST, ANNE (piano)

### 1959

THE VAN DER HARST QUARTET: Anne Van der Harst (p); Ray Horne (vib); John Bermingham (b); Gordon Lotta (d).

| | | |
|---|---|---|
| I Can't Get Started | World Record Club A1 | |
| Between the Devil and the | - | |
| Deep Blue Sea | | |
| Over the Rainbow | - | |
| I'll Remember April | - | |

## VARLEY, ANNE (piano)

AJ LAURIE BAND: Ken Sims (c); Terry Pitts (tb); Aj Laurie (cl); Anne Varley (p); Diz Disley (bj); Stan Leader (b); Viv Carter (d).

| | | |
|---|---|---|
| 898 | Blue Blood Blues | Esquire EP124 |
| 899 | There'll Come a Day | - |
| 900 | Keyhole Blues | - |
| 901 | Don't Go Away Nobody | - |

## VITO, ELAINE (harp)

July 5 or 6, 1960 - New York

James Moody (ts,as,fl); Hank Jones (p); John Beal (b); Osie Johnson (d); Leon Cohen (woodwinds); u (strings); Elaine Vito (h); Torrie Zito (arr,cond).

| | | |
|---|---|---|
| Dorothee | Argo LP 679 | |
| All My Life | - | |
| I Remember Clifford | - | |
| A Song of Love | - | |

## WALSH, KAY (trumpet)

See Collective Section.

## WALTON, BLANCHE SMITH (piano)

July 12, 1927 - Chicago

Frankie "Half Pint" Jaxon (vo) acc. by Blanch Smith Walton (p); Jasper Taylor (wb).

| | | |
|---|---|---|
| 12919-A | Can't You Wait Till You Get Home | Gennett 6214, Black Patti 8040, Supertone 9283 |
| 12920-A | I'm Gonna Steal You a Million Dollars | Gennett 6215, - Supertone 9283 |

July 22, 1927 - Chicago

same personnel.

| 12941-A | Willie the Weeper | Black Patti 8048 |
| --- | --- | --- |

**August 1, 1927 - Chicago**

Taylor out.

| 12959 | She's Got It | Gennett 6244 |
| --- | --- | --- |
| 12960 | I'm Gonna Dance Wit De Guy Wot Brung Me | - |

**August 3, 1927 - Chicago**

| 12966 | Corrine | Black Patti 8048 |
| --- | --- | --- |

## WATERS, PATTY (piano)

**December 19, 1965 - New York**

Patty Waters (p,vo).

| Moon Don't Come Up Tonight | ESP 1025 |
| --- | --- |
| Why Can't I Come to You | - |
| You Thrill Me | - |
| Sad Am I, Glad Am I | - |
| Why Is Love Such a Funny Thing | - |
| I Can't Forget You | - |
| You Loved Me | - |

Burton Greene (p,piano-harp); Steve Tintweiss (b); Tom Price (d) added.

| Black is the Color of My True Love's Hair | ESP 1025 |
| --- | --- |

## WATKINS, VIOLA (piano)

**1946 - New York City**

Viola Watkins (p,vo) acc. by THE HONEY DRIPS: details unknown.

| Somebody's Someone | Ebony 102 |
| --- | --- |
| I Guess I'm Not the Type | - |

**1947 - New York City**

Viola Watkins (p,vo) acc. by THE SUPER JAZZ MEN: details unknown.

| MF124 | It's Right Here for You | Super Disc 1047 |
| MF125 | You're In Love With Everyone | - |
| MF186 | Hey Stop Kissing My Sister | Super Disc 1052 |
| MF189 | Tonight You Belong to Me | - |
| MF212 | Now I Know | MGM 10232 |
| MF215 | I Wonder Why | - |
| | Hey Mama | MGM 10344 |
| | My Real Fine Man | - |

1949 - New York City

Viola Watkins (p,vo); acc. by u (g,b,d).

| JR186 | Cream Pie Daddy | Jubilee 5012 |
| JR187 | Am I Wasting My Time | - |
| JR188 | That's For Sure | Jubilee 5007 |
| JR189 | I Want You I Need You | Jubilee 5043 |
| JR190 | Put It Back Before I Miss It | - |
| JR191 | Red Riding Hood | Jubilee 5023 |
| JR192 | Jelly and Bread | Jubilee 5007 |

c. 1952 - New York City

Viola Watkins (p,vo) acc. by FRANK HUMPHRIES ORCHESTRA:  Frank Humphries (tp); others unknown.

| JR645 | Laughing At Life | Jubilee 5023 |

## WATSON, PAULA (piano)

1947 - Los Angeles

| SA595 | Pretty Papa Blues | Supreme 1507, Swing Time 252 |
| SA596 | A Little Bird Told Me | - - |

1947 - Los Angeles

Paula Watson (p,vo) acc. by Tiny Webb (g) and others.

| | Nightmare Boogie | Supreme 1510, Swing Time 252 |
| | You Broke Your Promise | Supreme 1512 |
| | I've Got the Sweetest Man Of All Things | - |
| | | Supreme 1518 |
| | Hidin' in the Sticks | - |

## WEBER, ANNETTE (organ)

See Collective Section.

WEBSTER, KATIE (piano)

1956 - Lake Charles

Elton Anderson (g,vo) acc. by Danny George (ts); Katie Webster (p); Sid
Lawrence (b); Roosevelt Griffin (d).

ACA3573, Shed So Many Tears          Vin 1001
4004
ACA3574, Roll On Train                   -
4005


c. 1958 - Crowley, Louisiana

Leroy Washington (g,vo) acc. by Katie Webster (p); Bobby McBride (b-g);
Warren Storm (d).

                Wild Cherry              Excello 2144, Stateside(E)S110008
                Be Kind                      -
                Chinatown Gal            Excello 2161
                Gimme My Right               -
                My True Life             Excello 2172
                Why Should I Cry             -


1958 - Crowley, Louisiana

Katie Webster, Ashton Conroy (p); Ashton Savoy (g,vo); Little Brother
Griffin (d).

                No Bread No Meat (vAS)   Flyright LP530
K1              Baby, Baby               Kry 100, Flyright 3503
K2              I Want You to Love Me        -          -  , PL530


1958-1959 - Crowley, Louisiana

JIMMY DOTSON AND THE BLUE BOYS:  Jimmy Dotson (vo); Bob McBride or Al
Foreman (g); Katie Webster (p); u (b-g); Warren Storm (d).

7030            Oh Baby                  Rocko 516
7031            I Need Your Love             -


1950-1960 - Lake Charles

Elton Anderson (g,vo) acc. by Danny George (ts); Katie Webster (p); Sid
Lawrence (b); Roosevelt Griffin (d).

19362           Cool Down Baby           Mercury 71542
19363           Secret of Love               -
19807           Walking Alone            Mercury 71643
19809           Crying Blues                 -
                I Love Cherie            Mercury 71778
                Please Accept My Love        -

**1961 - Crowley, Louisiana**

Slim Harpo (James Moore) (hca,vo) acc. by Katie Webster (p); Al Foreman, Bobby McBride (g); Warren Storm (d).

|  |  |
|---|---|
| My Home is a Prison | Excello LP 8003 |
| Bobby Sox Baby | - |

**1966 - Crowley, Louisiana**

Slim Harpo (hca,vo) acc. by James Johnson, Rudolph Richard (g); Katie Webster (p); Geese August (b); Sammy Kaye (d).

|  |  |  |
|---|---|---|
| Baby Scratch My Back | Excello 2273, | LR 8005 |
| I'm Gonna Miss You (Like the Devil) | - | - |
| Shake Your Hips | Excello 2278, | - |
| Midnight Blues | - | - |
| Wonderin' Blues | - | - |
| I'm Your Breadmaker | Excello 2282 | |
| Loving You | - | , CBS 66278 |

date unknown.

Lionel Torrence (Lionel Prevo) (ts,bars); Boo Woo Guidry (ts); Harry Simoneaux (bars); Katie Webster (p,vo); Al Foreman (g); Bobby McBride (b-g); Warren Storm (d).

| R7004 | Open Arms | Rocko 503 |
|---|---|---|
| A701 | Close to My Heart | Action 1000 |
| A702 | On the Sunny Side of the Street | - , Rocko 503 |

date unknown.

Katie Webster (p,vo) acc. by SHERMAN WEBSTER'S BAND: u (tp,saxes,g, b,d).

| LH1925 | Glory Of Love | Spot 1000, Flyright LP530 |
|---|---|---|
| LH1926 | The Katie Lee | - - |

date unknown.

Katie Webster (p,vo) with unknown accompaniment.

| R7024 | Goodbye Baby I'm Still Leaving You - Pt. 1 | Rocko 513, Flyright LP 530 |
|---|---|---|
| R7025 | Goodbye Baby I'm still Leaving You - Pt. 2 | - - |

date unknown.

(prob) Lionel Torrence (Lionel Prevo) (ts,bars); Boo Woo Guidry (ts);
Harry Simoneaux (bars); Katie Webster (p,vo); Al Foreman (g); Bobby
McBride (b-g); Warren Storm (d).

| Z7450 | Shooee Sweet Daddy | Zynn 505 |
| Z7451 | I Need You Baby, I Need You | — |

u (tuba) added.

| | Sunny Side of Love | Flyright LP 530 |

guitar out.

| | I Wanna Know | — |

saxes out.

| | I Feel So Low | — |

date unknown.

Katie Webster (p,vo) acc. by Lionel Torrence (Lionel Prevo) (ts); Peter
Gunther (bars); u (b,g,d).

| | Don't You Know | Flyright LP 530 |
| | Mama Don't Allow | — |

date unknown.

Katie Webster (p,vo).

| | Baby Come Over | Flyright LP 530 |

date unknown.

Katie Webster (p,vo) with unknown accompaniment.

| | Never Let Me Go | A. Bet 9420 |
| | Dearest Darling | — |
| | Lied Lied Lied | Goldband 1248 |
| | Family Rules | — |

date unknown.

Katie Webster (p,vo) acc. by u (g,d).

| | San Antonio Here I Come | Goldband 1252 |
| | Eldorado Katy | — |

date unknown.

Katie Webster (p,vo) with unknown accompaniment.

| | |
|---|---|
| Secret Love | Goldband 1252 |
| Love is the Answer | - |
| I Started Loving You Again | Goldband 1256 |
| Love Bliss Voodoo | - |

## WEBSTER, L'ANA (alto saxophone)

January 18, 1938 - New York City

MIKE RILEY AND HIS ROUND AND ROUND BOYS:  Mike Riley (tb,vo,dir); Harry Prebal, John Montelione (tp); George Tookey (cl,as); L'Ana Webster (as); Joe Butaski (p); Sam de Bonis (g); Pops Darrow (b); Bill Flanagan (d).

| | | |
|---|---|---|
| 63170-A | Cachita | Decca 1662 |
| 63171-A | Oooh Boom! | Decca 1655, F-6635, Br A-81551, Polydor A-61559 |
| 63172-A | You're Giving Me the Run Around | Decca 1655 |
| 63173-A | Oh, Dear, What Can the Matter Be | Decca 1662 |

See Collective Section for Additional Recordings

## WETZEL, BONNIE (bass)

See Collective Section.

## WHITE, GEORGIA (piano)

April 10, 1935 - Chicago

Georgia White (p,vo); u (g).

| | | |
|---|---|---|
| C9907-A | Dupree Blues | Decca 7100 |
| C9908-A | Dallas Man (Lost Lover Blues) | - |
| C9909-A | Your Worries Ain't Like Mine | Decca 7072 |
| C9910-A | You Done Lost Your Good Thing Now | - |

July 15, 1935 - Chicago

same personnel.

| | | |
|---|---|---|
| 90154-A | Honey Dripper Blues | Decca 7122 |
| 90155-A | Freddie Blues | - |
| 90156-A | Easy Rider Blues | Decca 7135 |
| 90157-A | Graveyard Blues | - |

September 7, 1935 - Chicago

| | | |
|---|---|---|
| 90309-A | Your Worries Ain't Like Mine | Decca 7143 |
| 90310-A | You Done Lost Your Good Thing Now | - |

January 16, 1936 - New York City

same personnel.

| | | |
|---|---|---|
| 60346-A | Can't Read, Can't Write | Decca 7166 |
| 60347-A | Tell Me Baby | Decca 7152 |

January 17, 1936 - New York City

same personnel.

| | | |
|---|---|---|
| 60352-C | There Ain't Gonna Be No Doggone Afterwhile | Decca 7174 |
| 60353-A | Someday, Sweetheart | Decca 7166 |

January 21, 1936 - New York City

same personnel.

| | | |
|---|---|---|
| 60374-A-B | If You Can't Get Five, Take Two | Decca 7149 |
| 60375-A | Rattlesnakin' Daddy | Decca 7174 |

January 24, 1936 - New York City

same personnel.

| | | |
|---|---|---|
| 60401-B | Get 'Em from the Peanut Man (Hot Nuts) | Decca 7152 |

April 1, 1938 - New York City

Georgia White (p,vo) acc. by Lonnie Johnson (g); u (b).

| | | |
|---|---|---|
| 63543-A | I'm Blue and Lonesome (Nobody Cares For Me) | Decca 7450 |
| 63547-A | Almost Afraid to Love | - |
| 53548-A | Too Much Trouble | Decca 7477 |
| 63549-A | Crazy Blues | Decca 7807 |

| 63550-A | Tain't Nobody's Business If I Do | Decca 7477 |
| 63551-A | Holding My Own | Decca 7521 |

October 21, 1938 - Chicago

Georgia White (p,vo) acc. by Ikey Robinson (g); John Lindsay (b).

| 91545-A | The Blues Ain't Nothin' But | Decca 7562 |
| 91546-A | Dead Man's Blues | Decca 7534 |
| 91547-A | Love Sick Blues | - |
| 91548-A | My Worried Mind Blues | Decca 7562 |

November 3, 1939 - Chicago

Georgia White (p,vo) acc. by u (as,d).

| 91868-A | Worried Head Blues | Decca 7807 |

March 11, 1941 - Chicago

Georgia White (p,vo) acc. by u (g,b).

| 93573-A | Mail Plane Blues | Decca 7866 |
| 93575-A | Mama Knows What Papa Wants When Papa's Feeling Blue | Decca 7841 |
| 93576-A | Come Around to My House | - |
| 93577-A | Territory Blues | Decca 7853 |
| 93578-A | When You're Away | - |

## WILLIAMS, DEVONIA (piano)

February 18, 1949 - Los Angeles

DEE WILLIAMS SEXTET: John Anderson (tp); Gene Montgomery (ts); Richard Brown (bars); Devonia Williams (p); Morris Edwards (b); Roy Porter (d).

| SLA505-3 | Dee's Boogie | Savoy 684 |
| SLA506-1 | Bongo Blues | - |
| SLA508-1 | Midnite Creep | Savoy 716 |
| SLA509-1 | Double Trouble Hop | - |

October 30, 1953 - Los Angeles

Lil Greenwood (vo) acc. by Devonia Williams (p); Jesse Ervin (g); Mario Delgarde (b); Al Wichard (d).

| F371 | All is Forgiven | Federal 12165 |
| F372 | I'll Go | Federal 12158 |

| F373 | Mercy Me | Federal 12165 |
|------|----------|---------------|
| F374 | I'm Crying | Federal 12158 |

## WILLIAMS, DELLA (guitar)

1961 - New Orleans

Della Williams (g,vo).

| | Motherless Children | Stv SLP 135 |
|--|---------------------|-------------|

## WILLIAMS, EDNA (trumpet)

See Collective Section.

## WILLIAMS, LOVEY (guitar)

Summer, 1968

Lovey Williams (g,vo).

| | Rootin' Ground Hog | Matchbox 226 |
|--|--------------------|--------------|
| | Train I Ride | - |
| | Honey I Ain't Goin' Outta That Door | Xtra 1105 |
| | Baby Let Me Ride in Your Automobile | - |
| | Coal Black Mare | - |
| | Majo Land | - |
| | Boogie Chillun | - |

## WILLIAMS, MARY LOU
## (piano, celeste, leader, arranger)

January, 1927 - Chicago

Jeanette James (vo) acc. by her SYNCO JAZZERS: Henry McCord (tp); Bradley Bullett (tb); John Williams (as,bass-sax); Mary Lou (Burley) Williams (p); Joe Williams (bj); Robert Price (d).

| 4117-2 | Midnight Stomp | Paramount 12470 |
|--------|----------------|-----------------|
| 4119-1 | Downhearted Mama | - |
| 4124-1-3 | The Bumps | Paramount 12451 |
| 4125-1-2 | What's That Thing | - |

February, 1927 - Chicago

JOHN WILLIAMS' SYNCO JAZZERS: Henry McCord (tp); Bradley Bullett (tb);

John Williams (as,bass-sax); Mary Lou (Burley) Williams (p); Joe Williams (bj); Robert Price (d).

| 4187-2 | Down in Gallion | Paramount 12457, Poydras 5, Ristic 9 |
| 4188-1-2 | Goose Grease |   -      -      - , Herwin 92018 |

**March 7, 1927 - Chicago**

same personnel.

| 12626-A | Pee Wee Blues | Gennett 6124, Black Patti 8009, Champion 15295, 40109 |
| 12627-A | Now Cut Loose | Gennett 6124, Black Patti 8009, Champion 15295, 40109 |

**November 7, 1929 - Kansas City**

ANDY KIRK AND HIS TWELVE CLOUDS OF JOY: Gene Prince, Harry Lawson (tp); Allen Durham (tb); Lawrence Freeman, John Williams, John Harrington (saxes); Claude Williams (vn); Mary Lou Williams (p); William Dirvin (bj); Andy Kirk (b); Edward McNeill (d); Billy Massey (vo).

| KC-593 | Cloudy | Brunswick 4653 |

**November 8, 1929 - Kansas City**

same personnel.

| KC-596 | Casey Jones Special | Brunswick 4653 |

**November 9, 1929 - Kansas City**

JOHN WILLIAMS AND HIS MEMPHIS STOMPERS: Andy Kirk (bass-sax); Gene Prince, Harry Lawson (tp); Allen Durham (tb); John Harrington (cl,as); John Williams (as,bars); Lawrence Freeman (ts); Claude Williams (vn); Mary Lou Williams (p); William Dirvin (bj,g); Edward McNeill (d).

| KC-600 | Somepin' Slow and Low | Vocalion 1453 |
| KC-601 | Lotta Sax Appeal | - |

**April 24, 1930 - Chicago**

Mary Lou Williams (p) solo.

| C-5724-C | Night Life | Brunswick 7178,80033,(E)01625, (F)500327,(G)A9507,UHCA 37, Stash ST 109 |
| C-5725-C | Drag 'Em | Brunswick 7178,(E)02507,UHCA 38 |

April 29-30, May 1, 1930 - Chicago

| | | |
|---|---|---|
| C-446-A | I Lost My Gal From Memphis | Brunswick 4803 |
| C-4462-A | Loose Ankles | - |
| C-4470 | Snag It | Brunswick 4878 |
| C-4471 | Sweet and Hot | - |
| C-4473 | Mary's Idea | Brunswick 4863, Perfect 15697 |
| C-4480 | Once or Twice | - - |

July 15, 1930 - Chicago

ANDY KIRK AND HIS TWELVE CLOUDS OF JOY:  Harry Lawson (tp); Allen Durham (tb); John Harrington (as,cl); Mary Lou Williams (p); William Dirvin (bj,g); Edward McNeill (d).

| | | |
|---|---|---|
| C-6017 | Gettin' Off a Mess | Brunswick 7180 |

October 9, 1930 - Chicago

Gene Prince, Harry Lawson (tp); Allen Durham (tb); Lawrence Freeman, John Harrington (saxes); Claude Williams (vn); Mary Lou Williams (p); William Dirvin (bj); Andy Kirk (b); Edward McNeil (d); Billy Massey (vo).

| | | |
|---|---|---|
| C-6430-A | Dallas Blues | Brunswick 6129,(F)A-500124, (G)A-9149 |
| C-6431 | Travelin' That Rocky Road | Brunswick 4981, 01054 |
| C-6432 | Honey, Just For You | - - |
| C-6435 | You Rascal, You | Brunswick 7180 |

December 15, 1930 - New York City

similar personnel.

| | | |
|---|---|---|
| E-35750 | Saturday | Brunswick 6027 |
| E-35751 | Sophomore | -  , Stash ST 109 |

March 2, 1931 - Camden, New Jersey

Blanche Calloway (vo) acc. by her JOY BOYS:  Harry Lawson, Edgar Battle, Clarence Smith (tp); Floyd Brady (tb); John Harrington (cl,as); John Williams (as); Lawrence Freeman (ts); Mary Lou Williams (p); Bill Dirvin (bj); Andy Kirk (tuba); Ben Thigpen (d).

| | | |
|---|---|---|
| 64068-1 | Casey Jones Blues | Victor 22640, HMV B-6114, K-6500,R-14588 |
| 64069-2 | There's Rhythm in the River | Victor 22641 |
| 64070-2 | I Need Lovin' | -  , Bluebird B-5334 |

March 2, 1936

ANDY KIRK AND HIS TWELVE CLOUDS OF JOY: Paul King, Earl Thompson, Harry
Lawson (tp); Ted Donnelly (tb); John Williams, John Harrington (s); Dick
Wilson (ts); Andy Kirk (bass-sax); Claude Williams (vn); Mary Lou
Williams (p); Ted Robinson (g); Booker Collins (b); Ben Thigpen (d,vo).

| 60852-C | Walkin' and Swingin' | Decca 809, Od 284210 |
|---------|----------------------|----------------------|
| 60853-A | Moten Swing | Decca 853,3517, Co DB-5015 |
| 60854-A | Lotta Sax Appeal | Decca 1046, 3883,   - |
| 60861-B-C | Git | Decca 931 |
| 60862-A | All the Jive is Gone | Decca 744, Co DB/MC-5025 |
| 60866-A | Bearcat Shuffle | Decca 1046, Co DB-5025,MZ-489 |
| 60867-A | Steppin' Pretty | Decca 931, Co DB-5023 |
| 60868-A | I'se a Muggin' | Decca 744, Co (E) DM-5004 |
| 60874-A | Christopher Columbus | Decca 729, Co DB-5000 |

March 6, 1936

same personnel.

| 60876-A | Corkey | Decca 772, Y-5112, Co DB-5021 |
|---------|--------|-------------------------------|
| 60877-A | Corny Rhythm | Decca 1021, Co (E) DB/MC 5018 |
| 60878-A | Overhand | Decca 781, 3385,Co MC-5013 |
| 60879-A | Isabelle | Decca 1021,   - |

April 3, 1936

same personnel.

| 60894-A | Swingin' For Joy | Decca 1155, Co (E) MC-5003, DW-4368, MZ-490 |
|---------|------------------|---------------------------------------------|
| 60895-A | Clean Pickin' | Decca 1155, Co (E) MC-5003, DW-4368, MZ-490 |

April 7, 1936

same personnel.

| 60961-C | Puddin' Head Serenade | Decca 1208, Co DB-5027 |
|---------|-----------------------|------------------------|
| 60972 | Until the Real Thing Comes Along | Decca 809, Od 284210 |
| 60973 | Blue Illusion | Decca 772, Y-5112, Co DB-5021 |
| 60974-A | Cloudy | Decca 1208, Co DB-5020 |

April 9, 1936 - New York

Ted Robinson (g); Mary Lou Williams (celeste); Booker Collins (b); Ben
Thigpen (d).

| 61023-A | Mary's Special | Decca 781, 3385, Co(E) MC-5013 |
|---------|----------------|--------------------------------|

February 15, 1937

ANDY KIRK AND HIS TWELVE CLOUDS OF JOY: Paul King, Earl Thompson, Harry Lawson, Henry Wells (tp); Ted Donnelly (tb); John Williams, John Harrington (s); Dick Wilson (ts); Andy Kirk (bass-sax); Mary Lou Williams (p); Ted Robinson (g); Booker Collins (b); Ben Thigpen (d,vo).

| 61003-A | Give Her a Pint (And She'll Tell It All) | Decca 853, Co DB-5029 |
|---|---|---|

1936-1937

same or similar personnel.

| 61463-A | 52nd Street | Decca 1146, M-39028, Br(E)02377 |
|---|---|---|
| 61464-A | A Lady Who Swings the Band | Decca 1085 |
| 61465-A | What Will I Tell My Heart | - | - |
| 61466-B | Dedicated to You | Decca 1146, Y-5179 |

February 15 ,1937

same or similar personnel.

| 61598-A | Wednesday Night Hop | Decca 1303,60522,Br(E)02519 |
|---|---|---|
| 61599-A | Skies Are Blue | Decca 1349,Br(E)02469,A-81275 |
| 61950-A | Downstream | Decca 1531, M-30084, Br(E)02441 |

July 26-27, 1937

Paul King, Earl Thompson, Harry Lawson (tp); Ted Donnelly, Henry Wells (tb); John Williams, John Harrington, Earl Miller (saxes); Dick Wilson (ts); Andy Kirk (bass-sax); Mary Lou Williams (p); Ted Robinson (g); Booker Collins (b); Ben Thigpen (d).

| 62446-A | A Mellow Bit of Rhythm | Decca 1579, M-30084, Br(E)02483, A-81300 |
|---|---|---|
| 62477 | In My Wildest Dreams | Decca 1479 |
| 62448-A | Better Luck Next Time | Decca 1422 |
| 62449-A | With Love In My Heart | Decca 1477 |
| 62453-B | What's Mine Is Yours | Decca 1827 |
| 62454-A | Why Can't We Do It Again | Decca 1477 |
| 62455-A | Key To My Heart | Decca 1710 |
| 62456-A | I Went To a Gypsy | Decca 1422 |
| 62457-A | It Must Be True | Decca 1827 |
| 62539-A | Little Joe From Chicago | Decca 1710, 3385, 25118, Br(E)02740, (G)82077 |

December 13, 1937

same personnel.

| | | | | |
|---|---|---|---|---|
| 62872-A | Lover Come Back To Me | Decca (G)82077 | 1163, | Br(E)02740, |
| 62873-A | Poor Butterfly | Decca (G)82077 | 1663, | - |
| 62874-A | Big Dipper | Decca (G)81521 | 1606, | Br(E)02687, |
| 62875-A | Bear Down | Decca (G)81521 | 1606, | - |

February 8, 1938

Pha Terrell (vo) added.

| | | |
|---|---|---|
| 64255-A | I Surrender Dear | Decca 1916 |
| 64256 | Twinklin' | Decca 2483, Br(E)02789, (G)82200, A-8357 |
| 63258-A | I'll Get By | Decca 1916 |
| 63777-A | Honey (vPT) | Decca 2326 |

September 9, 1938

same personnel.

| | | |
|---|---|---|
| 64613-A | Bless You My Dear | Decca 2204 |
| 64614-A | How Can We Be Wrong | Decca 2081 |
| 64615-A | Mess-A-Stomp | Decca 2204, M-30204, Br(E)20763, A-82105 |
| 64644-A | What Would People Say | Decca 2277 |
| 64645-A | How Much Do You Mean To Me | Decca 2081 |

September 14, 1938

same personnel.

| | | |
|---|---|---|
| 64622-A | The Pearls | Decca 2796, Y-5496, Br88060, (E)02836 |
| 64663-A | Mr. Freddy Blues | Decca 2797, Y-5721, Br02836 |
| 64664-A | Sweet (Patootie) Patunia | - - , Br(E)03009 |
| 64665-A | The Rocks | Decca 2796, Y-5496, Br88060, (E)03009 |

October 24-25, 1938

Clarence Trice, Earl Thompson, Harry Lawson (tp); Henry Wells, Ted Donnelly (tb); Johnny Williams, Buddy Miller, John Harrington, Dick Wilson (saxes); Mary Lou Williams (p); Ted Robinson (g); Booker Collins (b); Ben Thigpen (d).

| | | |
|---|---|---|
| 64694-A | Jump Jack Jump | Decca 2226, M-30204, BR(E)02707, (G)82000 |
| 64695 | Breeze | Decca 2261 |
| 64697-C | What a Life | Decca 2617 |

| 64698-A | Sittin' Around and Dreamin' | Decca 2261 |
|---------|------------------------------|------------|
| 64699-A | What's Your Story Morning Glory | Decca 3306, Y-5855 |

**December 5, 1938**

same personnel.

| 65778 | September in the Rain | Decca 2617 |
|-------|------------------------|------------|
| 64779-A | Clouds | Decca 2570 |
| 64780-A | Julius Caesar | Decca 2383 |
| 64781-A | Dunkin' a Doughnut | Decca 2723, Br(E)02936, (F)505263 |
| 64782 | Goodbye | Decca 2570 |
| 64783-A | Mary's Idea | Decca 2326, Br(E)02740,A-83077 |
| 64784-A | But It Didn't Mean a Thing | Decca 2277 |
| 64785-A | Say It Again | Decca 2774 |

**March 1, 1939**

Don Byas (ts) replaces Williams; Floyd Smith (g) replaces Robinson.

| 65188-A | You Set Me On Fire | Decca 2383 |
|---------|---------------------|------------|
| 65189-A | I'll Never Learn | Decca 2510 |
| 65190-A | Close To Five | Decca 2407, Y-5423,M-30290, M-30348,Br02763, A82105 |
| 65191-A | Floyd's Guitar Blues | Decca 2483, Br(E)02789, (G)82200, A-82457, Coral 160021 |

**March 22, 1939**

same personnel.

| 65249-A | Then I'll Be Happy | Decca 2723 |
|---------|---------------------|------------|
| 65250 | S'Posin' | Decca 2510 |
| 65261-A | I'll Never Fail You | Decca 2407, Y-5423 |

**March, 1939**

Mildred Bailey (vo) and her OXFORD GREYS: Mary Lou Williams (p); Floyd Smith (g); Johnny Williams (b); Eddie Dougherty (d).

| 24228-1 | There'll Be Some Changes Made | Vocalion 2568, Co35943 |
|---------|-------------------------------|------------------------|
| 24229-1 | Barrelhouse Music | Vocalion 4802, Br(G)A82178, Par(E)R2692 |
| 24230-1 | Arkansas Blues | Vocalion 4081, Cq 9217, Od 272261, A-2352, Par(E)R2685, Br A-82177 |
| 24231-1 | Gulf Coast Blues | Vocalion 4800 |
| 24231-2 | Gulf Coast Blues | - |

| 24232-1 | You Don't Know My Mind | Vocalion 4802, Br(G)A82178, |
| | Blues | Par(E)R2692, Od 272261 |
| 24233-1 | Prisoner of Love | Vocalion 5268, Co 35943 |

October 12, 1939 - New York

Mary Lou Williams (p) solo.

| 25470-1 | Little Joe From Chicago | Columbia 37334 |

November 15, 1939

(prob) Clarence Trice, Earl Thompson, Harry Lawson (tp); Henry Wells, Ted Donnelly (tb); Don Byas (ts); Buddy Miller, John Harrington, Dick Wilson (saxes); Mary Lou Williams (p); Floyd Smith (g); Booker Collins (b); Ben Thigpen (d).

| 66877-A | I'm Getting Nowhere With You | Decca 2957 |
| 66878-A | I Don't Stand a Ghost of a Chance With You | Decca 2915 |
| 66879-A | Please Don't Talk About Me When I'm Gone | Decca 3033, Coral 60048 |
| 66880 | Big Jim Blues | Decca 2915, BM-1165, Y-5585, Br(E)02936, (F)505263 |

January 2, 1940

June Richmond (vo) added.

| 67010-A-B | Wham (vJR) | Decca 2962, F-8062 |
| 67011-A | Love is the Thing | Decca 3033 |
| 67012-A | Why Go On Pretending | - |
| 67013-A | It Always Will Be You | Decca 2957 |

January 26, 1940 - New York City

SIX MEN AND A GIRL: Earl Thompson (tp); Buddy Miller (cl,as); Dick Wilson (ts); Mary Lou Williams (p); Floyd Smith (g); Booker Collins (b); Ben Thigpen (d0.

| US-1316-1 | Mary Lou Williams Blues | Varsity 8193 |
| US-1317-1 | Tea For Two | - |
| US-1318-1 | Scratchin' the Gravel | Varsity 8190 |
| US-1319-1 | Zonky | - |

May 5, 1940

Shorty Baker, Earl Thompson, Big Jim Lawson (tp); Don Byas, John Harrington, Dick Wilson, Andy Kirk (reeds); Henry Wells, Ted Donnelly (tb); Mary Lou Williams (p); Booker Collins (b); Boyd Smith (g); Ben Thigpen (d).

|  | Shiek of Araby | Everybody's EV3006 |
|--|----------------|--------------------|
|  | The Riff | - |
|  | Marchetta | - |

June 25, 1940

Harry Lawson, Harold Baker, Clarence Trice (tp); Ted Donnelly, Fred Robinson (tb); Rudy Powell, John Harrington, Dick Wilson, Edward Inge (saxes); Mary Lou Williams (p); Floyd Smith (g); Booker Collins (b); Ben Thigpen (d).

| 67893-A | Fine and Mellow | Decca 3282, Br(E)03076 |
|---------|-----------------|------------------------|
| 67894-A | Scratching the Gravel | Decca 3293, Br(E)03100, Stash ST 109 |
| 67895-A | Fifteen Minute Intermission | Decca 3282, Br(E)03076 |
| 67896-A | Take Those Blues Away | Decca 3293, Br(E)03100 |

July 8, 1940

Pha Terrell (vo) added.

| 67917-A | Now I Lay Me Down To Dream | Decca 3306 |
|---------|----------------------------|------------|
| 67918-A | No Greater Love (vPT) | Decca 3350 |
| 67919-A | Midnight Stroll | - |
| 67920-A | Little Miss | Decca 3491 |

November 7, 1940

Henry Wells (tb) replaces Robinson.

| 68317-A | The Count | Decca 18123, Y-6092, Br(E)03525 |
|---------|-----------|---------------------------------|
| 68318-A | Twelfth Street Rage | Decca 18123, BrA-82588, Br(E)03525 |
| 68319-A | When I Saw You | Decca 3491 |

November 18, 1940

same personnel.

| 68363-A | If I Feel This Way Tomorrow | Decca 3582 |
|---------|----------------------------|------------|
| 68364-A | Or Have I | - |
| 68365-A | Baby Dear | Decca 18122, Coral CP39, MCA510088 |
| 68366-A | Harmony Blues | Decca 18122,    -  ,MCA510088 |

January 3, 1941 - New York City

same personnel.

| | | |
|---|---|---|
| 68546-A | Cuban Boogie Woogie | Decca 3663, BM-1235, Br(E)03180 |
| 68547-A | A Dream Dropped In | Decca 3619 |
| 68548-A | Is It a Sin | - |
| 68549-A | Ring Dem Bells | Decca 3663,    - .    - |

July 17, 1941

Buddy Miller (sax) replaces Powell.

| | | |
|---|---|---|
| 69519-A | Big Time Crip | Decca 4042, Br 03293 |
| 69520-B | 47th Street Jive | -         - |
| 69521-A | I'm Misunderstood | Decca 4141 |
| 69522-A | No Answer | - |

March 12, 1944 - New York City

MARY LOU WILLIAMS AND HER ORCHESTRA:  Frank Newton (tp); Vic Dickenson (tb); Ed Hall (cl); Mary Lou Williams (p); Al Lucas (b); Jack Parker (d).

| | | |
|---|---|---|
| 651 | Lullably of the Leaves | Asch 1004, 4501 |
| 652 | Little Joe | Asch 1002, 4502, Folkways FP32, FJ2292 |
| 653 | Roll 'Em | Asch 1003,   - , V-Disc 375 |
| 656 | Satchel Mouth Baby | Asch 502 |
| 656-2 | Satchel Mouth Baby | Selmer Y-7229 |

Newton out.

| | | |
|---|---|---|
| | Yesterday's Kisses | Selmer Y-7229, Baronet TR3, Cupol 9005 |

June 5, 1944

Mary Lou Williams (p) solo.

| | | |
|---|---|---|
| 660 | Mary Lou's Boogie | Asch 1003, V-Disc 375 |
| 661 | Drag 'Em | Asch 1002, 4503 |
| 662 | St. Louis Blues | Asch 1004, 4501, Cupol 9005 |

June 5, 1944

MARY LOU WILLIAMS AND HER ORCHESTRA:  Dick Vance (tp); Vic Dickenson (tb); Claude Green (cl); Don Byas (ts); Mary Lou Williams (p); Al Lucas (b); Jack Parker (d).

| | | |
|---|---|---|
| 1234 | Man O' Mine | Asch 552-2, 1006, Stinson LP24 |
| 1235 | Stardust, Part 2 | Asch 552-1, 1005,    - |
| 1236 | Gjam Mili Jam Session | Asch 552-2, 1006,    -, V-Disc 375 |
| 1239 | Stardust, Part 1 | Asch 552-1, 1005,    - |

August 10, 1944 - New York City

MARY LOUS WILLIAMS TRIO:   Bill Coleman (tp,vo); Mary Lou Williams (p); Al Hall (b).

| 710 | Russian Lullably | Asch 351-1 |
| 711 | Blue Skies | - |
| 712 | Persian Rug | Asch 351-2 |
| 713 | Night and Day | - |
| 714 | You Know Baby (vBC) | Asch 351-3 |
| 715 | I Found a New Baby | - |

December 11, 1944 - New York

MARY LOU WILLIAMS AND HER ORCHESTRA:   Bill Coleman (tp); Mary Lou Williams (p); Jimmy Butt (b); Eddie Dougherty (d); Josh White (vo).

| 780 | The Minute Man (vJW) | Asch 2001, Folkways FA2966 |
| 781 | Froggy Bottom | -, Swingfan 101,  - |

December 15, 1944 - New York City

MARY LOU WILLIAMS AND HER ORCHESTRA:   Bill Coleman (tp); Claude Green (cl); Joe Evans (as); Coleman Hawkins (ts); Mary Lou Williams (p); Eddie Robinson (b); Denzil Best (d).

| 1237 | Lady Be Good (no cl,as) | Asch 552-3, 1007, Stinson LP24 |
| 1259 | Carcinoma (no cl,as,ts,d) | -         -          - |
| 1300 | Song In My Soul | Asch 1008, Stinson LP29 |
| 1301 | This and That | -          - |

Spring 1945

SIGNS OF THE ZODIAC:   Mary Lou Williams (p); Al Lucas (b); Jack Parker (d).

| ZO-2 | Taurus | Asch 620-1 |
| ZO-3 | Pisces | Asch 621-3 |
| ZO-4 | Gemini | Asch 620-2 |
| ZO-6 | Capricornus | Asch 621-2 |
| ZO-7 | Saggitarius | - |
| ZO-8-1 | Aquarius | Asch 621-3 |
| ZO-9 | Libra | Asch 621-1 |
| ZO-10-1 | Virgo | Asch 620-3 |
| ZO-11-1 | Aries (no d) | Asch 620-1 |
| ZO-12 | Scorpio | Asch 621-1 |

Mary Lou Williams (p) solo.

| ZO-20 | Cancer | Asch 620-2 |
| ZO-2 | Leo | Asch 620-3 |

June 29, 1945 - New York City

Mary Lou Williams (p) solo.

| | | |
|---|---|---|
| Stars | Selmer Y7134, Baronet TR5 | |
| Moon | – | – |
| Sunset | Selmer Y7135 | |
| Sunrise | – | |

August 5, 1945 - New York

Bill Coleman (tp); Mary Lou Williams (p); Al Hall (b); Specs Powell (d).

| | |
|---|---|
| Sleep | Jazz Pan LP11 |
| Gjon Mili Jam Session | – |

February 16, 1946 - New York

Mary Lou Williams (p) solo.

| | | |
|---|---|---|
| 235 | How High the Moon | Disc 5025 |
| 236 | The Man I Love | Disc 5026 |
| 237 | Cloudy | Disc 5025 |
| 238 | Blue Skies | Disc 5026, Selmer Y7133 |
| 239 | These Foolish Things | Disc 5027 |
| 240 | Lonley Moment | – |

1946-1947

MARY LOU WILLIAMS AND HER ORCHESTRA: including Kenny Dorham (tp); Mary Lou Williams (p); Johnny Smith (g); Graham Moncur (b).

| | | |
|---|---|---|
| Kool | Disc 5033, 833 | |
| Mary Lou | – | – |

1947 - New York

MARY LOU WILLIAMS ORCHESTRA: Irving Kustin, Leon Schwartz, Edward Sadowski (tp); Martin Glaser, Allan Feldman, Maurice Lopez, Orlando Wright (reeds); Frank Roth (p); Milton Orient (b); Jack Parker (d); Mary Lou Williams (leader,arr).

| | | | |
|---|---|---|---|
| 656 | Lonely Moments | Disc 6067, Folkways FA2966 | |
| 658 | Whistle Blues | – | – |

March 18, 1949 - New York City

MARY LOU WILLIAMS ORCHESTRA: Idrees Suliman (tp); Martin Glaser (b-cl); Allan Feldman (cl,as); Mary Lou Williams (p); Mundell Lowe (g); George Duvivier (b); Denzil Best (d); Kenny Hagwood (vo).

| K6016 | Tisherome | King EP-279, LP295-85, JS 612, |
| | | Vg(E)V2147 |
| K6017 | Knowledge | –   ,EP-279, – ,   –, |
| | | Vg(E)V2147 |
| K6018 | Oo Blaa Dee (vKH) | King EP-279, 15003, LP295-85 |
| | Shorty Boo | King JS 612,       – |

January 3, 1950 - New York City

MARY LOU WILLIAMS TRIO: Mary Lou Williams (p); Mundell Lowe (g); George Duvivier (b); Denzil Best (d).

| K6120 | Bye Bye Blues | King 4349, EP280, LP295-85, |
| | | Par(E)GEP8567, LP540 |
| K6121 | Moonglow | King EP280, LP295-85, |
| | | Par(E)GEP8567, LP40 |
| K6122 | Willow Weep For Me | King 4349, EP280, LP295-85, |
| | | Par(E)GEP8567, LP540 |
| K6123 | I'm in the Mood for Love | King EP280, LP295-85, |
| | | Par(E)GEP8567, LP540 |

March 7, 1951 - New York City

MARY LOU WILLIAMS TRIO: Mary Lou Williams (p); Carl Pruitt (b); Cill Clarke (d).

| | Mary's Waltz | Atlantic EP518, LP114 |
| | The Cream in My Coffee | –          – , LP 1271 |
| | Surrey With Fringe On Top | –          –      – |
| | S'Wonderful | –          –      – |
| | From This Moment On | Blue Star 236, Atl LP 114, – |
| | Pagliacci | –      – |
| | In the Purple Grotto | –      – |
| | Opus Z | –      – |

June 11, 1951 - New York City

MARY LOU WILLIAMS QUINTET: Skippy Williams (cl); Mary Lou Williams (p); Billy Taylor (b); Al Walker (d); Dave Lambert Singers (vocal group).

| NY151 | Walking | Circle 3008 |

June 15, 1951 - New York City

Mary Lou Williams (p); Billy Taylor (b); Willie Guerra (bgs).

| NY155 | The Sheik of Araby | Circle 3008, L412 |
| NY156 | When Dreams Come True | – |
| NY157 | Bobo | –, Gz 2024 |
| NY158 | Kool | –      – |
| NY159 | Lover Come Back to Me | Circle 3009,  – |
| NY160 | S'Posin' | –      – |

```
NY161      Handy Eyes (St. Louis Blues)              -
NY162      Tisherome                                 -
```

April 16, 1952 - New York

MARY LOU WILLIAMS TRIO: Mary Lou Williams (p) u (rhythm).

```
NY166      Yes We Have No Bananas      Circle/Blue Star (F)246
```

July 11, 1952 - New York City

MARY LOU WILLIAMS AND HER ORCHESTRA: Harold Baker (tp); Vic Dickenson
(tb); Morris Lane (ts); Mary Lou Williams (p); Nevell John (g); Eddie
Safranski (b); Don Lamond (d).

```
83158      Down Beat                   Brunswick 80123, BL 54000,
                                       Coral(E)LVA-9009
83160      Out of Nowhere                   -  , Brunswick BL 54000
83161      C Jam Blues                 Brunswick 80123,      -,
                                       Coral(E)LVA-9009
```

January 23, 1953 - London

MARY LOU WILLIAMS TRIO: Mary Lou Williams (p); Ken Napper (b); Allen
Ganley (d); Tony Scott (bgs).

```
           Titoros                     Vogue V2163,(E)LDE022,(F)LD124,
                                       Contemp C2507
           Lady Bird                   Vogue V2163,      -         -,
                                       Contemp C2507
           Don't Blame Me                   -          -          -
           They Can't Take That Away        -          -          -
           Koolbongo                        -          -          -
           Perdido                          -          -          -
           For You                          -          -          -
           Round About Midnight             -          -          -
```

March 19, 1953 - London

Mary Lou Williams (p); Jack Fallon (b); Gerry McLaughlin (d).

```
17685      Laughin Rag                 London (E) 1174
17686      Rag of Rags                      -
```

June 26, 1953 - London

Mary Lou Williams (p); Ray Dempsey (g); Rupert Nurse (b); Tony Kinsey
(d).

```
395        Melody Maker                Prestige LP 175
396        Musical Express                  -
```

| 397 | Sometimes I'm Happy | - |
| 398 | Monk's Tune | - |

**December 2, 1953 - Paris**

MARY LOU WILLIAMS-DON BYAS:   Don Byas (ts); Mary Lou Williams (p);
Gerard Pochonet (d); Buddy Banks (b).

| Why | Vogue (F) LD186 |
| Lullaby of the Leaves | - |
| Chika | - |
| Mary's Waltz | - |
| O.W. | - |
| Moonglow | - |
| N.M.E. (New Music Express) | - |

Byas out.

| Just You, Just Me | - |
| Boom Blues | - |

**Early 1954 - Paris**

Mary Lou Williams (p); Buddy Banks (b); Jean-Louis Viale (d).

| There's a Small Hotel | Blue Star (F) BLP 6841 |
| En Ce Temps La' | - |
| Lover | - |
| Between the Devil and the Deep Blue Sea | - |
| Carioca | - |
| Tire Tire L'aigville | - |
| Autumn in New York | - |
| Nicole | - |

**1954 - Paris**

Nelson Williams (tp); Ray Lwarence (ts); Mary Lou Williams (p); Buddy
Banks (b); Kansas Fields (d).

| Leg 'n' Lou | Club Francais du Disque J12 |
| Gravel | - |
| Nancy in Love With the Colonel | - |

Nelson Williams and Lawrence out.

| Swingin' For Guys | - |
| Memories of You | - |
| Avalon | - |

Jacques David (d) replaces Fields; Beryl Bryden (vo,wbd) added.

|  |  |
|---|---|
| Freight Train Blues | Club Francais du Disque J12 |
| Rock Me | - |

**1954 - Paris**

Mary Lou Williams (p) solo.

|  |  |
|---|---|
| Club Francais Boogie | Club Francais du Disque J12 |
| I Made You Love Paris | - |

**1954 - London**

MARY LOU WILLIAMS QUARTET: Mary Lou Williams (p); Lennie Bush (b); Tony Kinsey (d); Tony Scott (bgs).

|  |  |
|---|---|
| Azurte | Vogue (F) LDU 33339 |
| Twilight | - |
| Flying Home | - |
| Nickles | - |
| Yesterdays | - |
| The Man I Love | - |
| Just One of Those Things | - |
| Why | - |

**June, 1959 - New York**

Mary Lou Williams (p); Bruce Lawrence (b); Jack Parker (d).

| | | |
|---|---|---|
| 3R949 | Chuck-a-Lunk Jug Pt. 1 | Sue 715 |
| 3R950 | Chuck-a-Lunk Jug Pt. 2 | - |
| | Night and Day | Sue 724 |
| | I Got Rhythm | - |

**October 9, 1963 - New York**

BLACK CHRIST OF THE ANDES: Mary Lou Willliams (p); Howard Roberts and His Choral Group (vo).

|  |  |
|---|---|
| Black Christ of the Andes | Saba 15062ST |
| The Devil | - |

Mary Lou Williams (p); Ben Tucker (b); Percy Brice (d).

|  |  |
|---|---|
| It Ain't Necessarily So | Saba 15062ST |

Mary Lou Williams (p) solo.

|  |  |
|---|---|
| A Fungus Amongus | - |

**November 19, 1963 - New York**

Mary Lou Williams (p); Percy Heath (b); Tim Kennedy (d).

          A Grant Night for Swinging   Saba 16062ST
          My Blue Heaven                  -
          Dirge Blues                     -


June 20, 1965 - Pittsburg

   Mary Lou Williams (p); Larry Gales (b); Ben Riley (d).

          45° Angle                  RCA-Vic LPM/LSP 3499
          Joycie                         -


date unknown - Kansas City

   ANDY KIRK AND HIS TWELVE CLOUDS OF JOY:  Gene Prince, Harry Lawson (tp);
   Allen Durham (tb); Lawrence Freeman, John Williams, John Harrington
   (saxes); Claude Williams (vn); Mary Lou Williams (p); William Dirvin
   (bj); Andy Kirk (b); Edward McNeill (d); Billy Massey (vo).

   KC-591      Mees-A-Stomp            Brunswick 4694, A-500162,
                                       Vocalion 3255
   KC-592-A    Blue Clarinet Stomp     Brunswick 4694,   -,Vo 3255
   KC-618      Corky Stomp             Brunswick 4893, (E) 01211,
                                       (F) A-8825, (G) A8825
   KC-619      Froggy Bottom           Brunswick 4893, (E) 01211,
                                       (F) A-8825, (G) A8825


date unknown.

   MARY LOU WILLIAMS AND HER ORCHESTRA:   Bill Coleman (tp); Mary Lou
   Williams (p); Jimmy Butt (b); Eddie Dougherty (d); Josh White (vo).

          The Minute Man (vJW)       Asch 2001
          Froggy Bottom                  -


date unknown.

   Nora Lee King (vo) acc. by Mary Lou Williams (p).

   1228        Until My Baby Comes Home    Asch 550-2


date unknown.

   Mary Lou Williams (p) solo.

          Roll 'Em                   V-Disc 375, Caracol 423


date unknown.

   (prob) Charlie Shavers (tp); Trummy Young (tb); Mary Lou Williams (p); u
   (g,b,d).

Gjon Mili Jam Session          V-Disc 375, Caracol 423

date unknown.

Mary Lou Williams (p); Wendell Marshall (b); Osie Johnson (d); u (b-g).

|                        |                  |
|------------------------|------------------|
| Jericho                | Jazztone J1206   |
| Amy                    | -                |
| Roll 'Em               | -                |
| I Love You             | -                |
| Easy Blues             | -                |
| Fandangle              | -                |

Johnson out.

|                        |    |
|------------------------|----|
| I Love Him             | -  |
| Lullaby of the Leaves  | -  |

Mary Lou Williams (p) solo.

|                        |    |
|------------------------|----|
| Sweet Sue              | -  |
| Talk of the Town       | -  |
| Taurus                 | -  |
| Mama, Pin a Rose On Me | -  |


### WILLRICH, VIRGINIA (piano, accordian)

November 4, 1929 - New York

VIRGINIA WILLRICH AND HER TEXAS RANGERS: Charlie Teagarden (tp); Jack
Teagarden (tb); Virginia Willrich (p,acc); Dick McDonough (g); Jack
Willrich (d).

| 403227-B | Same Old Moon | Okeh 41328, MFC 1, Od A-189299 |
| 403228-C | Through (How Can You Say<br>We're Through) | -   -   - |


### WILLS, ALICE (trombone)

See Collective Section.


### WISE, LAURIE (guitar)

1966 - London

Elaine Delmar (vo) acc. by Moe Miller (FrH,tp); Tommy Whittle (ts);
Colin Beaton (p); Laurie Wise (g); John Borthwick (b); Harvey Bruns (d).

|                          |                        |
|--------------------------|------------------------|
| I'll Be Around           | Columbia (E) SX (SCX) 6044 |
| Winter of My Discontent  | -                      |

| | |
|---|---|
| Is It Always Like This | – |
| It's So Peaceful in the Country | – |
| While We're Young | – |
| Who Can I Turn To | – |
| You're Free | – |
| That's the Way it Goes | – |
| S... Is a Comin' In | – |
| The April Age | – |
| The Wrong Blues | – |
| The Lady Sings the Blues | – |

## ZIMMER, VICKI (piano)

1948

Vicki Zimmer (p,vo).

| | |
|---|---|
| He's a Bad Man | Bullet 286 |
| Take Another Guess | – |

## ZIRL, CECELIA (bass)

See Collective Section.

# 2
# Collective Section

April 2, 1920 - New York City

MORRISON'S JAZZ ORCHESTRA: George Morrison (vn,dir); Leo Davis (tp); Ed Carwell (tb); Jimmy Lunceford (as,vn); Cuthbert Byrd (as); Ed Kelly (ts); Desdemona Davies or Mary E. Kirk or Jesse Andrews (p); Lee Morrison (bj); Eugene Montgomery (d).

| | | |
|---|---|---|
| 79098-2 | I Know Why | Columbia A-2945 |

May, 1925 - Chicago

Ma Rainey (vo) acc. by her GEORGIA JAZZ BAND: Howard Scott (tp); George "Hooks" Tilford (c-mel sax,kazoo,slide whistle); Charlie Green (tb); Buster Bailey (cl); Lovie Austin or Lil Henderson (p); Kaiser Marshall or Happy Bolton (d).

| | | |
|---|---|---|
| 2136-1-2 | Army Camp Harmony Blues | Paramount 12284, Poydras 88 |
| | Explainin' the Blues | - - |

August, 1925 - Chicago

Ma Rainey (vo) acc. by her GEORGIA JAZZ BAND: Kid Henderson (c); Howard Scott (tp); Charlie Green (tb); Buster Bailey (cl); Lucien Brown (cl,as); Lovie Austin or Lil Henderson (p); George Williams (bj); Kaiser Marshall (d); Happy Bolton (d,chimes).

| | | |
|---|---|---|
| 2209-1-2 | Stormy Sea Blues | Paramount 12295 |
| 2210-2 | Rough and Tumble Blues | Paramount 12311 |
| 2211-1-2 | Night Time Blues | Paramount 12303 |
| 2212-2 | Levee Camp Moan | Paramount 12295 |
| 2213-2 | Four Day Honory Scat | Paramount 12303 |
| 2214-2 | Memphis Bound Blues | Paramount 12311 |

August, 1926 - Chicago

Ma Rainey (vo) acc. by her GEORGIA BAND: Kid Henderson or Homer Hobson (c); Albert Wynn (tb); William Clinton or Tom Brown (cl,as); u (musical saw); Lil Henderson, Lil Hardaway or Jimmy Flowers (p); W.J. Byrne, Rip Bassett or Silas White (bj); Fred Scott or Ben Thigpen (d).

| | | |
|---|---|---|
| 2627-1 | Down in the Basement | Paramount 12395 |
| 2628-1 | Sissy Blues | Paramount 12384 |
| 2629-2 | Broken Soul Blues | - |
| 2631-1 | Trust No Man | Paramount 12395 |

September 27, 1932 - New York City

Connie Boswell (vo) acc. by Bunny Berigan (tp); Tommy Dorsey (tb); Jimmy Dorsey (cl); Harry Hoffman (vn); Martha Boswell (p); Dick McDonough (g); Helvetia "Vet" Boswell (cello); Stan King (d).

B-12378-A  I'll Never Have to Dream          Brunswick 6405, 01382,
           Again                             SpEd5002-S
B-12379-A  Me Minus You                      Brunswick 6405, 01382,
                                             SpEd5002-S


July 12, 1934 - New York

Kay Walsh, Estella Slavin, Elvira Rohl (tp); Ruth McMurray, Althea
Heumann (tb); Ruth Bradley (cl,as,vo); Betty Sticht, Helen Ruth, Audrey
Hall (cl,as,ts); Jerrine Hyde, Mirriam Greenfield (p); Helen Baker (g);
Maria Lenz (b); Lil Singer (d); Ina Ray Hutton (dir,vo).

83377-1    How's About Tomorrow Night  Victor 24692


July 19, 1934 - New York

same personnel.

83604-1    And I Still Do (vRB)             Victor 24692


September 13, 1934 - New York

same personnel.

15914-1    Georgia's Gorgeous Gal           Vocalion 2801
           (vRB)
15915-1    Wild Party                       Vocalion 2816, Harrison LP-C
15916-1    Twenty-Four Hours in             Vocalion 2801
           Georgia (vIRH)


September 24, 1934 - New York

same personnel.

16012-1    Witch Doctor                     Vocalion 2816, Harrison LP-C


1936 - Hollywood

Lois Lamb, Marion Elzea, Juel Donahue (tp); Fy Hesser, Alice Wills,
Jessie Bailey (tb); Zacky Alexander, Betty Sticht, Betty Sattley, Rose
Ansidale (reeds); Betty Roudebush (p); Marion Gange (g); Marye Rivers
(b); Jean Skinner (d); Ina Ray Hutton (vo).

           Truckin'                         Bandstand BS7127


June 11, 1935 - New York City

MILLS CAVALCADE ORCHESTRA:  George Brunies (tb,dir); Florence Dieman,
Elvira Rohl (tp); Norman Conley, Althea Conley (tb); Jules Harrison,
Marie Carpenter (as); Evelyn Pennak, Herbie Haymer (ts); Henrietta

Borchard, Rudy Berson, Sid Sidney (vn); Gladys Mosier (p); Jessie Moore (b); Frank Carlson (d).

| CO-17587-1 Lovely Liza Lee | Columbia 3066-D, Par F-219 |
| CO-17589-1 Rhythm Lullaby | -       - |

September 19, 1940 - New York

Kay Walsh, Estella Slavin, Elvira Rohl (tp); Ruth McMurray, Althea Heumann (tb); Ruth Bradley (cl,as,vo); Betty Sticht, Helen Ruth, Audrey Hall (cl,as,ts); Jerrine Hyde, Mirriam Greenfield (p); Helen Baker (g); Maria Lenz (b); Lil Singer (d); Stewart Foster (vo); Ina Ray Hutton (dir,vo).

| 28661 | Gotta Have Your Love | Okeh 5830 |
| 2862-1 | Five O'Clock Whistle (vIRH) | Okeh 5852 |
| 2863-1 | Make Me Know It | - |
| 2864 | A Handful of Stars | Okeh 5830 |

July 15, 1941 - New York

same personnel.

| 30874-1 | What's the Good of Moonlight (vIRH) | Okeh 6335 |
| 30875-1 | At Last (vSF) | - |
| 30876-1 | Nobody's Sweetheart (vIRH) | Okeh 6380 |
| 30877-1 | Back in Your Own Backyard | - |

1945 - New York City

MARY LOU WILLIAMS' GIRL STARS: Marjorie Hyams (vib); Mary Lou Williams (p); Mary Osborne (g,vo); Bea (Billy) Taylor (b); Bridget O'Flynn (d).

| He's Funny That Way | Continental 6021 |
| D.D.T. | -  , Rmg RLP 032, JS 784 |
| Rumble Re-Bop | Continental 6032 |
| Blues at Mary Lou's | - |

March, 1945 - New York City

HIP CHICKS: Jean Starr (tp); L'Ana Hyams (Webster) (ts); Marjorie Hyams (vib); Vicki Zimmer (p); Marion Gange (g); Cecilia Zirl (b); Rose Gottesman (d); Vivian Garry (vo).

| I Surrender Dear | Black & White 1216 |
| Moonlight on Turban Bay (no vib) | - |
| Strip Tease | Black & White 1217 |
| Popsie | - |
| The Sergeant on Furlough | Black & White 1218 |
| Seven Riffs With the Right Woman | - |

1945 - Los Angeles

THE BLUES MAN:  Paul Howard (cl,ts); Nina Russell (org); Mata Roy (p);
George Vann (d,vo).

| | | |
|---|---|---|
| Kansas City Boogie | Juke Box UR101, Specialty 501 | |
| My Baby's Blues | - | - |
| Ice Cream Freezer | Specialty 508 | |
| Jumpin' at the Sunset | - | |
| Worryin' Blues | Specialty 509 | |
| All Alone Blues | - | |

July 24, 1946 - July

MARY LOU WILLIAM'S GIRL STARS:  Margie Hyams (vib); Mary Lou Williams
(p); Mary Osborne (g); June Rotenberg (b); Rose Gottesman (d).

| | | |
|---|---|---|
| PD6VB2523 | Fifth Dimension | Victor 27-1048, LPT31, Camden CAL 384, HMV DLP 1022 |
| PD6VB2524 | Harmony Grits | Victor 20-2174 |
| PD6VB2525 | It Must Be True | - |
| PD6VB2527 | Boogie Misterioso | Victor 40-0145, Camden CAE 418 |
| PD6VB2528 | Conversation (Jump Caprice) | Stash ST 109,                - |

September 5, 1946 - Los Angeles

VIVIAN GARRY QUINTET:  Edna Williams (tp); Emma Colbert (vn); Wini
Beatty (p); Vivian Garry (b,vo); Dody Jeshke (d).

| | | |
|---|---|---|
| D6VB2143 | I'm in the Mood For Love | Victor 20-2352 |
| D6VB2144 | Body and Soul | Victor 40-0144 |
| D6VB2145 | A Woman's Place Is In the Groove | - |
| D6VB2146 | Operation Mop | Victor 20-2352 |

October 7, 1946 - New York City

MARY LOU WILLIAMS TIRO:  Mary Lou Williams (p); June Rotenberg (b);
Bridget O'Flynn (d).

| | | |
|---|---|---|
| D6VB2528 | Humoresque | Victor 20-2025, Camden CAL384, (E)CDN 118, HMV X741 |
| D6VB2899 | Waltz Boogie | Victor 20-2025, Camden CAL384, HMV X741 |
| D6VB3024 | Hesitation Boogie | Victor 40-4043, LPM 2321 |

October 8, 1946 - New York City

Beryl Booker (p,vo); Mary Osborne (g); June Rotenberg (b).

| | | |
|---|---|---|
| D6VB3030 | Low Ceiling | Victor 40-0147 |
| D6VB3032 | I Only Have Eyes for You | Victor 20-3088, LPT 31, HMV DLP1022 |
| D6VB3033 | Don't Blame Me | Victor 40-0147 |

c. 1947

THE SEPIA TONES:  Paul Howard (cl,ts); Nina Russell (org); Mata Roy (p); George Vann (d).

| | |
|---|---|
| Boogie No. 1 | Juke Box VR 100 |
| Sophisticated Blues | - |
| When He Comes Home to Me vMR) | - |

October 7, 1949 - New York City

Jackie Cain (vo); Roy Kral (p,vo); Marilyn Beaout (cello); John Romano (g); Ken O'Brien (b); Elaine O'Brien (d).

| | | |
|---|---|---|
| A306 | Auld Lang Syne | Atlantic 664 |
| A307 | Afro-Desia | Atlantic 668 |
| A308 | Everlovin' Blues | Atlantic 664 |
| A309 | What Do You Think I Am | Atlantic 668 |

October 24, 1949 - New York City

Tiny Davis (tp,vo); Birdie Davis (as); Helen Cole (d); u (ts,p,b).

| | | |
|---|---|---|
| 75438 | Race Horse | Decca 48220, Br(G/F)87517 LPBM |
| 75439 | How About That Jive | Decca 48246 |
| 75440 | Draggin' My Heart Around | Decca 48122 |

October 27, 1949 - New York City

same personnel.

| | | |
|---|---|---|
| 75453 | I Never Get Tired of Doin' It | Decca 48122 |
| 75454 | Bug Juice | Decca 48220, Br(G/F)87517 LPBM |
| 75455 | Laura | Decca 48246 |

c. 1953

Teddi King (vo) acc. by Beryl Booker (p); Bonnie Wetzel (b); Elaine Leighton (d).

| | |
|---|---|
| Round Midnight | Stv SLP302 |
| I Concentrate on You | - |
| It Never Entered My Mind | - |
| What's New | - |

```
            Prelude to a Kiss              -
            Little Girl Blue               -
```

October 17, 1953 - New York

Marie Knight (vo) acc. by Annette Weber (org); James Roots (p); Sister
Rosetta Tharpe (g); James D. Richardson (b); Theodore Sanders (d).

```
85401     God Spoke to Me          Decca 48308, MCA(F)510129
85402     Calvary                  -
85403     I Tell It Wherever I Go  Decca 48320
85404     This Old Soul of Mine    -
```

1954 - New York City

Beryl Booker (p); Bonnie Wetzel (b); Elaine Leighton (d).

```
            Tenderly             Cadence C-1000, London(E)HB-A1054
            Body and Soul            -                        -
            Night and Day            -                        -
            My Funny Valentine       -                        -
            My Ideal                 -                        -
            I Don't Know Why         -                        -
```

1954 - Los Angeles

same personnel.

```
            Thou Swell           Discovery 176, DL3021
            Ebony                    -                  -
            Polka Dots and Moonbeams                    -
            That Old Gang of Mine                       -
            Symphony                                    -
            Booker T.                                   -
            An Old Piano Plays the Blues                -
```

January, 1954 - Live Concert - (prob) Cologne, Germany.

Billie Holiday (vo) acc. by Buddy DeFranco (cl); Red Norvo (vib); Sonny
Clark or Beryl Booker (p); Red Mitchell (b); Elaine Leighton (d).

```
            Billie's Blues       United Artists UAJ14014,
                                 UAS15014, UAE(E)ULP 1026,
                                 (G)69013
            Lover Come Back To Me  United Artists UAJ14014,
                                 UAS15014, UAE(E)ULP 1026,
                                 (G)69013
```

February, 1954 - Pairs

Beryl Booker (p); Bonnie Wetzel (b); Elaine Leighton (d).

|  |  |  |  |
|---|---|---|---|
| April in Paris | Vogue(F)LD203, Discovery DL3022 | | |
| Paris in the Spring | - | - | |
| The Last Time I Saw Paris | - | - | |
| I Love Paris | - | - | |
| Cheek To Cheek | - | - | |

Don Byas (ts) added.

|  |  |  |
|---|---|---|
| Makin' Whoopie | - | - |
| I Should Care | - | - |
| Beryl Booker's Byased Blues | - | - |

June 2, 1954 - New York City

CATS VS. CHICKS: Cats: Clark Terry (tp); Urbie Green (tb); Lucky Thompson (ts); Horace Silver (p); Tal Farlow (g); Percy Heath (b); Kenny Clarke (d). Chicks: Norma Carson (tp); Corkey (Hecht) Hale (h); Terry Pollard (vib); Mary Osborne (g); Bonnie Wetzel (b); Elaine Leighton (d).

|  |  |  |  |
|---|---|---|---|
| The Man I Love | MGM E225, E3614 | | |
| Cats Meet Chicks | - | - , MGM 3611 | |
| Mamblues | - | - , Stash ST 109 | |
| Anything You Can Do | - | - | - |

December, 1954 - New York City

Marian McPartland (p); Bill Crow (b); Ruth Negri (h); George Koutzon (cello).

| | | | |
|---|---|---|---|
| 20887 | Falling in Love with Love | Capitol T699, (E)LC6828 | |
| 20888 | Royal Garden Blues | - | - |
| 20889 | Everything But You | - | - |
| 20890 | I Could Write a Book | - | - |
| 20577 | Street of Dreams | Capitol T574 | |
| 20578 | Mad About the Boy | - | |
| 20579 | Let's Call the Whole Thing Off | - | |
| 20580 | I Told Every Little Star | - | |

Betty Glamann (h); Lucien Schmidt (cello) added.

| | | | |
|---|---|---|---|
| 20900 | Sand in My Shoes | Capitol T699, (E)LC6828 | |
| 20901 | Easy Come, Easy Go | - | - |
| 20902 | For All We Know | - | - |
| 20903 | Chelsea Bridge | - | - |

1955 - New York City

HARVEY LEONARD TRIO/SEXTET: Harvey Leonard (p); Anne Drevnak (b); Elaine Leighton (d). // Jerry Lloyd (tp); Frank Rehak (tb); Marty Lewis (ts); Harvey Leonard (p); Teddy Kotick (b); Bill Bradley (d).

|  |  |
|---|---|
| Woody'n You | Keynote LP 1102 |
| The Lady is a Tramp | - |

```
         Bee Cee Cee                         -
         Tiger's Tune                        -
         We'll Be Together Again             -
         The Tiger                           -
         Chippy'n                            -
         Autumn Nocturne                     -
         Alone Together                      -
         To Mickey's Memory                  -
```

November, 1955 - New York

Marian McPartland (p); Bill Crow (b); Margaret Ross, Ruth Negri (h); George Koutzon, Lucien Schmidt (cello);

```
20919    If I Love Again             Capitol T699
20920    I'll Be Around                   -
20921    Poor Little Rich Girl            -
```

Ross and Schmidt out.

```
20922    Struttin' With Some         Capitol T699
           Barbecue
```

January 16, 1957 - New York City

Max Cohn, George Ricci, Arnold Eidus, Isador Zir (strings); Margaret Ross (h); Marian McPartland (p); William Britto (b) Jimmy Campbell (d).

```
21324    This is New                 Capitol EAP1-895, T895
21325    After All                   Capitol EAP30895,  -
21326    Love Walked In              Capitol EAP1-895,  -
```

January 29, 1957 - New York City

same personnel.

```
21372    Little Girl Blue            Capitol EAP3-895, T895
21373    With You in My Mind         Capitol EAP2-895,  -
21374    Black is the Color          Capitol EAP3-895,  -
21375    Greensleeves                Capitol EAP1-895,  -
```

February 6, 1957 - New York City

Osie Johnson (d) replaces Campbell.

```
21388    I Remember You              Capitol EAP3-895, T895
21389    Autumn Nocturne             Capitol EAP2-895,  -
21390    Like a Ship Without a Sail  Capitol EAP1-895,  -
21391    For Elise                   Capitol EAP2-895,  -
```

July 6, 1957 - Newport Jazz Festival

DIZZY GILLESPIE AND HIS ORCHESTRA: Dizzy Gillespie, Ermet Perry, Carl Warwick, Talib Daawud (tp); Melba Liston, Al Grey, Ray Connor (tb); Jimmy Powell, Ernie Henry (as); Billy Mitchell, Benny Golson (ts); Pee Wee Moore (bars); Mary Lou Williams (p); Paul West (b); Charlie Persip (d).

|  | Zodiac Suite | Verve MGV8244 |
|---|---|---|
|  | Carioca | - |

May 26, 1959 - New York City

QUINCY JONES AND HIS ORCHESTRA: Harry Edison, Ernie Royal, Joe Wilder, Clark Terry (tp); Jimmy Cleveland, Urbie Green, Quentin Jackson, Melba Liston (tb); Julius Watkins (FrH); Phil Woods, Frank Wess (as); Benny Golson, Jerome Richardson (ts); Danny Banks (bars); Patti Bown (p); Kenny Burrell (g); Milt Hinton (b); Charlie Persip (d); Quincy Jones (arr,cond).

| 18642 | Moanin' | Mercury 71489,MG20444,(E)ZEP10047,<br>MMC14038,CMS18026,125055MGL,<br>135055MCY |
|---|---|---|

May 27-28, 1959 - New York City

QUINCY JONES AND HIS ORCHESTRA: Joe Newman, Ernie Royal, Joe Wilder, Clark Terry (tp); Jimmy Cleveland, Urbie Green, Quentin Jackson, Melba Liston (tb); Julius Watkins (FrH); Phil Woods, Frank Wess, (as); Benny Golson, Zoot Sims (ts); Sahib Shihab (bars); Patti Bown (p); Kenny Burrell (g); Milt Hinton (b); Sam Woodyard (d), Quincy Jones (arr,cond).

| 18643 | Happy Faces | Mercury MG20444, SR60129,<br>(E)MMC14038,CMS18026,12505MCL,<br>135055MCY |
|---|---|---|
| 18644 | Along Came Betty | Mercury MG20444, SR60129,<br>(E)MMC14038,CMS18026,12505MCL,<br>135055MCY |
| 18645 | I Remember Clifford | Mercury MG20444, SR60129,<br>(E)MMC14038,CMS18026,12505MCL,<br>135055MCY |
| 18646 | Whisper Not | Mercury MG20444, SR60129,<br>(E)MMC14038,CMS18026,12505MCL,<br>135055MCY |
| 18647 | The Gypsy | Mercury MG20444, SR60129,<br>(E)MMC14038,CMS18026,12505MCL,<br>135055MCY |
| 18648 | Tickle-Toe | Mercury MG20444, SR60129,<br>(E)MMC14038,CMS18026,12505MCL,<br>135055MCY |

June 16, 1959 - New York City

Harry Edison (tp) replaces Terry; Jerome Richardson (ts) replaces

Golson; Les Spann (g) replaces Burrell (g); Don Lamond (d) replaces Woodyard.

| 18716 | A Change of Pace | Mercury 71456,MG20444,SR60129, (E)MMC14038,CMS18026,12505MCL, 135055MCY |
| 18717 | Birth of a Band | Mercury 71456,MG20444,SR60129, (E)MMC14038,CMS18026,12505MCL, 135055MCY |

February 27, 1960 - Paris

| 20042 | Love is Here to Stay | Mercury 71665,MG20612,SR60612, AMT1111 |
| 20043 | Moonglow | Mercury 71665, - -, AMT1111 |

February 29, 1960 - Paris

same personnel.

| 20044 | Chinese Checkers | Mercury MG20612,SR60612, MMC14080,CMS18055 |

April 21, 1960 - Paris

same personnel.

| 20047 | A Sunday Kind of Love | Mercury MG20612,SR60612, MMC14080,CMS18055 |
| 20048 | The Midnight Sun Will Never Set | Mercury MG20612,SR60612, MMC14080,CMS18055 |

October 19, 1960 - New York City

Benny Bailey, Clyde Reasinger, Freddie Hubbard, Jerry Kail (tp); Melba Liston, Curtis Fuller, Quentin Jackson, Wayne Andre (tb); Phil Woods, Joe Lopez (as); Oliver Nelson, Jerome Richardson (ts); Sahib Shihab (bars); Patti Bown (p); Les Spann (g,fl); Buddy Catlett (b); Stu Martin (d).

| 25070 | G'Wan Train | Mercury 71737,MG20612,SR60612, MMC14080,CMS18055 |
| 20572 | You Turned the Tables on Me | Mercury MG20612,SR60612, MMC14080,CMS18055 |
| 25073 | Tone Poem | Mercury MG26012,SR60612, MMC14080 |
| 25078 | Pleasingly Plump | Mercury 71737 |

May 22, 1961 - New York City

DIZZY GILLESPIE BIG BAND: Dizzy Gillespie, Robert Nagle, Bernie Glow,

Ernie Royal, Nick Travis, Dock Severinson (tp); Jimmy Knepper, Urbie
Green, Paul Faulise, Dick Hixon (tb); Jimmy Buffington, John Barrows
(FrH); William Stanley, Harvey Phillips (tuba); Gloria Agostini, Laura
Newell (h); George Duvivier (b); Charlie Persip (d); J.J. Johnson (arr);
Gunther Schuller (cond).

| | | |
|---|---|---|
| The Sword of Orion | Verve MGV 8411 | |
| Jubelo | - | |
| Blues Mist | - | |
| Fantasia | - | |
| Horn of Plenty | - | |
| Ballade | - | |

July 3, 1961 - Newport Jazz Festival

QUINCY JONES AND HIS ORCHESTRA:  Jimmy Maxwell, Jimmy Nottingham, Joe
Newman, John Bello (tp); Curtis Fuuler, Britt Woodman, Melba Liston,
Paul Faulise (tb); Julius Watkins (FrH); Joe Lopez, Phil Woods (as);
Jerome Richardson, Eric Dixon (ts,fl); Pat Patrick (bars); Patti Bown
(p); Les Spann (g,fl); Art Davis (b); Stu Martin (d); Quincy Jones
(arr,cond).

| | | | | |
|---|---|---|---|---|
| 21119 | Meet B.B. | Mercury MG20653,SR60653,12500MCL | | |
| 21120 | G'Wan Train | - | - | - |
| 21121 | Evening in Paris | - | - | - |
| 21122 | Banja Luko | - | - | - |
| 21123 | Lester Leaps In | - | - | - |
| 21124 | Boy in the Tree | - | - | - |
| 1125 | Airmail Special | - | - | - |

October, 1961 - "Basin Street East" - New York City

Billy Eckstine (vo) acc. by QUINCY JONES' ORCHESTRA:  (prob) Joe Newman,
John Bello, Jimmy Maxwell, Jimmy Nottingham (tp); Curtis Fuller, Britt
Woodman, Melba Liston, Paul Faulise (tb); Joe Lopez, Phil Woods (as);
Jerome Richardson, Eric Dixon (ts); Julius Watkins (FrH); Patti Bown
(p); Les Spann (fl,g); Art Davis (b); Stu Martin (d).

| | |
|---|---|
| All Right Okay You Win | Mercury MG20675,SR60674, MMC14100,CMS18066 |
| Medley:  I'm Falling For You/Fool That I Am/ Everything I Have Is Yours/In the Still of the Night | Mercury MG20675,SR60674, MMC14100,CMS18066 |
| Ellington Medley:  Don't Get Around Much Anymore/ I'm Just a Lucky So And So/Caravan/Sophisticated Lady | Mercury MG20675,SR60674, MMC14100,CMS18066 |
| Work Song | Mercury MG20675,SR60674, MMC14100,CMS18066 |
| Ma She's Making Eyes At Me | Mercury MG20675,SR60674, MMC14100,CMS18066 |

December 18, 1961 - New York City

QUINCY JONES AND HIS ORCHESTRA: Thad Jones, Al Derisi, Freddie Hubbard, Snooky Young (tp); Rod Levitt, Melba Liston, Billy Byers, Paul Faulise (tb); Julius Watkins (FrH); Phil Woods, Jerome Richardson (as); Eric Dixon, Oliver Nelson (ts); Patti Bown (p); Milt Hinton (b); Bill English (d); Quincy Jones (arr,cond).

| | | |
|---|---|---|
| Hard Sock Dance | Impulse A(S)11, HMV CLP1581, SCD1462 | |
| Little Karen | - - - | |
| Robot Portrait | - - - | |

December 22, 1962 - New York City

Snooky Young, Thad Jones, Joe Newman, Ernie Royal (tp); Melba Liston, Curtis Fuller, Paul Faulise, Tom Mitchell, Billy Byers (tb); Julius Watkins, Jimmy Buffington, Earl Chapin, Ray Alonge (FrH): Harvey Phillips (tuba); Phil Woods (as); Jerome Richardson (as,ts); Oliver Nelson (ts); Patti Bown (p); Milt Hinton (b); Osie Johnson (d); Gloria Agostini (h); Quincy Jones (arr,cond).

| | | |
|---|---|---|
| Quintessence | Impulse 206,A(S)11,HMV CLP1581, SCD1462 | |
| Invitation | - - - - | |
| Straight No Chaser | - - - - | |

Early 1962 - New York City

BILLY BYERS CONDUCTING QUINCY JONES' ORCHESTRA: Ernie Royal, Doc Severinson, Joe Newman, Clark Terry (tp); Jimmy Cleveland, Melba Liston, Wayne Andre, Tony Studd (tb); Jimmy Buffington, Ray Alonge, Don Corrado, Bob Northern (FrH); Harvey Philips (tuba); Jerry Dodgion (as,cl,fl); Eric Dixon (ts,fl); Sol Schlinger (bars,b-cl); Patti Bown (p); Milt Hinton (b); Osie Johnson (d); Ed Shaughnessy, Eddie Costa (perc).

| | | |
|---|---|---|
| 23261 | Mood Indigo | Mercury MG2028, SR 6028 |
| 23262 | Just Squeeze Me | - - |
| 23263 | All Too Soon | - - |
| 23264 | Solitude | - - |

Jack Rains (tb) replaces Andre; Julius Watkins (tuba) replaces Corrato, Spencer Sinatra (ts) replaces Dixon.

| | | |
|---|---|---|
| 23268 | Take the A Train | Mercury MG2028, SR 6028 |
| 23269 | Chelsea Bridge | - - |
| 23270 | I'm Beginning to See the Light | - - |

Al De Risie (tp) replaces Severinson; Eric Dixon (ts) replaces Sinatra.

| | | |
|---|---|---|
| 23332 | Don't Get Around Much | Mercury MG2028, SR 6028 |
| 23333 | Sophisticated Lady | - - |
| 23334 | Caravan | - - |

October 12, 1962 - Town Hall - New York

Clark Terry, Ernie Royal, Snooky Young, Richard Williams, Rolf Ericson,
Ed Amour (tp); Britt Woodman, Quentin Jackson, Willie Dennis, Eddie
Bert, Jimmy Cleveland, Jimmy Knepper (tb); Don Butterfield (tuba); Eric
Dolphy, Charlie Marian, Buddy Collette, Charles McPherson, Zoot Sims,
Pepper Adams, Jerome Richardson (saxes, woodwinds); Toshiko Mariano
(Akiyoshi), Julie Byard (p); Teddy Charles (vib); Les Spann (g); Charlie
Mingus, Milt Hinton (b); Danny Richmond (d); Melba Liston (arr,cond);
Bob Hammer (arr).

| | | |
|---|---|---|
| Epitaph Pt. 1 | United Artists UAJ 14024 | |
| Epitaph Pt. 2 | - | |
| Freedom | - | |
| Please Don't Come Back From the Moon | - | |
| My Search (arrBH) | - | |
| Finale (In a Mellow Tone) | - | |

April 9, 1963 - New York

QUINCY JONES AND HIS ORCHESTRA: Joe Newman, Clark Terry, Ernie Royal,
Snooky Young, Jimmy Nottingham, Al Derisi (tp); Billy Byers, Paul
Faulise, Jimmy Cleveland, Quentin Jackson, Kai Winding, Tom Mithcell,
Santo Russo, Melba Liston (tb); Julius Watkins, Jimmy Buffington, Ray
Alonge, Bob Northern, Earl Chapin, Paul Ingraham, Fred Klein, Willie
Ruff (FrH); Bill Stanley, Jay McAllister (tuba); Phil Woods, Zoot Sims,
Roland Kirk, James Moody, Walt Levinsky, Frank Wess, Al Cohn, Romeo
Penque, Budd Johnson, Seldon Powell, Jerome Richardson (reeds); Lalo
Schiffrin, Bobby Scott, Patti Bown (p,org); Kenny Burrell, Jim Hall,
Wayne Wright, Sam Herman (g); Milt Hinton, Art Davis, George Duvivier,
Ben Tucker, Major Holley, Chris White (b); Rudy Collins, Ossie Johnson,
Ed Shaughnessy (d); Charles McCoy (hca); James Johnson (tympany);
Charles Gomez, Jack Del Rio, Jose Paula, Bill Costa, George Devers
(perc); Quincy Jones (arr,cond).

| | | |
|---|---|---|
| 22890 | Back at the Children Shack | Mercury MG20799 |
| 22891 | Comin' Home Baby | - |
| 22892 | Gravy Waltz | - |

April 10, 1963 - New York

same personnel.

| | | |
|---|---|---|
| 22894 | Exodus | Mercury MG20799 |
| 22895 | Jive Samba | - |
| 22896 | Walk on the Wild Side | - |

April 11, 1963 - New York

same personnel.

| | | |
|---|---|---|
| 22897 | Take Five | Mercury MG20799 |
| 22898 | Cast Your Fate to the Wind | - |

```
22899    Bossa Nova USA                    -
22900    Watermelon Man                    -
```

October 9, 1967

Budd Johnson (b-cl,ts); Mary Lou Williams (p); Grant Green (g); Larry Gales (b); Perry Brice (d); Jimmy Mitchell (solo-vo); George Gordon Singers (vocal group); Melba Liston (arr,cond).

```
         Anima Christi             Saba 15062ST
         Praise the Lord           -
```

November 5, 1964 - Los Angeles

PAUL HORN QUINTET AND LALO SCHIFFRIN'S ORCHESTRA: Paul Horn (as,cl,b--fl); Lynn Blessing (vib); Mike Lang (p); Bill Plummer (b); Larry Bunker (d), Al Porcino, Conte Condoli (tp); Dorothy Remsen, Ann Stockton (h); Ken Watson, Emil Richards, Frank Flynn, Milt Holland (perc); u (vocal choir).

```
35522    Kyric                     RCA Victor LPM (S) 3414
35523    Agnus Dei                 -
35524    Gloria                    -
35525    Interludium               -
```

November 6, 1964 - Los Angeles

same personnel.

```
35526    Offertory                 RCA Victor LPM (S) 3414
35527    Sanctus                   -
35528    Credo                     -
35529    Prayer                    -
```

April 19, 1966 - New York

Thad Jones, Joe Newman, Jimmy Nottingham, Ernie Royal, Clark Terry (tp); Melba Liston, Quentin Jackson, Paul Faulise, Tom McIntosh (tb); Phil Woods, Jerry Dodgion (as); Jerome Richardson, Bob Gibson (ts); Danny Banks (bars); Shirley Scott (org); Atilla Zoller (g); George Duvivier (b); Grady Tate (d); Oliver Nelson (arr,cond).

```
90530    Sophisticated Swing       Impulse A(S)9119
90531    Roll 'Em                  -
(0532    Sometimes I'm Happy        -
90533    For Dancers Only          -
```

June 10, 1968 - New York

Edward Williams, Dud Bascomb (tp); Melba Liston, Quentin Jackson (tb); Gene Walker (as); Freddie McCoy (vib); Joanne Brackeen (el-p,org); Wally

Richardson (g); Jimmy Lewis (el-b); Bernard Purdie (d); Montego Joe (cga).

        Don't Tell Me That          Prestige PRLP7582
        MacArthur Park                 -

# Index

Adami, Madame (p) - 3
Agostini, Gloria (h) - 3, 301, 302
Akiyoshi, Toshiko (Mariano) (p) - 5, 303
Alexander, Zacky (reeds) - 292
Amadio, Judy (fl) - 8
Ambrose, Amanda (p) - 9
Ansidale, Rose (reeds) - 292
Armstrong, Lil Hardin (p) - 11
Ashby, Dorothy (h) - 26
Austin, Lovie (p) - 28, 291

Bailey, Jessie (reeds) - 292
Baker, Helen (g) - 292, 293
Barrett, "Sweet" Emma (p) - 38
Barton, Lynn (tb) - 41
Barton, Willene (ts) - 41
Beaout, Marilyn (cello) - 295
Beatty, Wini (p) - 294
Beaucamp, Martha (sax) - 42
Berman, Ruth (h) - 42
Birdson, Blanche (h) - 42
Bley, Carla (p) - 43
Blunt, Hilary (g) - 44
Booker, Beryl (p) - 44, 294, 295, 296
Booker, Connie Mae (p) - 45
Borchard, Henrietta (vn) 292-293
Boswell, Helvetia "Vet" (cello) - 291
Boswell, Martha (p,cello,celeste) - 45, 291
Bown, Patti (p) - 51, 598, 299,, 300, 301, 302, 303
Brackeen, Joanne (p,org) - 57, 304
Bradley, Ruth (cl,as) - 292, 293
Brim, Grace (hca) - 59
Brown, Cleo (p) - 59
Brown, Louise (p) - 61
Bryant, Clora (tp) - 61

Cantine, Sarah (p) - 62
Capers, Valerie (p) - 62
Carlisle, Una Mae (p) - 62
Carpenter, Marie (as) - 292
Carr, Lady Will (p) - 64
Carr, Wynona (p,g) - 65
Carroll, Barbara (p) - 66
Carson, Norma (tp) - 297
Charters, Ann (p) - 71
Chatman, Christine (p) - 72
Clark, Cortelia (g) - 73
Coates, Dorothy Love (p) - 74
Colbert, Emma (vn) - 294
Cole, Helen (d) - 295
Coleman, Gloria (org) - 74
Conley, Althea (tb) - 292
Collins, Joyce (p) - 75
Crawford, Lillian (p) - 76
Creath, Marge (p) - 76

Dabney, Elisha "Bartley" (tb) - 76
Dane, Barbara (g) - 76
Davies, Desdemona (p) - 291
Davies, Ramona (p) - 77
Davis, Birdie (as) - 295
Davis, Martha (p) - 81
Davis, Tiny (tp) - 295
Dearie, Blossom (p) - 83
Dickerson, Aletha (p) - 86
Dieman, Florence (tp) - 292
Dixon, Lucille (b) - 87
Donahue, Juel (tp) - 292
Donald, Barbara (tp) - 87
Donegan, Dorothy (p) - 88
Dranes, Juanita "Arizona" (p) - 90
Drevnak, Anne (b) - 297
Dukes, Aggie (p) - 91

Edwards, Bernice (p) - 91
Elliott, Elaine (p) - 92
Elzea, Marion (tp) - 292
Ershoff, Elizabeth (h) - 93

Franklin, Aretha (p) - 93
Freeman, Sharon (FrH) - 95

Gange, Marion (g) - 292, 293
Garry, Vivian (b) - 96, 293, 294
Geller, Lorraine (p) - 97
Getz, Jane (p) - 99
Gibson, Marge (b) - 100
Girard, Adele (h) - 100
Glamann, Betty (h) - 103, 297
Goossens, Marie (h) - 104
Gottesman, Rose (d) - 293, 294
Gray, Kitty (p) - 104
Green, Vivian (p) - 105
Greenfield, Mirriam (p) - 292, 293
Griffith, Shirley (g) - 106

Hale, Corky (Hecht) (p,h,fl) - 106, 297
Hall, Audrey (reeds) - 292, 293
Hampton, Carmelita (bars) - 107
Handy, Katherine (p) - 107
Hardaway, Lil (p) - 107, 291
Harris, Nancy (p) - 109
Hemingway, Jane (p) - 109
Henderson, Leora (tp) - 109
Henderson, Lil (p) - 109, 291
Henderson, Rosa (p) - 110
Hesser, Fy (tb) - 292
Heumann, Althea (tb) - 292, 293
Hill, Rosa Lee (g) - 110
Hill, Ruth (h) - 110
Hinton, Algia Mae (g) - 111
Hipp, Jutta (p) - 112

Hoffman, Jean (p) - 114
Hope, Mary (p) - 115
Horn, Shirley (p) - 116
Horsey, Mabel (p) - 117
Howard, Camille (p) - 118
Howard, Louella (fl) - 123
Hutton, Ina Ray (ldr) - 292, 293
Hyams, Marjorie (vib) - 123, 293, 294
Hyde, Jerrine (p) - 292, 293

Jacobs, Julie (oboe,EngH) - 126
Jenkins, Ann (p) - 127
Jenkins, Myrtle (p) - 127
Jeshke, Dody (d) - 294
Johnk, Katherine (h) - 127
Johnson, Edith North (p) - 128
Johnson, Louise (p) - 128
Johnson, Margaret "Queenie" (p) - 128
Jones, Bertha Lee (g) - 129
Jones, Betty Hall (p) - 120
Jones, Brenda (b) - 130
Jones, Dolly (c) - 131
Julye, Kathryne (h) - 131

Kelly, Jo Ann (g) - 132
Kimball, Jeanette (Salvant) (p) - 132
Kirk, Mary E. (p) - 291
Koehler, Carmelita (cello) - 137
Korchinska, Maria (h) - 137

Lamb, Lois (tp) - 292
Lee, Barbara (as) - 138
Lee, Carroll (p) - 138
Lee, Julia (p) - 139
Lee, Perri (org) - 142
Leighton, Elaine (d) - 142, 295, 296, 297
Lenz, Maria (b) - 292, 293
Lewis, Clara (p) - 143
Lewis, Helen (p) - 143
Lewis, Mildred (p) - 144
Liston, Melba (tb,cond,arr) - 144, 298, 299, 300, 301, 302, 303, 304
Lutcher, Nellie (p) - 157

McDonald, Joyce (p) - 161
McFarland, Elaine (p) - 161
McFarland, Loretta (h) - 162
McLawler Sarah (org) - 162
McLeod, Alice (Coltrane) (p,org,vib,h) - 164
McManus, Sue (bj) - 167
McMurray, Ruth (tb) - 292, 293
McPartland, Marian (p) - 167, 297, 298
Marcus, Marie (p) - 174
Marshall, Bessie (p) - 176
Martin, Madonna (p) - 176
Minnie, Memphis (g) - 177
Miller, Betty (p) - 186

Mosier, Gladys (p) - 293
Murphy, Rose (p) - 187

Negri, Ruth (h) - 297, 298
Newell, Laura (h) - 188, 301
Noel, Hattie (p) - 189
Norris, Catherine (cello) - 189

O'Brien, Elaine (d) - 295
Odetta (g) - 189
O'Hara, Betty (v-tb) - 190
O'Flynn, Bridget (d) - 293, 294
Osborne, Mary (g) - 190, 293, 294, 297

Palmer, Gladys (p) - 195
Peacock, Mary (b) - 195
Pennak, Evelyn (ts) - 202
Pierce, Mae (g) - 196
Pitts, Trudy (org) - 196
Pollard, Terry (p,vib) - 198, 297
Pope, Melba (p) - 198
Porter, Helen (d) - 199
Potts, Martha (p) - 199
Putman, Janet (h) - 200

Ray, Carline (b) - 204
Redd, Vi (as,sop) - 204
Remsen, Dorothy (h) - 205
Rivers, Marye (b) - 292
Robinson, Aletha (p) - 207
Rogers, Billie (tp) - 207
Rohl, Elvira (tp) - 292, 293
Ross, Margaret (h) - 209, 298
Rotenberg, June (b) - 294
Roudebush, Betty (p) - 292
Roy, Mata (p) - 294, 295
Rubin, Queenie Ada (p) - 213
Russell, Nina (org) - 294, 295
Ruth, Helen (cl,as,ts) - 292, 293
Ryan, Babs (p) - 215

Sattley, Betty (reeds) - 292
Saunders, Nettie (p) - 215
Schwartz, Julie (as) - 215
Scott, Dot (p) - 215
Scott, Hazel (p) - 217
Scott, Rhoda (org) - 219
Scott, Shirley (org) - 220, 304
Shaw, Sister Rosa (g) - 233
Simone, Nina (p) - 233
Singer, Lil (d) - 292, 293
Skinner, Jean (d) - 292
Slavin, Estella (tp) - 292, 293
Smith, Betty (ts) - 240
Smith, Dorothea (g) - 241
Smith, Dottie (d) - 242

Smith, Elizabeth (uk) - 242
Smith, Ethel (org) - 242
Smith, Laverne (p) - 242
Smock, Emma Ginger (vn) - 243
Snow, Valaida (tp) - 243
Sortier, Amanda (wb) - 247
Soyer, Janet (h) - 247
Spivey, Victoria (p,org,uk) - 248
Starr, Jean (tp) - 293
Sticht, Betty (cl,as,ts) - 292, 293
Stobart, Kathy (ts) - 251
Stockton, Ann Mason (h) - 253

Teagarden, Norma (p) - 254
Terrell, Sister O.M. (g) - 255
Terry, Thelma (b) - 255
Tharpe, Sister Rosetta (g,p) - 256, 296
Thomas, Lilette (p) - 261
Thompson, Barbara (fl,pic,sop) - 261
Thompson, Loretta (h) - 261

Van Der Harst, Anne (p) - 262
Varley, Anne (p) - 263
Vito, Elaine (h) - 263

Walsh, Kay (tp) - 292, 293
Walton, Blanche Smith (p) - 263
Waters, Patty (p) - 264
Watkins, Viola (p) - 264
Watson, Paula (p) - 265
Weber, Annette (org) - 296
Webster, Katie (p) - 266
Webster, L'Ana (as) - 269, 293
Wetzel, Bonnie (b) - 295, 296, 297
White, Georgia (p) - 269
Williams, Devonia (p) - 271
Williams, Della (g) - 272
Williams, Edna (tp) - 294
Williams, Lovey (g) - 272
Williams, Mary Lou (p,celeste,ldr,arr) - 272, 293, 294, 298, 304
Willrich, Virginia (p,acc) - 289
Wills, Alice (tb) - 292
Wise, Laurie (g) - 289

Zimmer, Vicki (p) - 290, 293
Zirl, Cecelia (b) - 293

**About the Compiler**

Jan Leder is a jazz flutist and composer who performs in the New York City area.